A LONG WAY TO GO

IRREGULAR MIGRATION PATTERNS, PROCESSES, DRIVERS AND DECISION-MAKING

A LONG WAY TO GO

IRREGULAR MIGRATION PATTERNS, PROCESSES, DRIVERS AND DECISION-MAKING

EDITED BY MARIE MCAULIFFE
AND KHALID KOSER

Australian
National
University

PRESS

ANU PRESS

Published by ANU Press
The Australian National University
Acton ACT 2601, Australia
Email: anupress@anu.edu.au
This title is also available online at press.anu.edu.au

A catalogue record for this
book is available from the
National Library of Australia

NATIONAL
LIBRARY
OF AUSTRALIA

ISBN(s): 9781760461775 (print)
9781760461782 (eBook)

Cover design and layout by ANU Press. Cover photograph adapted from: *Sydney, Australia* by NASA Goddard Space Flight Center, flic.kr/p/cE8dwS.

Contents

List of Figures

List of Tables

List of Acronyms

ANAO	Australian National Audit Office
BFE	Bureau of Foreign Employment (Sri Lanka)
CEAS	Common European Asylum System
DFAT	Department of Foreign Affairs and Trade (Australia)
DIAC	Department of Immigration and Citizenship (Australia)
DIBP	Department of Immigration and Border Protection (Australia)
DIE	Department of Immigration and Emigration (Sri Lanka)
EC	European Commission
EU	European Union
Frontex	European Agency for the Management of Operational Coordination at the External Borders of the Member States of the European Union
GCIM	Global Commission on International Migration
GDP	gross domestic product
GFC	global financial crisis
GN	Grama Niladhari
GSM	General Skilled Migration
HD	human development
HDI	Human Development Index
ICG	International Crisis Group
IDMC	Internal Displacement Monitoring Centre
IDP	internally displaced person
ILO	International Labor Organization

IMA	irregular maritime arrival
IOM	International Organization for Migration
IZA	Institute for the Study of Labor
LTTE	Liberation Tigers of Tamil Eelam
MV	motor vessel
NGO	non-governmental organisation
OCHA	Office for the Coordination of Humanitarian Affairs
OECD	Organisation for Economic Co-operation and Development
PAC	Pacific Access Category
PV	protection visa holder
QUT	Queensland University of Technology
RSF	Reporters Without Borders (Reporters Sans Frontiéres)
SHP	Special Humanitarian Program
SIEV	suspected illegal entry vessels
SP	service provider
SVP	Swiss People's Party
SWP	Seasonal Worker Program
TPS	Temporary Protected Status
TPV	temporary protection visas
UAM	unaccompanied asylum-seeking minor
UASC	unaccompanied or separated children
UNDESA	United Nations Department of Economic and Social Affairs
UNDP	United Nations Development Programme
UNHCR	United Nations High Commissioner for Refugees
UNODC	United Nations Office on Drugs and Crime
VOA	visa on arrival

Contributors[1]

Ignacio Correa-Velez is currently Associate Professor at the School of Public Health and Social Work, Queensland University of Technology, Brisbane, Australia. He has a background in Family Medicine and Population Health. Between 2004 and 2011, Dr Correa-Velez was Research Fellow and Deputy Director of the La Trobe Refugee Research Centre, La Trobe University, Melbourne, Australia. His research interests include refugee and asylum seeker health and settlement, health inequalities, social determinants of health, mental health and human rights.

Lakshman Dissanayake is the Vice Chancellor of the University of Colombo in Sri Lanka. Professor Dissanayake holds a Bachelor of Development Studies with First Class Honours, a Postgraduate Diploma in Population Studies (both from the University of Colombo), a Master of Arts in Demography from the Vrije Universitiet Brussels and a PhD from the University of Adelaide in Australia. He is a Visiting Professor, Faculty of Health Sciences, Leeds Beckett University (UK) and Adjunct Member of the Australian Population and Migration Research Center, University of Adelaide. He is a Fellow of the Royal Society of Arts (UK).

Tim Hatton is Professor of Economics at the University of Essex (UK) and Emeritus Professor at The Australian National University (ANU). His research focus is the causes and effects of international migration, in both historical and contemporary contexts. He has published extensively on the great transatlantic migrations of the late nineteenth century and their role in the development of the Atlantic economy. More recently, he has analysed trends in asylum applications to the countries of the EU, the development of asylum policy and changes in public opinion towards

---

1   The opinions, comments and analyses expressed in this publication are those of the authors and do not necessarily represent the views of the department or any of the organisations or institutions with which the authors are affiliated.

immigrants and refugees. His book *Seeking Asylum: Trends and Policies in the OECD* (2011) is available online at the Centre for Economic Policy Research (London).

Graeme Hugo AO, 1946 to 2015, was University Professorial Research Fellow, Professor of the Department of Geography, Environment and Population and Director of the Australian Population and Migration Research Centre at the University of Adelaide. His research interests were in population issues in Australia and South East Asia, especially migration. He was the author of over 400 books, articles in scholarly journals and chapters in books, as well as a large number of conference papers and reports. In 2002, he secured an ARC Federation Fellowship over five years for his research project, 'The new paradigm of international migration to and from Australia: Dimensions, causes and implications'. In 2009, he was awarded an ARC Australian Professorial Fellowship over five years for his research project 'Circular migration in Asia, the Pacific and Australia: Empirical, theoretical and policy dimensions'.

Dinuk Jayasuriya is a Visiting Fellow at the Development Policy Centre, ANU, with a research focus on evaluations, migration and mental health. Dr Jayasuriya has previously led surveys of over 60,000 households in Afghanistan, Bangladesh, Malaysia, Pakistan, Papua New Guinea, the Philippines, Solomon Islands and Sri Lanka. Dinuk has consulted for the Department of Immigration and Border Protection, the World Bank, International Finance Corporation, AusAID and multiple Red Cross Societies.

Katharine Knoetze is a registered psychologist with experience as a clinician in counselling and psychiatric settings. From 2008 to 2015 Katharine worked in the field of refugee-related trauma. Some of this work was conducted at the Queensland Program of Assistance to Survivors of Torture and Trauma. This provided her with extensive experience working with individuals from culturally and linguistically diverse backgrounds, and the opportunity to learn from her clients about culture-specific explanatory models of distress.

Khalid Koser MBE is Extraordinary Professor in Conflict, Peace and Security in the Faculty of Humanities and Sciences at Maastricht University. He has published over 100 books, articles and chapters on refugees, migration, and asylum, including the International Organization for Migration's (IOM) *World Migration Report in 2010*. He is editor of the *Journal of Refugee Studies*. Dr Koser is also Non-Resident Fellow at the Lowy Institute for Foreign Policy, Associate Fellow at the Geneva Centre for Security Policy, Associate Fellow at Chatham House, Research Associate at the Graduate Institute of International and Development Studies in Geneva, and co-chair of the World Economic Forum Global Future Council on Migration.

Katie Kuschminder is a NWO Rubicon Research Fellow at the Global Governance Programme, Robert Schuman Centre for Advanced Studies, European University Institute in Florence, Italy and an affiliated researcher at Maastricht Graduate School of Governance and United Nations University – Maastricht Economic and Social Research Institute on Innovation and Technology (UNU-MERIT). Katie's current research focuses on forced, irregular and return migration. Katie holds a PhD in migration studies from Maastricht University.

Craig Loschmann is a research fellow at the Maastricht Graduate School of Governance and UNU-MERIT. His research over the years has focused primarily on the causes and consequences of forced migration in the contexts of Afghanistan and the African Great Lakes region. His current interests are in the influence of refugee populations on host communities, and the impact of mass return in post-conflict settings. Craig has consulted on numerous migration-related projects for organisations like the United Nations High Commissioner for Refugees (UNHCR), IOM, International Labor Organization (ILO) and Organisation for Economic Co-operation and Development (OECD), among others, and has conducted fieldwork in Burundi and Rwanda. He holds Masters degrees in Economics and International Political Economy and Development from Fordham University, and a PhD from the Maastricht Graduate School of Governance and UNU-MERIT.

Marie McAuliffe is the head of the migration policy research division at IOM in Geneva. She is a senior fellow at the Global Migration Centre at the Graduate Institute of International and Development Studies in Geneva, a visiting scholar at the Population Institute at Hacettepe University in Ankara, and is on leave from the Department of Immigration and Border Protection. She is a member of the scientific committee of the Swiss Network for International Studies and of the international advisory board of the Asia in Global Affairs research forum in Kolkata. Marie also co-convenes IOM's Migration Research Leaders' Syndicate in support of the 2018 Global Compact for Migration. She is co-editor of IOM's *World Migration Report 2018* (with Martin Ruhs) and is on the editorial board of the scientific journal *International Migration*. For three years (2012–2014) Marie directed the Australian irregular migration research program. In late 2014, she was awarded a Sir Roland Wilson scholarship to complete her doctoral research at the ANU School of Demography.

Victoria Mence is a senior researcher and analyst with a focus on human displacement and irregular migration issues. She has worked for the Australian Government on humanitarian resettlement and international migration since 2007. Victoria has lectured in human rights theory and interdisciplinary epistemology at the University of Sydney. She holds a Bachelor of Social Sciences from the University of Sydney and a Graduate Certificate in Studies from ANU with a major in international law.

Joseph Moloney was Policy Officer at the Australian Catholic Migrant and Refugee Office from 2011 to 2014. In this role, he researched both voluntary and forced migration in the Asia–Pacific region with a specific focus on migration to Australia. Using applied economic analysis, Joe researched the role of asylum policy and its impact on asylum flows. He also explored the role of alternative migration streams such as family, skilled and humanitarian protection visas, and the impact these alternative visas have on asylum flows.

Caven Jonathan Napitupulu is a PhD candidate at the Department of Geography, Environment and Population at the University of Adelaide and at the final stage of writing his dissertation on transit migration in Indonesia. He obtained a Master of Public Administration from the Flinders University of South Australia and a Diploma from the Indonesian Immigration Academy. His research interests are in refugee issues. He works as an Indonesian immigration officer, is currently posted at the International Cooperation Desk in Jakarta and is involved in international government forums on refugees.

Mariana Nardone is currently a CONICET Postdoc Fellow at the Institute for Social Sciences Research at Universidad del Salvador (Argentina). She holds a Bachelor of Sociology from Universidad del Salvador, a Master of Design and Management of Social Programs, and a PhD in Social Sciences (FLACSO-Argentina). Her work in academic, government, nongovernment and international organisations includes teaching, research and consultancy. Her research interests are in refugee studies, non-governmental organisations and social networks. Between 2013 and 2015, Dr Nardone was a Research Fellow at the School of Public Health and Social Work, Queensland University of Technology in Australia. Between 2016 and 2017, she was a Postdoctoral Fellow at the Centre for Global Cooperation Research (Universität Duisburg-Essen, Germany).

Alex Parrinder was formerly assistant director and acting director of the Department of Immigration and Border Protection's irregular migration research program. He worked on international migration research and policy for the department for nine years prior to taking up positions at the Australian Research Council and the Department of Education and Training. He holds a Bachelor of Asian Studies (Honours) and Bachelor of Laws from ANU.

Melissa Siegel is Professor of Migration Studies and Head of Migration Studies at the Maastricht Graduate School of Governance and UNU-MERIT. She is the Co-Director of the Maastricht Center for Citizenship, Migration and Development and holds the Chairmanship of the United Nations University Migration Network. She has worked on or headed projects for many governments and international organisations and teaches at the graduate and undergraduate level around the world. Her main research interests are in the causes and consequences of migration.

George Tan is Research Affiliate at the Hugo Centre for Migration and Population Research and teaches in the Department of Geography, Environment and Population at the University of Adelaide. Dr Tan has a background in demography and migration and is particularly interested in the demographic, social and spatial implications of international student mobility, skilled migration and refugees/asylum seekers. He has worked on and led research projects relating to migration, not only for a wide range of government bodies such as the Department of Immigration and Border Protection, Fair Work Ombudsman and the Government of South Australia, but also for international organisations such as IOM.

Warren Weeks is the founder and CEO of Cubit Media Research, a privately held research company that specialises in applying big data technologies and behavioural modelling to the in-depth analysis of global media content. His undergraduate studies were in the areas of motivational psychology, information systems and marketing. He holds a postgraduate diploma in business from Monash University and an executive MBA from the University of Queensland. He is a fellow of the Australian Institute of Management, a guest lecturer at Melbourne University, and a long-time supporter of that institution's student mentoring program.

Foreword

Mark Matthews

In this information age, characterised by near-instant communication at a global level, public policy has become a matter of understanding, using and, in turn, being affected by these global information flows—potentially in unexpected ways. The objectives that national governments, and international governance arrangements, seek to achieve can be both aided and thwarted by the rapid and comprehensive dissemination of information. This information helps the people on whom behaviour-influencing policies focus to grasp what may happen to them soon and to react quickly. Potentially, this easy access to information helps those on whom policy focuses to anticipate what may come next by observing patterns and analysing what is driving these patterns. Anthony Giddens (1987) has framed this issue thus: the understanding of what governments are trying to do that is achieved by the people whose behaviours governments seek to influence, reciprocally, allows these people to act in ways that make a previously valid theory about why they act as they do become *untrue*. He calls this the 'double hermeneutic'. Governments try to learn-by-doing, but those people whose behaviours governments seek to shape can 'learn-by-undoing'.

This double hermeneutic driving learning-by-undoing constrains public policy effectiveness—imposing limits to the return on investment on what is currently referred to as 'evidence-based policymaking'. Accumulating more evidence on the causes and effects that governments seek to modify will only be fruitful if learning-by-undoing is weak. If learning-by-undoing is strong, and assisted by the transparency and accountability that is another feature of modern governance, then collecting and analysing more data and placing these results in the public domain will, in itself, most likely disappoint policymakers as unintended consequences generate nasty surprises (what was expected to work did not work). Consequently, we need enough evidence to make sufficient sense of things to make well-judged decisions on difficult and risky matters, but we should beware of extrapolating this productive relationship in a manner that assumes that even more evidence will result in even better policy decisions. Learning-by-undoing means that this accumulating evidence can, above a threshold, start to increase rather than reduce unintended consequences in public policy. The result is decreasing marginal returns to investment in more evidence as a basis for policy decisions.

Irregular migration is a contemporary manifestation of this challenge. Modern communications at a global level makes it easier to grasp the gradients of safety, wellbeing and future prospects that crisscross the world. People are more aware of why they don't want to be where they are, where they would like to go and how they might get there. As the chapters in this book demonstrate, people's expectations and decisions are shaped by the ever-increasing volume of information from many sources, in what is becoming a key feature of the information age. Rapidly updated and pervasive electronic information is now an integral component of both licit and illicit (e.g. people smuggling business) transnational value chains that link individual nations' jurisdictions.

For governments seeking to grapple with these challenges, robust evidence is a necessary but not a sufficient condition for acting. However, for governments, this pervasive and near-instant communication at a global level is also a tool for policy delivery. Clearly communicating policy intentions changes the expectations of the people and groups governments seek to influence—whilst the clients of people smugglers may be understandably desperate, the people smuggling businesses are able to factor this information on new policy stances into their tactics and strategies—potentially leading to faster changes in behaviours than occurs when those behaviours simply react to what is happening rather than what is expected to happen in the future. Illicit market processes factor these risks into the values of assets and investments just as effectively as licit market processes.

This book reflects an innovative effort to strengthen government–academic collaboration against this complex, important and often very saddening background. Conscious of the usefulness of improving the evidence-base on irregular migration, we jointly set about putting in place a program, known as the Collaborative Research Program on the International Movement of People. Developed in Australia as a pilot initiative, this innovative government–academic partnership has attracted attention in other countries (and amongst international organisations) as a viable model for investigating issues of collective international concern. If implemented on a larger scale as a multilateral initiative, this approach could reduce duplication amongst nationally commissioned studies and help to exploit the synergies between each nation's own work on irregular migration.

The Research Program was intended to make progress in helping to enrich the evidence-base via building an effective partnership between government and academia. The program was co-managed by the Crawford School of Public Policy at The Australian National University and the Australian Government's Department of Immigration and Border Protection. From the university side of things, it was refreshing to work closely, and in a trusted manner, with practitioners in government—to balance academic research interests and incentives against the differing interests and incentives in government. Above all, this collaboration highlighted to me the 'bell curved' nature of the return on investment in creating more evidence: we set about increasing the availability of evidence on irregular migration and, in so doing and by virtue of the close collaboration with practitioners, learned a little more about the diminishing marginal returns to investment that can set in as a result of learning-by-undoing.

The collected papers in this book stand as a record of both the substantive achievements in research on irregular migration and as a testimonial to the potential that exists for strengthened government–academic collaboration to have the 'dual-use' impact of seeking to directly inform policy whilst also strengthening academic research capability.

Looking to the future, there may be new ways of approaching the policy utility of evidence.

First, enhanced information flows can create a 'tug of war' between factors that limit policy effectiveness (via learning-by-undoing) and those that increase it (via the ways in which expectations revalue assets and investments in the illicit domain). This may open up new perspectives on evidence and analysis. Rather than treating evidence too narrowly, as information on what has happened so far (and may be happening at the moment), we may be able to offset the diminishing marginal returns to investment in evidence and analysis by paying more attention to the forward-looking expectational dimension: focusing on a better understanding how information flows on emerging policy stances are likely to shape irregular migration in the future. This perspective is better positioned to inform 'strategic insights' in public policy.

Second, the intertwined licit and illicit activities that comprise the transnational value chains shaping irregular migration suggest that adopting such a perspective may strengthen our understanding of how irregular migration is evolving. As a key focus for analysis, these value chains that span different national jurisdictions, and that can be rerouted in response to nationally based policy initiatives, provide a useful complement to nation-state perspectives. This systemic approach would be particularly valuable if it were also framed in a forward-looking manner—focused on anticipating what may happen based upon the analysis of accumulated experience to date. We need a better balance between intelligence and strategic insights on what may happen in the future and robust evidence on what has happened so far. The experience reflected in this book highlights the utility of government–academic collaborations that develop a better balance between evidence and strategic insights. This re-balancing requires academics to be more willing to move out of the comfort zone of analysing evidence of what has happened so far and into the challenging domain of insights into what may happen next—some are comfortable in this domain, but others less so. This process can be assisted by doing far more to frame strategic insight in a scientific manner—as testable hypotheses rather than simply as opinion and speculation. Of course, the challenge of learning-by-undoing means that some of these hypotheses may need to be kept confidential to government for a defined period …

This pragmatic collaborative approach could be particularly useful to policymakers by helping to future-proof their interventions—reducing the risk of designing policy on the basis of what used to work rather than what may work better in the future.

Dr Mark Matthews
SDG-Economic Development, UK
Former Executive Director of the HC Coombs Policy Forum
The Australian National University

Reference list

Giddens, A. (1987). *Social theory and modern sociology*. Cambridge: Polity.

Preface

Marie McAuliffe and Khalid Koser

In its August 2012 report, the Expert Panel on Asylum Seekers noted that 'the evidence on the drivers and impacts of forced migration is incomplete, and more intuitive than factual. As a result, the policymaking process is forced to rely on partial and largely qualitative information, rather than a solid base of measurement and analysis. Addressing this gap in evidence and knowledge is a priority'. The expert panel went on to recommend that a research program on irregular migration be established in support of the development of a stronger evidence-base to inform policy deliberations. The expert panel envisaged that, among other things, the program would 'focus on the drivers and determinants of irregular migration, including why people decide to leave their home countries, how they travel between source, transit and destination countries, and the irregular and regular migration pathways used by asylum seekers' (Expert Panel on Asylum Seekers, 2012, p. 46).

The Australian Government agreed to all 22 of the panel's recommendations, including the establishment of an irregular migration research program. As part of the research program, an occasional paper series was established, with the initial paper, *Establishing an evidence-base for future policy development on irregular migration to Australia*, being the overarching 'lead' paper for the series (Koser & McAuliffe, 2013). This paper was designed to help identify gaps in knowledge and research in the Australian context by comparing it to international research, and to make recommendations about how to fill these gaps, drawing on international experience. The paper was the template for the research program, helping guide the program managers and advisers as they commissioned empirical research on irregular migration to Australia.

Just over five years later, this book compiles occasional papers commissioned under the irregular migration research program established in response to the expert panel's recommendation. The papers selected for inclusion provide empirical research and analysis on aspects of irregular migration, and have been ordered according to the migration cycle, with contextual chapters provided initially, followed by chapters on migrant decision-making, migration processes, return migration and finally future-focused migration thematic chapters.

The idea for this book came out of a November 2014 research workshop on irregular migration hosted by The Australian National University's Crawford School of Public Policy in partnership with the Department of Immigration and Border Protection. The ANU-DIBP research workshop was the second under this unique joint collaboration and it brought together researchers and policymakers as well as international and Australian members of the department's research advisory groups (listed below).

After two stimulating and intense days of discussions on research proposals under development, updates from researchers who were then in the field, analysis of administrative data as well as final presentations of research findings, there was a sense that the collaboration was bearing fruit, but that the research gains needed to be shared more widely. It seemed fitting that a book proposal be submitted to ANU Press, in the hope that by bringing selected papers commissioned under the research program together in one book, a wider audience would be reached. The editors and contributors as well as the research advisory group members are hopeful that this objective will be achieved as we seek to make a contribution to an under-researched and often misunderstood aspect of international migration.

Acknowledgements

The editors would like to thank ANU Press, Professor Tom Kompas, two anonymous peer reviewers of the draft manuscript, the chapter authors and Simon Hay, as well as the members of the Joint Project Management Team who oversaw the ANU-DIBP Collaborative Research Program (Mark Matthews (co-Chair), Marie McAuliffe (co-Chair), Peter Hughes, Andrew Podger, and Janice Wykes). Special thanks are also due to Christopher Ritchie (DIBP) and Jonathan Cheng (ANU) who supported the program and helped turn the idea for this book into a reality. We gratefully acknowledge the financial support of the Department of Immigration and Border Protection for this volume.

Our acknowledgements are also due to members of both advisory bodies established to support the irregular migration research program, listed below (as at June 2015). We are particularly grateful to the more active members who provided ongoing advice and played a critical role in reviewing occasional papers and other work, including Md Jalal Abbasi-Shavazi, Gervais Appave, Richard Bedford, Tim Hatton, Peter Hughes, Khalid Koser, Maryanne Loughry, Aloysious Mowe, Kathleen Newland and Anna Triandafyllidou. We have been deeply saddened by the passing of our colleague and friend Graeme Hugo, who was an active member of our advisory group as well as a contributor to this volume. Assistance from Janet Wall and University of Adelaide staff in finalising chapters by Professor Hugo is gratefully acknowledged.

Irregular Migration Research Advisory Group

- Professor Mohammad Jalal Abbasi-Shavazi, Professor of Demography, University of Tehran and Adjunct Professor, Crawford School of Public Policy, The Australian National University

- Thomas Albrecht (Observer), Regional Representative, United Nations High Commissioner for Refugees

- Joseph Appiah, Chief of Mission, Australia, International Organization for Migration

- Andrew Goledzinowski AM, Ambassador for People Smuggling Issues, Department of Foreign Affairs and Trade

- Professor Tim Hatton, Professor of Economics, Crawford School of Public Policy, The Australian National University

- Peter Hughes, Program Visitor, Regulatory Institutions Network, School of Regulation, Justice and Diplomacy, The Australian National University

- Lisa King, Director, Strategic Communications, Joint Agency Task Force, Operation Sovereign Borders

- Dr Maryanne Loughry, Associate Director, Jesuit Refugee Service

- Marie McAuliffe, Sir Roland Wilson PhD Scholar, School of Demography, The Australian National University

- Fr Aloysious Mowe, Director, Jesuit Refugee Service

- Ashton Robinson, Assistant Secretary-General, Middle East, Africa and Transnational Issues Branch, Office of National Assessments

- Rachael Spalding, First Assistant Secretary, Strategic Policy and Planning Division, Department of Immigration and Border Protection (Chair)
- Janice Wykes, Assistant Secretary, Policy Research & Statistics Branch, Department of Immigration and Border Protection

Previous members

- Dr Derek Bopping, then Director, Intelligence Analysis Unit, Customs and Border Protection Service
- Professor Stephen Castles, Research Chair in Sociology, University of Sydney (resigned membership)
- Craig Chittick, then Ambassador for People Smuggling Issues, Department of Foreign Affairs and Trade
- Mark Getchell, then Chief of Mission, Australia, International Organization for Migration
- Professor Graeme Hugo, Director, Australian Population and Migration Research Centre, University of Adelaide
- Chris O'Keeffe, then Director, Strategic Communications, Joint Agency Task Force, Operation Sovereign Borders
- Dr Wendy Southern (former Chair), then Deputy Secretary, Policy and Programme Management Group, Department of Immigration and Border Protection
- Mardi Stewart, then Director, Strategic Communications, Joint Agency Task Force, Operation Sovereign Borders
- Rick Towle (Observer), then Regional Representative, United Nations High Commissioner for Refugees
- Janice Wykes, then Assistant Secretary, Policy Research & Statistics Branch, Department of Immigration and Border Protection

Irregular Migration Research International Reference Panel

- Gervais Appave, Special Policy Adviser to the Director General, International Organization for Migration
- Professor Richard Bedford, Professor of Population Geography, National Institute of Demographic and Economic Analysis, University of Waikato

- Professor Supang Chantavanich, Director, Asian Research Centre for Migration, Chulalongkorn University
- Professor Lakshman Dissanayake, Department of Demography, University of Colombo
- Professor Khalid Koser, Extraordinary Professor of Conflict, Peace and Security, Maastricht University
- Professor Susan Martin, Director, Institute for the Study of International Migration, Georgetown University
- Marie McAuliffe, Sir Roland Wilson PhD Scholar, School of Demography, The Australian National University
- Kathleen Newland, Director of Migrants, Migration, and Development and Refugee Protection Programs, Migration Policy Institute
- Rachael Spalding, First Assistant Secretary, Strategic Policy and Planning Division, Department of Immigration and Border Protection (Chair)
- Professor Anna Triandafyllidou, Director, Global Governance Programme, Robert Schuman Centre for Advanced Studies, European University Institute.

Previous members

- Dr Jeff Crisp, Research and Evaluation, United Nations High Commissioner for Refugees, Geneva (resigned membership)
- Dr Wendy Southern (former Chair), then Deputy Secretary, Policy and Programme Management Group, Department of Immigration and Border Protection

Reference list

Expert Panel on Asylum Seekers. (2012). *Report of the expert panel on asylum seekers*. Canberra: Australian Government.

Koser, K., & McAuliffe, M. (2013). *Establishing an evidence-base for future policy development on irregular migration to Australia*. Irregular Migration Research Program, Occasional Paper Series 01. Canberra, Australian Department of Immigration and Citizenship.

1

Introduction

Marie McAuliffe and Khalid Koser

In modern Western history, for the most part, the prevailing governance of international migration has generally served many nations reasonably well, including Australia. Orderly movement has been largely the norm and has contributed to growth in economies, increased human development, the capacity to protect large numbers of people facing persecution, and the ability of hundreds of millions of people to forge meaningful lives abroad. Concomitantly, there is a perception that other countries and regions, particularly some non-industrialised nations and peoples, have perhaps not fared as well and the benefits of international migration could perhaps be described as uneven.

Against this backdrop, there is growing concern that the less desirable aspects of international migration are increasing in significance and magnitude: the growth in irregular migration (including people smuggling and human trafficking); the increasing restrictiveness of migration-receiving countries' entry policies; a sense that national identities are being threatened (not just that they are changing); rising exploitation of migrants all the way along the migration pathway; and increasing harm to migrants, including substantial numbers of deaths during journeys (Brian & Laczko, 2014), all threaten the overall dividends of international migration.

Of particular importance to states is the need is to manage irregular migration. Irregular migration has in recent decades become a significant public policy issue and the focus of considerable human, financial, diplomatic, physical/capital, technological, intelligence, operational and other resources. In part, many of the negative issues associated with irregular migration, and the pressing need to respond to it, perhaps revolve around its scale as well as its potential scale. From the little we know about actual international irregular migration flows, the combination of increasing international movements and a perception that there is growing desire for international migration has the capacity to influence policy responses. There has at times been a focus within some destination countries on deterring irregular migrants, perhaps without appreciating fully why or how migration occurs. In this sense, there is good reason to develop a better understanding of irregular migration flows—their scale, pace, diversity, demography and extent, as well as the mixed motivations and multiple factors underpinning them.

To do so effectively, it is important to analyse irregular migration flows within a broader context of other transnational phenomena and global forces that are acting to shape, fundamentally alter and even enhance flows in dynamic ways. By better understanding irregular migration processes and the factors underpinning them we are better able to anticipate the consequences of policy, and to formulate effective multidimensional responses that can enhance migrant wellbeing, manage borders, assist states hosting large numbers of people in need of protection and provide opportunities to increase human development in key locations. This book is about people, often far from Australia, making difficult migration decisions, embarking on dangerous and sometimes high-risk journeys to Australia, and about how we might better understand the constraints they face, the factors that influence them and the migration journeys they undertake.

Irregular migration as an enduring and complex public policy issue

The multiple complex forces of globalisation interact with migration dynamics to influence international migration patterns and trends. Increasing urbanisation, fluctuating economic circumstances, geopolitical insecurity and conflict, development disparities, environmental impacts, population growth and demographic change all influence the movement of people, along with factors such as increasing access to transportation, telecommunications, social networks and proximity to viable migration pathways and agents. Within this context, irregular migration is a contested topic with significant national, regional and global implications, particularly in Europe but also in other parts of the world. This form of migration presents ongoing challenges and continues to raise compelling humanitarian, political, social, economic and security concerns. It can be daunting for policymakers to try to balance these concerns while developing effective and sustainable strategies to manage irregular migration and borders.

The need for policy-relevant research on irregular migration cannot be overstated. Examination of the many factors underpinning irregular movement is important to the development of a better understanding of multicausality and its interconnected dimensions. Scholars have recognised that research that is not explicitly policy oriented is also crucial, particularly forced migration research that looks beyond the policy frames of reference to explore less visible aspects of this form of migration (Bakewell, 2008).

As an immigration nation surrounded by sea, Australia's border-related operational capacities, both offshore and onshore, have evolved over decades to become among the more advanced in the world. Regular migration is planned and regulated in an orderly and predictable manner. Further, the dimensions, characteristics and history of international managed migration in the Australian context are comprehensively researched, and a strong evidence-base exists to inform policy. In contrast, irregular migration tends to be disorderly, unpredictable and unregulated. Irregular migration thus raises central concerns for governments that want to maintain public confidence in the state's capacity to protect sovereignty and manage borders.

Defining irregular migration

There is a wide range of definitions of 'irregular' migrants, including those who have purposefully crossed a border without authorisation, those who have inadvertently or unknowingly crossed a border without authorisation, those who have become irregular sometime after entering a country regularly, those who have been trafficked, and those who have been born into irregularity. For the purpose of this book, the term 'irregular migration' is mainly limited to the migration processes involved in travelling to and entering a country irregularly. We are, therefore, interested in intentional migration embarked upon to gain irregular entry into a country, regardless of whether this has been unassisted, with the help of a smuggler or has been as a result of human trafficking. The management and support of irregular migrants within a destination country is beyond this book's scope.

We have chosen this focus for three main reasons. First, the increasing number of people crossing borders irregularly poses significant and increasingly complex policy and operational challenges for many states throughout the world, and some of the responses that have been implemented are clearly not working as intended. Second, the irregular migration journey is widely recognised as dangerous, often costly and sometimes deadly for migrants. While there is widespread support for reducing irregular migration in principle, the nature of policy responses is often hotly contested. Policy responses that balance the rights and needs of migrants with those of nation states and their need to protect sovereignty, and that uphold international legal obligations can be difficult to achieve. Third, policy responses addressing other aspects of irregular migration (e.g. those who become irregular after entering legally) are necessarily different to those aimed at influencing migration patterns and processes.

Estimating irregular migration

Determining flows of irregular migrants is inherently difficult. Kraler and Reichel (2011) argued that 'wild assumptions, estimates and number games are made in regard to irregular migration flows' (p. 97). Nevertheless, sound attempts to quantify irregular movements can provide clear benefits to national governments, regional and local governments, international organisations, service providers, employers and others. If such actors can better understand the number of people engaging in irregular migration, they will be better able to develop responses and mitigation strategies able to manage the many potentially conflicting interests. These different interests may range from those of governments focused on border management, civil society actors focused on safeguarding migrants as far as possible from exploitation and other forms of vulnerability, and service providers seeking to support irregular migrants in transit or destination countries.

Australia seems to hold a fairly atypical place among industrialised destination countries, in that in Australia it is possible to record and/or estimate irregular migration flows reasonably well. Australia's geography, sea borders and relative isolation from regions that have traditionally experienced large-scale human displacement and acute refugee flows has meant that Australia has developed over recent decades a perhaps unique ability among industrialised countries to manage international people movement. As a corollary, Australia has, out of necessity, developed border management practices that have extended its virtual border well beyond its physical border as a means of facilitating travel to what is— from much of the world's perspective—an isolated location. Almost all international travel to Australia is by air. Multilayered processes have been developed focusing on the management of cross-border movements with virtually no regulations or processes in place to manage internal migration through, for example, national identity cards, registration processes, internal 'passports', and other forms of regulation and restriction (Koser & McAuliffe, 2013).

With the regulation of international air travel, and considerable investment in technology and international cooperation in this regard, there has been a fairly constant low number of irregular air arrivals of between one and two thousand per year. This contrasts with the peak–lull dynamic of irregular maritime arrivals (Figure 1.1). In addition, the number of irregular migrants living in Australia is very low (around 62,700 or 0.26 per cent of the population) compared to other countries, including the US (around 12 million or 3.85 per cent), and South Africa (between 3–5 million or around 7.5 per cent) (McAuliffe & Mence, 2014; Department of Immigration and Border Protection [DIBP], 2014).

Further, irregular air arrivals (i.e. those refused immigration clearance at airports) represented a very small proportion of all air arrivals (around 0.013 per cent in 2011–12, or 2,048 of around 15.920 million air arrivals), whereas irregular maritime arrivals are a much greater proportion of all maritime arrivals (8,371 or 3.1 per cent of 478,000 maritime arrivals in 2011–12).[1] Very few irregular air arrivals lodge asylum claims, and so do not pose the same policy challenges as those who arrive irregularly by sea. In 2011–12, of the 2,048 irregular air arrivals, just 26 people made

---

1   Maritime arrivals are derived from DIBP's Annual report of 2011–12 (pp. 151 and 219).

protection claims at the border (Koser & McAuliffe, 2013). In contrast, almost all of those who have arrived irregularly by sea in recent years have submitted asylum claims, in the majority of cases successfully.

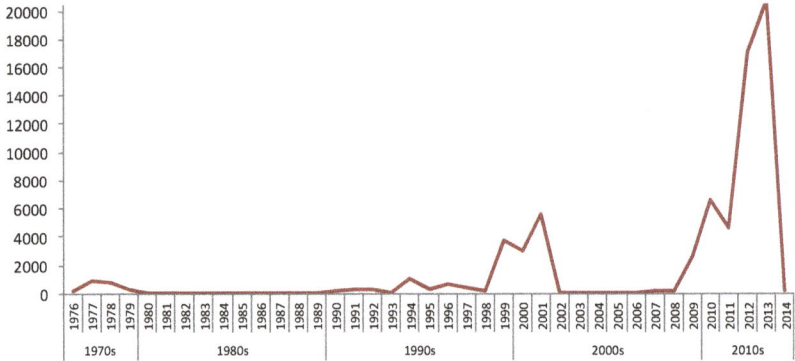

Figure 1.1: Number of irregular maritime arrivals to Australia, 1976–2014

Source: McAuliffe and Mence (2014), updated.

In terms of asylum seekers who arrived in an authorised manner on a visitor or other type of visa, there would appear to be some underlying differences between these asylum seekers and those who arrive unauthorised. In addition to demographic differences (most notably citizenship), behaviours and/or motivations appear to be somewhat divergent. For example, in many cases they apply for asylum years after they have arrived in Australia. Analysis of 2011–12 program data shows that the median time between arrival and application for a protection visa for those who arrived by air in an authorised manner was 321 days. In relation to some student visa citizenship groups, median times were over 1,000 days (Koser & McAuliffe, 2013, p. 6).

Irregular maritime arrivals in the Australian context have become a lightning rod for political, public and academic debate. Australia is not alone in this regard: in receiving countries such as Italy, Greece, Spain and Malta, the phenomenon is high on the immigration agenda where it remains contested and contentious. The International Organization for Migration (IOM) estimated that in 2015 over one million people arrived in Europe irregularly by sea, where the discourse has become increasingly polarised.

Research issues

Part of the problem with the debates about irregular migration is a lack of information and data on aspects of its manifestation, as well as of its consequences. This is particularly so in the Asia–Pacific region where information and data has tended to be fragmented, anecdotal and sometimes based on assumptions. Research on the topic can sometimes reflect polarised positions. In addition, research is commonly undertaken within discrete theoretical disciplines or analytical frameworks, such as economics, sociology, demography, anthropology, national sovereignty and security, international (refugee) law and human rights (Brettell & Hollifield, 2015), which all contribute valuable insights but do not always adequately capture the multifaceted and dynamic nature of migration processes, including from migrants' perspectives, that multidisciplinary research and analysis is often able to illuminate.

There has also been an emphasis on the interests and concerns of receiving countries, with less attention given to origin, transit and refugee host countries, let alone the migrants themselves or their families. This can inhibit a more nuanced understanding of the characteristics of populations on the move and the reasons for changing migration patterns. Further, given the largely invisible, often clandestine nature of irregular migration, the difficulty of systematically measuring, researching and understanding movements is considerable. Data on irregular movements within the Asia–Pacific region are generally not available; research is challenging, expensive and sensitive. In other regions, such as the Horn of Africa, efforts to overcome such difficulties are bearing fruit and the scale of irregular movement, smuggling, trafficking and exploitation of migrants is being reported.

Irregular maritime migration flows to Australia have been a contentious academic and public policy issue for several decades. Much of the focus of the discourse on, and research into, this discrete type of irregular migration has been on the treatment of asylum seekers and refugees who make up these irregular flows. There is a considerable body of literature and commentary on these aspects, including on the critical areas of human rights, normative frameworks, mental health, settlement and integration, international relations and domestic politics. These areas of research and scholarly enquiry are extremely important; they are also fairly mature.

There is a substantial body of work that exists on these aspects of irregular maritime migration to Australia, but much less enquiry into the migration patterns, processes, drivers and decision-making underpinning movement.

The contributions in this volume aim to rectify some of the imbalance in migration research by presenting empirical research findings on irregular migration undertaken in origin, transit and destination countries using a range of methods and employing interdisciplinary approaches. The chapters in this book originate from the Irregular Migration Research Program's occasional paper series (see background discussion in the Preface), and are rooted in a particular period of time, namely 2012 to 2014. References to recent developments are made in relevant chapters, such as the reduction in irregular maritime arrivals to Australia in 2014 and the increase in arrivals to Europe in 2015; however, the main emphasis remains on the period from which this volume emerged.

Reference list

Bakewell, O. (2008). Research beyond the categories: The importance of policy irrelevant research into forced migration. *Journal of Refugee Studies, 21*(4), 432–453. doi.org/10.1093/jrs/fen042

Brettell, C., & Hollifield, J. (Eds). (2015). *Migration theory: Talking across disciplines.* New York: Routledge.

Brian, T., & Laczko, F. (Eds). (2014). *Fatal journeys: Tracking lives lost during migration.* Geneva: International Organization for Migration.

Castles, S. (2002). *Environmental change and forced migration: making sense of the debate.* New Issues in Refugee Research, working paper no. 70. Geneva: United Nations High Commissioner for Refugees.

Clarke, J. (2000). The problems of evaluating numbers of illegal migrants in the European Union. In P. de Bruycker (Ed.), *Regularisations of illegal immigrants in the European Union* (pp. 13–22). Brussels: Bruylant.

Department of Immigration and Border Protection (2012) *Annual report 2011–12.* DIBP: Canberra.

Department of Immigration and Border Protection. (2014). *Australia's Migration Trends 2013–14.* Canberra: Author.

Koser, K., & McAuliffe, M. (2013). *Establishing an evidence-base for future policy development on irregular migration to Australia*. Irregular Migration Research Program, occasional paper series 01. Canberra: Australian Department of Immigration and Citizenship.

Kraler, A., & Reichel, D. (2011). Measuring irregular migration and population flows—what available data can tell. *International Migration 49*(5), 97–128. doi.org/10.1111/j.1468-2435.2011.00699.x

McAuliffe, M., & Mence, V. (2014). *Global irregular maritime migration: Current and future challenges*. Irregular Migration Research Program, occasional paper series 07. Canberra: Australian Department of Immigration and Border Protection.

.

2

Irregular maritime migration as a global phenomenon

Marie McAuliffe and Victoria Mence[1]

The estimated number of international migrants has increased dramatically over the past 55 years, from estimates of around 77 million in 1960 to around 244 million in 2015 (United Nations Department of Economic and Social Affairs [UNDESA], 2016). During that time, the pace of movement has increased as more and more international travel links have emerged. There has been an expansion in migration pathways as access to air travel has increased, resulting in much greater diversity among international travellers (International Migration Institute [IMI], 2006, p. 2).

The volume of cross-border movements that many countries around the world are facing is increasing, and shows no signs of abating. In the US, it is estimated that up to 360 million cross-border movements occurred in 2013 (US Customs and Border Protection, 2014). In Australia, 14.5 million cross-border movements were recorded in program year 1996–97 compared to 31.6 million in 2011–12. The current estimate is that by 2020 Australia will experience 50 million movements per year across its border. Countries in Asia are also experiencing increases in movement, including labour migration to the economies of Singapore,

---

1   The authors are grateful for research assistance from Simone Gangell and Paul Hayes in the preparation of this chapter.

Malaysia, South Korea and Thailand (Hugo, 2014). As access to international movement has increased, states have sought to implement a range of strategies to manage this increase in scale, pace and diversity. Immigration and border management policies and practices have rapidly evolved to meet changes in global circumstances and perceptions of risk associated with the movement of large numbers of people.

Alongside increased global mobility more generally, there has been, over recent years, an increase in refugees and asylum seekers globally. For example, United Nations High Commissioner for Refugees (UNHCR) data indicate that in 2000 there were around 19 million displaced persons[2] worldwide, compared to 59.5 million in 2014 (UNHCR, 2015).[3] There has also been a substantial increase in the number of displaced persons[4] since the recent global low of 2003. The overall global population of displaced persons more than doubled between 2003 and 2014, from 14.8 to 59.5 million people.

Against this backdrop of increasing movement and human displacement, irregular migration poses enduring challenges, and irregular maritime migration most markedly. The humanitarian crisis in the summer of 2015 involving the maritime (and subsequently land) movements of hundreds of thousands of people from Syria, Afghanistan and elsewhere via North Africa and Turkey highlighted the considerable and highly visible policy challenges raised by irregular maritime migration.

While it is acknowledged that there are limitations in seeking to distinguish global irregular maritime migration from other forms of irregular migration as well as from broader asylum-related migration flows, it is also important to note that it is a phenomenon with attributes that are distinguishable from irregular migration by land and air. This paper attempts to articulate the key aspects of this phenomenon.

In preparing this chapter, one of the key issues it raised was the relatively minor focus irregular maritime migration has received in the academic literature compared to other related topics. Perhaps one of the reasons for

2   This figure comprises refugees, asylum seekers, internally displaced persons, stateless persons and various other populations of concern to UNHCR.
3   This figure includes 10.5 million refugees, 925,000 asylum seekers and 17.6 million internally displaced persons.
4   For the present purpose, 'displaced persons' comprise refugees, asylum seekers, internally displaced persons (IDPs), stateless persons and 'others' of concern. Other aggregate figures used by UNHCR may also include populations of returned refugees and returned IDPs.

a more subdued level of academic enquiry is feasibility. While there can be no doubt that irregular maritime migration is a high profile, visually powerful form of irregular migration, the ability to conduct research on its various aspects is undoubtedly challenging. First, access to potential or actual irregular migrants who are willing to engage with researchers can be very difficult. The sensitive and profound nature of their experiences poses particular challenges. Second, the criminal aspects of irregular maritime migration have meant that aspects of counter people smuggling, transnational criminal networks and disruption are often unable to be examined fully due to the inability of accessing classified information, which is not readily available outside government (Koser, 2010). Third, the polarised nature of the public discourse surrounding irregular migration (and maritime migration in particular) makes examination of the topic in a balanced way difficult.

The somewhat more limited level of academic enquiry on the specific topic of global irregular maritime migration perhaps also needs to be viewed in relation to the seemingly, at times, frantic pace and significant focus it has been afforded in terms of policy deliberations of governments around the world, including those characterised as 'source', 'transit' and 'destination' countries. Attempts to study correlation and causality in complex and turbulent policy environments are likely to be compromised.

In terms of the structure of the chapter, the second section below discusses irregular migration, including definitions and data issues. The third section provides an overview of irregular maritime migration flows in key hotspots globally. The fourth section briefly outlines the multifaceted nature of irregular maritime migration. The fifth and final section concludes by highlighting some of the policy challenges in responding to irregular maritime migration.

The broader irregular migration context

Irregular maritime migration is commonly examined in academic literature as one element of the much broader occurrence of irregular migration, which in turn is a feature of modern migration patterns in an era of increased globalisation. The origins of irregular migration, and its links to forces driving the dramatic increase in international migration in the latter part of the twentieth century, are important themes in the literature. The increase in regular migration and the correspondingly rise of irregular migration has, in the view of many commentators, an irresistible momentum that is likely to continue (Koser, 2005, p. 7).

The increase in irregular migration is regarded by many commentators as an inevitable consequence of a globalised economy founded on integrated markets that fuel high labour demands and high levels of immigration (Castles, 2004; Hollifield, 2004). Hollifield looked at what he called the 'liberal' paradox whereby rich developed countries promote and embrace open channels of trade, money and labour (particularly by highly skilled migrants) whereas the mass movement of unskilled workers willing to work for low wages, also necessary to a globalised economy, face highly regulated migration controls. This tension between immigration restrictions and the demand for labour has, in Hollifield's view, driven the increase in irregular migration (Hollifield, 2004, p. 905).

For people facing very difficult (and possibly life-threatening) circumstances—including persecution, poverty, endemic corruption as well as lack of health care, education, employment and/or housing —and who have the ability to migrate, industrialised countries with good human rights records, sound economies and functioning civil societies will remain desirable destinations as they offer, in comparison to other countries, a higher standard of living and security as well as the ability to remit funds to people remaining in the country of origin. As noted by Terrazas (2011, p. 3), '[t]he notion that international migration is somehow related to the well-being of countries of origin is deeply intuitive'.

The substantial literature on the relationship between development and movement indicates that the ability to migrate is a significant issue. The ability to migrate is not related to the 'strength' of needs or the depth of direness faced, and some groups most in need do not have the resources or ability to migrate. Carling, for example, argued that those affected by extreme conditions such as warfare can have the strongest migration aspirations but a lack of ability to do so: a group he calls the 'involuntarily immobile' (Carling, 2002). Other significant research has found that as human development increases, and access to education, income, housing, transport and technology improves, the ability of people to migrate increases and populations become more mobile—the so-called 'hump migration' theory (Martin & Taylor, 1996; Skeldon, 1997; Zelinsky, 1971). De Haas has argued that the relationship between development, economic growth and migration is fundamentally nonlinear so that, for example, while 'a lack of freedoms is likely to fuel migration aspirations, the same lack of freedoms may simultaneously decrease people's capabilities to migrate' (de Haas, 2011, p. 14).

The securitisation of migration

In the academic literature, international migration has been characterised as a non-traditional security issue in the post–Cold War period, along with other phenomena such as food and energy access, international terrorism, drug trafficking and transnational crime. A school of academic thought—the Copenhagen School—conceptualised 'securitisation' as the characterisation of danger and threat of a particular kind via a speech act that moved 'security' from the military realm to other realms, such as migration (Weaver, 1995).

The end of the Cold War, and the related demise of a powerful external threat to the security of the West, enabled the emergence of threats, or perceived threats, that involved non-state actors. This had implications for a range of global and international issues, particularly those that were not (adequately) regulated between states, or those that operated outside of states' control, such as international terrorism. Migrant smuggling and human trafficking are other examples of threats involving non-state actors that would appear to be largely beyond regulation.

Faist argued that one of the effects of the events of 11 September, 2001 was that it reinforced the trend towards securitising migration, which directly resulted in increased migration control, significant investment in border management systems and substantial institutional responses (such as the formation of the US Department of Homeland Security, which incorporated the former Immigration and Nationalisation Service), most notably in the US but more generally throughout the Western world (Faist, 2004). In Miggiano's view, the intensification of border controls is an overt demonstration of the securitisation of migration processes that is especially apparent with the deployment of military resources to manage sea borders (Miggiano, 2009, pp. 1–8).

Relatedly, public administration of migration has changed over time, with greater focus being afforded to security aspects, as reflected in the changed roles and responsibilities of government departments and agencies.

Migration has increasingly become a focus of security-related agencies, although the implications resulting from the changing focus for migration as a public policy issue remain unclear (Koser, 2012).

Some of the other consequences of securitising migration discussed in the literature include aspects related to migrant integration (Ceyhan & Tsoukala, 2002; Huysmans, 2000; Mulvey, 2010) as well as the heightened expectations of the public that governments should, and are able to, control transnational movements across their borders (Faist, 2004, p. 4). Issues of human security are also addressed, as well as the tensions between national security concerns and human security, which 'broadens the scope of security analysis and policy from territorial security to the security of people' (Gomez & Gasper, 2013), especially in relation to migration policies and the negative impacts on migrants (Doneys, 2011).

The implications for the management of irregular migration are potentially profound. There is no doubt that the phenomenon is currently portrayed as a security issue in destination countries, and some argue that the impact of the securitisation of migration in the twenty-first century is on course to intensify (Humphrey, 2013).

The role of telecommunications and the media

The role of telecommunications and the media's portrayals of migration should not be underestimated, particularly in the context of increasing migration flows and the technological advances in communications contributing to globalisation (Hopkins, 2009). Coverage of migration in various media, such as newspapers and television, has been noted for its polarisation, particularly in Europe. Key findings by academics indicate that references to migration in the media are generally episodic rather than consistent, increasingly focused on irregular migration, and are often associated with topics of criminality or border protection (Kim, Carvalho, Davis, & Mullins, 2011; Pickering, 2001; Threadgold, 2009). The securitisation of migration in recent times is prevalent in media coverage on migration (Global Commission on International Migration [GCIM], 2005; Koser, 2012).

A more recent issue concerning irregular migration and media coverage is the possibility that public information could be exploited by people smugglers. With the launch of Operation Sovereign Borders in September

2013, the Australian Government restricted the dissemination of information on operational matters, citing public interest immunity. The decision to not release operational information was based on the grounds that such information would place people involved in operations at risk and unnecessarily cause damage to Australia's national security, defence and international relations (Morrison, 2014). Part of the rationale was also that such information would provide migrant smugglers with the opportunity to avoid detection or to precipitate a search and rescue response (Campbell, 2014).

Improved telecommunications provide migrants greater access to information, and act to strengthen social bonds between diaspora and countries of origin. Access to remittances via enhanced technology is also likely to be relevant to particular groups. As highlighted by Vertovec (as cited in Nedelcu, 2012, p. 1341):

> [Information communications technologies] enable new forms of migrant transnationalism characterised not only by the growing intensity of transnational exchanges and activities, but also by a ubiquitous system of communication that allows migrants to connect with multiple, geographically distant and culturally distinct worlds to which they identify and participate on a daily basis.

Family, friends and community members who have migrated internationally inspire potential migrants to achieve the same outcome and can provide tangible assistance to migrate, including information, funds and advice. Together with enhanced 'real time' communications technology, these networks provide potential migrants with an improved ability to assess their migration options. It is important, however, not to overestimate the impact of newer communications technologies. Despite the internet being considered a global communications medium, for example, access to the internet is still limited in many locations. This makes accurate measurement of its level of influence difficult (Rabogoshvili, 2012). Further, access alone does not ensure adoption of new technologies. Differential access by race, class, sex and ethnicity are factors in technological engagement (Panagakos & Horst, 2006). Access to mobile telephones, however, appears to have increased dramatically, as can be seen in Figure 2.1.

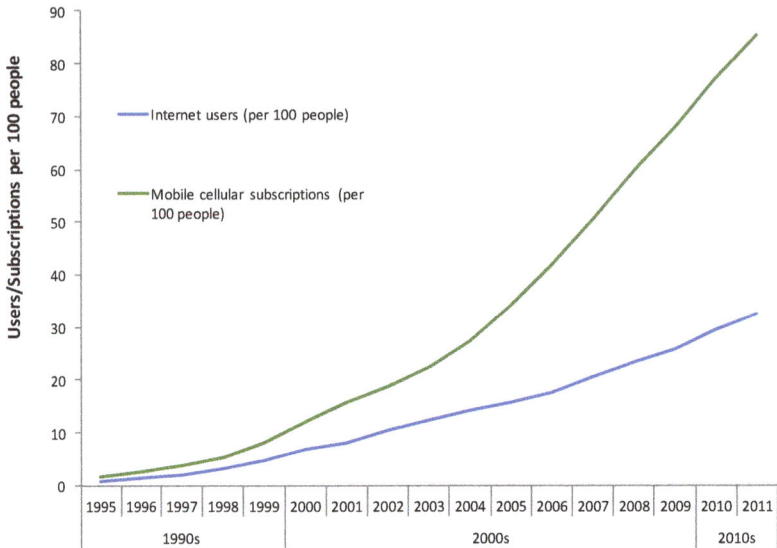

Figure 2.1: Global internet and mobile telephone access

Source: Data extracted from World Bank (2015). A similar version of this graph was published by The Brookings Institution on 25 February, 2014, www.brookings.edu/research/interactives/2014/snapshot-6-rorschach-tests-international-order.

Interconnectedness, diaspora and mobility

The influence of diaspora has long been considered a factor in migration, including irregular migration. Diaspora provide social networks for potential irregular migrants, which can serve as 'feedback mechanisms' (Banerjee, 1983; Crisp, 1999; Meyer, 2001). These networks consist mostly of family, friends, community or religious organisations, as well as people smugglers and others who assist in the migration journey (Koser & Pinkerton, 2002). Once established, social networks may facilitate further migration, including affecting destination choice, providing information and material assistance, and offering a source of emotional support.

While empirical evidence about the role of social networks in irregular migration is more limited (Crisp, 1999; de Haas, 2011; Staring, 2004), it is probable that transnational networks play a vital role in helping people circumnavigate the challenges involved in irregular migration (Crisp, 1999). It has been noted that such networks are especially important in providing the organisational infrastructure required for people to migrate clandestinely or irregularly, i.e. through people smuggling, the trafficking of persons or the irregular movement of asylum seekers.

In addition to facilitating the migration process itself, transnational social networks provide irregular migrants with subsistence and support upon arrival (Crisp, 1999). Important for any migrant, the provision of support in the form of possible sources of income and assistance is particularly vital for illegal migrants (Blaschke, 1998), who are more restricted from accessing employment opportunities or possibly even their own financial holdings in their country of origin.

Interconnections between diaspora and communities in their country of origin are perhaps stronger than ever before as a result of increased access and technological improvements in telecommunications and travel. The use of the internet in particular has been viewed to have strengthened transnational networks, putting those who have migrated in contact not only with their immediate family and friends, but with 'virtual ethnic communities' on the basis of common descent (Conversi, 2012).

For all that is known about the influence of diaspora on migration, there is much that is assumed, particularly relating to irregular migration. The difficulties with conducting research on irregular migration discussed in the introduction of this paper have resulted in a knowledge gap regarding irregular migrants' decision-making processes that, if filled, would reveal more about the role of diaspora in irregular migration.

Data and definitions

According to the latest UNDESA Population Division report on international migration, in 2015 an estimated 244 million people, or 3.3 per cent of the world's population, were international migrants, compared with 175 million in 2000 and 154 million in 1990. Between 1990 and 2013, the estimated number of international migrants worldwide rose by over 77 million or by 50 per cent. Much of this growth occurred between 2000 and 2010 (UNDESA, 2016).

In terms of the proportion of migrants that are thought to travel irregularly, broad estimates are available to provide indications of irregular migration globally. The United Nations, for example, has estimated that globally there are approximately 30 to 40 million irregular or undocumented migrants, a number that equates to between 15 and 20 per cent of all international migrants (UNDESA, 2003).

Some commentators question the utility of attempting to quantify irregular migration, citing the practical difficulties as well as the underlying rationale for collecting and citing such statistics, which can amount to alarmism (Castles, 2002; Clarke, 2000). There are, however, clear benefits in attempting to quantify irregular movements, including from the perspectives of national governments, regional and local governments, international organisations, service providers, employers and others. A better understanding of irregular migration, including in relation to quantity, allows for the development of responses and mitigation strategies as a means of managing the multitude of potentially conflicting interests.

Challenges in defining and quantifying irregular migration

Understanding the scale and nature of irregular migration is important, not only in national and regional contexts but also in a global context, as a means of identifying trends and patterns for a range of policy, economic and geopolitical reasons. There are, however, significant challenges in establishing reliable estimates upon which meaningful analysis and useful comparisons can be made (Koser, 2010). A summary of these challenges is included in Table 2.1, which highlights the inherent difficulties in accurately placing the quantum of irregular migration in a broader context.

Table 2.1: Difficulties in measuring irregular migration

Aggregating data	Tends to disguise the complexity of irregular migration, e.g. 'mixed flows' consists of economic migrants and those fleeing persecution Lack of comparable data both over time and between locations
Media	Media tendency to focus on the highest available estimate Statistics may be used more to alarm than inform
Confusion in definitions	Irregular migration covers a range of people who can be in an irregular situation for different reasons, and people can switch from a regular to irregular status, or vice versa
Stocks and flows	Can be difficult to differentiate between the two and discern what is actually being counted Flows usually only focus on entries, not exits or return flows Stocks assume permanence, when migrants may leave, change their status or die Impossible to combine both stocks and flows to gain a total estimate
Data accessibility	Often collected by enforcement agencies and not made publicly available
Sensitivities around human rights	There may be some nondisclosure of irregular migrants by various parties (e.g. employers) making quantifying the number of irregular migrants difficult

Source: Koser (2010).

Part of the difficulty is related to definitional issues, which may differ by jurisdiction, as well as the wide-ranging nature of 'irregular' status, which can result, for example, from people entering countries undetected through sophisticated smuggling operations as well as from minor administrative issues that have the effect of rendering a person irregular. A useful summary of the main categories of irregular migrants is summarised in Table 2.2, highlighting the complexity of 'irregularity', which clearly has its more benign forms, particularly when viewed in the border management and/ or security context.

Table 2.2: Definition of irregular migration

In principle, irregular migration populations can be divided into five categories:	
1	Migrants who have illegally entered the country by either physically evading formal immigration control or presenting false papers.
2	Migrants who legally entered the country for a fixed period which has expired; they did not renew their permission to stay and are therefore unlawful overstayers.
3	Migrants who are lawfully entitled to reside in the country, but are in breach of some visa condition, notably by working more than their immigration status permits.
4	Asylum seekers who legally entered the country to pursue a case for refugee status, but who remain despite a final decision refusing them a continuing right to remain.
5	Children born in the country to such 'irregular migrants', who also lack a right to remain although they are not themselves migrants.

Source: Gordon, Scanlon, Travers, and Whitehead (2009).

Difficulties in quantifying irregular migration notwithstanding, it can be an important exercise, not least because it highlights the very substantial differences in estimates. In this regard, the imprecise nature of the task of quantification becomes apparent, and the need to treat data on irregular migration with caution is underscored. For example, estimates on the number of irregular migrants in Europe has varied widely from two to eight million (Koser, 2005). Recent reports estimate that there are around 12 million in the US (Hoefer, Rytina, & Baker, 2011). Some reports estimate that there are 'several' million irregular migrants in South and South East Asia, and between three and five million in South Africa (Koser, 2005). Further information on the estimated number of irregular migrants in selected locations is in Table 2.3.

Table 2.3: Estimated size of irregular migrant populations by region/country

Region/country	Time period	Estimated population (stock)	Source
European Union	2007	4.5 million	(a)
	2008	1.9–3.8 million	(b)
	2008	8 million	(c)
United Kingdom	2007	417,000–863,000	(d)
	2009	750,000	(e)
Italy	2008	651,000	(f)
	2010	544,000	(g)
	2011	<500,000	(g)
Greece	2011	172,000–390,000	(f)
Spain	2009	300,000–390,000	(f)
United States	2007	12.2 million	(g)
	2010	10.8–11.2 million	(h)
	2012	11.7 million	(g)
South Africa	2005	3–5 million	(i)
Saudi Arabia	2013	1 million+	(j)
Yemen	2013	25,000+	(k)
Australia	2010	53,900	(l)
	2011	58,400	(m)

Source: (a) Council of Europe (2007), p. 8. (b) Clandestino Project (2009b), p. 4. (c) Frontex (2010), p. 9. (d) Gordon et al. (2009), p. 7. (e) Koser (2010), p. 186. (f) Clandestino Project (2009a), p. 1. (g) European Migration Network, (2012), p. 213. (g) Passel, Cohn, & Gonzalez-Barrera (2013). (h) Rosenblum (2012). (i) Koser (2005). (j) Walker (2013). (k) Regional Mixed Migration Secretariat (2013). (l) Department of Immigration and Border Protection (DIBP) (2010). (m) Australian National Audit Office (ANAO) (2013), p. 39.

In a global context, irregular migration to Australia constitutes a very small proportion of all irregular migration, especially when compared to the US and Europe. More than five million temporary entrants visited Australia in 2012–13, with 16,460 persons recorded who did not leave when their visas expired. In the same period, some 25,100 people arrived irregularly by boat.

Irregular maritime migration flows

Unlike other forms of irregular migration, the numbers of irregular maritime migrants moving from poor, less developed and/or conflict ridden countries in Asia, Africa, Latin America and the Middle East to developed countries, such as the flows heading for the US, Europe and Australia, are relatively well documented. One of the reasons that this movement is monitored so closely is that it is highly visible. It also tends to be a focus of intense public interest. As a consequence, there has been in more recent times the development of highly regulated border management processes that have increased the capacity to count and report on the scope of irregular maritime flows.

The US Coast Guard, for example, reports precise figures going back to 1995. The EU's Frontex has increased its capacity, especially since 2008, to report on the number of persons detected while undertaking maritime migration in the Mediterranean and North Atlantic. In the Indian Ocean, the number of irregular migrants heading to Australia is recorded in some detail, although public reporting has tended to be at the aggregate level. These flows are typical of the focus on 'South–North' movement, and highlight the interest in monitoring irregular maritime migration the North.

The appetite for monitoring and reporting on such flows would appear to be considerable. There is also an issue of capability. Highly industrialised, richer destination countries, as opposed to poorer, less developed destination countries, have greater capacity to monitor and report on irregular maritime migration. Perhaps the largest, most significant flows of irregular maritime migrants occur well outside the three 'South–North' hotspots of the US, Europe and Australia, as the examples of Indonesia–Malaysia maritime migration and Africa–Middle East maritime migration discussed below appear to indicate, notwithstanding the lack of reliable statistics.

The scale of irregular maritime migration is difficult to quantify outside of the main South–North migration corridors. That said, even as recently as 10 years ago, such movement into Europe was not monitored and reported on in the highly systematised way it is today through Frontex. Overall, irregular maritime migration is able to be quantified in specific locations, namely the Caribbean Sea to the US, the Mediterranean Sea to Europe and the Indian Ocean to Australia. In recent years, Canada has experienced incidents of large noncommercial vessels of several hundred passengers arranged by smugglers, although this has been limited (e.g. the MVs [motor vessels] Sun Sea and Ocean Lady in 2009).

Data tends to capture interdictions/detections, and so clearly does not capture all attempts (successful or otherwise). It is likely that there are successful undetected maritime ventures in all contexts, but arguably this is less likely in some circumstances. For example, it is possible that failing to be intercepted off the northwest coast of Australia by authorities may result in irregular migrants perishing in the very harsh and isolated coastal regions; the need to be detected by authorities is a genuine one.

South–North irregular maritime migration: US, Europe and Australia

The Caribbean is the major region for undocumented maritime migrants attempting to enter the US, predominantly from Haiti, Cuba and the Dominican Republic. Since 1982, almost 50 per cent of migrants interdicted at sea were Haitians (118,700), followed by Cubans (29 per cent or 70,700 migrants) and migrants from the Dominican Republic (15 per cent or 36,600 migrants). Trend data, as shown in Figure 2.2, illustrates the very substantial increases in the early to mid-1990s, and the subsequent tapering off of interdictions.

Information gathering on irregular migration into the EU, either by land, air or sea, has been coordinated by Frontex since it began operations in 2005. Prior to this, each member state was responsible for its own marine surveillance along the EU's southern borders. As a result, historical statistics on the number of detections of illegal entry by sea are difficult to aggregate. Frontex data indicate that there were peaks and troughs in maritime migration since 2009, until the dramatic increase in 2015. Between 2009 and 2014, the number of maritime irregular detections had been low (mainly under 40,000 per quarter). Then, in 2015, more than 850,000 travelled through the Eastern Mediterranean route from Turkey to Greece (Frontex, 2015).

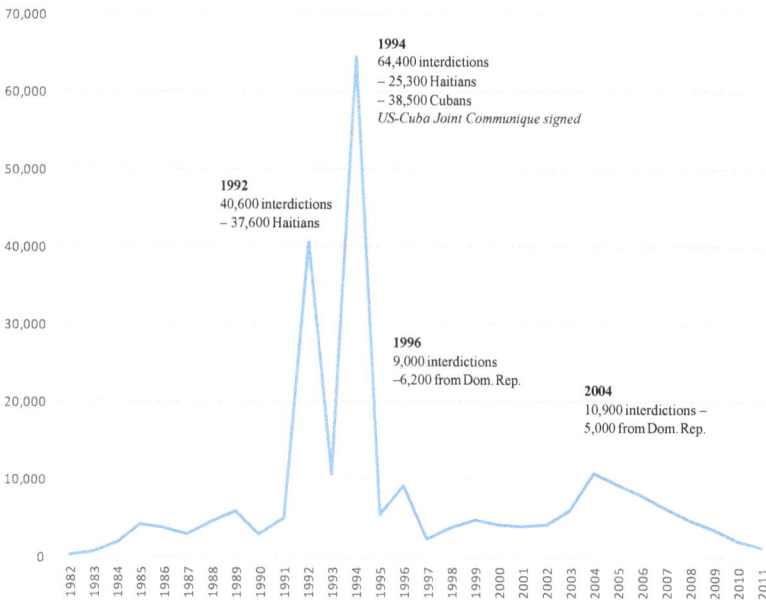

Figure 2.2: Maritime migrant interdictions since 1982 by fiscal year
Source: Adapted from United States Coast Guard (2014).

Since the mid-1970s, Australia has received over 69,000 irregular maritime arrivals (IMAs). The vast majority of these (71 per cent, almost 49,000) arrived in the last four calendar years. The year 2013 experienced the largest volume of IMAs to Australia ever recorded, with over 20,700 arrivals. A total of 41 citizenship groups have arrived in Australia since 2008. Figure 2.3 shows the trend of IMAs to Australia since the 1970s. The significant decline at the end of 2013 reflects the measures taken by the Australian Government that resulted in only 157 IMAs arriving in 2014.

Analysis of official data published by Australia, the US and the EU suggests a differentiation in the way irregular migrants enter key destination countries, predominantly reflecting geography. Figure 2.4 shows that the vast majority of irregular migrants detected in 2012 were attempting to enter Australia by sea (92 per cent). By comparison, the majority of detected irregular migrants to the US were by land. In the EU, land travel comprised a higher proportion of irregular migration than sea travel, noting that air detection statistics were not available. Ideally, trend analysis would be able to provide a fuller picture of the relativities within regions, and more accurately highlight differences between regions, particularly given the fluctuations in Europe between land and sea detections.

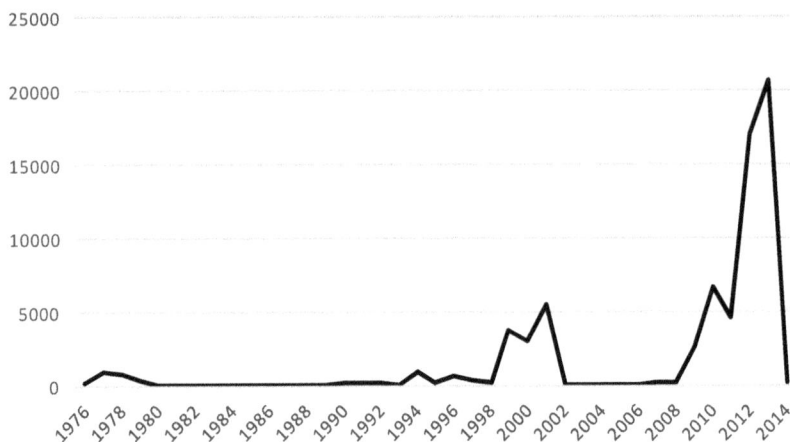

Figure 2.3: Number of IMAs to Australia, 1976–2014
Source: Adapted from Phillips & Spinks (2013); updated using unpublished departmental data.

Based on most accounts, the scale of detected and undetected irregular migration (South to North) and number of unauthorised persons at any given time in the US and Europe is substantial and indicates that irregular maritime migration at the borders constitutes a small part of irregular migration. In contrast, the situation in Australia is different—as an island continent, geography, sea borders and relative isolation provide Australia with a unique ability among industrialised countries to manage its border. Australia does not have the vast and porous land borders that characterise the border management problems faced by the US and Europe, and maritime migration is the main manifestation of irregular migration in the Australian context.

Placing irregular maritime movements in the context of irregular migration more broadly is an important step in assessing the significance of irregular maritime migration, particularly in relation to calibrating policy responses. While this is not a straightforward exercise, and should be treated with some caution, Figure 2.4 does highlight the different dynamics occurring in different national and regional settings. This perhaps may go some way to explain the levels of focus afforded to the different forms of irregular migration.

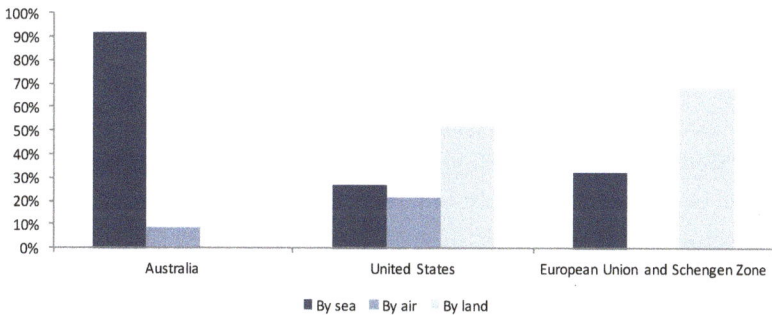

Figure 2.4: Proportion of detected irregular arrivals by region and mode of travel around 2012

Source: Data for Australia was sourced from the Department of Immigration and Citizenship (DIAC) (2012–13). Data for the US was sourced Simanski and Sapp (2012). Data for the EU was sourced from Frontex (2013).

Note: Sea arrivals for Australia were based on 25,000 irregular maritime arrivals (excluding vessel crew members) and excluded a small number of illegal foreign fishers and people who arrived on a scheduled cargo or cruise vessel and were refused entry at a seaport. Air arrivals were based on those who arrived on a scheduled flight and were subsequently refused entry at an airport. Data for the US relates to approximately 193,000 aliens determined inadmissible at a US border. It excluded some 360,000 persons apprehended at border control points, as a breakdown of these persons by mode of travel was unavailable. Data for the EU relates to over 72,000 illegal border crossings between border control points for 27 countries in the EU and 3 Schengen associated countries (Norway, Iceland and Switzerland). Data for unauthorised air arrivals for the entire EU was unavailable. The proportions are for illustrative purposes only, and are based on the number of detected irregular arrivals by mode of travel. The data does not include estimates for undetected border crossings, and does not take into account variations in proportions over time. Note that the graph refers to proportions, not absolute volumes. The reference period for Australia is Australian Financial Year 2012–13;[5] the US is Fiscal Year 2012;[6] the EU is calendar year 2012.

Further examples of irregular maritime migration: Horn of Africa and South East Asia

Another region of substantial irregular maritime activity, involving migrants mainly from Ethiopia and Somalia, is the Gulf of Aden and the Red Sea between the Horn of Africa to Yemen. The organisation responsible for recording this movement is the Regional Mixed Migration Secretariat. The capture of data has improved steadily since 2010. While the reporting may not capture every movement the numbers reported give

---

5   Australian Financial Year 2012–13 is 1 July 2012 to 30 June 2013.
6   United States Fiscal Year 2012 is 1 October 2011 to 30 September 2012.

a clear indication that the scope of irregular maritime movement involved is substantial. Around 500,000 people are estimated to have crossed the Gulf of Aden between 2007 and 2013.

Other flows tend to be more clandestine. Based on the migration characteristics of various citizenship groups and their inability to access regular travel pathways, there are thought to be significant numbers of people moving by boat in the South East Asian region. Many of these people appear to be undocumented migrant workers seeking work in neighbouring countries. Others travel to Indonesia from where they join boats to Australia. The true scale of this movement is thought to be substantial and used mainly by those who lack the capacity to travel via regular pathways, although the numbers are difficult to track and there is limited data to report. There are estimated, however, to be around two million irregular migrants in Malaysia alone (International Organization for Migration [IOM], 2010).

Media reporting on sudden flashpoints or hot spots is triggered, more often than not, by tragic incidents such as boats sinking, loss of life at sea or a sudden and unexpected upsurge in movement. Extensive media reports, for example, indicate that since the dramatic increase in interethnic violence in Rakhine province in Myanmar from mid-2012, there has been a substantial increase in the maritime migration of Rohingya from Myanmar and neighbouring Bangladesh to Thailand, Malaysia, Indonesia and beyond. This flow became a humanitarian crisis in May 2015 when thousands of Rohingya and Bengali migrants were stranded at sea, having been pushed back by Thai, Indonesian and Malaysian authorities.

The multifaceted nature of irregular maritime migration

In seeking to understand the complexity of irregular maritime migration as a dynamic global phenomenon occurring within broader global forces, it is important to critically examine some of its key aspects. While it is beyond the scope of this chapter to examine the multitude of issues that may relate to the phenomenon, an attempt to draw out the key aspects has been made. These are discussed in this section and include: geography and mode of transport; non-state actors and migrant smuggling; international obligations and state sovereignty; and migrants' motivations.

Geography and mode of transport

Geography plays a fundamental role in irregular migration flows. The physical proximity of source and destination countries as well as the nature of their geographic positioning—land borders, sea/ocean channels—is a significant factor in people movement. The ease (or otherwise) by which people are able to travel irregularly using different modes of transport is an important factor. For example, around 266,000 Mexicans are estimated to have been apprehended trying to enter the US overland in 2012 (Passel, Cohn, & Gonzalez-Barrera, 2013), whereas 79 Mexicans were intercepted by US Coastguards in 2012 (United States Coast Guard, 2014).

While not wishing to overgeneralise, and noting that all forms of irregular movement would involve considerable challenges and difficulties for migrants, the ability to undertake land border crossings (however perilous) is likely to involve a reduced level of organisation and logistical support compared to maritime migration. First, maritime migration usually involves groups of people rather than individuals and so requires at least a basic level of organisation. Second, infrastructure in the form of a seaworthy vessel is required to make the journey, involving logistics and cost. Land border crossings, on the other hand, can be undertaken by individuals and do not require the same level of infrastructure and organisational support.

This has implications for direct movements between source and destination countries—the huge volume across the US–Mexican land border being a case in point—as well as for the relative ease in which transit countries can be entered. Transit countries with long porous land borders (e.g. Libya, Egypt, Morocco) may perhaps pose fewer constraints than transit countries with different geography (e.g. Indonesia, Malaysia). Many irregular maritime migrants to Spain, for example, travel from different locations in sub-Saharan Africa through land borders of Morocco before travelling by sea to Spain or entering via the Spanish enclaves Ceuta and Melilla (de Haas, 2005). Movement to Australia, on the other hand, presents a unique dynamic in that not only is Australia without a land border, but as well its main transit country (Indonesia) has limited land borders given its island composition.

The fundamental role of physical geography, while able to be overcome via air travel, is arguably a more important aspect now compared to 15 to 20 years ago, and prior to the significant increase in screening of air travellers

(Faist, 2004). It is likely with the recent advances in border control and identity verification technology, air travel offers fewer opportunities for irregular migrants seeking to enter destination countries, although people using genuine travel documentation based on a fraudulent identity remain a considerable challenge, one that is being increasingly addressed through the use of biometric technology.

It is possible that, overall, the tightening of air travel has had an impact on irregular migration via other modes (land and sea). There is no doubt that irregular migration by land border crossing and maritime venture continue to be viewed as viable options by migrants, agents and smugglers where these options are available, and particularly given that citizens of many countries who travel irregularly are unable to access regular migration pathways (see Table 2.1). In addition, and as discussed above, a certain level of organisational capability needs to be in place to support irregular maritime migration, and while this may act as a constraint, it may also enable/encourage the expansion of unregulated actors (e.g. organisers, smugglers and corrupt officials).

Non-state actors and migrant smuggling

There has been substantial research and enquiry into migrant smuggling processes and dynamics, predominantly in relation to migrant smuggling into Europe, and in the context of the Protocol against the Smuggling of Migrants by Land, Sea and Air. In a 2011 report by the United Nations Office on Drugs and Crime (UNODC), a global review of migrant smuggling revealed a number of dynamics and characteristics that highlight the considerable challenges in tackling and reducing smuggling—see the summary of the UNODC report below. More recently, the UNODC has highlighted the significant role corruption plays in migrant smuggling, noting that (UNODC, 2011, p. 3):

> Migrant smuggling could not occur on the large scale that it so often does without collusion between corrupt officials and criminals. Corruption seriously undermines national and international efforts to prevent and control the smuggling of migrants … [it] may occur in countries of origin, transit, or destination. It may be systemic, institutional or individual.

The organisational capabilities of non-state actors involved in irregular migration, including corrupt officials, agents, organisers and smugglers, has undoubtedly been assisted by changes in telecommunications, which offer greater opportunities for people to participate successfully in the movement of people irregularly. In this sense, smuggling networks are able to occur largely outside of effective state regulation, allowing perhaps a greater degree of 'opportunism' by a wider range of actors than has occurred in the past. The notion of organised, 'apex' smuggling systems that are controlled by mafia-type bosses has largely given way to recognition that smuggling involves less organised, highly agile networks of relationships (Pastore, Monzini, & Sciortino, 2006, p. 109):

> the evolutions of the smuggling industry does [*sic*] not seem to produce highly structured and hierarchically governed organisations, but rather flexible coalitions managed through contractual agreements and repeated interactions.

Targeting of operational and policy responses to reduce the viability of migrant smuggling for the range of actors involved has been a key focus of governments, including in relation to irregular maritime migration (Koser, 2011). Such responses will undoubtedly continue to be central components in strategic and tactical efforts to reduce irregular maritime migration.

Other commentators have drawn attention to the need for more systematic change to underlying markets as a key component to reducing irregular migration, and have characterised some employers as 'bad actors' and suggested that 'markets—not criminal masterminds, syndicates or networks—drive illegality' (Papademetriou, 2014, p. 2). In the context of the somewhat limited data on stocks and flows of irregular migrants, as described above, it could be hypothesised that structural labour market issues are more of an issue for some markets that have a greater reliance on irregular migration (e.g. the US and parts of Europe) compared to other markets (e.g. Australia).

International obligations and state sovereignty

The tensions between state action and international legal obligations and responsibilities are a recurring theme throughout the literature. While detailed legal and technical analysis is beyond the scope of this chapter, there are some aspects worth highlighting that demonstrate that the problems are complex and not easily reconciled.

Irregular maritime migration, in many respects, encapsulates one of the most contentious fault lines between state sovereignty and international legal obligations and responsibilities. Strong links tend to be made by governments between migration control, border protection and state sovereignty. Governments are often very concerned to demonstrate that they have a firm grip on the movement of people across borders—a (legitimate) sovereign right that tends to be jealously guarded (Brouwer & Kumin, 2003; van Selm & Cooper, 2005). 'Control over migration is interpreted … as being somehow intrinsic to what is it to be a nation, to "stateness" and to the core of membership and national identity' (Dauvergne, 2003, p. 2).

Irregular maritime migration invokes a range of international norms and conventions in relation to human rights, law of the sea, including rescue at sea, and criminality associated with migrant smuggling and trafficking— all of which makes for a complex mix (de Bruycker, di Bartolomeo, & Fargues, 2013; Miltner, 2006). Given its visibility, and the attention irregular migration by sea attracts, the imperative to demonstrate state control of maritime borders is particularly sensitive. However, reconciling state practices to stem the flow of irregular maritime migration with international legal responsibilities and obligations is complicated by conflicting interests, blurred lines of responsibility and overlapping issues (Mallia, 2003). For example, in Europe, confusion and disagreements over territorial boundaries at sea and state responsibility for search and rescue are proving difficult to resolve. There are concerns that the confusion over who has responsibility among states undermines international cooperation to protect life at sea, seen by many as a fundamental humanitarian consideration (Annan, 2014; Mallia, 2003).

State measures to control irregular maritime migration can, and do, often clash with humanitarian considerations inherent in multiple international legal instruments that are activated in relation to irregular maritime migration, including in relation to nonrefoulement. Reconciling these conflicting interests is a fundamental challenge for all stakeholders involved. Critics of restrictive measures that are increasingly focused on preventing migrant flows from reaching their destination or from departing source and transit countries suggest that this fails to address the protection concerns of refugees caught up in irregular maritime migration flows (Dauvergne, 2003; Gammeltoft-Hansen, 2008).

Gammeltoft-Hansen (2008) suggested that this extraterritorial shift to focus on measures that attempt to deflect or prevent movement is regarded by some commentators as a geographical relocation of the border, with the potential to relocate the limits of sovereignty in relation to border control. Striking a balance between state sovereignty and international legal frameworks in the context of the increasing trend towards extraterritorialism in relation to irregular maritime migration, and the complex set of issues involved, is thought to be a key global challenge of the future.

Irregular maritime migration presents an undeniably visual manifestation of irregular migration and as such triggers some fundamental political and policy concerns relating to states' international protection obligations, sovereignty, border control and security, and as such demands the attention of governments (Koser & McAuliffe, 2013; Koser, 2010; Watson, 2009). The potential and actual impacts on bilateral relationships as well as regional and broader international relationships and reputations are also key considerations for governments, including as they relate to sovereignty issues.

There is a strong sense that, notwithstanding different interests, values and priorities, as Newland pointed out, 'international migration has surpassed the ability of any one country to manage unilaterally' (Newland, 2010, p. 336). The transnational nature of irregular maritime migration demands government-to-government cooperation, including in a multilayered or tiered fashion. Engagement via multilateral forums as well as regional consultative processes are important means of understanding and working through points of convergence and divergence; these forms of engagement can also act to support or enhance bilateral cooperation.

Migrants' motivations

A number of complex, interrelated factors impact on the movement of irregular asylum and non-asylum migration flows, and in relation to why people migrate (Castles, 2013; de Haas, 2011; Havinga & Böcker, 1999; Koser, 2011; Middleton 2005; Neumayer, 2004). Historically, academic and nonacademic writing has been dominated by the 'push–pull' model, with its roots in Ravenstein's laws of migration from the 1880s.

Today, among policymakers, the 'push–pull' theory continues to dominate, possibly because of the attractiveness it offers as a conceptually linear model. The model also downplays migrant agency, with migrants being 'pushed' and 'pulled' from and to locations. Perhaps a century ago it was highly relevant in social, economic, technological and geopolitical terms, and it offered a way of explaining and understanding migration. It is less relevant today, including because of the substantial social, economic, technological and geopolitical changes that have ensued in most parts of the world and that are enabling much greater transnational interaction.

Hein de Haas has argued that 'people will only migrate if they perceive better opportunities elsewhere and have the capabilities to move' (de Haas, 2011, p. 14). Through a range of dynamics (or 'enabling' factors), including diaspora and other migrant networks, de Haas argued that migrants' agency and counterstrategies can effectively undermine states' attempts to control migration. It is important to note that de Haas' theoretical discussion was not specific to irregular migration; however, he argued that refugee and asylum flows also involve agency and that 'the "voluntary"–"forced" migration dichotomy is simplistic because it assumes that one category of migrants enjoys total freedom and the other category has no choice or agency at all' (de Haas, 2011, p. 14).

Adhikari's research on the relative impact of a range of factors on migrants' decision-making in Nepal highlights that migrant agency, even in extreme conflict situations, is present, and that decisions on movement were based on more than just the threat to one's life and included factors related to economic livelihoods and social networks (Adhikari, 2013). He highlighted the need for further research into the survival strategies people adopt once they decide to stay in war zones.

Much of the irregular maritime migration flows, including to Europe, Yemen, Australia and the US, are not sudden onset (although there are exceptions from time to time, such as the 2011 Libya crisis), and do involve migrant agency, and possibly considered, long-term decision-making processes. The number of factors impacting on movement and decision-making highlights the complex nature of irregular maritime migration. It is also important to acknowledge that none of the factors are likely to be static, and some of them can change decisively and rapidly, undoubtedly adding to the complexity of irregular migration.

The 'mixed' composition of irregular migrant populations, as opposed to past assumptions that irregular migration flows were composed primarily of asylum seekers, is a significant and important characteristic of modern manifestations of irregular migration (Miltner, 2006; Papastavridis, 2007). One of the more significant conundrums highlighted by irregular maritime migration is the 'migration–asylum nexus'. In the midst of the irregular migration flows of migrant workers are people who have moved because of war, ethnic or political persecution and meet the criteria as refugees. To add to the complexity, the boundaries between each group can be blurred or even change over time with migrant workers becoming refugees or vice versa (Koser, 2013).

On the one hand, the humanitarian crisis in Syria provides a very stark illustration of the fundamental need for the protection of people in fear for their lives, and of the ongoing and perhaps growing need for an effective international system that provides refugee protection. There is a clear imperative for states and international organisations to respond quickly and decisively in such situations.

When examining irregular maritime movement involving asylum seekers, onwards movement is an important consideration, as are the reasons underpinning movement. It is, in this context, useful to acknowledge Johansson's distinction between anticipatory refugee movement and acute or spontaneous movements (Johansson, 1990). As highlighted by Koser and McAuliffe, '[for] IMAs in Australia, who have undertaken long and relatively expensive journeys from their origin countries, and transited other countries where they might have remained in an irregular situation … the choice of Australia for most … appears to be deliberate' (2013, p. 13). Much of the movement to Australia in recent years has been anticipatory rather than acute. This, in turn, and given the substantial distances travelled from source through (multiple) transit countries to Australia, means that both the decision to leave and the choice of destination are highly relevant topics of research in the Australian context.

A further line of enquiry relevant to the examination of global irregular maritime migration is the extent to which communities actively use migration as a strategy for survival and/or to improve individual and collective outcomes. This conceptualisation of migration as a social strategy acknowledges that there are often many reasons underpinning migration that are not static but dynamic in nature, depending on prevailing circumstances. Monsutti, for example, has argued that in relation to Hazaras, no hard and fast distinction can be made between refugees and economic migrants, and that a 'migration continuum' exists that has developed as part of a broader strategy of survival (2005, pp. 168–69):

> Afghans give different and usually plural reasons for their decision to migrate: perhaps an outbreak of fighting, a threat from a personal enemy, the danger of bombing or compulsory conscription; perhaps the search for work or opportunities to trade, the need for medical treatment, or the undertaking of a pilgrimage.

When viewed as a social strategy, the existence of migration pathways and networks, including to and within destination countries, is almost certainly likely to have an impact on the tendency and ability of groups of people to migrate successfully. Migration as part of historical and cultural norms is an aspect that is prevalent in some academic discussion (Monsutti, 2005).

Some evidence of the many reasons underpinning asylum flows and the search for a better life are evident in empirical research conducted under the Irregular Migration Research Program (as described in the Preface and Introduction), and as discussed in Chapter 3 (Sri Lankan survey results) and Chapter 11 (survey of IMAs granted protection).

Conclusions

Irregular maritime migration is intrinsically linked to a range of other phenomena—regular migration, other forms of irregular migration, human development, improvements in telecommunications and the securitisation of migration. The complex, multifaceted nature of irregular maritime migration renders it a particularly challenging issue for many states around the world. The geopolitical implications now and into the future are potentially profound as origin, transit and destination states work to better manage movements and seek to avoid deaths at sea and reduce migrant vulnerability.

When examined as a global phenomenon, it is evident that South–North irregular maritime migration flows are highly visible and well documented, especially compared to other (larger) flows, including in South East Asia, Africa and the Middle East. A better understanding of the scale and nature of flows in other parts of the world, including in relation to the issues that migrants face, may raise additional challenges with broader implications for global migration movements.

There is a sense that the willingness of states to engage in forms of cooperation and collaboration on irregular maritime migration that do not involve the formulation of restrictive responses has diminished over time (Castles, 2004; de Haas, 2011). This diminution is reflective of current global and geopolitical dynamics, and in particular a growing sense of the potential for significantly increased 'unmanaged' migration in light of increased international movement (GCIM, 2005). The collaboration involved in managing earlier displacement—the Comprehensive Plan of Action in South East Asia to deal with flows from Vietnam and Laos being one example—appears, in a general sense, to have increasingly given way to state-centric hardening of positions.

Where there are 'pockets' or discrete groups that are able to be managed, it would appear that there is a greater degree of willingness to engage collaboratively in a positive sense in attempts to manage displacement. One such example of this can be seen in relation to states' handling of stateless groups, where the size of the stateless groups appears to be a factor (among others) in states' willingness to collaborate to find solutions with the assistance of the UNHCR. A second factor related to cooperation would appear to be related to whether the displacement issue is entrenched and/ or enduring, or more akin to an acute, sudden-onset displacement. This is perhaps best highlighted by large-scale displacement in Libya and Syria, which resulted in significant humanitarian support being provided from a range of actors, particularly at the outset. It remains to be seen how this will eventually unfold in Europe if the recent significant increases from Syria, Afghanistan, Iraq and elsewhere continue into the coming years.

In global and international discussions, it would appear that the appetite for a greater degree of convergence of approaches to restrictive migration policies, recognising migrant rights and increasing human development may well be increasing, notwithstanding the inherent difficulties in navigating a path that is able to achieve aspects of all three objectives. This will continue to be a challenge for individual nation states and regions as the global discourse evolves and expectations change. It may well be that in the future not only will migrants' aspirations increase, but significant populations may find that their capability to migrate may also increase. For some of these people, irregular maritime migration may well prove the only viable migration option.

Notwithstanding considerable challenges, it is worth reflecting on the policy and operational response capacities of some nation states to effectively harness resources (including financial, human, intellectual, technological and social, etc.) to deal with complex and difficult issues. There would appear to be a strong appetite for agile responses based on a good understanding of evidence, options, implications and risk, including in global and regional forums. One of the challenges for policymakers is to be able to deliver on all of these aspects in dynamic environments, and in an era of greater contestability.

Reference list

Adhikari, P. (2013). Conflict-induced displacement, understanding the causes of flight. *American Journal of Political Science, 57*(1), 82–89. doi.org/10.1111/j.1540-5907.2012.00598.x

Australian National Audit Office. (2013). Individual management services provided to people in immigration detention. Canberra: ANAO.

Banerjee, B. (1983). Social networks in the migration process: Empirical evidence on chain migration in India. *The Journal of Developing Areas, 17*(2), 185–96.

Blaschke, J. (1998, 29 June – 3 July). *Addressing the employment of migrants in an irregular situation: the case of Germany.* Paper presented at the technical symposium on international migration and development, The Hague.

Brouwer, A., & Kumin. J. (2003). Interception and asylum: Where migration control and human rights collide. *Interception and Asylum, 21*(4), 6–24.

Campbell, A. (2014). Public interest immunity claim, January 31, 2014, Legal and Constitutional Affairs References Committee. *Hansard—Parliament of Australia.*

Carling, J. (2002). Migration in the age of involuntary immobility. *Journal of Ethnic and Migration Studies, 28*(1), 5–42. doi.org/10.1080/13691830120103912

Castles, S. (2002). *Environmental change and forced migration: making sense of the debate.* New issues in refugee research, working paper no. 70. Geneva: United Nations High Commissioner for Refugees.

Castles, S. (2004). Why migration policies fail. *Ethnic and Racial Studies, 27*(2), 205–227. doi.org/10.1080/0141987042000177306

Castles, S. (2013). The forces driving global migration. *Journal of Intercultural Studies, 34*(2), 122–40. doi.org/10.1080/07256868.201 3.781916

Ceyhan, A., & Tsoukala, A. (2002). The securitization of migration in western societies: Ambivalent discourses and policies. *Alternatives, 27*(Special Issue), 21–39. doi.org/10.1177/03043754020270s103

Clandestino Project. (2009a). *Database on irregular migration, stocks of irregular migrants: Estimates for Spain.* Retrieved from irregular-migration.net/typo3_upload/groups/31/3.Database_on_IrregMig/3.2.Stock_Tables/Spain_Estimates_IrregularMigration_Nov09_2.pdf.

Clandestino Project. (2009b). *Policy brief: Size and development of irregular migration to the EU.* Retrieved from irregular-migration.net/fileadmin/irregular-migration/dateien/4.Background_Information/4.2.Policy_Briefs_EN/ComparativePolicyBrief_SizeOfIrregularMigration_Clandestino_Nov09_2.pdf.

Clarke, J. (2000). The problems of evaluating numbers of illegal migrants in the European Union. In P. de Bruycker (Ed.), *Regularisations of illegal immigrants in the European Union.* Brussels: Bruylant.

Conversi, D. (2012). Irresponsible radicalisation: Diasporas, globalisation and long-distance nationalism in the digital age. *Journal of Ethnic and Migration Studies, 38*(9), 1357–79. doi.org/10.1080/1369183X.2012.698204

Council of Europe. (2007). *The Human Rights of Irregular Migrants in Europe.* Commissaire aux droits de l'homme issue paper 1. Brussels: Council of Europe. Retrieved from rm.coe.int/16806da797.

Crisp, J. (1999). *Policy challenges of the new diasporas: migrant networks and their impact on asylum flows and regimes.* ESRC transnational communities programme working paper. Oxford, University of Oxford.

Dauvergne C. (2003, April). *Challenges to sovereignty: Migration laws for the 21st century.* Paper presented at the 13th Commonwealth law conference, Melbourne.

de Bruycker, P., di Bartolomeo, A., & Fargues, P. (2013). *Migrants smuggled by sea to the EU: Facts, laws and policy options.* Migration Policy Centre research report. Florence: European University Institute.

de Haas, H. (2005). *Morocco: From Emigration Country to Africa's Migration Passage to Europe.* Washington DC: Migration Policy Institute. Retrieved from www.migrationpolicy.org/article/morocco-emigration-country-africas-migration-passage-europe.

de Haas, H. (2011). *The determinants of International migration: conceptualising policy, origin & destination effects.* Working paper. Oxford: International Migration Institute. Retrieved from www.imi.ox.ac.uk/publications/wp-32-11.

Department of Immigration and Border Protection. (2010). *Fact sheet 86—Overstayers and other unlawful non-citizens.* Canberra: Author.

Department of Immigration and Citizenship. (2012–13). *Annual report.* Canberra: Commonwealth of Australia.

Doneys, P. (2011). En-gendering insecurities: The case of the migration policy regime in Thailand. *International Journal of Social Quality, 1*(2), 50–65. doi.org/10.3167/IJSQ.2011.010205

European Migration Network. (2012). *Practical measures to reduce irregular migration,* European Migration Network synthesis report. Retrieved from ec.europa.eu/home-affairs/sites/homeaffairs/files/what-we-do/networks/european_migration_network/reports/docs/emn-studies/irregular-migration/00a_emn_synthesis_report_irregular_migration_october_2012_en.pdf.

Faist, T. (2004). *The migration-security nexus: International migration and security before and after 9/11.* Willy Brandt series of working papers in international migration and ethnic relations. Sweden: Malmo University.

Frontex (European Agency for the Management of Operational Coordination at the External Borders of the Member States of the European Union). (2010). *Frontex annual risk analysis 2010.* Warsaw, Poland: Frontex.

Frontex (European Agency for the Management of Operational Coordination at the External Borders of the Member States of the European Union). (2013). *Frontex annual risk analysis 2013.* Warsaw, Poland: Frontex.

Frontex (European Agency for the Management of Operational Coordination at the External Borders of the Member States of the European Union). (2015). *Frontex annual risk analysis 2014*, Warsaw, Poland: Frontex.

Gammeltoft-Hansen, T. (2008). *The refugee, the sovereign and the sea: EU interdiction policies in the Mediterranean*. Danish Institute for International Studies (DIIS) working paper 6, Copenhagen.

Global Commission on International Migration. (2005). *Migration in an interconnected world: New directions for action*. Geneva: Author.

Gomez, O.A., & Gasper, D. (2013) *Human security: A thematic Guidance note for regional and national human development report teams*. New York: United Nations Development Programme.

Gordon, I., Scanlon, K., Travers, T., & Whitehead, C. (2009). *Economic Impact on London and the UK of an Earned Regularisation of Irregular Migrants in the UK*. London: Greater London Authority.

Havinga, T., & Böcker, A. (1999). Country of asylum by choice or by chance: asylum-seekers in Belgium, the Netherland and the UK. *Journal of Ethnic and Migration Studies, 25*(1), 43–61. doi.org/10.108 0/1369183X.1999.9976671

Hoefer, M., Rytina, N., & Baker, B. (2011). *Estimates of the unauthorized immigrant population residing in the United States*. Office of Immigration Statistics, US Department of Homeland Security. Retrieved from www.dhs.gov/sites/default/files/publications/Unauthorized%20 Immigrant%20Population%20Estimates%20in%20the%20US%20 January%202011_0.pdf.

Hollifield, J. (2004). The emerging migration state. *The International Migration Review, 38*(3), 885–912. doi.org/10.1111/j.1747-7379. 2004.tb00223.x

Hopkins, L. (2009). Media and migration: a review of the field. *Australian Journal of Communication, 36*(2), 35–54.

Hugo, G. (2014) The changing dynamics of ASEAN international migration. *Malaysian Journal of Economic Studies 51*(1): 43–67.

Humphrey, M. (2013). Migration, security and insecurity. *Journal of Intercultural Studies, 34*(2), 178–95. doi.org/10.1080/07256868.201 3.781982

Huysmans, J. (2000). The European Union and the securitization of migration. *Journal of Common Market Studies, 38*(5), 751–77. doi.org/ 10.1111/1468-5965.00263

International Migration Institute. (2006). *Towards a new agenda for international migration research*. Oxford: Author. Retrieved from www. imi.ox.ac.uk/publications/towards-a-new-agenda-for-international-migration-research.

International Organization for Migration. (2010). *Labour migration from Indonesia*. Jakarta: Author.

Johansson, R. (1990). The refugee experience in Europe after World War II: Some theoretical and empirical considerations. In Rystad, G. (Ed.), *The uprooted: Forced migration as international problem in the post war era* (pp. 227–62). Lund: Lund University Press.

Kim, S., Carvalho, J., Davis, A., & Mullins, A. (2011). The view of the border: News framing of the definition, causes, and solutions to illegal immigration. *Mass Communication and Society, 14*, 292–314. doi.org/ 10.1080/15205431003743679

Koser, K. (2005, September). *Irregular migration, state security and human security*. Paper prepared for the policy analysis and research programme of the Global Commission on International Migration. Geneva: GCIM. Retrieved from www.peacepalacelibrary.nl/ebooks/files/GCIM_TP5.pdf.

Koser, K. (2010). Dimensions and dynamics of irregular migration. *Population, Space and Place, 16*(3), 181–93. doi.org/10.1002/psp.587

Koser, K. (2011). The smuggling of refugees. In D. Kyle, & R. Koslowski (Eds), *Global human smuggling* (pp. 257–72). Baltimore, MD: Johns Hopkins University Press.

Koser, K., & McAuliffe, M. (2013). *Establishing an evidence-base for future policy development on irregular migration to Australia*. Irregular Migration Research Program, Occasional Paper Series 01. Canberra:

Australian Department of Immigration and Citizenship. Retrieved from www.border.gov.au/ReportsandPublications/Documents/research/evidence-base-for-future-policy.pdf.

Koser, K., & Pinkerton, C. (2002). *The social networks of asylum seekers and the dissemination of information about countries of asylum*. London: UK Home Office.

Mallia, P. (2003). *The challenges of irregular migration*. Jean Monnet occasional papers no. 4. Malta: Institute for European Studies.

Martin, P., & Taylor, J. (1996). The anatomy of a migration hump. In Taylor, J. (Ed.), *Development strategy, employment, and migration: Insights from models* (pp. 43–62). Paris: OECD Development Centre.

Meyer, J. B. (2001). *Network approach versus brain drain: Lessons from the diaspora*. International Migration, 39. Oxford: Blackwell Publishers Ltd.

Middleton, D. (2005). *Why asylum seekers seek refuge in particular destination countries: an exploration of key determinants*. Global Migration Perspectives, No. 34. Geneva: Global Commission on International Migration. Retrieved from www.refworld.org/docid/42ce54774.html.

Miggiano, L. (2009, November). *States of exception: securitisation and irregular migration in the Mediterranean*. New issues in refugee research, no. 177. Geneva: United Nations High Commissioner for Refugees. Retrieved from www.refworld.org/docid/4c232575a.html.

Miltner, B. (2006). Irregular maritime migration: Refugee protection issues in rescue and interception. *Fordham International Law Journal, 30*(1), 75–125.

Monsutti, A. (2005). *War and migration: Social networks and economic strategies of the Hazaras of Afghanistan*. London: Routledge.

Morrison, S. (2014). Public interest immunity claim, January 31, 2014, Legal and Constitutional Affairs References Committee. *Hansard— Parliament of Australia*.

Mulvey, G. (2010). When policy creates politics: The problematizing of immigration and the consequences for refugee integration in the UK. *Journal of Refugee Studies, 23*, 437–62. doi.org/10.1093/jrs/feq045

Nedelcu, M. (2012). Migrants' new transnational habitus: Rethinking migration through a cosmopolitan lens in the digital age. *Journal of Ethnic and Migration Studies, 38*(9), 1339–56. doi.org/10.1080/1369 183X.2012.698203

Neumayer, E. (2004). Asylum destination choice—What makes some West European countries more attractive than others? *European Union Politics, 5*(2), 155–80. doi.org/10.1177/1465116504042444

Newland, K. (2010). The governance of international migration: Mechanisms, processes and institutions. *Global Governance, 16,* 331–43.

Panagakos, A., & Horst, H. (2006). Return to Cyberia: Technology and the social worlds of transnational migrants. *Global Networks, 6*(2), 109–24.

Papademetriou, D. (2014). *Curbing the influence of 'bad actors' in international migration.* Washington DC: Migration Policy Institute. Retrieved from www.migrationpolicy.org/research/curbing-influence-bad-actors-international-migration.

Papastavridis, E. (2007, 28–29 September). *Interception of human beings on the high seas under the law of the sea convention.* Paper presented at the second European Society of International Law (ESIL) research forum, Budapest.

Passel, J., Cohn, D., & Gonzalez-Barrera, A. (2013). *Population decline of unauthorized immigrants stalls, may have reversed.* Washington DC: Pew Research Centre. Retrieved from www.pewhispanic.org/2013/09/23/population-decline-of-unauthorized-immigrants-stalls-may-have-reversed/.

Pastore, F., Monzini, P., & Sciortino, G. (2006). Schengen's soft underbelly? Irregular migration and human smuggling across land and sea borders to Italy. *International Migration, 44*(4), 95–119. doi.org/10.1111/j.1468-2435.2006.00381.x

Phillips, J., & Spinks, H. (2013). *Boat arrivals in Australia since 1976.* Parliamentary library research paper. Canberra: Parliament of Australia. Retrieved from www.aph.gov.au/About_Parliament/Parliamentary_Departments/Parliamentary_Library/pubs/rp/rp1314/BoatArrivals.

Pickering, S. (2001). Common sense and original deviancy: News discourse and asylum seekers in Australia. *Journal of Refugee Studies, 14*(2), 169–86. doi.org/10.1093/jrs/14.2.169

Rabogoshvili, A. (2012). Chinese migration to Russia as revealed by narratives in Chinese cyberspace. *Journal of Current Chinese Affairs, 41*(2), 9–36.

Regional Mixed Migration Secretariat. (2013). *Responses to mixed migration in the Horn of Africa and Yemen: Policies and assistance responses in a fast-changing context.* Nairobi: Author.

Rosenblum, M. (2012). *Border security: Immigration enforcement between ports of entry.* Washington DC: Congressional Research Service.

Simanski, J., & Sapp, L. (2012). *Immigration enforcement actions: 2012.* US Department of Homeland Security, Annual Report. Retrieved from www.dhs.gov/sites/default/files/publications/Enforcement_Actions _2012.pdf.

Skeldon, R. (1997). *Migration and development: A global perspective.* Essex: Longman.

Staring, R. (2004). Facilitating the arrival of illegal immigrants in the Netherlands: Irregular chain migration versus smuggling chains. *Journal of International Migration and Integration, 5*(3), 273–94. doi.org/10.1007/s12134-004-1015-9

Terrazas, A. (2011). *Migration and development: Policy perspectives from the United States.* Washington DC: Migration Policy Institute.

Threadgold, T. (2009). *The media and migration in the United Kingdom, 1999 to 2009.* Washington DC: Migration Policy Institute.

United Nations Department of Economic and Social Affairs. (2003). *Trends in total migrant stock: The 2003 revision.* New York: Author.

United Nations Department of Economic and Social Affairs. (2016). *Trends in international migrant stock: The 2015 revision.* New York: Author. Retrieved from www.un.org/en/development/ desa/population/migration/data/estimates2/index.shtml.

United Nations High Commissioner for Refugees. (2015). *UNHCR Population Statistics database.* Retrieved from popstats.unhcr.org/.

United Nations Office on Drugs and Crime. (2011). *Smuggling of migrants: A global review and annotated bibliography of recent publications.* New York: United Nations. Retrieved from www.unodc.org/documents/human-trafficking/Migrant-Smuggling/Smuggling_of_Migrants_A_Global_Review.pdf.

United States Coast Guard. (2014). *Maritime Migrant Interdictions: 1982 - Present.* Washington DC: Author.

United States Customs and Border Protection. (2014). CBP releases fiscal year 2013 statistics. *Access 3*(2), 1. Retrieved from www.cbp.gov/sites/default/files/assets/documents/2017-Mar/cbpaccessv3.02-012414.pdf.

van Selm, J., & Cooper, B. (Eds). (2005). *The new 'boat people': Ensuring safety and determining status.* Washington DC: Migration Policy Institute. Retrieved from www.migrationpolicy.org/research/new-boat-people-ensuring-safety-and-determining-status.

Vertovec, S. (2009). *Transnationalism.* London and New York: Routledge.

Watson, S. (2009). *The securitisation of human migration: Digging moats and sinking boats.* London: Routledge.

Weaver, O. (1995). Securitization and desecuritization. In Lipschultz, R. (Ed.), *On security.* New York: Columbia University Press.

World Bank. (2015). *World Bank world development indicators.* Retrieved October 21, 2015 from data.worldbank.org.

Zelinsky, Z. (1971). The hypothesis of the mobility transition. *Geographical Review 61*(2), 219–49. doi.org/10.2307/213996

Media

Annan, K. (2014, 2 January). Sympathy for the migrant. Project Syndicate. Retrieved from www.project-syndicate.org/commentary/kofi-a-annan-calls-for-a-new-understanding-of-migration-as-an-essential-part-of-the-human-experience.

Koser, K. (2011, 31 March). When is migration a security issue? Brookings blog. Retrieved from www.brookings.edu/research/opinions/2011/03/31-libya-migration-koser.

Koser, K. (2012, 15 August). *Securitizing migration: A good or bad idea?* (International Relations and Security Network, Zurich, Interviewers) [audio recording]. Retrieved from www.video.ethz.ch/campus/isn/e64b372e-c59e-4fbb-a091-6bfe68d9a17f.html.

Koser, K. (2013). Australia missing the lessons of Lampedusa. The Interpreter. Retrieved from www.lowyinstitute.org/the-interpreter/australia-missing-lessons-lampedusa.

Walker, I. (2013, 13 August). Saudi Arabia and its immigrants. The Centre of Migration Policy & Society blog. Retrieved from www.compas.ox.ac.uk/2013/saudi-arabia-and-its-immigrants/.

3

Placing Sri Lankan maritime arrivals in a broader migration context

Dinuk Jayasuriya and Marie McAuliffe[1]

Our examination of irregular maritime arrival (IMA) flows to Australia from Sri Lanka places emphasis on both origin country and global migration dynamics. This approach recognises broader migration and mobility that a more asylum-/refugee-specific focused approach has the potential to either underemphasise or miss entirely. Taking a broader view also has the potential to allow for a greater appreciation of Australia's comparative position in a global context, which is perhaps useful given the, at times, 'Australia-centric' view of IMA flows.

This chapter places the unusual 2012 'spike' of Sri Lankan IMAs to Australia in a broader migration context as a means to better understand the Sri Lankan migration dynamics at both the macro level and at the micro (i.e. individual) level. It does not delve into all aspects of Sri Lankan migration—such as the irregular migration of migrant workers, for example—which, while potentially interesting, are beyond the scope of this chapter.

---

1   The authors are grateful for research assistance from Simone Gangell, Paul Hayes and Victoria Mence in the preparation of this chapter.

We draw on two surveys undertaken in January and May of 2013, of 8,800 people in Sri Lanka, to show that while potential irregular migrants indicated that they would like to travel for reasons such as wanting a better future and economic prosperity, which are conceivably similar to those of regular migrants, these are not the only reasons. Rather, consistent with recent literature, our chapter paints a multidimensional picture showing that some potential irregular migrants from Sri Lanka wanted to travel for economic reasons and/or due to allegations of torture and persecution.[2]

The provision of information and evidence of Sri Lanka's place in a global migration context (including historically), as well as how some Sri Lankans view irregular migration, hopefully provides some illustration of why a strong appreciation of time and place in migration dynamics is important in improving our understanding of migration patterns and processes. This chapter does not attempt to cover all aspects related to Sri Lankan IMA flows in more recent times. It does, however, draw on a range of data and information relevant to the development of a deeper understanding of the events of 2012, when thousands of Sri Lankan IMAs travelled to Australia.

Sri Lanka and migration

Migration flows of Sri Lankan citizens to other countries can be broadly grouped into the following categories: temporary work (skilled, semi-skilled and unskilled workers); settlement (mostly skilled migrants); education (mainly for tertiary studies); political reasons (asylum seekers); and tourism, including pilgrimages to India and Nepal (International Organization for Migration [IOM] & Institute of Policy Studies of Sri Lanka [IPS], 2008).

Sri Lankan nationals who exit Sri Lanka are required to complete an embarkation card, and foreigners an arrival card for surrender to immigration officials. There are only a small number of entry/exit points for managing passenger movements in Sri Lanka, including one major and one minor international airport located in Colombo and a recently constructed international airport in the country's south. There are seven major sea ports around the country (Department of Immigration and Emigration [DIE], 2013).

---

2   These allegations are not necessarily of state-sponsored torture and persecution.

In 2011, Sri Lanka recorded 1,206,135 arrivals of Sri Lankan citizens and 1,235,228 departures (DIE, 2011a; 2011b). Of those Sri Lankans departing, 262,960 (21 per cent) were for foreign employment (Bureau of Foreign Employment [BFE], 2012).

Sri Lankan temporary and permanent emigration for employment

In 2011, 262,960 Sri Lankans departed for work abroad with an almost linear increase between 1990 and 2011 (refer Figure 3.1). This growth exceeds population growth; departures for employment increased 305 per cent between 1991 and 2011, compared with a 20 per cent growth in Sri Lanka's population over the same period (BFE, 2011; World Bank, 2013a). In 1991, 0.38 per cent of the population travelled overseas for work, increasing to 1.26 per cent of the population in 2011. Sri Lankans departing for employment outside Sri Lanka are required to register with the Sri Lanka Bureau of Foreign Employment.

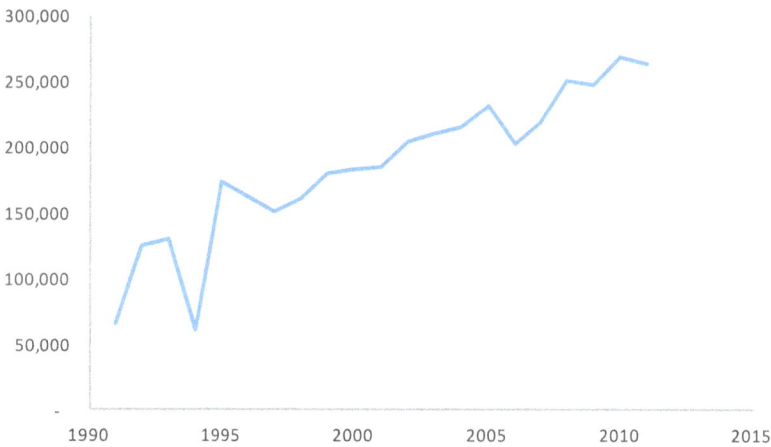

Figure 3.1: Departures for foreign employment
Source: Adapted from BFE (2012).

In 2010, almost 90 per cent of Sri Lankan men and almost 94 per cent of Sri Lankan women who sought temporary or permanent emigration for employment did so in the Middle Eastern countries of Saudi Arabia, Qatar, Kuwait, Lebanon, Jordan, Oman, Bahrain and the United Arab Emirates (DIE, 2010).

The importance of these destination countries as sources of income is reflected in the increase in remittances from the Middle East since 1990. In 2011, remittances from the Middle East accounted for 60 per cent of total remittances to Sri Lanka (as shown in Figure 3.2).

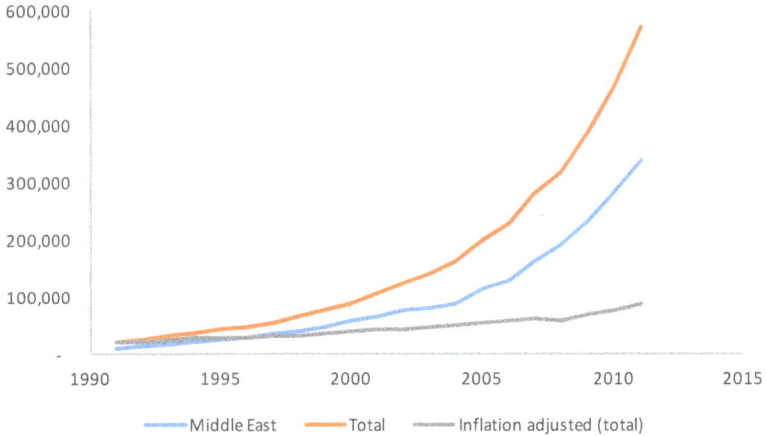

Figure 3.2: Remittances globally and from the Middle East
Source: Adapted from BFE (2012) and World Bank (2013a).

The increase in remittances has had a flow-on effect to the national economy, accounting for almost 50 per cent of export earnings in 2011 (BFE, 2012), and being approximately five times greater than the value of Foreign Direct Investments into Sri Lanka (World Bank, 2013a; World Bank, 2012).

Sri Lankan emigration for study

Education is very important for Sri Lankans, as demonstrated by the numerous newspaper, radio and billboard advertisements in Sri Lanka promoting potential places of study, both in Sri Lanka and overseas. A degree from a university outside of Sri Lanka is highly valued, with over 60 organisations, or 'education agents', providing advice on overseas study options (Australian Council for Private Education and Training, n.d.). Yet the absolute number of students travelling overseas for study to countries belonging to the Organisation for Economic Co-operation and Development (OECD) is relatively low. Table 3.1 shows a steady increase from 2004 until 2009, with Australia being the number one destination. Sri Lankans travelling overseas for study are not required to register with any government authority.

Table 3.1: International students from Sri Lanka in OECD countries

Destination	2004	2005	2006	2007	2008	2009
Australia	2,117	2,082	2,499	3,550	4,073	4,296
UK	2,267	2,419	2,765	3,005	3,141	3,553
US	1,964	2,081	2,234	2,425	2,594	2,927
Japan	615	765	867	1,155	1,197	1,098
Canada	161	-	252	186	271	309
Total	7,603	7,855	9,125	10,915	12,049	13,065

Source: Adapted from OECD (2012).

Sri Lankan diaspora communities

In 2010, there were nearly two million people in the Sri Lankan diaspora, with approximately 54 per cent of them living in the Middle East and approximately 34 per cent living in industrialised countries (World Bank, 2010).[3] There are two distinct groups within this population. Sri Lankan Tamils constitute the overwhelming majority of diaspora communities found in industrialised countries, while migrant workers (such as those to the Middle East) are largely Sinhalese (International Crisis Group [ICG], 2010).

The Sri Lankan diaspora has been increasing steadily over the last decade. To illustrate, in OECD countries alone the diaspora has increased from an estimated 300,000 people in 2000 to almost 700,000 in 2010 (refer Figure 3.3).

The countries with the largest diaspora in 2010 were Canada, the UK, Italy and Australia (refer Table 3.2).

In 2010, Australia was ranked number four on the list with an estimated 78,098 people in the Sri Lankan diaspora.[3] By mid-2013, the diaspora was estimated to be 130,000 by the Australian Department of Foreign Affairs and Trade (DFAT) (DFAT, n.d.). In 2011, the Sri Lankan community was the 13th largest migrant group in Australia, equivalent to 1.6 per cent of Australia's overseas-born population and 0.4 per cent of Australia's total population (Department of Immigration and Citizenship [DIAC], 2012). According to census data, around 50,151 Australians were Tamil speaking (Special Broadcasting Service [SBS], 2013).

---

3   World Bank and UN data only refer to Sri Lankan–born people and not people of Sri Lankan ancestry.

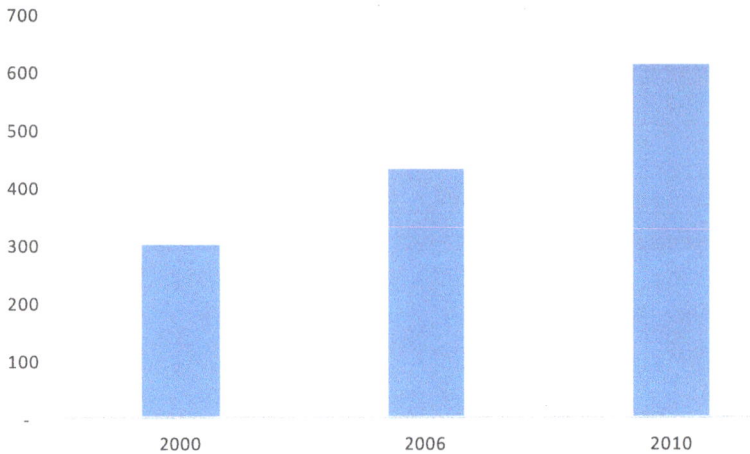

Figure 3.3: Sri Lankan diaspora in all OECD countries, 2000, 2006 and 2010

Source: OECD (2012) and adapted from World Bank (2010).

Table 3.2: Top 10 industrialised countries for the Sri Lankan diaspora, 2010

Rank	Country	Diaspora in 2010
1	Canada	123,012
2	UK	113,448
3	Italy	79,400
4	Australia	78,098
5	Germany	47,813
6	France	43,712
7	US	34,572
8	Switzerland	25,186
9	Norway	11,561
10	Netherlands	9,727

Source: World Bank (2010).

Sri Lankan Tamil diaspora

Prior to Sri Lankan independence in 1948, there were some Sri Lankan Tamils living in Malaysia and Singapore, primarily as migrant workers in British Malaya (ICG, 2010). It was only after the 1983 riots that Tamils migrated en masse, largely as refugees to industrialised countries. Currently, there are estimated to be approximately one million Sri Lankan Tamils residing outside Sri Lanka, which is substantial when considering the Sri Lankan Tamil population in Sri Lanka is 2.3 million people (ICG, 2010; Department of Census and Statistics, 2012). Countries with significant (estimated) Sri Lankan Tamil populations include: Canada (200,000–300,000); UK (180,000); Germany (60,000); Switzerland (47,000); Australia (40,000); France (40,000–50,000); US (25,000); the Netherlands (20,000); and Malaysia (20,000) (ICG, 2010). A smaller number of the Sri Lankan Tamil diaspora live in the Middle East, South Africa and the Gulf States.

Diaspora and remittances

Remittances from industrialised countries with a large Sri Lankan diaspora have increased rapidly in the recent past, from USD1,429 million in 2010 to USD1,776 million in 2011 and USD2,161 million in 2012 (refer Figure 3.4). In 2012, remittances from the Sri Lankan diaspora in industrialised countries represented 34 per cent of all remittances globally.

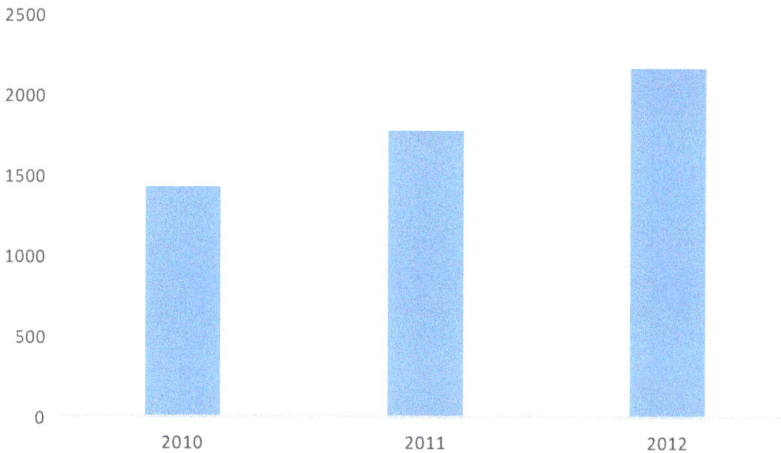

Figure 3.4: Remittances from OECD countries, 2010, 2011 and 2012
Source: Adapted from World Bank (2011, 2012, 2013b).

As might be expected, the top 10 industrialised countries for the Sri Lankan diaspora (for 2010) feature in the top 10 sources of remittances from industrialised countries (for 2012), almost in the same order (refer Tables 3.2 and 3.3). What is surprising is that the average remittance per person from OECD countries in 2010 was USD2,281, which was only slightly lower than the average remittance per person of USD2,329 from Middle Eastern countries.

Table 3.3: Top 10 sources of remittances to Sri Lanka, 2012 (industrialised countries only)

Rank	Country	Remittances (millions USD)
1	Canada	444
2	UK	399
3	Australia	279
4	Italy	272
5	Germany	173
6	France	154
7	US	132
8	Switzerland	99
9	Norway	48
10	Netherlands	36

Source: World Bank (2013b).

Prior to the defeat of the Liberation Tigers of Tamil Eelam (LTTE), the diaspora contributed an estimated USD200 million a year to the LTTE (ICG, 2010). For the past 25 years, the Sri Lankan Tamil diaspora has contributed to shaping the Sri Lankan political landscape through its financial and ideological support of the armed struggle for an independent Tamil state. Many in the diaspora were thought to have supported the LTTE; however, others were allegedly subject to extortion, intimidation and physical violence in order to silence criticism and secure financing (Human Rights Watch [HRW], 2006).

Sri Lanka and asylum seekers and refugees: Source, transit and destination

Given its recent past, Sri Lanka has primarily been a 'source' country of asylum seekers and refugees. That said, the labelling of 'source', 'host', 'transit' and 'destination' countries can be multidimensional, with countries fulfilling several of these broad categories at the one time. In addition, countries can quickly move from one category to another depending on prevailing security and political circumstances. Syria, for example, was until relatively recently a major 'host' country, primarily of Iraqi refugees; whereas it is now a major 'source' country due to the severity of its civil conflict.

Asylum seekers and refugees in Sri Lanka

Sri Lanka is not a party to the 1951 Refugee Convention or its 1967 Protocol, nor does it have specific legislation or administrative mechanisms governing asylum and refugee affairs. The Sri Lankan Government relies on the United Nations High Commissioner for Refugees (UNHCR) to register and assess asylum seekers. The UNHCR has been involved in Sri Lanka since 1987 when the organisation was invited by the Sri Lankan Government to facilitate large-scale repatriation of Sri Lankan refugees from India. The UNHCR, under an agreement with the government, undertakes refugee status determination processes in Sri Lanka.

According to UNHCR data, there are (at any one time) only a small number of asylum seekers and refugees in Sri Lanka. At the end of 2012, there were 110 refugees and 263 asylum seekers registered in Sri Lanka (UNHCR, 2013). UNHCR data on asylum applications submitted in Sri Lanka between 2005 and 2012 shows that the vast majority of asylum seekers were Pakistani. Data also reveals that there has been a slight increase in asylum applications over the last two years (as shown in Figure 3.5) from non-Pakistani applicants.

Refugees are not permitted to reside or work in Sri Lanka, and very few refugees choose to repatriate back to their country of origin. Resettlement, therefore, remains the main durable solution for them. In 2012, 178 refugees in Sri Lanka were resettled to the US and Canada (UNHCR, 2013).

According to some in the Sri Lankan Government, Sri Lanka is increasingly becoming a transit and destination country for irregular migrants and asylum seekers, as reflected in recent public comments by Sri Lankan ministers on the 'deportation' of asylum seekers in Sri Lanka (Powell, 2013). According to the Sri Lankan Department of Immigration and Emigration, Sri Lanka has become a transit country for asylum seekers from Pakistan and Afghanistan trying to reach Australia (Integrated Regional Information Networks [IRIN], 2012b).

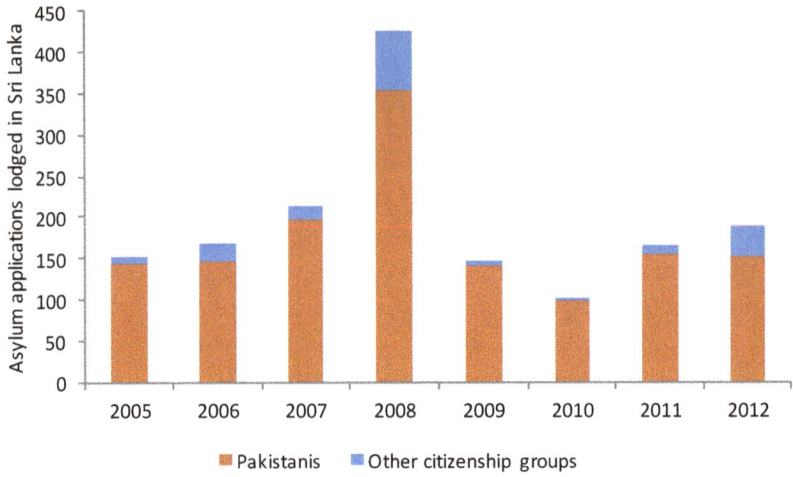

Figure 3.5: Asylum applications submitted in Sri Lanka, 2005–12
Source: UNHCR (n.d.).

Internally displaced persons in Sri Lanka

The number of internally displaced persons (IDPs) in Sri Lanka has gradually reduced since the end of the civil conflict in 2009. UNHCR has estimated that by the end of September 2012, some 468,000 people had returned to their places of origin (UNHCR, 2013). The closure in September 2012 of the government's 700-hectare IDP site 'Menik Farm' in northern Vavuniya district (the largest operational camp) highlighted the post-conflict transition that has occurred over time as people have gradually been resettled. At its peak, 'Menik Farm' housed 225,000 people (UNHCR, 2012). As of December 2012, 9,800 remained in IDP camps throughout Sri Lanka (Internal Displacement Monitoring Centre [IDMC], 2013).

Estimates of the number of IDPs in Sri Lanka have varied. The main sources of internal displacement statistics are government and the United Nations Office for the Coordination of Humanitarian Affairs (OCHA). As of January 2011, the OCHA estimated that around 273,772 Sri Lankans continued to be displaced (Association of Tamils of Sri Lanka in the USA, 2012). Some months on, IDMC (2013) estimated that (at 31 December, 2011), around 95,000 people were still displaced in Sri Lanka. IDMC noted that the Sri Lankan Government has kept some IDPs' areas of origin closed because of national security and/or danger to the public, including because of incomplete landmine clearance activity. As of the end of 2012, there were 93,447 IDPs, including people living inside and outside of camps (UNHCR, 2012). Given the substantial numbers of people that have been internally resettled, the UNHCR has indicated in its South Asia operations profile that during 2013 it will continue to promote the reintegration of refugee and IDP returnees, while winding down its direct engagement in the IDP situation (UNHCR, 2013).

Sri Lankan asylum seekers and refugees around the world

Sri Lanka's history of civil conflict is reflected in its status as a significant source country of asylum seekers and refugees. Given the nature of the civil conflict, Sri Lankan asylum flows have mainly comprised Tamils. According to UNHCR, as of December 2012, there were 132,749 Sri Lankan refugees and 13,975 asylum seekers worldwide (UNHCR, 2013). This placed Sri Lanka in the top 18 origin countries of the world's asylum seekers and refugees.

India has historically been, and continues to be, the main host country of Sri Lankan refugees. At the end of 2012, it hosted some 67,165 Sri Lankan (predominantly Tamil) refugees (UNHCR, 2013). The majority of India's UNHCR-registered Sri Lankan refugees lived in around 100 camps in the southern Indian state of Tamil Nadu. However, estimates of the number of Sri Lankans with pending asylum claims in Tamil Nadu vary considerably between organisations, from around 100,000 to 200,000 (ICG, 2010; IRIN, 2012a).

Outside of the thousands of Sri Lankan refugees hosted in India, Sri Lankan asylum seekers historically have travelled to specific destination countries. As shown in Table 3.4, the main asylum destination countries in 2012 were Australia, Malaysia, UK, France, Switzerland and Canada. These countries all have significant Sri Lankan diaspora.

Sri Lankan asylum claims in industrialised countries dropped from a high of about 14,500 applications in 2001 to around 5,500 per year between 2003 and 2006 (when there was a ceasefire between Sri Lanka and the LTTE). The UK, Canada and France collectively received 71 per cent of Sri Lankan asylum claims in 2001 (more than 10,000 of the 14,500 applications). In the lead-up to the end of the civil war in 2009, Sri Lankan asylum claims grew, as shown in Figure 3.6.

Table 3.4: Sri Lankan global asylum applications, 2012 (selected countries)

Destination	Asylum applications in 2012
Australia	2,309
Malaysia	1,910
UK	1,840
France	1,738
Switzerland	1,610
Canada	1,189
Germany	994
Japan	476
Indonesia	404
Korea	232
Nauru	216
Netherlands	140

Source: UNHCR (n.d.).

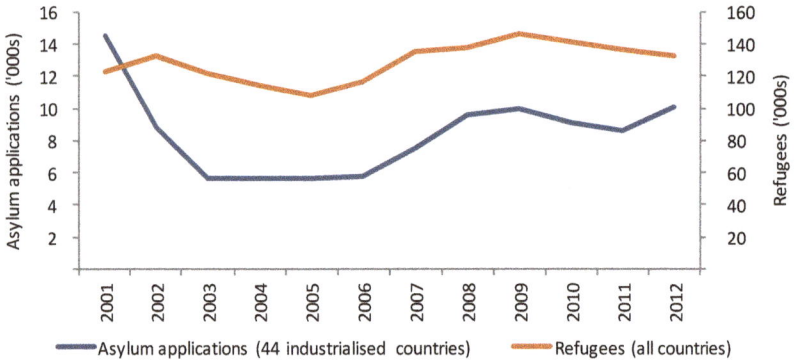

Figure 3.6: Sri Lankan asylum seekers and refugees, 2001–12
Source: UNHCR (2013); UNHCR (2002–13); UNHCR (n.d.).

Regular and irregular migration of Sri Lankans to Australia

As is the case with most other citizenship groups, the vast majority of Sri Lankan arrivals enter Australia on temporary visas, as can be seen in Figure 3.7. In 2012–13, 22,503 temporary entry visas were granted to Sri Lankan nationals, with visitors accounting for 73 per cent of visas granted. Other categories included student visas (2,899 or 13 per cent) and temporary work visas (1,014 or 5 per cent).

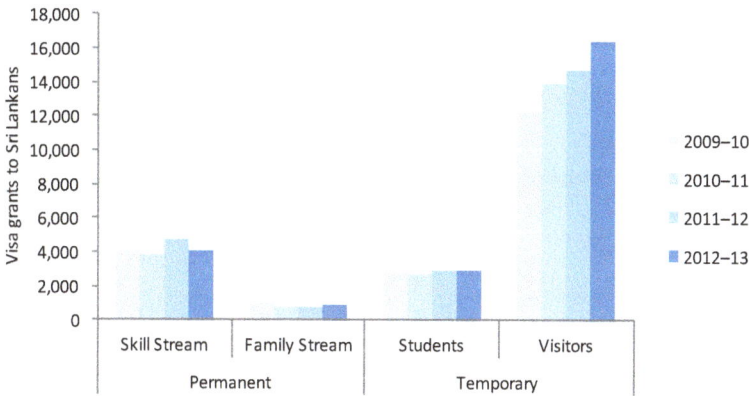

Figure 3.7: Australian visas granted to Sri Lankans, 2009–10 to 2012–13
Source: DIAC (2013).

Sri Lankan permanent migration to Australia

Sri Lankans first started emigrating to Australia in large numbers in the mid-1980s as a response to protracted conflict between the LTTE and government forces. Even though hostilities have formally ceased, the number of Sri Lankans choosing to live in Australia has continued to grow, with almost 5,000 Sri Lankans in 2012–13 migrating under Australia's Migration Program (comprising the Family and Skill Streams), compared with 2,000 a decade ago. Since 2007–08, Sri Lanka has consistently been one of Australia's top 10 source migrant countries.

Skilled migration remains the main route for Sri Lankan nationals seeking permanent residency in Australia, accounting for 80 per cent of permanent visas granted to Sri Lankan nationals under the Migration Program in the decade to 2012–13. Sri Lankans were ranked eighth out of 175 citizenship groups granted visas under the Migration Program's Skill Stream in 2012–13, with 4,078 skilled visas granted to Sri Lankans.

The majority of Sri Lankan skilled migrants arrive under the General Skilled Migration (GSM) component of the Skill Stream, which provides permanent residence to skilled migrants who do not have an employer sponsoring them. In 2012–13, 3,228 GSM visas were issued to Sri Lankans, representing 79 per cent of all permanent skilled visas for Sri Lankans in that year. The main occupations of those granted a GSM visa included information and communications technology professionals, accountants, and engineering professionals.

Family migration to Australia facilitates the entry of close family members of Australian citizens, permanent residents and eligible New Zealand citizens. In 2012–13, 883 Sri Lankan nationals were granted permanent residency under the Migration Program's Family Stream, ranking 13th among 176 citizenship groups represented in the Family Stream in that year.

Australia's Humanitarian Program is designed to ensure Australia can respond effectively to global humanitarian situations and that support services are available to meet the specific needs of these entrants. Sri Lankans have not been a major source group for Australia's Humanitarian Program, with just over a thousand Sri Lankans resettled under this program over the last 10 years. The majority (around 75 per cent) of visas granted to Sri Lankans under the offshore Humanitarian Program over the last five years were to the immediate ('split') family of Sri Lankan IMAs under the Special Humanitarian Program (SHP).

In 2012–13, 363 Sri Lankans were granted onshore protection visas (including both IMAs and non-IMAs), and 40 were granted offshore protection visas. The number of offshore resettlement grants to Sri Lankan citizens has decreased by 55 per cent from 88 in 2011–12. This accorded with previous years: 288 granted in 2010–11; 184 in 2009–10 and 215 in 2008–09, which is a reflection of the settling of hostilities since 2009. It is also a reflection of broader changes to the SHP. In addition, the number of onshore protection visas granted to Sri Lankans in 2012–13 has decreased by 14 per cent from the previous program year.

Sri Lankan asylum seekers to Australia

The significant decrease in Sri Lankan asylum claims globally, from 2002 onwards, coincided with the 2002 signing of the permanent ceasefire agreement between the Sri Lankan Government and the LTTE. Global asylum claims began to rise again in 2008 as the conflict escalated in the lead-up to the LTTE defeat in 2009.

This was reflected in asylum applications made in Australia. In 2008–09, Sri Lankans who arrived regularly by air (non-IMAs) made 478 applications for asylum. Subsequently, Sri Lankan non-IMA applications have generally declined over time: 328 in 2009–10; 160 in 2010–11; 138 in 2011–12 and 169 in 2012–13, while overall non-IMA application numbers have increased. Sri Lanka was ranked 14th among non-IMA asylum nationalities in 2012–13.

In 2009, Sri Lankan IMAs to Australia also increased but subsequently decreased and remained at low levels. The very dramatic increase in Sri Lankan IMA flows to Australia in 2012, however, signalled a departure from previous trends and was out of step with Sri Lankan asylum claims globally. To place the increase in context, in 2011 there were just over 200 IMAs from Sri Lanka, whereas in 2012 more than 6,400 Sri Lankan IMAs arrived in Australia, most of whom arrived in the second half of the year (refer Figure 3.8).

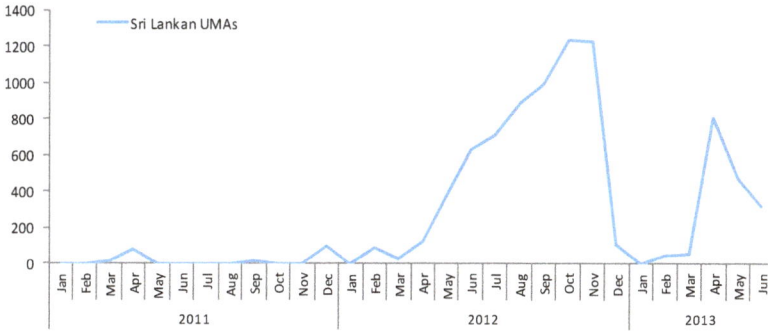

Figure 3.8: Sri Lankan irregular maritime arrivals, January 2011 – June 2013

Source: Department of Immigration and Border Protection (DIBP) (n.d.).

Note: By the end of 2012, many IMAs had not at that stage lodged applications for asylum, hence they were not captured in UNHCR asylum applications data in Table 3.4.

The large majority of IMAs from Sri Lanka were Tamils. However, in 2012, approximately 13 per cent of IMAs were Sinhalese, increasing from 0 per cent in 2011. Partly reflecting the changes in IMA dynamics and volume, returns to Sri Lanka following enhanced screening increased in volume. Between July 2012 and the end of May 2013, 162 voluntary and 965 involuntary returns to Sri Lanka occurred (Parliament of Australia, 2013).

In contrast to the Australian experience, other key Sri Lankan destination countries experienced decreases, plateaus or minor increases in 2012 (see Figures 3.9 and 3.10). Further to this, and unlike earlier IMA flows, in addition to protection issues, economic conditions and prospects were thought to be drivers for irregular maritime movement to Australia, especially for ethnic Sinhalese, who began arriving in significant numbers for the first time.

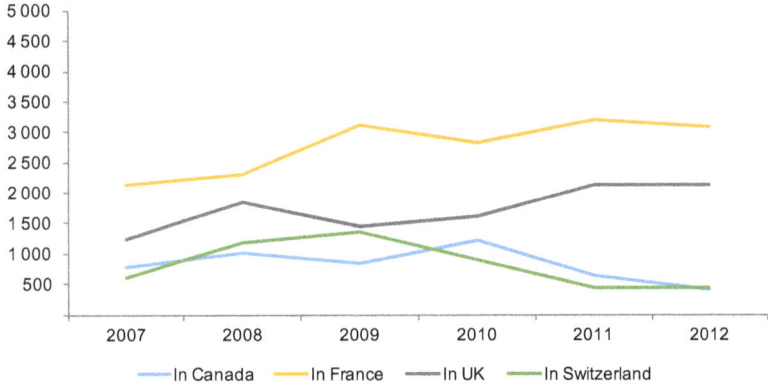

Figure 3.9: Sri Lankan asylum seekers: Key destination countries, 2007–12

Source: UNHCR (2002–13).

Figure 3.9 reveals the significant increase in Sri Lankan asylum seekers that occurred in Australia did not occur in other key destination countries. When Sri Lankan asylum applications submitted in all 44 industrialised countries are examined, a similar picture emerges (as shown in Figure 3.10).

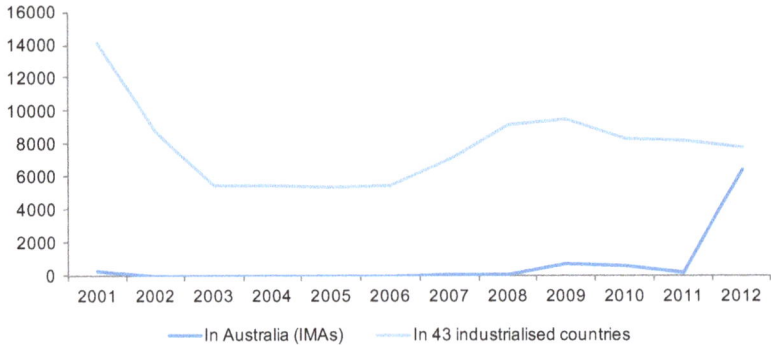

Figure 3.10: Asylum applications in 43 industrialised countries and IMAs, 2001–12

Source: UNHCR (2002–13); DIBP (n.d.).

Note: The 43 industrialised countries are all 44 industrialised countries listed in the UNHCR report except Australia.

Reasons potential irregular migrants from Sri Lanka choose to travel to destination countries

In 2012, some people believed Sri Lankan IMAs entered Australia for economic reasons (March, 2012). This is hardly surprising, since literature suggests economic factors are an important reason people seek asylum (Neumayer, 2005), and Australia has been one of the few OECD countries where the economy has remained resilient throughout the global financial crisis (GFC). Others claimed Sri Lankans entered due to humanitarian reasons, citing political persecution and torture (Doherty, 2012). Yet, according to literature, the reasons were likely to be multidimensional (Monsutti, 2005), with neither economic prospects nor humanitarian issues representing the only reason for an IMA to enter Australia.

Surveys conducted in Sri Lanka during January and May 2013 under the Irregular Migration Research Program sought the views of potential irregular migrants themselves. Both surveys involved a pilot of over 400 people and a final survey of over 4,000 people using iPad technology (hence a total of 8,800 people were surveyed over two waves). Districts, the largest administrative unit in Sri Lanka, were selected based on source locations of irregular migrants. Simple random sampling was then employed to select Divisional Secretariats (DSs), the second largest administrative unit and Grama Niladhari (GNs), the lowest administrative unit. Households within GNs were selected randomly when possible. Data was weighted to consider nonresponse, ethnicity, IMA source location and gender.[4]

The surveys asked respondents about their intentions as they related to migration to Australia by boat. Based on responses to survey questions, respondents were then categorised according to degree of intention. In essence, 'non-intenders' indicated no intention to travel, 'intenders' expressed a desire to travel overseas by boat, 'active intenders' demonstrated

---

4   Male responses were given greater weighting than female responses (by a ratio of 89:11), as males overwhelmingly represent IMA. Greater weightings were also provided for districts that were source areas for IMAs. Ethnicity was weighted such that it was reflective of the populations in the districts surveyed (these were predominately Tamil, with all but one of the five districts surveyed having Tamil populations greater than 80 per cent). Areas with higher nonresponse were given greater weighting (although levels of nonresponse were largely consistent across districts).

action by having made plans to travel and 'paid intenders' had made a payment towards such travel.[5] The focus of the results presented in this chapter is on 'intenders', given the low sample sizes and hence relatively larger margins of error involved in analysing the subsamples 'active intenders' and 'paid intenders'.

Intention to travel to Australia via irregular maritime migration

Figure 3.11 illustrates reasons captured during the surveys as to why 'intenders' want to leave Sri Lanka and enter Australia. Note that the sample size is too small to allow categorisation according to ethnicity.[6]

A very high proportion of respondents (89 per cent) who were categorised as 'intenders' indicated that they desired to travel to Australia by boat for asylum to 'give their families a better future'. While acknowledging that this was a very broad response option that is multidimensional in nature, it is worth highlighting that the response reflects two key aspects in the decision-making of potential irregular migrants: a wish for a better future; and a desire to create that future for their families.

When this result is examined in conjunction with the next two highest ranking results—'Australia's job opportunities' (86 per cent) and 'lack of job opportunities in Sri Lanka' (84 per cent)—it is possible that many respondents view the attainment of a better future as being linked, in part, to employment and the ability to earn an income. The importance of remittances to the Sri Lankan economy and, therefore, Sri Lankan families, means that it is possible that 'giving their families a better future' includes family members that would remain in Sri Lanka.

---

5   In January 2013, 'intenders', 'active intenders' and 'paid intenders' represented an estimated 7.92 per cent, 1.46 per cent and 0.22 cent of the population in the districts surveyed respectively. This reduced to 4.53 per cent, 0.54 per cent and 0.16 per cent across 'intenders', 'active intenders' and 'paid intenders' respectively during the May 2013 survey.
6   'Intenders' represent a small percentage of the total sample and hence a further breakdown across ethnicity would increase the margins of error.

To give their families 'a better' future	89%
Australia's job opportunities	86%
Lack of job opportunities in Sri Lanka	84%
It's too difficult to enter Australia using legal channels	63%
People smugglers are telling the truth	56%
Australia's accepting immigration program	54%
It's easier to travel to Australia than other countries	49%
Previous friends and family members being accepted in Australia	48%
Persecution in Sri Lanka	37%
Torture in Sri Lanka	35%
Do not know any other way to travel to Australia	29%

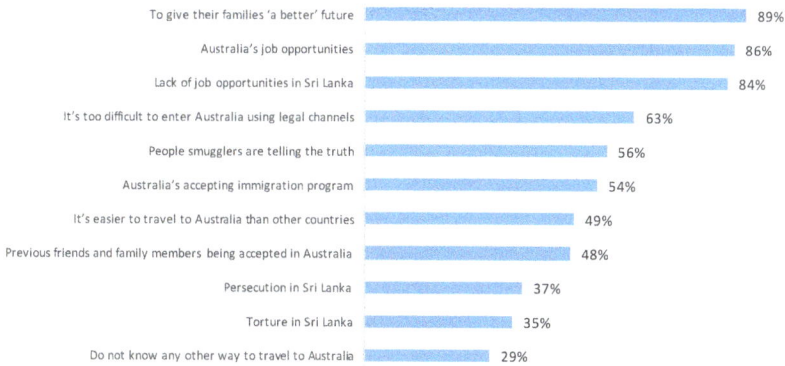

Figure 3.11: Reasons why 'intenders' want to leave Sri Lanka and enter Australia via boat
Source: 2013 Sri Lanka survey.

Economic factors, however, are unlikely to be the only reasons for wanting a better life. People who referred to persecution or torture amounted to almost 40 per cent of respondents. Notwithstanding the English definitions of 'torture' and 'persecution', these are ambiguous terms in Tamil and Sinhala. For example, 'torture' may refer to torture or violence from domestic partners rather than from state agents as might be assumed, while persecution may refer to Northern Tamils 'persecuting' Southern Tamils or vice versa with no consideration of whether or not the state could provide effective protection in such circumstances (Jayasuriya & Gibson, 2013). Further research is required to gain a better understanding of potential irregular migrants' views on more precise meanings of 'torture' and 'persecution'.

The difficulties involved with entering Australia using legal channels (63 per cent) could be due to the requirements necessary for skilled and other migration, and the challenges of being accepted via Australia's Humanitarian Program. Further, while people smugglers are criminals and may lie to increase the number of clients, they may also have successfully facilitated previous transfers of irregular migrants to Australia via boat. This could point to the reason why 'people smugglers' are known as 'agents' by some Sri Lankans and why 56 per cent of 'intenders' believe people smugglers tell the truth.

It seems significant that over 50 per cent of people stated 'Australia's accepting immigration program' as a reason why they chose Australia as a destination. However, the most attractive features of the immigration policy have not been identified. Moreover, an 'accepting immigration program' could conceivably refer to the Skilled Migration Program, the numerous advertisements encouraging students to travel to Australia or possibly the way asylum seekers are treated in Australia. Further research is clearly required to determine which aspects of Australia's immigration program are most attractive.

The fact that 49 per cent of 'intenders' believe it is easier to travel to Australia than to other countries may be surprising, given the documented deaths of asylum seekers at sea and the close proximity to other potential countries such as India. However, many Sri Lankans living in coastal towns are fisherman, and hence spending two weeks to a month at sea, which is approximately how long it takes to travel from Sri Lanka to Australia by boat, is unlikely to be an issue. Note that while India is certainly easier to travel to than Australia, survey results indicate that India is not a 'preferred' destination (refer Figure 3.14).

That 48 per cent of 'intenders' say previous friends and family being accepted in Australia is a reason for wanting to travel to Australia is reasonable and consistent with similar studies highlighting the importance for asylum seekers of relatives who live in destination countries (Robinson & Segrott, 2002). Moreover, future asylum seekers may believe that they have similar chances of resettlement, that they will have an inside track on the process and that they potentially have a strong support network if they are granted protection.

While 29 per cent of 'intenders' state not knowing any other way to travel to Australia is a reason for travelling by boat, it is conceivable that more than 29 per cent actually do not know about other forms of travel— even if it's not a stated reason. Indeed, the chances of potential irregular migrants entering through regular programs are likely to be minimal.

Examination of 'economic intenders'

Economic factors were clearly one reason the large majority of people (approximately 85 per cent) intended leaving Sri Lanka to travel to Australia. Yet many of these people also had other reasons for travel, and it would be unwise to not recognise the multidimensional factors involved in migrant decision-making.

To highlight this point, Figure 3.12 replicates Figure 3.11 but restricts the analysis to 'economic intenders' (those who stated they intended to leave Sri Lanka because of lack of job opportunities or intended to travel to Australia for job opportunities). Figure 3.13 shows 'economic intenders' also had other reasons for seeking asylum; i.e. these people are not only 'intenders' due to economic reasons.

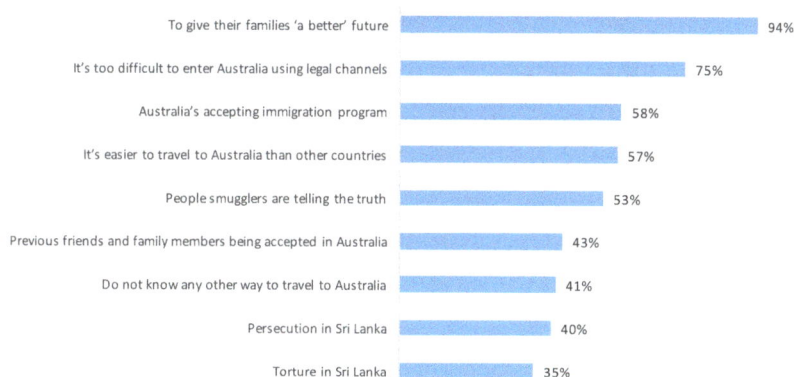

To give their families 'a better' future	94%
It's too difficult to enter Australia using legal channels	75%
Australia's accepting immigration program	58%
It's easier to travel to Australia than other countries	57%
People smugglers are telling the truth	53%
Previous friends and family members being accepted in Australia	43%
Do not know any other way to travel to Australia	41%
Persecution in Sri Lanka	40%
Torture in Sri Lanka	35%

Figure 3.12: Reasons why 'intenders' wanted to leave Sri Lanka and why they wanted to enter Australia via boat—sample restricted to 'economic intenders'[7]
Source: 2013 Sri Lanka survey.

The reasons why 'economic intenders' desire to travel to Australia by boat (Figure 3.12) were similar to all 'intenders' (Figure 3.11). Of interest is that among 'economic intenders', those who referred to persecution or torture amounted to approximately 42 per cent, suggesting at least 58 per cent of the 'economic intenders' potentially wanted to travel to Australia for non-protection reasons.

A key limitation of this survey data is that analysis focuses on people with an 'intention' (i.e. 'intenders') to travel overseas for asylum and not people with a demonstrated 'action' (i.e. 'active intenders') or people who have 'committed' to travelling overseas for asylum (i.e. 'paid intenders'). Results relating to 'intenders', 'active intenders' and 'paid intenders' are likely to vary significantly. To illustrate, among 'active intenders' considering travelling to Australia for economic reasons, the number who referred to persecution or torture increased to 66 per cent, suggesting that the

---

7   Data was pooled from the January and May surveys to increase the sample size of 'intenders' to Australia; however, this still produces a margin of error of approximately 5.4 per cent.

remaining 34 per cent may have intended travelling for reasons that did not overtly include protection-related concerns. Future research should consider a larger sample size that is likely to capture a larger absolute number of 'active intenders' and 'paid intenders'.

Additionally, Figures 3.11 and 3.12 list reasons why 'intenders' desire to travel to Australia by boat without demonstrating their relative importance. To illustrate, while economic reasons and persecution may be important drivers, the presence of family and friends in Australia may be a key determinant. Future research is required to analyse the relative importance of drivers and determinants. Finally, future research should consider presenting a more comprehensive list of possible factors influencing irregular migration.

Australia relative to the rest of the world

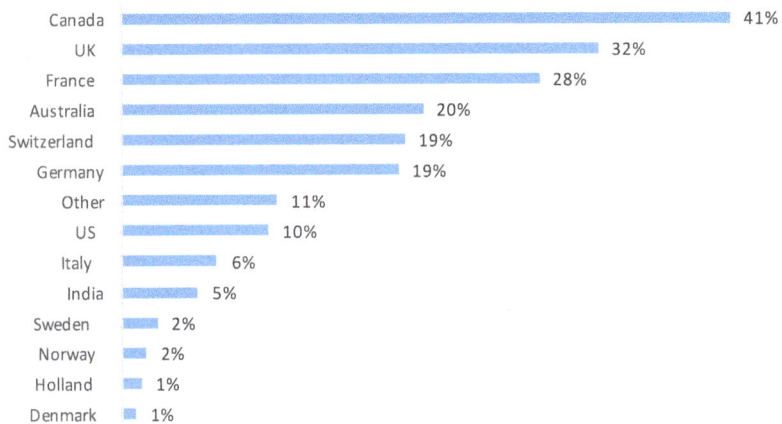

Country	Percentage
Canada	41%
UK	32%
France	28%
Australia	20%
Switzerland	19%
Germany	19%
Other	11%
US	10%
Italy	6%
India	5%
Sweden	2%
Norway	2%
Holland	1%
Denmark	1%

Figure 3.13: Intenders' preferred destinations

Source: 2013 Sri Lanka survey.

Note: Individuals could indicate a 'preference' to travel to more than one country while they have an 'intention' to travel to just one country. Results are subject to a margin of error of approximately 4.2 per cent.

The May 2013 survey data found that 41 per cent of 'intenders' wanted to travel to Canada for asylum, followed by the UK (32 per cent) and France (28 per cent). Australia ranked 4th out of 13 countries listed, at 20 per cent (refer Figure 3.14). This suggests that while Australia is still a preferred destination for asylum seekers from Sri Lanka, its importance may be diminishing. Australia's position relative to other countries could be due to a host of reasons including but not limited to geography, diaspora links, immigration policies and practices, and economic performance. Additional research is required to distil the relative importance of the multiple factors influencing decisions about potential migrants' preferred destinations.

Some reasons why 'intenders' wanted to travel to destination countries (anywhere in the world) are illustrated in Figure 3.14.

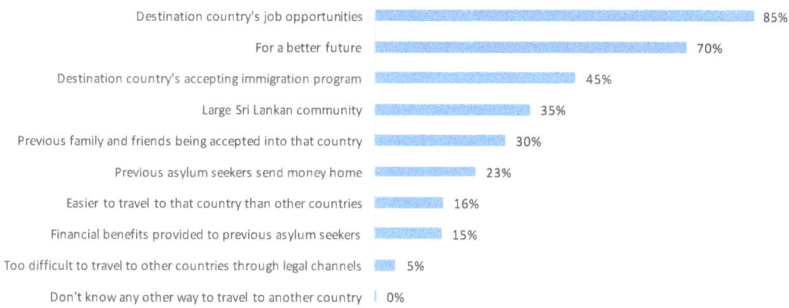

Destination country's job opportunities	85%
For a better future	70%
Destination country's accepting immigration program	45%
Large Sri Lankan community	35%
Previous family and friends being accepted into that country	30%
Previous asylum seekers send money home	23%
Easier to travel to that country than other countries	16%
Financial benefits provided to previous asylum seekers	15%
Too difficult to travel to other countries through legal channels	5%
Don't know any other way to travel to another country	0%

Figure 3.14: Reasons why 'intenders' are attracted to destination countries (all countries)

Source: 2013 Sri Lanka survey.

Note: Results are subject to a margin of error of approximately 4.2 per cent.

The results show that economic factors are the main reason 'intenders' are attracted to a destination country. Note that these options were not shown to respondents during the survey, suggesting results may be different if multiple-choice options were provided. For example, intuitively, ease of travel is an important reason why one might choose a certain country, yet only 16 per cent of people suggested this as an answer. Perhaps if respondents had been presented with pre-determined options, more people would have selected ease of travel. Further, unlike in Figures 3.9 and 3.10, the results also do not highlight why a person may want to leave Sri Lanka.

Conclusions

Many Sri Lankans travel overseas for regular and irregular migration purposes. In 2011, approximately 260,000 migrants travelled overseas for temporary or permanent employment opportunities. Most of the foreign workers were Sinhalese, and the large majority of Sinhalese workers migrated to Middle Eastern countries. In contrast, Tamils comprised the bulk of Sri Lanka's diaspora in industrialised countries, and made up the majority of asylum seekers and refugees.

In 2012, just over 15,000 Sri Lankans were asylum seekers globally, with Australia ranked as the number one destination. When focusing on IMAs, Australia experienced a highly unusual jump from under 100 arrivals from the first quarter of 2012 to around 2,600 in the third quarter of 2012. This number was also unusual when compared to asylum applications globally, with other countries experiencing decreases, plateaus or minor increases in 2012.

Surveys undertaken in high IMA source areas of Sri Lanka during January and May of 2013 revealed that the reasons people intended to travel by boat to Australia involved multiple, interrelated factors, including factors related to protection, visa access, employment, people smuggling, geography and family/community links. The most prominent factors related primarily to economic prosperity. This is unsurprising, given economic factors were also the primary reason for people desiring to travel to other countries. Of more interest is that, among people travelling for economic reasons, results show at least 58 per cent of people with a desire ('intenders'), and at least 36 per cent of people with plans in place ('active intenders'), to travel by boat to Australia, appeared to do so for non-protection reasons. That said, further research is required for a more precise analysis of the drivers and determinants of 'active intenders' and 'paid intenders'.

The survey findings are consistent with Koser's discussion of a paradigm shift involving the convergence of 'political refugees and economic migrants into a single migration route', as asylum seeking (Koser, 2001). Seeking asylum via irregular migration channels can be an effective strategy whereby people, including genuine asylum seekers, can gain a legitimate migration status relatively swiftly that would be virtually impossible to obtain by staying where they are or attempting to move via regular pathways.

The survey results in this chapter highlight the multidimensional factors potential irregular migrants take into account when assessing and reassessing whether to, and where to, migrate. Further examination of both potential and actual migrants' views (including IMAs) would allow for a deeper understanding of the drivers and motivations of those Sri Lankans who migrate irregularly by maritime means. Another useful research focus would be the possible decision-making factors involved in the decisions of potential irregular migrants not to migrate, including those who may be facing protection issues. Adhikari's research on the impact of a range of factors on potential refugee decision-making in Nepal highlights that individual decision-making, even in extreme conflict situations, is based on more than just the threat to one's life, and includes factors related to economic livelihoods and social networks (Adhikari, 2012).

Reference list

Adhikari, P. (2012). Conflict induced displacement: Understanding the causes of flight. *American Journal of Political Science, 57*(1), 82–89. doi.org/10.1111/j.1540-5907.2012.00598.x

Association of Tamils of Sri Lanka in the USA. (2012). 2012 UNHCR country operations profile—Sri Lanka. Retrieved April 19, 2012 from Ilankai Tamil Sangam: www.sangam.org/2012/04/UNHCR_Profile.php.

Australian Council for Private Education and Training. (n.d.). Education agents in Sri Lanka. Retrieved July 15, 2013 from www.acpet.edu.au (service available only to members).

Bureau of Foreign Employment (Sri Lanka). (2011). *Annual statistical report of foreign employment—2010*. Colombo: Author.

Bureau of Foreign Employment (Sri Lanka). (2012). *Annual statistical report of foreign employment—2011*. Colombo: Author.

Department of Census and Statistics (Sri Lanka). (2012). *Population by ethnic group according to districts, 2012*. Retrieved July 2013 from Population & housing data 2012 (provisional): www.statistics.gov.lk/PopHouSat/CPH2011/index.php?fileName=pop42&gp=Activities&tpl=3.

Department of Foreign Affairs and Trade (Australia). (n.d.). *Sri Lanka country brief*. Retrieved from dfat.gov.au/geo/sri-lanka/pages/sri-lanka-country-brief.aspx.

Department of Immigration and Border Protection (Australia). (n.d.). Unpublished data on irregular maritime arrivals, 2011–13.

Department of Immigration and Citizenship (Australia). (2012). *Country profile, Sri Lanka*. Canberra: Author.

Department of Immigration and Citizenship (Australia). (2013). *Statistics*. Canberra: Author.

Department of Immigration and Emigration (Sri Lanka). (2010). *Departures for foreign employment through all sources by country and sex 2006–2010 (provisional)*. Retrieved July 4, 2013 from National Centre for Migration Statistics: www.statistics.gov.lk/ncms/RepNTab/Tables/SLBFE/tab9.pdf.

Department of Immigration and Emigration (Sri Lanka). (2011a). *Arrivals by nationality and month—2011*. Retrieved July 4, 2013 from National Centre for Migration Statistics: www.statistics.gov.lk/NCMS/RepNTab/Tables/DIE/2011Arr.pdf.

Department of Immigration and Emigration (Sri Lanka). (2011b). *Departures by nationality and month—2011*. Retrieved July 4, 2013 from National Centre for Migration Statistics: www.statistics.gov.lk/NCMS/RepNTab/Tables/DIE/2011Dep.pdf.

Department of Immigration and Emigration (Sri Lanka). (2013). *About us/border management*. Retrieved July 4, 2013 from www.immigration.gov.lk/web/index.php?option=com_content&view=article&id=132&Itemid=59&lang=en.

Doherty, B. (2012, July 24). Sent home to 'arrest, torture'. *Sydney Morning Herald*. Retrieved October 10, 2013 from www.smh.com.au/federal-politics/political-news/sent-home-to-arrest-torture-20120723-22kur.html.

Human Rights Watch. (2006). *Funding the 'final war': LTTE intimidation and extortion in the Tamil diaspora*. Retrieved from www.hrw.org/report/2006/03/14/funding-final-war/ltte-intimidation-and-extortion-tamil-diaspora.

Integrated Regional Information Networks. (2012a). Sri Lanka: Tamil refugees slowly return from India. Retrieved July 16, 2013 from www.refworld.org/docid/4f0fed552.html.

Integrated Regional Information Networks. (2012b). Sri Lanka: More people boarding boats to Australia. Retrieved July 16, 2013 from: www.irinnews.org/report/95855/sri-lanka-more-people-boarding-boats-to-australia.

Internal Displacement Monitoring Centre. (2013). Numbers of IDPs in Sri Lanka. Retrieved from www.internal-displacement.org.

International Crisis Group. (2010). *The Sri Lankan Tamil diaspora after the LTTE*. Asia Report No. 186. Colombo/Brussels: Author.

International Organization for Migration, & Institute of Policy Studies of Sri Lanka. (2008). *International migration outlook—Sri Lanka*. Colombo: International Organization for Migration.

Jayasuriya, D., & Gibson, J. (2013, February 28). *Elephants, tigers and safety in post-conflict Sri Lanka*. Development Policy Centre Discussion Paper No. 27. Canberra: The Australian National University.

Koser, K. (2001). New approaches to asylum? *International Migration, 39*(6), 85–102. doi.org/10.1111/1468-2435.00180

March, S. (2012, November 7). Sri Lankans heading to Australia 'economic migrants', not refugees: IOM. Retrieved from ABC News: www.abc.net.au/news/2012-11-06/an-sri-lankans-27economic-migrants272c-not-refugees/4355860.

Monsutti, A. (2005). *War and migration: Social networks and economic strategies of the Hazaras of Afghanistan*. New York and London: Routledge. doi.org/10.1525/ae.2006.33.4.4049

Neumayer, E. (2005). Bogus refugees? The determinants of asylum migration to Western Europe. *International Studies Quarterly, 49*(3), 389–410. doi.org/10.1111/j.1468-2478.2005.00370.x

Organisation for Economic Co-operation and Development. (2012). *Key statistics on diaspora from Sri Lanka. Connecting with emigrants*. Paris: Author. doi.org/10.1787/9789264177949-graph30-en

Parliament of Australia. (2013, 28 May). Commonwealth senate estimates, legal and constitutional affairs legislation committee hearing (pp. 52–53, 115–16). Canberra: Author. Retrieved from www.aph.gov.au/hansard.

Powell, L. (2013, March 17). Sri Lankan minister calls for deportation of Maldivian asylum seekers. Minivan News. Retrieved August 25, 2017 from minivannewsarchive.com/date/2013/03/17.

Robinson, V., & Segrott, J. (2002). *Understanding the decision making of asylum seekers*. Home Office Research Study 243. London: Home Office.

Special Broadcasting Service. (2013). Census explorer. Retrieved August 13, 2013 from www.sbs.com.au/yourlanguage/tamil/censusexplorer.

United Nations High Commissioner for Refugees. (2002–13). *Asylum levels and trends in industrialized countries* (various eds). Geneva: Author.

United Nations High Commissioner for Refugees. (2012). Sri Lanka's displacement nears end with closure of Menik Farm. Retrieved July 5, 2013 from www.unhcr.org/en-au/news/latest/2012/9/506443d89/sri-lankas-displacement-chapter-nears-end-closure-menik-farm.html.

United Nations High Commissioner for Refugees. (2013, March). UNHCR Sri Lanka Fact Sheet. Sri Lanka. Retrieved July 16, 2013 from www.unhcr.org/561681326.pdf.

United Nations High Commissioner for Refugees. (n.d.). *UNHCR statistical online population database*. Data extracted July 5, 2015. Retrieved from popstats.unhcr.org.

World Bank. (2010). Bilateral migration matrix 2009. Retrieved August 24, 2017 from www.worldbank.org/en/topic/migration remittancesdiasporaissues/brief/migration-remittances-data.

World Bank. (2011). Bilateral remittance matrix 2010. Retrieved August 24, 2017 from www.worldbank.org/en/topic/migration remittancesdiasporaissues/brief/migration-remittances-data.

World Bank. (2012). Bilateral remittance matrix 2011. Retrieved August 24, 2017 from www.worldbank.org/en/topic/migration remittancesdiasporaissues/brief/migration-remittances-data.

World Bank. (2013a). World development indicators. Retrieved August 24, 2017 from www.worldbank.org/en/topic/migration remittancesdiasporaissues/brief/migration-remittances-data.

World Bank. (2013b). Bilateral remittance matrix 2012. Retrieved August 24, 2017 from www.worldbank.org/en/topic/migration remittancesdiasporaissues/brief/migration-remittances-data.

4

The root causes of movement: Exploring the determinants of irregular migration from Afghanistan

Craig Loschmann, Katie Kuschminder and Melissa Siegel

Introduction

The occurrence of migration outside of an official system is prevalent throughout the world. Although the precise number of irregular migrants is not known, the International Organization for Migration (IOM) estimated that 10 to 15 per cent of the world's 214 million international migrants in 2010 could be categorised as irregular (IOM, 2010, p. 29). The United Nations Development Programme (UNDP) puts that figure closer to a third, within developing countries alone (UNDP, 2009, p. 23). As a matter of concern for the individual, those embarking on such a journey expose themselves to great risk outside the authority of any formal institution. From the states' perspective, the extent of irregular migration and its political sensitivity can pose great dilemmas for policymakers trying to respond to such flows. Considering the scope and relevance of the issue, the lack of analysis on irregular migration is surprising.

This chapter explores irregular migration from the (post-)conflict environment of Afghanistan. Our analytical methods are two-fold: first, we sketch a descriptive profile of irregular migrants in order to gain insight into the features of the particular context in question; and second, we empirically model the determinants of irregular migration through standard regression analysis. Regarding the latter, irregular migration is often considered to be simply driven by a lack of ability to migrate through regular channels. While there may be some truth to such a notion, certain characteristics of migrants may also influence decision-making processes. We therefore investigate the role premigration circumstances play, but also look at other relevant migration-related factors, including the period in which migration occurred, destination and principal reasons for migrating, among others.

For both the descriptive and empirical analyses, we rely on a dataset originating from a household survey conducted in Afghanistan in April and May 2011. The survey captured information on 2,005 households across 100 communities. For our purposes, some 16 per cent of all adults observed in the sample are identified as 'irregular', meaning they are either current irregular migrants or former irregular migrants who have since returned.

The remainder of this chapter is structured as follows. We next provide a brief conceptual overview of irregular migration, including definitions and a discussion on determinants. We then outline recent migration trends in Afghanistan in order to better understand the context within which our study is embedded. Following that, we describe our sample and present a descriptive profile of irregular migrants, before moving on to the empirical analysis of the determinants of irregular migration from Afghanistan. Finally, we conclude with a brief discussion of the study's main findings.

Irregular migration: Definitions and caveats

Critical to defining 'irregular migration' is the recognition of multiple routes into irregularity (Uehling, 2004). The three main routes include individuals entering a country without proper authority, either through clandestine entry or with fraudulent documents; individuals entering with authority, but overstaying their authority; and individuals deliberately utilising the asylum system. The primary distinction of significance for most receiving states is that between irregular entry and irregular stay (de Haas, 2008). This chapter focuses on irregular entry, and so an 'irregular migrant' is defined as someone 'crossing borders without proper authority, or violating conditions for entering another country' (Jordan & Düvell, 2002, p. 15).

In the case at hand, our perspective is that of the country of origin, meaning we look at individuals leaving Afghanistan without proper documentation. Therefore, in practice, we define an irregular migrant within our dataset as an individual who has migrated abroad without official documentation (e.g. tourist visa, work visa, student visa, United Nations High Commissioner for Refugees [UNHCR] refugee status). As such, we do not capture other forms of irregularity like overstaying a visa or abuse of the asylum system, or irregular migrants who become regular through a regularisation scheme. Furthermore, we are unable to identify irregular movement involving smugglers or traffickers.

Beyond terminology, when reflecting on what may influence an individual to migrate irregularly, one must recognise that in most cases migration in general is not driven by a single motivating factor but rather an array of factors which traverse social, economic, environmental and political considerations (de Haas, 2011; Koser & McAulliffe, 2013). For instance, an individual may seek asylum abroad from political persecution, even though the underlying trigger to migrate may relate to another factor, such as a lack of work opportunities, resulting in a mixed migration motivation. Regardless of the myriad motivations that may drive migration, it seems likely that economic interests are a fundamental factor in decision-making processes (Battistella, 2008).

Moreover, when looking specifically at irregular migration, one must appreciate the parallels with regular migration in that we can expect both to be very much related to the interconnected social, political and economic forces operating in both host and sending countries (van Hear, Bakewell, & Long, 2012). For example, when the demand for foreign labour is not met by the supply of labour migration through formal channels, people routinely find their own informal, and often creative, ways to meet that demand. Indeed, Portes (1978) found that one of the key defining characteristics of irregular immigration to the US was that such migrants were 'individuals who move with the sole purpose of selling their work capacity' (p. 472). This consequently leads to the conclusion that the pull of a favourable labour market causes both regular and irregular migration, making distinct identification of the determinants of irregular migration in exclusion a challenge.

Still, even though it may not be difficult to imagine many of the same factors influencing both irregular and regular migration, there is also indication that the drivers of irregular migration in particular may be specific to the context. Orennius (2001), for example, found that there were five primary factors driving irregular migration from Mexico to the US, a context noticeably different to that of Afghanistan yet still informative: first, the history of migration between the two countries; second, the importance of established networks; third, the availability of smugglers to assist crossing the border; fourth, the large wage gap between the two countries; and fifth, the immigration policies of both countries. Although there are several similarities between the determinants of regular and irregular flows, irregular migration episodes may have certain defining characteristics, and individuals choosing to migrate through irregular channels may embody particular features which influence their decision-making process.

Migration trends in Afghanistan

Often, migration in the Afghan context is viewed solely in relation to the most recent period of conflict, overlooking the fact that cross-border movement in the region has a deep-rooted historical precedence. Prior to the Soviet invasion of 1979, Afghans enjoyed an almost unrestricted ability to move back and forth between both Pakistan and Iran, much of the time for temporary or seasonal employment opportunities (Stitger, 2006). The pull from stronger neighbouring labour markets along with close social and cultural ties helped establish robust social networks across locations (Monsutti, 2006). These networks were utilised and strengthened in the subsequent years of conflict, when many were forced to flee Afghanistan because of extreme insecurity and general hardship.

The conflict in Afghanistan over the last four decades has resulted in one of the worst episodes of protracted forced displacement, both externally and internally, in recent memory. During the Soviet presence over much of the 1980s an estimated 5.8 million people fled to Pakistan and Iran, while another 2 million are believed to have been internally displaced (Strand et al., 2008; Kuschminder & Dora, 2009). Even though the Soviet withdrawal by the end of the decade offered a brief period of respite, in terms of those seeking refuge abroad, the optimism for calm quickly subsided with heavy infighting between rival mujahedeen factions and the

Soviet-backed Najibullah regime. In the years up until the government's eventual fall in 1992, the official number of refugees peaked at just over 6.3 million (UNHCR, 2013a).

When the government finally did succumb, Afghanistan experienced a massive return, with more than half of those abroad at the time repatriating within two years. As the Taliban came to power in 1996, however, this considerable inflow came to a halt, only to be reignited following the removal of their regime by international forces in 2001. The promise of change that came along with the international community's presence in the country post-2001 led to large-scale repatriation, with around 2 million Afghans estimated to have returned in 2002 alone and another 3.7 million since then (UNHCR, 2015). Nonetheless, the Afghan refugee population still remains among the largest in the world, with nearly 2.5 million located in Pakistan and Iran (ibid.). Moreover, the heightened insecurity in recent years has led to a noticeable reduction in the number of people voluntarily repatriating.

Besides official refugees, the number of undocumented Afghans within the immediate region is sizeable. Movement to and from both Pakistan and Iran is fairly fluid, with many lured by job opportunities (Koser, 2014). In Iran alone, an estimated 1.4 million Afghans live without documentation, while another one million are believed to reside in Pakistan (UNHCR, 2013b). Migration outside the region, on the other hand, is relatively small, yet still significant, and in large part is made up of the better educated and highly skilled with the resources and wherewithal to embark on such a journey (Koser, 2014). Nevertheless, the total number of asylum claims by Afghans in mostly industrialised nations has risen in recent years, in response to intensifying violence and possibly in anticipation of the political and security transition that took place in 2014. Estimates show around 85,000 individuals applied for asylum in that year, up from around 75,000 in 2013 and 62,000 in 2012 (UNHCR, 2015).

Overall, migration trends in Afghanistan need to be considered in relation to the context of the moment. Over the last 35 years, mobility has been a fundamental survival strategy for many Afghan families (Monsutti, 2006). Migratory flows have fluctuated greatly, depending on the level of insecurity and the livelihood opportunities available. In light of the most recent transition, whether this modest slowdown in return and rise in requests for asylum turns into a greater trend, and whether such movement takes place outside of regular channels, depends on any number of structural factors both within and outside of Afghanistan, as well as the characteristics of the potential migrant.

The survey sample

This analysis draws on data from a household survey collected for the IS Academy: Migration and Development 'A World in Motion' project.[1] The objective of the questionnaire was to explore a diverse set of themes related to the relationship between migration and development processes. A range of separate modules provide in-depth information on both individuals and households including general socioeconomic characteristics, migration histories, future migration plans, return migration, remittances, transnational ties and more.

The data collection took place in April and May 2011. While a purely random sample was not possible due to the limitations of conducting fieldwork in high-risk areas of Afghanistan, particular attention was paid to capturing the diversity of the Afghan population in order to increase the representativeness of the sample. In this regard, the five provinces of Kabul, Herat, Balkh, Nangarhar and Kandahar were chosen because of their highly populated urban centres, and the fact that they represent around one third of the entire population. Moreover, they are geographically spread across the five main regions of the country, which allows for a greater representativeness of differing sociodemographic profiles and contextual factors that may influence migration behaviour. Within each province, stratification between urban, semi-rural and rural districts was applied as a way to capture different socioeconomic groups.[2] Specific communities within these districts were then identified as the primary sampling unit to be eligible for enumeration at random, following official administrative records provided by the Central Statistics

---

1   Unless otherwose noted, this dataset is the source for all figures and tables in this chapter. For more information about the dataset, see the project homepage: migration.unu.edu/research/migration-and-development/is-academy-on-migration-and-development-migration-a-world-in-motion.html#outline.
2   Urban refers to those communities which are the district capital; semi-rural refers to those communities which share a common border with the district capital; and rural refers to those communities with no common border with the district capital.

Organization of Afghanistan. Additionally, the surveying of households followed a random starting point and fixed interval sampling methodology to increase representativeness within the primary sampling unit.

The sample captures information on individuals within 2,005 households from 100 communities. Table 4.1 provides an overview by regularity status. The vast majority of those individuals with a migration experience migrated without official documentation and therefore irregularly. This is consistent with what we already know of migration in Afghanistan, where movement to and from neighbouring countries outside of any regulated system is common. Whether such individuals were current migrants, meaning they resided abroad for three months or more at the time of the survey, or were once migrants but had since returned is inconsequential to our analysis given the information provided from our questionnaire allows us to group them together based on relevant characteristics. Still, the imbalance between regular and irregular migrants makes comparison between these two groups problematic. Accordingly, the following descriptive profile focuses exclusively on irregular migrants.

Table 4.1: Overview by regularity status

Regularity status	Frequency	Per cent
Nonmigrant	6,195	82.57
Regular migrant*	86	1.15
Irregular migrant*	1,222	16.29
Total	7,503	100.00

Note: *Current and return migrants, aggregated. Per cent figures rounded to two decimals.

Descriptive profile

This section highlights premigration features of irregular migrants, including socioeconomic status prior to movement as well as migration-related factors pertaining to the irregular migration episode. We additionally look at the potential for irregular migration in the future, based on migration intentions. Before that, however, we provide an overview of migration and return flows of our sample based on time of departure and return.

Figure 4.1 depicts a narrative consistent with what we know about the ebb and flow of migration both from and back to Afghanistan. Migration in the pre-1992 period was prevalent due to conflict with the Soviet Union, slightly less so between 1992 and 1996 following the removal of the Najibullah regime, and higher once again in the Taliban years leading up to 2001. The expulsion of the Taliban, however, led to a dip in departures as the number of those leaving in the sample reached its lowest point between 2002 and 2006, yet this decline reversed in the final 5-year time period ending in 2011. Return migration, on the other hand, neatly mirrors these outflows. Return flows in our sample were trivial in the pre-1992 period, and increased between 1992 and 1996 before cooling off in the Taliban years up until 2001. The initial post-2001 period, however, witnessed substantial return, with the number repatriating reaching its peak, only to subside again in the final period between 2007 and 2011.

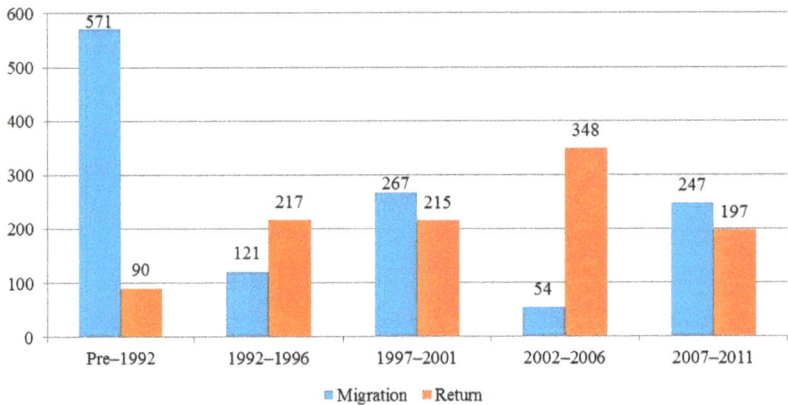

Figure 4.1: Migration and return flows

In terms of the premigration characteristics of irregular migrants, we find that 65 per cent of those with an irregular migration experience were heads of households, more than 80 per cent were male and the average age at departure was 23 years. Figures 4.2 and 4.3 highlight educational attainment and employment status, respectively, of irregular migrants prior to migrating. Figure 4.2 shows that nearly three quarters of our sample had no formal education prior to moving, whereas 14 per cent report primary, 15 per cent secondary and 1 per cent had tertiary level education. The proportion of irregular migrants in our sample with no formal education nearly matches the official measure of the adult Afghan population without any formal schooling at around 75 per cent (Central Statistics Organization, 2014, p. 68).

Figure 4.3 indicates that a fifth of respondents were employed prior to migrating, while 27 per cent were unemployed and 11 per cent were subsistence farmers. On the other hand, around 40 per cent of the responses were not applicable to employment status, meaning these respondents were either in education, retired, permanently sick or disabled, in community or military service or doing housework. If we take these two indicators to characterise socioeconomic status prior to migration, the results suggest those moving irregularly are generally in a disadvantaged position in society. Indeed, the vast majority of migration without documentation is undertaken by those in the sample with no formal education, and with little to no work experience.

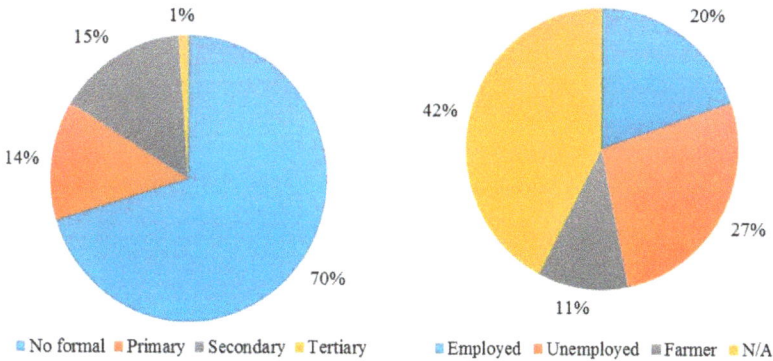

Figure 4.2: Educational attainment   Figure 4.3: Employment status

Information on the irregular migration episode helps shed light on migration decision-making processes. Figure 4.4 illustrates the main reasons for migrating by period of migration. Unsurprisingly, we see that prior to the 2001 NATO-led intervention, the vast majority of respondents moved because of security or political considerations.

This is in stark contrast to those leaving just after the international community's arrival and up until 2006, where absolute numbers were far lower and where the predominant reason for moving relates to employment. This trend only intensifies in the last period between 2007 and 2011, with 87 per cent of respondents during this time citing employment as the main reason for migration. Of those responses considered within the 'other' category, reasons for migrating included family reunification or formation (marriage), education, environmental disaster, moving with family and health.

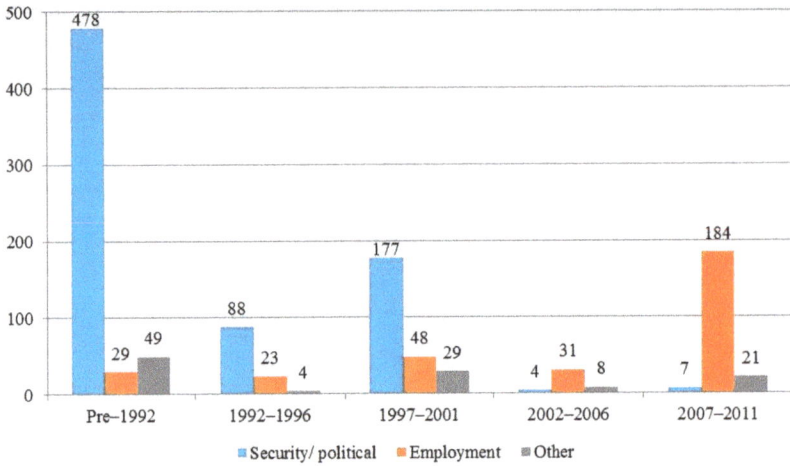

Figure 4.4: Main reason for migration

When it comes to where irregular migrants moved, as expected, nearly all indicated Pakistan or Iran, with 55 per cent going to the former and 43 per cent going to the latter. Of the two per cent who responded 'elsewhere', most specified European countries, including the UK, Belgium and Greece, and there were only a few cases of movement to Saudi Arabia and Tajikistan.

Figure 4.5 provides the main reason for choosing destination by irregular migrants, broken down by each location. Those moving to Pakistan did so mainly because of easy access and entry into the country, though around a quarter cited better working or living conditions. For Iran, however, the main reason is split between easy access or entry and better working or living conditions, suggesting greater job opportunities in comparison to the Pakistani labour market. Lastly, when considering the few moving to locations outside of Iran or Pakistan, better work or living conditions is the predominant reason. Of those who indicated 'other' reasons, responses included 'family or friends already there' and 'to study'.

Besides the individual irregular migrants' motivations for migrating, we are also able to investigate other people involved in both the decision to migrate and act of migration itself. Three quarters of irregular migrants report family members involved in the migration decision, while 19 per cent made the decision alone and 6 per cent counted on friends or others. Furthermore, 63 per cent of respondents migrated with family, while just over a quarter made the journey alone and 11 per cent with friends or others. However, when disaggregating by the period of migration, the share of respondents migrating with family is far lower in the post-2001 period compared to the pre-2001 period, 21 per cent compared with 77 per cent respectively, suggesting again that movement since the Taliban's removal is less about entire families fleeing for safety and more about a search for livelihood.

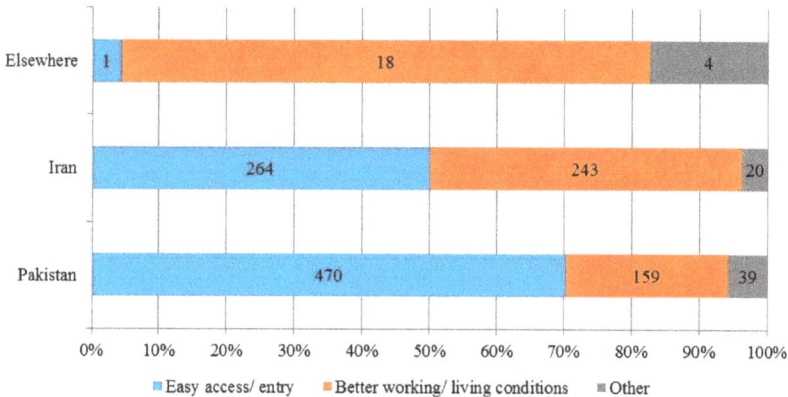

Figure 4.5: Main reason for choosing destination

Turning our attention to social networks, we look at both the contact respondents had with family or friends living abroad prior to migration as well as the financial support they received prior to migration. Only 13 per cent of all irregular migrants had contact with anyone abroad prior to embarking on the journey, suggesting the influence of cross-border networks in this particular case is not as crucial in the decision-making process as is often speculated. A third of respondents relied on either gifts or loans from friends and family to finance their journey in comparison with using savings or selling assets, indicating support at origin was significant for some. However, disaggregating by the period of migration again shows that financial support was much more likely in the post-2001 period in comparison to the pre-2001 period—56 per cent compared with 26 per cent respectively—potentially illustrating that migration motivated by a livelihood strategy is associated with a more robust social network of support.

Finally, we are also able to examine potential future flows of irregular migrants by considering migration aspirations at the time of survey. While 845 individuals in our sample reported having concrete plans to live in another country at some point in the future, only 8 per cent of that group were in possession of a valid passport at that time. Of those individuals with migration intentions, 63 per cent intended to move to the 'West', including, in order of priority, the Netherlands, Canada, the UK, Germany, the US and Australia. Conversely, nearly a quarter planned on moving to a 'non-Western' country like Saudi Arabia or the United Arab Emirates, while the remaining 14 per cent cited Iran or Pakistan. When differentiating by whether the respondent had a passport, no clear distinction arises in terms of destination choice. Moreover, when distinguishing by the reason for choosing that particular destination, nearly all respondents indicate better working or living conditions.

Empirical analysis

This section provides a more detailed empirical analysis using standard regression techniques to identify the determinants of irregular migration from Afghanistan. As mentioned earlier, the extreme imbalance between irregular and regular migrants in our sample complicates our ability to appropriately model determinants for both groups. We therefore provide two separate comparisons: the first, more robust, comparing irregular migrants and nonmigrants; and the second, more tentative comparing irregular migrants and regular migrants. In addition, we also provide the same two comparisons but restrict our sample to those who departed post-2001.

Our empirical approach is to use two separate probit models to estimate the predicted probability of an individual being an irregular migrant in general when comparing to nonmigrants, and in particular when comparing to regular migrants. The formal expression of the probit model is:

$$P(M_i=1 \mid X_i) = \Phi \beta_i X_i$$

where M_i indicates the binary dependent variable of individual i taking the value of 1 if s/he is an irregular migrant, or 0 whether s/he is a nonmigrant and regular migrant respectively. X_i is a series of independent variables comprised of basic individual and migration-related characteristics included strictly in the second model. Moreover, β_i represents the regression parameter to be estimated and Φ indicates the cumulative normal distribution function. All models are estimated using robust standard errors clustered at the household level, and we report the marginal effects along with their standard errors for easier interpretation.

Table 4.2 presents the results of the two separate probit models using the whole sample, estimating the predicted probability of an individual being an irregular migrant both generally and in particular.[3] Beginning with the general model comparing irregular migrants to nonmigrants, a few statistically significant findings stand out. First, a household head and male respondent is on the margin 24 and 2 percentage points more likely to be an irregular migrant, respectively, while older individuals are slightly less likely. Compared to those with no formal education, respondents with some form of educational attainment are less likely to be irregular migrants and the scale of the marginal effect increases with each level. An individual with tertiary education, for example, is 5 percentage points less likely to be an irregular migrant. In terms of employment status, the unemployed are 11 percentage points more likely to be irregular migrants compared to their employed counterparts, whereas the same relationship albeit to a smaller scale exists for subsistence farmers and those with a nonapplicable employment status.

Table 4.2: Probit model

	General		Particular	
Dependent variable	Irregular migrants		Irregular migrants	
Base	Nonmigrants		Regular migrants	
	Marginal effect	SE	Marginal effect	SE
Household head	0.2442***	(0.0098)	0.0030	(0.0138)
Male	0.0203**	(0.0084)	0.0250*	(0.0151)
Age^	−0.0078***	(0.0003)	−0.0001	(0.0004)
Educational attainment^				
No formal	Reference	(.)	Reference	(.)
Primary	−0.0247***	(0.0084)	−0.0115	(0.0149)
Secondary	−0.0451***	(0.0066)	−0.0047	(0.0133)
Tertiary	−0.0547***	(0.0127)	−0.1070	(0.1060)
Employment status^				
Employed	Reference	(.)	Reference	(.)
Unemployed	0.1121***	(0.0191)	0.0281*	(0.0160)
Subsistence farmer	0.0520***	(0.0155)	−0.0176	(0.0262)
Not applicable	0.0235***	(0.0075)	0.0202	(0.0133)
Household size	0.0029***	(0.0011)	−0.0006	(0.0018)

3   Summary statistics for all covariates used in the model can be found in Table A1 of the appendix.

Dependent variable	General		Particular	
	Irregular migrants		Irregular migrants	
Base	Nonmigrants		Regular migrants	
	Marginal effect	SE	Marginal effect	SE
Ethnicity				
Pashtun	Reference	(.)	Reference	(.)
Tajik	0.0105	(0.0072)	0.0067	(0.0133)
Hazara	0.0595***	(0.0195)	−0.0119	(0.0288)
Other	−0.0109	(0.0128)	0.0172	(0.0217)
District type				
Urban	Reference	(.)	Reference	(.)
Semi-rural	−0.0037	(0.0070)	0.0096	(0.0100)
Rural	0.0099	(0.0075)	−0.0108	(0.0139)
Province				
Nangarhar	Reference	(.)	Reference	(.)
Kabul	0.0201**	(0.0096)	−0.0494***	(0.0187)
Herat	0.0086	(0.0100)	−0.0327	(0.0208)
Balkh	0.0028	(0.0118)	−0.0146	(0.0126)
Kandahar	−0.0358***	(0.0072)	−0.0168	(0.0150)
Migration post-2001			−0.0592***	(0.0166)
Destination				
Pakistan			Reference	(.)
Iran			−0.0163	(0.0158)
Other			−0.3619***	(0.1240)
Migration reason				
Security/political			Reference	(.)
Employment			−0.0026	(0.0161)
Other			−0.0073	(0.0216)
Destination reason				
Easy access/entry			Reference	(.)
Better conditions			−0.0156	(0.0116)
Other			−0.0007	(0.0178)
Migration decision				
Family			Reference	(.)
Alone			0.0107	(0.0114)
Friends/other			−0.0037	(0.0293)

Dependent variable	General		Particular	
	Irregular migrants		Irregular migrants	
Base	Nonmigrants		Regular migrants	
	Marginal effect	SE	Marginal effect	SE
Migrated with				
Family			Reference	(.)
Alone			0.0377**	(0.0164)
Friend/other			0.0559***	(0.0120)
Social networks abroad			−0.0179	(0.0124)
Method to finance trip				
Savings/sold assets			Reference	(.)
Gifts/loans			0.0245**	(0.0107)
Other			0.0147	(0.0179)
R2 adjusted	0.3625		0.2300	
N	7294		1187	

Note: ^ indicates information for regular and irregular migrants is prior to migration.
* p<0.10, ** p<0.05, *** p<0.01

Looking at some of the standard control variables, those respondents originating from a larger household are slightly more probable to be irregular migrants. Hazaras are 6 percentage points more likely to be irregular in comparison to the Pashtun reference group. As for location, there is no statistically significant difference regarding the type of district one originates from, yet an individual from Kabul is 2 percentage points more likely to be an irregular migrant while those from Kandahar are 4 percentage points less likely in comparison to respondents from Nangarhar.

In the next model, comparing irregular migrants to regular migrants, we observe many of those statistically significant variables from the general model lose significance. Of the basic and premigration individual characteristics, only being male and unemployed leads to a respondent being marginally more likely to be an irregular migrant, both by 3 percentage points. Additionally, an individual from Kabul is now less likely to be an irregular migrant in contrast to that which is seen in the general model. Focusing specifically on those migration-related characteristics, we find respondents who moved after 2001 were 6 percentage points less likely to be irregular migrants in comparison to those who moved before international intervention.

There is no statistically significant difference between Iran and Pakistan; however, those migrating further abroad are much less likely, by 36 percentage points, to be irregular compared to the reference group. Moreover, we see no statistical significance when it comes to the reason one decides to migrate or why one chooses a specific destination, nor depending on who was involved in the migration decision. On the other hand, migrating alone as well as with a friend or other acquaintance is positively correlated with being an irregular migrant in comparison to those who made the journey with family, by 4 and 6 percentage points respectively. Likewise, being supported by family or friends through either a gift or loan in order to finance the migratory trip is associated with being slightly more likely to be an irregular migrant, by 2 percentage points, in relation to those who relied on savings or sold assets.

Despite irregular migration post-2001 being less prevalent than in the period prior, as indicated in the previous model there is reason to believe the nature of flows during this interval is fundamentally distinct in comparison to migration pre-2001. With this in mind, Table 4.3 presents the results of the same two models but with a restricted sample for those who departed post-2001.[4] Beginning once again with the general model, we find similarly that a household head and male respondent is more likely to be an irregular migrant. Still, the marginal scale of the variable indicating head of household is much lower than before, suggesting a slight change regarding which member migrates within the household. Age at departure still shows a negative sign despite being negligible. Concerning educational attainment, here only those respondents with secondary and tertiary qualifications are less likely to be irregular migrants, with the marginal scale again lower than that found earlier. With regard to employment status, now only a subsistence farmer is less likely to be an irregular migrant in comparison to an employed individual, again with marginal effects dampened.

---

4   Summary statistics for all covariates used in the model can be found in Table A2 of the appendix.

Table 4.3: Probit model, post-2001

	General, post-2001		Particular, post-2001	
Dependent variable	Irregular migrants		Irregular migrants	
Base	Nonmigrants		Regular migrants	
	Marginal effect	SE	Marginal effect	SE
Household head	0.0084***	(0.0026)	−0.0005	(0.0440)
Male	0.0274***	(0.0041)	0.1313**	(0.0562)
Age^	−0.0009***	(0.0001)	−0.0015	(0.0015)
Educational attainment^				
No formal	Reference	(.)	Reference	(.)
Primary	−0.0034	(0.0024)	−0.0588	(0.0538)
Secondary	−0.0068***	(0.0021)	0.0122	(0.0289)
Tertiary	−0.0108***	(0.0027)	−0.0857	(0.1966)
Employment status^				
Employed	Reference	(.)	Reference	(.)
Unemployed	0.0057	(0.0063)	0.0971***	(0.0364)
Subsistence farmer	−0.0104***	(0.0029)	0.0520	(0.0811)
Not applicable	−0.0040	(0.0028)	0.0583	(0.0416)
Household size	0.0006*	(0.0004)	−0.0008	(0.0056)
Ethnicity				
Pashtun	Reference	(.)	Reference	(.)
Tajik	0.0024	(0.0025)	0.0160	(0.0387)
Hazara	0.0150*	(0.0084)	−0.1458	(0.1296)
Other	−0.0060**	(0.0025)	0.0000	(.)
District type				
Urban	Reference	(.)	Reference	(.)
Semi-rural	0.0001	(0.0020)	0.0062	(0.0324)
Rural	0.0126***	(0.0034)	−0.0305	(0.0457)
Province				
Nangarhar	Reference	(.)	Reference	(.)
Kabul	0.0048*	(0.0028)	−0.0987	(0.0627)
Herat	0.0293***	(0.0059)	−0.0805	(0.0521)
Balkh	0.0204***	(0.0058)	−0.0351	(0.0254)
Kandahar	−0.0043**	(0.0018)	−0.0274	(0.0602)

Dependent variable	General, post-2001 Irregular migrants		Particular, post-2001 Irregular migrants	
Base	Nonmigrants		Regular migrants	
	Marginal effect	SE	Marginal effect	SE
Destination				
Pakistan			Reference	(.)
Iran			–0.0232	(0.0309)
Other			–0.6232***	(0.1813)
Migration reason				
Security/political			Reference	(.)
Employment			0.0209	(0.0663)
Other			0.0767	(0.0626)
Destination reason				
Easy access/entry			Reference	(.)
Better conditions			–0.0101	(0.0278)
Other			–0.0829	(0.0862)
Migration decision				
Family			Reference	(.)
Alone			–0.0080	(0.0329)
Friends/other			0.0000	(.)
Migrated with				
Family			Reference	(.)
Alone			0.1294	(0.1014)
Friend/other			0.2171**	(0.0884)
Social networks abroad			–0.0320	(0.0355)
Method to finance trip				
Savings/sold assets			Reference	(.)
Gifts/loans			0.1045**	(0.0471)
Other			0.0958	(0.0603)
R2 adjusted	0.2463		0.3847	
N	6421		272	

Note: ^ indicates information for regular and irregular migrants is prior to migration.
* $p<0.10$, ** $p<0.05$, *** $p<0.01$

Regarding control variables, most results are similar, yet with a lower marginal effect despite a few variables gaining statistical significance. In reference to those variables specifying location, it seems an individual from a rural district as well as from Herat and Balkh provinces is now slightly more likely to be an irregular migrant. Considering that migration post-2001 is motivated more by employment opportunities abroad, it is unsurprising that rural households now are more likely to be the origin of irregular migrants than their urban counterparts. Moreover, the statistical significance of provinces like Herat and Balkh post-2001 may indicate a more recent dispersion from where irregular migrants originate.

Finally, looking at the particular model again we see once more that most of those statistically significant variables in the general model lose significance. Still, being male and unemployed remain statistically significant and positive, and actually gain in scale in comparison to the situation when the whole sample is in the analysis. Additionally, considering migration flows are more likely driven by employment since 2001, the 10 per cent marginal effect for the unemployed variable is telling. Beyond this result, however, all other statistically significant results are similar to what was seen before, including destination other than Pakistan or Iran, migrating with a friend or other acquaintance and relying on gifts or loans in order to finance the trip. Nevertheless, the marginal effect for each is amplified compared to the model using the whole sample, with the latter two again potentially indicating a greater social element to the migration event when motivated by the search for livelihood opportunities.

Conclusions

Despite the widespread occurrence of irregular migration in both the developed and developing world, there is a gap in understanding the specific determinants of irregular migration. This study has aimed to contribute to filling this research gap by exploring the determinants of irregular migration within the (post-)conflict environment of Afghanistan, taking both a descriptive and empirical approach. Relying on a unique dataset, we first profile irregular migrants in our sample and second model the determinants of being an irregular migrant for both the whole sample and those who migrated post-2001.

The descriptive profile paints a consistent picture regarding what we know about the history of migration in Afghanistan. Over the last 35 years, migration has ebbed and flowed in response to both insecurity and the lack of livelihood opportunities. Despite the rise and fall in migration flows, irregular cross-border movement has been common throughout this time period, especially to and from neighbouring Pakistan and Iran. The results highlight that the vast majority of migration from Afghanistan has been, and will continue to be, irregular.

The descriptive analysis indicates that those who move irregularly are predominately of a lower socioeconomic status, with little to no schooling and limited work experience. Moreover, the main reason for migrating has shifted over time. Unsurprisingly, migration was primarily motivated by security or political considerations prior to 2001, whereas since then it has been primarily driven by the search for employment. This emphasis on migration for livelihood is greater for those moving to Iran for those moving to Pakistan, which may indicate the greater demand for low-skilled labour in Iran due to the nature of its economy. Likewise, the fact that migrating alone is more prevalent post-2001, and that the trip is also more likely financed through gifts or loans from family and friends, gives credence to the notion of migration for livelihood potentially being based on a strategy at the household level. Finally, taking into consideration the intentions to migrate of those individuals without an official passport suggests irregular migration is likely to continue into the near future.

As for the empirical analysis focusing on the determinants of migration, we notice a number of premigration characteristics of statistical significance. In the general model, individuals with a lower educational background are consistently more likely to be irregular migrants compared to nonmigrants. There is also evidence in both the general and particular models that those with less employment experience are more likely to migrate, yet the statistical significance varies across specification. Regarding location, it seems the origin of irregular migrants has dispersed more recently to include mostly rural areas and more provinces.

When it comes to migration-related factors, we find irregular migration to be less likely in the post-2001 period than in the previous period, even though it still dominates overall flows. Moreover, our analysis finds evidence that those individuals migrating beyond neighbouring Pakistan and Iran, which in this case was primarily to various European countries and Saudi Arabia, are less likely to have made the journey through irregular channels. It is important to note, however, that most research on irregular Afghan migration to other countries, such as Australia and those in Europe, does find that the majority of these flows are irregular (Boland, 2010; Koser & McAuliffe, 2013; Vervliet, Vanobbergen, Broekaert, & Derluyn, 2015). Even though the number of individuals in our sample that did move outside of Pakistan and Iran is limited, this finding may still indicate the difficulties in doing so given the associated costs and distance. Additionally, those respondents migrating with a friend or other acquaintance are more likely to be irregular migrants in comparison to those individuals migrating with family, while the same goes for those relying on financial support from family or friends to finance the journey. This last finding again potentially indicates the importance of social networks when migration is motivated by the search for employment, possibly as part of an implicit household strategy to diversify the overall sources of livelihood.

Reference list

Battistella, G. (2008). Irregular migration. In Appave, G., & Cholewinski, R. (Eds), *World migration 2008* (pp. 201–34). Washington DC: Inter-American Development Bank.

Boland, K. (2010). *Children on the move between Afghanistan and western countries*. Geneva: United Nations Children's Fund.

Central Statistics Organization. (2014). *National Risk and Vulnerability Assessment 2011/2012. Afghanistan Living Conditions Survey*. Kabul: Author.

de Haas, H. (2008). *Irregular migration from West Africa to the Maghreb and the European Union: An overview of recent trends*. Geneva: International Organization for Migration.

de Haas, H. (2011). *The determinants of international migration: Conceptualizing policy, origin and destination effects*. Determinants of International Migration, project paper no. 2. Oxford: International Migration Institute.

International Organization for Migration. (2010). *World Migration Report 2010*. Geneva: Author.

Jordan, B., & Düvell, F. (2002). *Irregular migration: Dilemmas of transnational mobility*. Aldershot: Edward Elgar.

Koser, K. (2014). *Transition, crisis and mobility in Afghanistan: Rhetoric and reality*. Geneva: International Organization for Migration.

Koser, K., & McAuliffe, M. (2013). *Establishing an evidence-base for future policy development on irregular migration to Australia.* Irregular Migration Research Program, Occasional Paper Series 01. Canberra: Australian Department of Immigration and Citizenship. Retrieved from www.border.gov.au/ReportsandPublications/Documents/research/evidence-base-for-future-policy.pdf.

Kuschminder, K., & Dora, M. (2009). *Migration in Afghanistan: History, current trends and future prospects.* Paper series: Migration and development country profiles. Maastricht: Maastricht Graduate School of Governance.

Monsutti, A. (2006). *Afghan transnational networks: Looking beyond repatriation.* Kabul: Afghan Research and Evaluation Unit.

Orrenius, P. M. (2001). Illegal immigration and enforcement along the US–Mexico border: An overview. *Economic and Financial Review, 1*(1), 2–11.

Portes, A. (1978). Introduction: toward a structural analysis of illegal (undocumented) immigration. *International Migration Review, 12*(4), 469–84. doi.org/10.2307/2545446

Stitger, E. (2006). Afghan migratory strategies—An assessment of repatriation and sustainable return in response to the convention plus. *Refugee Survey Quarterly, 25*(2): 109–22. doi.org/10.1093/rsq/hdi0129

Strand, A., Akbari, A., Chaudhary, T. W., Harpviken, K. B., Sarwari, A., & Suhrke, A. (2008). *Return in Dignity, Return to What? Review of the Voluntary Return Programme to Afghanistan.* Bergen: Chr. Michelsen Institute.

Uehling, G. (2004). *Unwanted migration: combating and unwittingly creating irregular migration in Ukraine.* New Issues in Refugee Research, working paper no. 109. Geneva: United Nations High Commissioner for Refugees.

United Nations Development Programme. (2009). *Human development report 2009. Overcoming barriers: Human mobility and development.* Geneva: Author. doi.org/10.18356/9d335cec-en

United Nations High Commissioner for Refugees. (2013a). *Global trends 2012—Displacement: The new 21st century challenge.* Geneva: Author.

United Nations High Commissioner for Refugees. (2013b). *Solutions strategy for Afghan refugees: Summary progress report*. Geneva: Author.

United Nations High Commissioner for Refugees. (2015). *UNHCR statistical online population database*. Data extracted July 23, 2015. Retrieved from popstats.unhcr.org.

van Hear, N., Bakewell, O., & Long, K. (2012). *Drivers of migration*. Migrating out of poverty, working paper no. 1. Oxford: University of Oxford.

Vervliet, M., Vanobbergen, B., Broekaert, E., & Derluyn, I. (2015). The aspirations of Afghan unaccompanied refugee minors before departure and on arrival in the host country. *Childhood, 22*(3), 1–16.

Appendix

Table A1: Summary statistics

Variable	Nonmigrant		Regular migrant		Irregular migrant	
	Mean	SD	Mean	SD	Mean	SD
Household head	0.19	(0.39)	0.37	(0.49)	0.65	(0.48)
Male	0.48	(0.50)	0.72	(0.45)	0.82	(0.39)
Age^	34.16	(15.99)	25.53	(12.09)	23.37	(13.13)
Educational attainment^						
No formal	0.67	(0.47)	0.59	(0.49)	0.70	(0.46)
Primary	0.11	(0.31)	0.16	(0.37)	0.13	(0.34)
Secondary	0.19	(0.39)	0.21	(0.41)	0.15	(0.36)
Tertiary	0.03	(0.16)	0.03	(0.18)	0.01	(0.11)
Employment status^						
Employed	0.23	(0.42)	0.42	(0.50)	0.27	(0.45)
Unemployed	0.04	(0.20)	0.05	(0.21)	0.12	(0.33)
Subsistence farmer	0.04	(0.19)	0.09	(0.29)	0.11	(0.31)
Not applicable	0.69	(0.46)	0.44	(0.50)	0.50	(0.50)
Household size	8.29	(2.81)	8.20	(2.58)	7.72	(2.75)
Ethnicity						
Pashtun	0.47	(0.50)	0.37	(0.49)	0.45	(0.50)
Tajik	0.41	(0.49)	0.44	(0.50)	0.42	(0.49)

Variable	Nonmigrant		Regular migrant		Irregular migrant	
	Mean	SD	Mean	SD	Mean	SD
Hazara	0.05	(0.22)	0.17	(0.38)	0.08	(0.27)
Other	0.06	(0.24)	0.01	(0.11)	0.05	(0.21)
District type						
Urban	0.51	(0.50)	0.50	(0.50)	0.49	(0.50)
Semi-rural	0.24	(0.42)	0.20	(0.40)	0.26	(0.44)
Rural	0.26	(0.44)	0.30	(0.46)	0.25	(0.44)
Province						
Nangarhar	0.22	(0.42)	0.14	(0.35)	0.24	(0.42)
Kabul	0.21	(0.40)	0.31	(0.47)	0.22	(0.41)
Herat	0.17	(0.37)	0.19	(0.39)	0.20	(0.40)
Balkh	0.20	(0.40)	0.29	(0.46)	0.19	(0.39)
Kandahar	0.21	(0.40)	0.07	(0.26)	0.15	(0.36)
Migration post-2001			0.57	(0.50)	0.22	(0.41)
Destination						
Pakistan			0.25	(0.44)	0.55	(0.50)
Iran			0.60	(0.49)	0.43	(0.50)
Other			0.15	(0.36)	0.02	(0.14)
Migration reason						
Security/political			0.40	(0.49)	0.63	(0.48)
Employment			0.47	(0.50)	0.28	(0.45)
Other			0.14	(0.35)	0.10	(0.29)
Destination reason						
Easy access/entry			0.33	(0.47)	0.60	(0.49)
Better conditions			0.58	(0.50)	0.35	(0.48)
Other			0.09	(0.29)	0.05	(0.22)
Migration decision						
Family			0.77	(0.42)	0.75	(0.43)
Alone			0.20	(0.40)	0.19	(0.39)
Friends/other			0.02	(0.15)	0.07	(0.25)
Migration with						
Family			0.62	(0.49)	0.63	(0.48)
Alone			0.35	(0.48)	0.25	(0.43)
Friend/other			0.03	(0.18)	0.12	(0.32)
Social networks abroad			0.19	(0.39)	0.13	(0.34)

	Nonmigrant		Regular migrant		Irregular migrant	
Variable	Mean	SD	Mean	SD	Mean	SD
Method to finance trip						
Savings/sold assets			0.58	(0.50)	0.60	(0.49)
Gifts/loans			0.31	(0.47)	0.33	(0.47)
Other			0.10	(0.31)	0.07	(0.25)

Note: ^ indicates information for regular and irregular migrants is prior to migration.

Table A2: Summary statistics, post-2001

	Nonmigrant		Regular migrant		Irregular migrant	
Variable	Mean	SD	Mean	SD	Mean	SD
Household head	0.19	(0.39)	0.22	(0.42)	0.30	(0.46)
Male	0.48	(0.50)	0.70	(0.47)	0.93	(0.26)
Age^	34.17	(15.99)	27.42	(10.72)	24.85	(9.61)
Educational attainment^						
No formal	0.67	(0.47)	0.52	(0.51)	0.58	(0.50)
Primary	0.11	(0.31)	0.24	(0.43)	0.18	(0.39)
Secondary	0.19	(0.39)	0.22	(0.42)	0.23	(0.42)
Tertiary	0.03	(0.16)	0.02	(0.15)	0.01	(0.09)
Employment status^						
Employed	0.23	(0.42)	0.47	(0.50)	0.42	(0.49)
Unemployed	0.04	(0.19)	0.02	(0.15)	0.04	(0.19)
Subsistence farmer	0.04	(0.20)	0.04	(0.21)	0.09	(0.29)
Not applicable	0.69	(0.46)	0.47	(0.50)	0.45	(0.50)
Household size	8.29	(2.81)	8.17	(2.54)	8.02	(2.73)
Ethnicity						
Pashtun	0.47	(0.50)	0.28	(0.46)	0.26	(0.44)
Tajik	0.41	(0.49)	0.50	(0.51)	0.59	(0.49)
Hazara	0.05	(0.22)	0.22	(0.42)	0.10	(0.30)
Other	0.06	(0.24)	0.00	(0.00)	0.04	(0.20)
District type						
Urban	0.51	(0.50)	0.54	(0.50)	0.40	(0.49)
Semi-rural	0.24	(0.42)	0.20	(0.40)	0.20	(0.40)
Rural	0.26	(0.44)	0.26	(0.44)	0.41	(0.49)
Province						
Nangarhar	0.22	(0.42)	0.17	(0.38)	0.11	(0.32)

	Nonmigrant		Regular migrant		Irregular migrant	
Variable	Mean	SD	Mean	SD	Mean	SD
Kabul	0.21	(0.40)	0.15	(0.36)	0.18	(0.38)
Herat	0.17	(0.37)	0.24	(0.43)	0.34	(0.47)
Balkh	0.20	(0.40)	0.41	(0.50)	0.33	(0.47)
Kandahar	0.21	(0.40)	0.02	(0.15)	0.04	(0.20)
Destination						
Pakistan			1.00	(0.00)	1.00	(0.00)
Iran			0.07	(0.25)	0.13	(0.34)
Other			0.66	(0.48)	0.81	(0.39)
Migration reason						
Security/political			0.27	(0.45)	0.05	(0.23)
Employment			0.13	(0.34)	0.04	(0.20)
Other			0.72	(0.46)	0.84	(0.36)
Destination reason						
Easy access/entry			0.15	(0.36)	0.11	(0.32)
Better conditions			0.24	(0.43)	0.41	(0.49)
Other			0.59	(0.50)	0.55	(0.50)
Migration decision						
Family			0.17	(0.38)	0.04	(0.20)
Alone			0.69	(0.47)	0.63	(0.48)
Friends/other			0.00	(0.00)	0.04	(0.19)
Migration with						
Family			0.31	(0.47)	0.33	(0.47)
Alone			0.48	(0.51)	0.16	(0.37)
Friend/other			0.04	(0.21)	0.29	(0.45)
Social networks abroad			0.22	(0.42)	0.14	(0.35)
Method to finance trip			0.48	(0.51)	0.55	(0.50)
Savings/sold assets			0.57	(0.50)	0.25	(0.44)
Gifts/loans			0.35	(0.48)	0.60	(0.49)
Other			0.09	(0.28)	0.15	(0.36)

Note: ^ indicates information for regular and irregular migrants is prior to migration.

5

Seeking the views of irregular migrants: Decision-making, drivers and migration journeys

Marie McAuliffe[1]

A substantial body of research indicates that a number of complex, interrelated factors impact on the movement of irregular asylum and non-asylum migration flows (Castles, 2013; de Haas, 2011; Havinga & Böcker, 1999; Koser, 2011; Middleton, 2005; Neumayer, 2004). In some of the literature, the factors related to asylum seeker migration have been characterised as either 'push' or 'pull' factors, both in terms of the decision to migrate as well as choice of destination country (Havinga & Böcker, 1999; Neumayer, 2004; Zimmermann, 1996). Generally, push factors from the country of origin include: the political and security situation in-country (home and/or host country); the state of the economy, and access to income; the outlook for the future, and in particular the prevailing pessimism (Adhikari, 2013; Hatton, 2011; Theilemann, 2006). Pull factors, on the other hand, include: asylum seeker policies in destination countries; how welcoming destination countries are perceived to be; perceptions of destination countries' acceptance of refugees; the state of

_____

1   The author is grateful for research assistance from Simone Gangell and Paul Hayes in the preparation of this chapter.

the economies of destination countries; and the existence of diaspora and communities in destination countries (Koser, 1997; Koser & Pinkerton, 2002; Neumayer, 2004; Theilemann, 2006; Toshkov, 2012).

There is also a range of 'enabling' factors that act to facilitate flows, and that are less prevalent in the literature.[2] These enabling factors cannot be characterised by the linear push–pull construct, but act to facilitate or underpin movement. Enabling factors include:

- geography and the ease of travelling to specific destination countries (Havinger & Böcker, 1999; Monsutti, 2010);
- the ability to travel through transit countries (e.g. facilitative visa arrangements) and proximity to established migration networks (and, in some cases, a related lack of ability to gain visas for lawful entry to destination countries);
- diaspora populations with the ability and resources to assist others in their communities around the world to migrate (Doraï, 2011; Koser & Pinkerton, 2002);
- an increased ability to self-fund travel, as human development and greater access to resources increases (de Haas, 2010);
- enhanced 'real time' communications technology to provide better information for decision-making both of potential irregular immigrants and people smugglers (e.g. blogs, social media, news reporting of events); and
- a global asylum system that was established decades ago to address a particular set of circumstances, and may not have evolved sufficiently to reflect significant changes in the environment (e.g. refusal of countries to accept the return of their nationals, and the lack of any ability to make countries accept the return of their citizens) (Hamlin, 2012; Hatton, 2011; Jones, 2009).

The number of factors impacting on decision-making highlights the complex nature of irregular migration. It is also important to acknowledge that none of the factors are likely to be static, and some of them can change decisively and rapidly, undoubtedly adding to the complexity of migrant decision-making.

---

2   One exception being de Haas (2010).

There is a body of literature on decision-making by asylum seekers and potential asylum seekers; however, there are two important points to note about the research that has been conducted so far on this topic (Koser & McAuliffe, 2013). First, the focus of this research has been largely limited to 'choice of destination', with very little examination of the decision-making processes associated with the decision to leave a country of origin. On the one hand, this is partly due to a view that, in relation to asylum seekers, forced migration is occurring. The associated assumption is that asylum seekers have a lack of agency, thereby effectively rendering research on this aspect of decision-making largely irrelevant (Koser & Pinkerton, 2002; Robinson & Segrott, 2002; Spinks, 2013). Forced migration is characterised as being driven by 'push' factors, so that when situations in countries become intolerable asylum seekers are compelled to move across borders.

In addition to the forced migration perspective, the primary focus on choice of destination as opposed to the decision to leave origin countries is likely to be related to the broader policy and political environment of the time. This is especially so in the European context, where much of the research on asylum seeker decision-making has been situated (Brekke & Aarset, 2009; Neumayer, 2004; Robinson & Segrott, 2002; van Liempt & Doomernik, 2006). Neumayer, for example, summarises:

> Asylum seekers coming to Western Europe have preferred some destination countries over others. Austria, Germany, Sweden and Switzerland were the main destination countries relative to their population size in the 1980s and 1990s, whereas Finland, Italy, Portugal and Spain took on very few asylum seekers. … [T]he objective is to explain the choice amongst the various countries on offer as their destination for those asylum seekers coming to Western Europe. I want to explore to what extent one can explain the relative attractiveness of destination countries.

Second, given that much of the research on decision-making is European, it is not able to adequately account for the particularities of the Australian situation, especially Australia's geography and lack of proximity to similar destination countries. That is not to say that the European research is not relevant, for many aspects undoubtedly are. It is, however, prudent to be cautious about aspects of its applicability to the Australia context. In an absence of Australian empirical research, there has been a tendency for researchers and commentators to apply European research findings to the Australian context. In a recent paper published by the Australian Parliamentary Library, for example, Spinks (2013) states that 'decisions about where to go are not always made by refugees themselves but rather are often determined, or at least heavily influenced, by others. In some cases, the decision is made by a family member, but for many the destination is chosen by the 'agent' or people smuggler engaged to get them to a place (any place) of safety' (p. 9). The evidence provided by the survey results to be discussed in this chapter calls this into question. Table 5.6, for example, shows that 79 per cent of respondents reported being involved in the final decision to travel to Australia, and that 16 per cent of respondents reported that people who helped with travel (e.g. people smugglers) were involved in the final decision to travel to Australia.

The significant influence of agents is highlighted in European research on asylum seekers' decision-making (Koser, 2008; Robinson & Segrott, 2002; van Liempt & Doomernik, 2006). It is possible that the entrenched smuggling networks that have supported irregular migration flows into Europe for decades may render potential migrants less able to exercise agency in terms of where to travel, particularly given the many countries smugglers can ultimately send migrants. This would appear to be less relevant in the Australian context, however, given that Australia is effectively at the 'end of the line'. As highlighted by Koser and McAuliffe (2013), for irregular maritime arrivals (IMAs) 'in Australia, who have undertaken long and relatively expensive journeys from their origin countries, and transited other countries where they might have remained in an irregular situation … the choice of Australia for most … appears to be deliberate' (p. 13). In this sense, it is useful to acknowledge Johansson's distinction between anticipatory refugee movement and acute or spontaneous movements (Johansson, 1990). When examining asylum seeker movement to Australia, much of the movement in recent years has been anticipatory rather than acute. This, in turn, and given the substantial distances travelled from source through (multiple) transit countries to Australia, means that both the decision to leave and the choice of destination are highly relevant topics of research in the Australian context.

Within this context, this chapter provides unique insights into how maritime asylum seekers to Australia contemplated and undertook migration journeys. As the first quantitative empirical research in Australia that has sought the views of IMAs, the study upon which this chapter is based has drawn on the existing European research, but also reflects the different dynamics that the Australian context presents. Seeking irregular migrants' views on the decision-making processes related to both the decision to leave and the choice of destination are key aspects of the survey, as are the roles of people other than the migrant in decision-making (including agents).

Methods

The scope of the survey was all adult IMAs who had been granted a protection visa between 6 July, 2011 and 31 December, 2012 (inclusive), and were based in Sydney, Melbourne or Brisbane. This population totalled 4,725 IMAs. The population was defined in order to minimise, as far as possible, problems of recall by limiting the scope to people who had recently travelled as IMAs. That said, issues of recall necessarily remain for this type of research.

IMAs who had not been granted a permanent visa during this period were out of scope. This approach ensured that all people in the survey had certainty about their status in Australia. The scope did not include people found not to be in need of protection, noting that merits and judicial review processes may take considerable periods of time, and a negative primary decision may not reflect a person's final status. In addition, the survey population did not include any persons under the age of 18 due to particular sensitivities concerning interviewing minors. People who were under the age of 18 at the time of travel but had since turned 18 were in scope.

The survey sample was drawn from two of the Department of Immigration and Border Protection's databases: the settlement database and the adult migrant English program database. The survey sample was drawn in two stages. The first group was drawn on 16 April 2013, and this was supplemented by a further group drawn in mid-June 2013.

A stratified sample was selected from the databases. The sample was stratified by citizenship (Afghan, Iranian, Pakistani, Sri Lankan and other[3]) and location (New South Wales, Queensland and Victoria). The sampling rates varied between the strata, including because of variability in contact detail accuracy. To gain the same accuracy for estimates for a small population (e.g. Sri Lankans) a much higher sampling rate was required

---

3   A sufficient subsample of Iraqis was not able to be obtained. Iraqis were included in the 'other' category.

than for a larger population. The stratification process has not introduced a bias in the population estimates because the responses are appropriately weighted to take these differing sample rates into account. Further details of the survey methodology are outlined in McAuliffe (2013).

Utilising technology to support self-completion

Due to the challenges inherent in seeking honest, candid information about experiences that may have involved trauma, vulnerability and high-risk behaviour, specific measures were employed as a means of reducing response bias and non-sampling error.

First, the survey was designed as a self-completion survey. The self-completion of sensitive questions has been found to increase the level of reporting in a survey by reducing the social desirability effects relative to the administration of the same questions by an interviewer (Tourangeau & Smith, 1996). Given the sensitive nature of some of the questions, the potential for interviewer bias to affect the results was a significant issue. Interviewer bias can be due to the actual characteristics of the interviewer (e.g. sex, age, perceived social status) or because respondents may be reluctant to reveal beliefs unlikely to be endorsed by an interviewer (Bowling, 2005).

In the IMA survey context, a traditional interviewer survey approach involving bilingual interviewers would be likely to have an impact on bias. This is, in part, due to the specific languages groups required to support an interviewer mode of delivery. Given the history of some IMAs groups, the bilingual interviewers required to conduct the interviews would (for some key citizenship groups) be likely to have their own experiences and views of irregular maritime migration, either due their own personal experiences (they may have themselves been IMAs) or those of their family, friends or other community members. Self-completion allowed for much-reduced interaction by removing the need for an interviewer to conduct the survey and ask questions.

The use of computer-based technology involving self-completion was chosen as it has been found to be effective in eliciting honest, open answers from participants in other surveys involving highly sensitive issues (Tourangeau & Smith, 1996; Seebregtsa et al., 2009). For example, in a survey on rape in South Africa, participants were asked questions via a tablet computer-based survey on their experiences as both a perpetrator, and a victim, of rape (Jewkes, Sikweyiya, Morrell, & Dunkle, 2009). The results showed that a substantial proportion of men indicated that they themselves had raped, and this finding was in contrast to studies based on other research methodologies.

The survey was conducted using a tablet computer preloaded with the questionnaire translated in the primary language of the participant. The survey was self-completed, rather than interview based, with the questions available in English, Arabic, Dari, Farsi, Hazaragi, Tamil and Urdu. The technology allowed respondents to switch between languages in 'real time'. A 'skip' option allowed participants to skip questions they did not want to answer. The respondent was in control of the pace of the survey and was able to pause, reread a question, or think about an answer, a factor which has been seen to improve the quality of answers in self-administered questionnaires (Hox, Kef, & de Leeuw, 2003).

In recognition of potential literacy and technological access issues, bilingual assistants were engaged to provide initial guidance to the participant on how to complete the questionnaire on the tablet computer. The assistants remained available to provide assistance for completion of a question if requested, but did not interview the respondent. This allowed participants to complete the survey anonymously.

The approach involving the provision of bilingual assistants recognised that an unsupported web-based administration would be likely to fail because of the particular characteristics of the population. While this approach may have had an impact on response bias due to the presence of an assistant, the much-reduced interaction (compared to a traditional interviewer) will have undoubtedly had a positive impact on the reporting of sensitive responses. Computer-based self-completion also assists in reducing non-sampling errors, such as missing values and incorrect coding, compared to other survey delivery methods (Bernabe-Ortiz et al., 2008).

There are a number of methodological limitations entailed in the approach that was adopted. Issues of recall, for example, are likely to have an impact on survey results. However, this would equally be the case for other methodologies, such as structured interviews and focus groups.

Much effort was expended on being able to elicit sensitive information through the use of computer-based self-completion surveying. The approach does not allow, however, for exploration of detailed questioning of aspects of respondents' experiences, such as would be the case through structured interviewing.

Survey results

A quantitative survey of IMAs, with a specific focus on pre-arrival experiences, was considered an important means to build an aspect of the evidence-base. Surveys of this nature are able to identify patterns, including by determining how widely certain processes are undertaken or what characteristics feature in a particular process (Sayer, 1992, p. 243).

This section provides a summary of the key results of the survey. The results in this chapter are primarily reported at the aggregate level; that is all respondents, rather than subsamples with particular characteristics. Selected results by some citizenship groups (Afghans, Iranians, Pakistanis and Sri Lankans) as well as age have been included to highlight specific demographic differences.

The survey comprised 44 multipart questions on respondents':

- host country experiences;
- circumstances in home and/or host country;
- decisions to leave;
- choice of destination;
- travel to Australia;
- Australian experiences; and
- demographic characteristics.

Host country experiences

To better understand the experiences of survey participants, it was important to identify their migration histories. People who commenced their journey to Australia from their country of birth would be likely to have a different set of experiences to those who had spent time in host or transit countries, noting that the distinction between 'host' and 'transit' can be blurry, and is largely based on a time dimension. Respondents who indicated they had spent at least 12 months in a country other than their country of birth were asked to respond to a series of questions relating to their experiences in that country.

This subsample comprised 327 respondents, or almost one third of the sample. Discussion of survey results in this section is limited to the subsample, not the entire sample, and has been referred to as 'host' country experiences.

The main host countries identified by respondents were Pakistan (60 per cent) and Iran (24 per cent). Other less prominent countries included Indonesia (4 per cent), India (3 per cent), and Iraq (3 per cent). These results appear to be directly related to the citizenship composition of the 'hosted' subsample: the majority of Afghans (57 per cent) indicated they had lived in a country other than their birth country prior to travelling to Australia. Iranian respondents reported very low levels of having lived in a host country (5 per cent). These results accord with the United Nations High Commissioner for Refugees (UNHCR) data on hosted refugee populations (UNHCR, 2013).

These results show that of the four main citizenship groups (Afghans, Iranians, Pakistanis and Sri Lankans), all groups reported 90 per cent or more having been born in their stated country of citizenship. Small proportions of Afghan respondents reported that they were born in Pakistan (3 per cent) and Iran (2 per cent). Seven per cent of Pakistani citizens reported having been born in Afghanistan. The results indicate, for example, that most Afghan respondents were born in Afghanistan and had been living in a host country prior to travelling to Australia.

The average time spent in a host country was 20.5 years. Eleven per cent had spent 5 years or less in a host country, with almost half (44 per cent) having spent more than 20 years in a host country. The vast majority (82 per cent) indicated that they had had no contact with UNHCR while living in a host country, with just 3 per cent having indicated that they had been recognised as a refugee.

The majority of the host country subsample (60 per cent) reported that they had worked illegally while residing in a host country, with 19 per cent having indicated that they worked legally. While not necessarily related, this more or less aligned with the response to questions about their legal status in a host country, with 19 per cent indicating that they had some form of legal status (e.g. registration with UNHCR), while the overwhelming majority (79 per cent) advised that they had no legal status. In addition, just over one in 10 indicated they had been deported by their host country at least once. Around 30 per cent of hosted respondents indicated they had travelled back to their country of birth at least once. This was most common among Afghans (31 per cent), and is likely to have involved both voluntary and involuntary movement in light of the deportation results. This is consistent with recognised circulatory migration patterns of Hazaras in the region (Monsutti, 2005, pp. 168–69).

Circumstances in country of origin

The survey sought respondents' views on three specific aspects of their lives in their country of origin: their 'social proximity' (Fussell & Massey, 2004) to migration (including direct migration experiences, as well as those of family, friends and others in their communities); the extent of their links to diaspora in Australia; and the problems they faced prior to leaving. For the purposes of this chapter, the term 'origin country' has been used to encompass both 'home' countries (i.e. relevant to people residing in their country of citizenship prior to travel) and 'host' countries (i.e. relevant to people residing in countries other than their country of citizenship). In the survey, 'residence' was defined as being 12 months or more (not including time spent in detention).

Social proximity to migration

The survey results showed that respondents had, on average, a reasonable social proximity to migration prior to leaving their home or host country to travel to Australia. In other words, social proximity related to the extent to which respondents knew of people who had migrated (or attempted to), or had previously migrated themselves (or attempted to).

Social proximity to migration tended to diminish the closer the respondent was in social terms to the actual migrant group. For example, around a third of respondents indicated that it was common for people to travel to another country for work (32 per cent), and that their ethnic group travelled to other countries for work (34 per cent), compared to friends (17 per cent) and family members (13 per cent) who had migrated for work.

As shown in Table 5.1, respondents were less sure about being able to answer the more general questions (28–31 per cent chose the 'not sure' option), compared to more specific questions on friends (10 per cent not sure) and family (5 per cent not sure) who had travelled to another country for work.

Table 5.1: Social proximity to migration and travel for work

Measure	Yes (%)	No (%)	Not sure (%)	No answer (%)	Total (%)
In [origin country], was it common for people to travel to another country to find work?	32	36	31	1	100
Did the majority of [your ethnic] community travel to another country to find work?	34	38	29	1	100
Did you have any friends who travelled to another country to find work?	17	73	10	1	100
Did you have any family members who travelled to another country to find work?	13	83	5	1	100
Prior to leaving [origin country], had you ever applied for a visa to travel to any other country?	9	87	3	0	100
Prior to leaving [origin country], did you know of people who had travelled to another country without a visa?	18	68	14	1	100

Source: IMA survey.

When results were examined by the four citizenship groups, there was not much variation in relation to family members who had travelled to another country to find work, nor in relation to applying for visas themselves. There was, however, variation in response to the more general questions about 'ethnic groups' and 'people', with Sri Lankans having reported much higher responses against these two groups (65 per cent and 73 per cent, respectively). Sri Lankans were also less likely to report having had friends who had travelled (2 per cent).

With regard to knowing people who had travelled to other countries without a visa, Afghans were more likely to report this (23 per cent), and Sri Lankans and Pakistanis much less likely (2 per cent and 3 per cent, respectively). Afghans reported that the countries people travelled to in these circumstances included Iran, Pakistan, Afghanistan, Turkey and Australia.

Links to diaspora in Australia

Another factor with the potential to affect decision-making is the extent to which potential migrants had personal links to family members, friends and others in destination countries. Results showed that around 22 per cent of respondents indicated that they had relatives in Australia before they left their origin country. When other social links to Australia were examined, the results showed that 37 per cent had relatives, friends, friends of relatives/friends or fellow ethnic community members in Australia prior to their departure. When examined by citizenship, Afghans (43 per cent) and Pakistanis (38 per cent) were more likely than Iranians (24 per cent) to have links to Australia. Further breakdowns by citizenship group are shown in Figure 5.1.

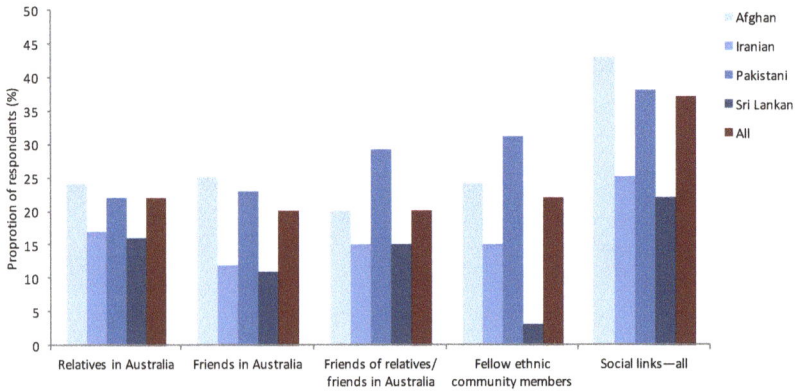

Figure 5.1: Respondents' links to Australia prior to departing origin country

Source: IMA survey (n=1,008).

Note: 'Social links—all' includes relatives, friends, friends of relatives/friends or fellow ethnic community members in Australia.

Prevailing conditions

When asked about the problems faced in their country of origin, an overwhelming majority of respondents indicated there were many problems facing them, and that these problems were varied in nature and involved protection and non-protection problems. The most prominent problems included ethnic-based discrimination (62 per cent), general insecurity (60 per cent), religious discrimination (59 per cent), serious harassment (53 per cent), persecution (51 per cent), political oppression

(40 per cent), corruption (34 per cent), poor education facilities (30 per cent), lack of job opportunities (27 per cent), unemployment (27 per cent), and poverty (23 per cent).

Respondents' reporting of the top three problems facing them provided further clarity of the severity of the multitude of problems facing them, with protection-based reasons featuring heavily (see Table 5.2). Non-protection reasons also featured, and included general insecurity (32 per cent), widespread violence (10 per cent), unemployment (8 per cent), lack of job opportunities (7 per cent), and loss of home (6 per cent).

When examined by citizenship, for example, Pakistanis and Afghans were more likely to report religious discrimination than others (85 per cent and 74 per cent respectively), and Sri Lankans and Afghans were more likely to report persecution on the basis of ethnicity (89 per cent and 80 per cent, respectively). Sri Lankans were also much more likely than others to report 'eviction/loss of home/nowhere to live' as a problem (69 per cent). Further analysis of these results is likely to reveal a complex picture that will vary by citizenship and ethnicity. This would be further enhanced through the completion of future surveys so that changes over time could be analysed.

Table 5.2: Problems faced by respondents in country of origin prior to travel: Protection and non-protection

	ALL (%)	Afghans (%)	Iranians (%)	Pakistanis[2] (%)	Sri Lankans[2] (%)
Protection					
Discrimination against [ethnicity] people	62	80	22	66	89
Religious discrimination	59	74	42	85	60
Serious harassment	53	59	52	24	72
Persecution	51	55	41	42	71
Political oppression	40	32	57	41	73
Torture	39	39	41	28	81
Non-protection[1]					
General insecurity	60	63	54	54	83
Widespread violence	39	38	36	38	68
Unemployment	27	20	27	3*	16*
Poor education facilities	30	29	20	13*	30
Lack of job opportunities	27	18	29	2*	26

	ALL (%)	Afghans (%)	Iranians (%)	Pakistanis[2] (%)	Sri Lankans[2] (%)
Eviction/loss of home/ nowhere to live	20	18	8	<1*	69
Corruption	34	31	38	17*	42
Poverty	23	18	16	2*	25
Poor health facilities	22	22	10	3*	38
Other					
Other	2	1*	2*	1*	<1*
Threat to life[3]	<1*	<1*	<1*	0	0
Prefer not to say	<1*	0	<1*	0	0

Source: IMA survey. (n=1,008). Multiple response question.

Note: (1) It is possible that some 'non-protection' factors (e.g. 'eviction/loss of home/ nowhere to live') could be protection-related, depending on the exact nature of claims made. For the purposes of this chapter, these factors have been interpreted as being non-protection factors. (2) These citizenship groups have low sample sizes and results for these groups should be treated with caution. (3) 'Threat to life' was coded based on open responses from the 'Other' field. For the purposes of this analysis, it is considered as a protection factor. Estimates based on less than 20 unweighted responses have been asterisked.

Decision-making

To better understand the range of factors involved in irregular migration decision-making processes, the survey asked questions about both the decision to leave and the choice of destination. It asked respondents about their involvement, the involvement of other people, and the sources of information used in these decisions. The survey also asked respondents about the reasons they left their country of origin to travel to Australia, and about any specific events that triggered their departure. Noting that all respondents had been granted protection in Australia, responses related to different forms of persecution ranked highly. The range of reasons for leaving selected by respondents, however, appears to indicate the complexity involved in the decision to leave, particularly in light of the prevalence of both protection and non-protection reasons for leaving origin countries.

Overall, responses showed that both 'push' and 'pull' factors were taken into account in decision-making, and that both 'protection' and 'non-protection' reasons for movement applied. Responses to questions about people involved the decision to leave and choice of destination indicate that there are some differences in these decision-making processes, including in relation to the involvement of specific groups of people such as friends and family in origin countries, and people who help with travel (e.g. people smugglers). The differences in results are discussed below.

Reasons for leaving country of origin

The most common reasons respondents selected for leaving their country of origin were religious persecution (51 per cent), persecution against people of the respondent's ethnicity (52 per cent) and general insecurity/conflict (42 per cent). General persecution (32 per cent), political persecution (25 per cent), an issue with the origin country's authorities (16 per cent) and persecution against women (14 per cent) also featured (see Table 5.3).

Many respondents also reported 'pull' factors among their reasons for leaving to travel to Australia, particularly perceptions of Australia's attitude towards asylum seekers and refugees, with 30 per cent selecting 'Australia treats asylum seekers well' and 23 per cent selecting 'Australia accepts refugees'.

Twenty-four per cent responded that they left to travel to Australia for 'a better life'. This response option was imprecise in that it is likely to refer to a range of protection and/or non-protection reasons, and may also encompass both 'push' and/or 'pull' factors. However, it was included in the survey because it is a phrase that is often used by migrants themselves. Further analysis of this variable against other variables is likely to be of interest.

Of the non-protection reasons, the most common reason for leaving was general insecurity/conflict (42 per cent). Other non-protection reasons included 'better education services' (15 per cent), 'better health services' (9 per cent), 'lack of economic opportunity' (9 per cent), 'to get Australian citizenship' (9 per cent), 'better housing' (8 per cent) and 'to work' (7 per cent).

Consistent with results concerning the problems faced in origin countries, when the reasons for leaving were examined by citizenship, Pakistanis and Afghans were more likely to report religious persecution than others (82 per cent and 68 per cent, respectively), and Sri Lankans and Afghans were more likely to report persecution on the basis of ethnicity (84 per cent and 69 per cent, respectively). Sri Lankans and Iranians were also more likely than other groups to report political persecution (70 per cent and 49 per cent, respectively) as a reason for leaving.

Respondents' reporting of the top three reasons for leaving provided further clarity, with protection-based reasons featuring heavily. Non-protection reasons also featured, and included general insecurity (30 per cent), 'Australia treats asylum seekers well' (15 per cent), 'for a better life' (13 per cent), issue with the country's authorities (10 per cent), and better education services (7 per cent).

Table 5.3: Reasons for leaving country of origin: Protection and non-protection

	ALL (%)	Afghans (%)	Iranians (%)	Pakistanis[2] (%)	Sri Lankans[2] (%)
Protection					
Persecution against [Ethnicity] people	52	69	18	63	84
Religious persecution	51	68	33	82	45
General persecution	32	28	35	24*	64
Political persecution	25	11	49	23*	70
Australia accepts refugees	23	24	12	25*	19*
Persecution based against women	14	7	21	6*	59
Non-protection[1]					
General insecurity/conflict	42	41	40	43	69
Australia treats asylum seekers well	30	30	21	32	20
For a better life	24	18	24	13*	12*
Issue with the country's authorities	16	7	32	1*	40
For better education services	15	12	14	4*	8*
To get Australian citizenship	9	5*	3*	0	4*
To work	7	4*	4*	1*	2*
For better health services	9	5	5*	1*	2*
Lack of economic opportunity	9	5	11	2*	14*
For better housing	8	6	2*	2*	<1*
To join family/community	3	2*	<1*	0	3*
Australia is safe	<1*	<1*	0	0	<1*

	ALL (%)	Afghans (%)	Iranians (%)	Pakistanis[2] (%)	Sri Lankans[2] (%)
Other					
I don't know, I was a child	<1*	<1*	<1*	0	0
Other	3	3*	2*	1*	0
Threat to life[3]	3	4*	0	3*	0
None of these	3	3*	5*	0	3*

Source: IMA survey (n=1,008). Multiple response question.

Note: (1) It is possible that some 'non-protection' factors (e.g. 'issue with country's authorities') could be protection-related, depending on the exact nature of claims made. For the purposes of this chapter, these factors have been interpreted as being non-protection factors. (2) These citizenship groups have low sample sizes and results for these groups should be treated with caution. (3) 'Threat to life' was coded based on open responses from the 'Other' field. For the purposes of this analysis, it is considered as a protection factor. Estimates based on less than 20 unweighted responses have been asterisked.

The vast majority of respondents (85 per cent) indicated that they faced both protection and non-protection-related problems in their country of origin and/or left their origin country for both protection and non-protection reasons (see Table 5.4).

When examined by citizenship, the results show that there was not a great deal of variation between citizenship groups, the exception being Sri Lankan respondents, who were more likely to have reported both protection and non-protection factors (96 per cent).

Table 5.4: Problems faced in origin country and/or reasons for leaving country of origin: Protection and non-protection factors[1]

	ALL (%)	Afghans (%)	Iranians (%)	Pakistanis[3] (%)	Sri Lankans[3] (%)
Both protection and non-protection	85	86	81	85	96
Protection only	9	11	8	15*	0
Non-protection only[2]	3	1*	4*	0	2*
Other/none/no answer	3	2*	7*	0	2*
Total	100	100	100	100	100

Source: IMA survey (n=1,008).

Notes: (1) Protection problems and reasons included: all forms of persecution, religious discrimination, ethnic discrimination, serious harassment, political oppression, torture, 'Australia accepts refugees', 'threat to life'. Non-protection problems and reasons included: lack of economic/job opportunity; unemployment; general insecurity/conflict; widespread violence, corruption, poverty, for better housing; eviction/loss of home; to work; to join family/community; poor/better health services; poor/better education services; for a better life; issue with country's authorities; to get Australian citizenship; 'Australia treats asylum seekers well'. (2) It is possible that some 'non-protection' reasons could be protection-related, depending on the exact nature of claims made. For the purposes of the survey, the problems/reasons in note 2 have been interpreted as being non-protection. (3) These citizenship groups have low sample sizes and results for these groups should be treated with caution. Estimates based on less than 20 unweighted responses have been asterisked.

Departure triggers

Acknowledging that decision-making factors are not static and can change decisively and rapidly, the survey asked respondents whether any particular events triggered their departure. The results suggest that while the underlying reasons respondents decided to leave may have been present for a period of time, in most instances a specific incident triggered their departure.

Sixty-eight per cent responded that a significant security threat or incident triggered their departure. Events affecting respondents' family and friends, namely a threat against family/children (31 per cent) and the loss of a close family member/friend (18 per cent) ranked second and third respectively.

The next most common responses were the imminent threat of deportation (18 per cent), loss, or threat of losing home or shelter (14 per cent) and loss, or threat of losing job or income (11 per cent). In relation to the role of people smugglers, three per cent of respondents answered that being approached by an agent (e.g. people smuggler) was a trigger.

People involved in the decision to leave

The responses to questions about the people involved in the final decision to leave indicated that friends and/or family in the country of origin played an important role and that, to a lesser extent, people smugglers were involved. A not insubstantial proportion of respondents indicated that they themselves were not involved in the final decision to leave (12 per cent). Eighty-two per cent responded that they were themselves involved in the final decision. When examined by citizenship, Iranians were more likely to not have been involved (19 per cent), along with Afghans (11 per cent) compared to Sri Lankans (4 per cent). In light of the survey results on who respondents travelled with—which show that Iranian respondents were more likely to have travelled in family groups— the higher Iranian results may be related to the age and/or sex of the respondents.

Responses to questions on the involvement of friends and family in the decision to leave varied with respect to location. Forty per cent indicated that friends/family in their country of origin were involved in the decision, with only 6 per cent having indicated that friends/family in other countries were involved and 5 per cent that friends/family in Australia were involved.

Finally, 11 per cent of respondents indicated that people who helped them travel (e.g. people smugglers) were involved in the decision to leave. Sri Lankans were more likely to report the involvement of people smugglers (20 per cent).

The choice of destination

The survey sought respondents' perspectives on Australia as a destination country and the reasons they travelled to Australia, with questions about their consideration of destination countries, as well as the sources of information and methods of access they used when making the decision.

When asked to select the countries they considered travelling to, 47 per cent of respondents selected Australia, and 33 per cent selected the option, 'I did not consider any particular countries'. Canada and the UK (6 per cent and 5 per cent, respectively) were the next most common responses.

Respondents who selected Australia were then asked about the reasons they considered travelling to Australia over other possible countries (see Table 5.5). The most common responses were that 'Australia was accepting refugees' (65 per cent) and that it 'does not return refugees' (46 per cent). The responses 'other countries were not accepting refugees' (18 per cent) and 'other countries were returning refugees' (17 per cent) ranked fourth and fifth respectively. The third ranked response was 'because my family would be able to follow me to Australia' (24 per cent). Table 5.5 provides the full list of responses.

The survey also asked respondents about the main reasons they ended up travelling to Australia from their origin country (as opposed to selecting Australia relative to another country). The attractiveness of Australia appeared to lessen: 'Australia was accepting refugees' dropped to 33 per cent and 'Australia does not return refugees' dropped to 22 per cent, although they were still highly ranked. Despite similarity to the reasons given for considering Australia, the results to this question indicate that there are different dynamics involved in this aspect of decision-making. Forty per cent indicated that none of the response options applied, indicating that the question was not sufficiently tested and essentially failed. While it is extremely difficult to speculate about the reasons that did apply and were not reflected in the survey question, it is possible that the impact of people assisting with travel (e.g. people smugglers) could be a reason, noting that respondents indicated that these people were more involved in the decision about where to migrate than the decision to leave the origin country.

Table 5.5: Respondents' consideration of Australia as a destination country and reasons for travelling to Australia

Reason	Why did you consider travelling to Australia over other countries?	What were the main reasons you ended up travelling to Australia?
Australia was accepting refugees	65	31
Australia does not return refugees	46	22
Because my family would be able to follow me to Australia	24	9
Other countries were not accepting refugees	18	8
Other countries were returning refugees	17	7
There is work in Australia	13	4
Because it is easier to travel to Australia than other countries	14	7
To be with my family	8	2
To be with [ethnicity] people	6	4
I did not have family in other countries	5	4
I did not have friends in other countries	4	3
Australia is safe	3	2
To be with friends	3	1
[Ethnicity] people are not in other countries	2	1
Threat to life	1	3
Other	3	6
None of these	11	40
No answer	0	5

Source: IMA survey (n=454 to 554).

These responses indicate there would be value in further research into Australia's position as a destination country in the complex global migration context, including how Australia is perceived in comparison to other destination countries.

Using questions structured in the same way as those about the decision to leave (see the section on 'reasons for leaving country of origin', above) the survey asked about the people involved in the choice of destination, including the role of friends and family in origin countries, diaspora and agents (e.g. people smugglers).

Seventy-nine per cent responded that they were themselves involved in the final decision that Australia would be the final destination, while 13 per cent responded that they were not involved. This is similar to the result on respondent involvement in the final decision to leave (12 per cent were not involved), and again Iranians were more likely to have indicated that they were not involved in the destination decision (19 per cent).

The involvement of friends/family in the decision again varied with respect to location. Twenty-nine per cent responded that friends/family in origin countries were involved in the final decision, while 6 per cent responded that friends/family in Australia were involved and 4 per cent responded that friends/family in other countries were involved.

Overall, 15 per cent of respondents indicated that people who helped them travel (e.g. people smugglers) were involved in the decision that Australia would be their final destination. Iranians were more likely to have reported the involvement of these people (25 per cent), and Afghans less likely (9 per cent).

Sources of information about Australia

Respondents most commonly reported that they relied on friends and family in their country of origin (23 per cent) and people who helped them travel (e.g. people smugglers) (15 per cent) for information about Australia, prior to making the final decision that Australia would be their final destination. Only 5 per cent responded that they relied on social media (e.g. Facebook) for information, with 47 per cent indicating that they did not use social media. Similar to other results, Iranian respondents (24 per cent) were more likely to have reported reliance on people who helped them travel (e.g. people smugglers).

In relation to information sources from Australia, 12 per cent of respondents reported relying on official information from the Australian Government, and 7 per cent on friends/family in Australia.

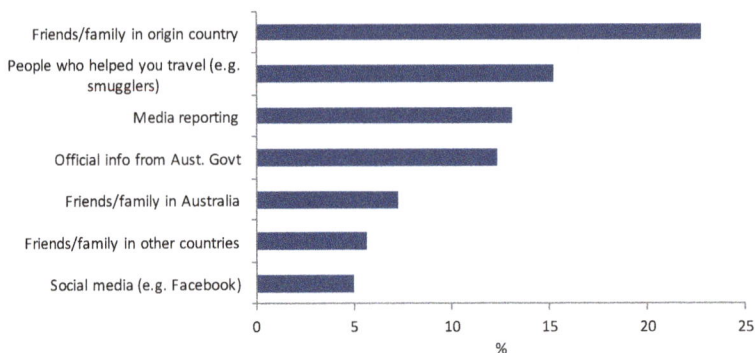

Figure 5.2: Sources of information relied upon when making the final decision that Australia would be the destination

Source: IMA survey (n=1,008).

Differences in decision-making processes: The decision to leave and choice of destination

The survey responses indicated that there were some differences in decision-making processes in relation to the decision to leave the country of origin and the choice of destination. For example, friends/family in origin countries were more likely to have been involved in the decision to leave than they were in the choice of destination, while the opposite is true for people who helped the respondents to travel (e.g. people smugglers).

Table 5.6: People involved in decision-making processes

	Decision to leave origin country (%)	Decision to go to Australia (%)
Respondent	82	79
Friends/family in origin country	40	28
Friends/family in Australia*	5	6
Friends/family in other countries*	6	4
People who helped with travel (e.g. people smugglers)*	11	15

Source: IMA survey (n=1,008).

Note: *Some respondents indicated that some circumstances did not apply (e.g. they did not have family/friends in Australia). The percentages are based on the total responses, including responses that indicated that circumstances did not apply.

There were also some differences in decision-making processes when individual and collective decision-making was examined. As shown in Figure 5.3, a higher proportion of respondents indicated that they made the decision to travel to Australia by themselves compared to the decision to leave the country of origin.

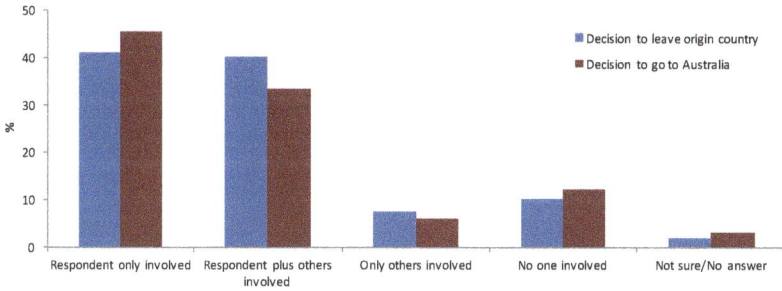

Figure 5.3: Individual and collective decision-making: Decision to leave and decision to travel to Australia

Source: IMA survey (n=1,008).

Additional research into the circumstances in which people are not involved in the final decision to leave would provide a better understanding of the role of collective decision-making on migration, and may also provide insights into issues of potential vulnerability involved in irregular migration.

Travelling to Australia

The survey also explored respondents' experiences of their journey to Australia. The questions examined connections to a range of different groups, such as people who had helped them travel (e.g. people smugglers), as well as practices they adopted en route and how safe these practices made respondents feel while travelling. Almost two thirds of respondents travelled without friends or family, and around 30 per cent reported having travelled with family. There was significant variation by citizenship, as shown in Figure 5.4, with Iranians much more likely to have reported having travelled with family (54 per cent) compared to other citizenship groups: Afghans (6 per cent); Pakistanis (11 per cent); Sri Lankans (19 per cent).

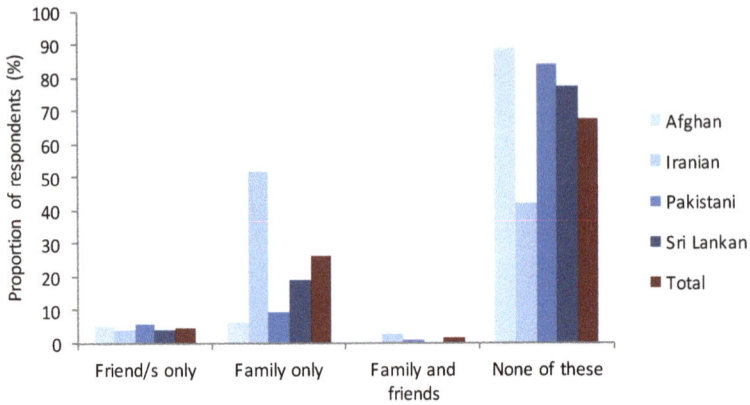

Figure 5.4: Respondents' travelling companions
Source: IMA survey (n=1,008).

In terms of assistance respondents received to travel to Australia, agents (e.g. people smugglers) previously unknown to the respondent provided the most help (43 per cent of respondents received help). Friends and family in origin countries also provided assistance, although there was variation by citizenship, with Pakistanis and Sri Lankans reporting greater assistance from this group (45 per cent and 41 per cent respectively; see Figure 5.5).

Assistance was also provided by agents (e.g. people smugglers) previously known to the respondent, although this was more common for Iranians. Respondents indicated that family/friends in Australia and other countries did not tend to help with travel (6 per cent and 3 per cent respectively).

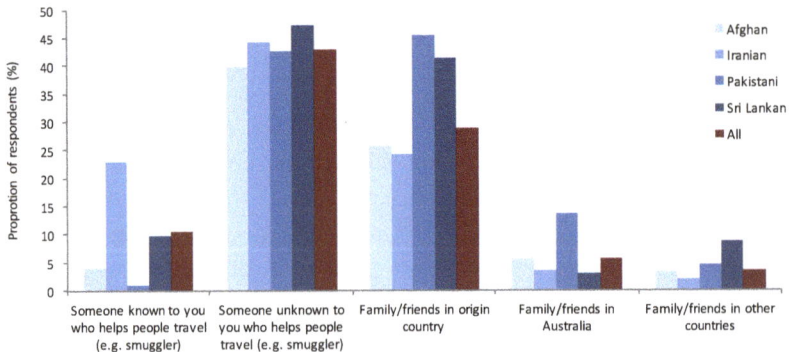

Figure 5.5: Assistance respondents received to travel to Australia
Source: IMA survey (n=1,008).

The average amount invested in travel to Australia was around USD12,600, with some marginal variation by citizenship: USD13,500 for Afghans; USD12,200 for Iranians; USD11,000 for Pakistanis; USD9,200 for Sri Lankans. Travel was predominantly funded by respondents' immediate families (including self-funding) (82 per cent); 10 per cent had been funded by family/friends in their origin country, and 2 per cent by family/friends in Australia. Eighteen per cent indicated that they (or their families) were still in debt, although Sri Lankans were more likely to report this (36 per cent).

Most respondents (91 per cent) indicated that they had travelled through Indonesia on their way to Australia; 55 per cent transited Malaysia, 23 per cent transited Thailand, 13 per cent transited Pakistan and 8 per cent transited the United Arab Emirates. Only 3 per cent of respondents indicated that they had travelled directly to Australia. When examined by citizenship, as shown in Figure 5.6, many Pakistanis and Afghans indicated that they had travelled to Australia via multiple transit countries, whereas nearly half of the Sri Lankans indicated that they had travelled directly.

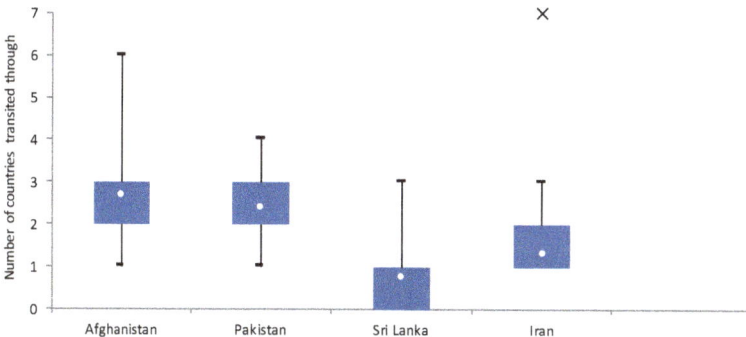

Figure 5.6: Number of transit countries by citizenship

Source: IMA survey (n=1,008).

Notes: ● is the mean number of transit countries; × refers to an outlier. The box represents the interquartile range (the 25th to 75th percentile). The black line represents the minimum and maximum values.

Practices en route

Consistent with anecdotal information, the journey to Australia, for many respondents, involved crossing multiple borders, spending time in countries with no legal status and relying on strangers to progress the next stage of their journey. This suggests a high degree of risk, fear and uncertainty for those who made the journey, as evident from the survey results. Fifty-four per cent of all respondents indicated that they were smuggled across other countries' borders at some stage of their journey. When the results are examined by citizenship group, substantial differences emerged, with 73 per cent of Afghans and 70 per cent of Pakistanis having reported being smuggled. The results were much lower for Iranians (24 per cent) and Sri Lankans (4 per cent), noting that around half of the Sri Lankan respondents reported having travelled directly to Australia.

Nineteen per cent of respondents reported having paid bribes to officials; however, this was much higher among Iranians (39 per cent) compared to other citizenship groups (10 per cent for Pakistanis and Afghans).

Many respondents (41 per cent) reported having travelled on a false passport at some stage during their journey to Australia (a further 17 per cent were not sure if their passport was valid or false), with 74 per cent of those indicating that using a false passport had made them feel very or quite unsafe. In contrast, and not surprisingly, of those who had valid visas to enter transit countries (39 per cent), the majority reported that this had made them feel very or quite safe (62 per cent).

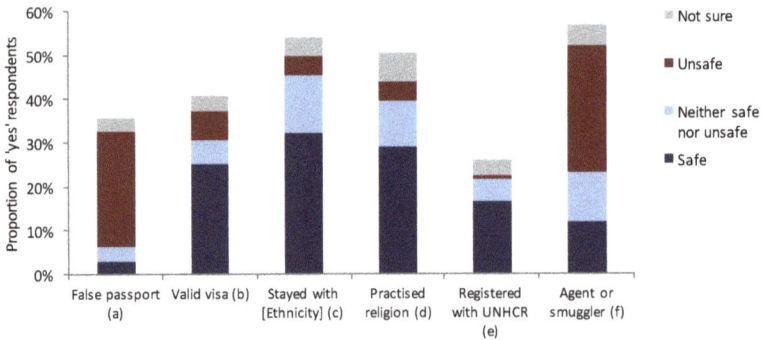

Figure 5.7: Aspects of feeling safe during journey to Australia

Source: IMA survey (n=1,008).

Notes: (a) Used a false passport during your journey to Australia (n=357); (b) Had a visa to validly enter a transit country during your journey to Australia (n=399); (c) Stayed with [Ethnicity] people during your journey to Australia (n=537); (d) Able to practice your religion in transit countries during your journey to Australia (n=501); (e) Registered with UNHCR during your journey to Australia (n=257); (f) Used the services of someone who helps people to travel during your journey to Australia (n=557).

Some practices appeared to increase the sense of safety during the journey, such as contact with members of their ethnic community (59 per cent felt very or quite safe), or practising their religion (57 per cent felt very or quite safe). Just over one quarter of respondents registered with UNHCR during the journey to Australia. Overall this provided a sense of safety (63 per cent felt very or quite safe). Four per cent of those registered with UNHCR reported this had made them feel unsafe. A majority of respondents (56 per cent) indicated that they had used the services of someone who helps people travel (e.g. people smuggler) during their journey. Around half of these respondents indicated that this had made them feel quite or very unsafe during their journey to Australia.

Australian experiences

The survey sought the views of respondents on whether they engaged in specific activities after arriving in Australia, including communicating with family and friends in various locations, travelling back to their origin country to visit, and providing remittances. Forty per cent indicated that they did not undertake any such activities, and 9 per cent chose not to respond. The most prevalent activity reported was the provision of money to family and/or friends in their home country (35 per cent), with 7 per cent having indicated that they send money to people in other countries.

In reflecting on the journey to Australia, the vast majority of respondents indicated that the journey to Australia was more difficult or much more difficult (83 per cent) than they had expected—see Figure 5.8. Very few respondents (1 per cent) indicated than the journey was easier or much easier than expected. This accorded with respondents' reported experiences en route, particularly in relation to how unsafe they felt during their journey when using a people smuggler(s). The implications of the disparity between potential migrants' views of what the migration journey is likely to entail compared to the reality of the journey are potentially profound.

It would be useful to examine this issue in more detail, noting there was not significant variation between citizenship groups, the notable exception being Sri Lankans, 96 per cent of whom reported that the journey was much more difficult than expected (with another 3 per cent reporting it was more difficult than expected). Further analysis of survey data, supplemented with qualitative research, would enhance the understanding of migrants' journeys, which in turn would assist in enhancing informed choice of migrants and reducing vulnerability en route.

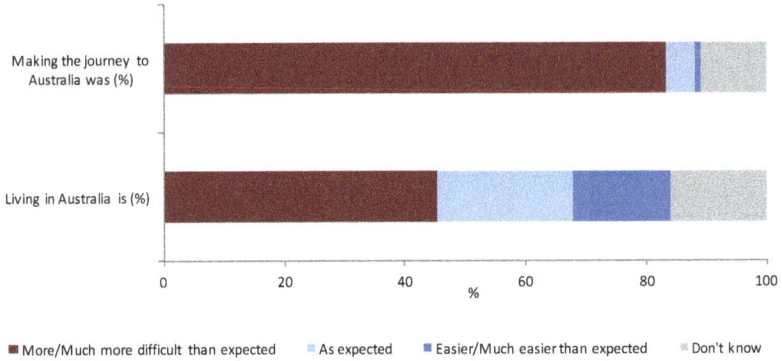

Figure 5.8: Experiences of the journey to, and life in, Australia
Source: IMA survey (n=1,008).

A slightly higher proportion of respondents (45 per cent) found that living in Australia was more difficult or much more difficult than expected compared to those that found it as expected, easier or much easier (39 per cent). There was significant variation by citizenship group. As shown in Figure 5.9, Sri Lankans were more likely to have reported life in Australia as being easier or much easier (80 per cent) compared to Iranians (4 per cent), Afghans (15 per cent) and Pakistanis (25 per cent).

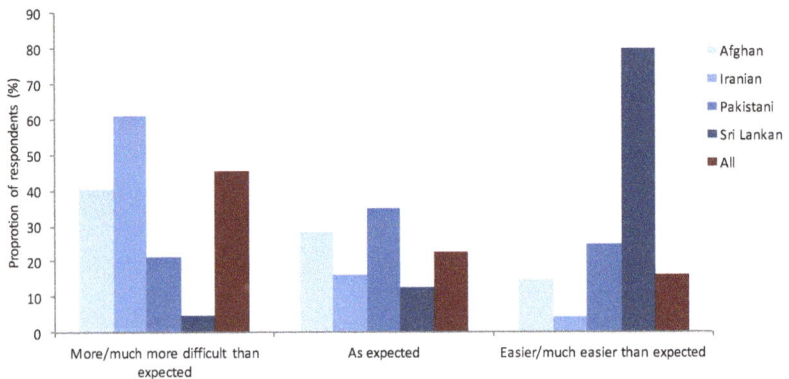

Figure 5.9: Respondents' perceptions of living in Australia
Source: IMA survey (n=1,008).

The fact that most Sri Lankans found living in Australia easier than expected may be related to their English language ability. Eighty-one per cent of Sri Lankan respondents stated that English was their primary language, compared with less than 1 per cent for Afghans, and 5 per cent for both Iranians and Pakistanis. Figure 5.10 shows that there is a correlation between respondents who perceived living in Australia to be easier than expected and those who stated that English is one of their primary languages. The survey asked respondents to list their 'primary language(s)'. It did not take into account actual competency levels, or those who spoke English but did not consider English as a primary language. Examination of respondents' perceptions of life in Australia showed no correlation with the existence of social links to Australia, or being employed in Australia.

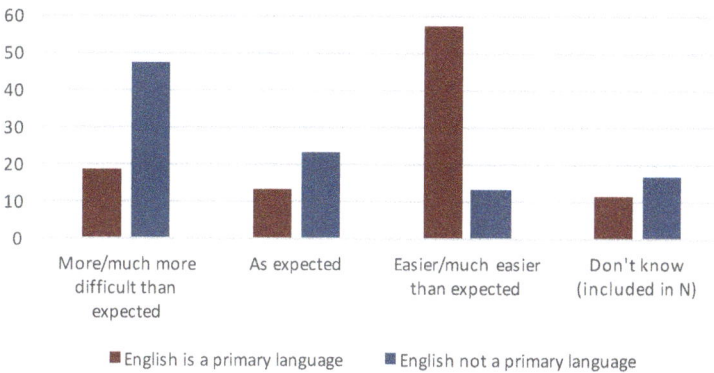

Figure 5.10: Respondents' perceptions of living in Australia by primary language
Source: IMA survey (n=980).

Findings

One of the most significant findings of the IMA survey is that it clearly shows that IMAs are not a homogenous group. While there may well be some similarities in terms of some specific demographic characteristics, for example in relation to sex, the IMA survey results show that there are very substantial differences in both the demographic characteristics and the experiences of different groups of IMAs. This chapter has highlighted some of the substantial differences in patterns and processes of different IMA groups, mainly by citizenship—for example, Afghans and Pakistanis reported greater links to Australia prior to travel; Iranians and Sri Lankans reported greater involvement of agents who helped them travel (e.g. people smugglers); Iranians tended to travel with family members, while Afghans predominantly travelled without family or friends.

A more nuanced understanding of the very different migration processes experienced by different groups of irregular migrants, including in relation to decision-making, has implications for policy deliberations. For example, the extent and nature of collective decision-making has potential implications for decision-making in relation to the promotion and take-up of assisted voluntary return packages for those found not to be in need of protection. Information on return packages, for example, could also be usefully communicated to others involved in decision-making.

One of the notable differences between citizenship groups was the likelihood of having lived in a host country prior to migrating. Overall, a 'hosted' respondent was typically an Afghan born in Afghanistan, having lived in Pakistan or Iran for many years (with some moving between Afghanistan and their host country), and who was likely to have worked illegally and not have had any contact with UNHCR. These characteristics accord with research on Afghan migration survival strategies, and the tendency of particular groups to engage in circular migratory patterns through the region as a means of economic and cultural survival. Monsutti, for example, has argued that in relation to Hazaras, no hard and fast distinction can be made between refugees and economic migrants and that a 'migration continuum' exists that has developed as part of a broader strategy of survival (Monsutti, 2005, pp. 168–69). Further, he states that 'Afghans give different and usually plural reasons for their decision to migrate: perhaps an outbreak of fighting, a threat from a personal enemy, the danger of bombing or compulsory conscription; perhaps the search for work or opportunities to trade, the need for medical treatment, or the undertaking of a pilgrimage' (2005, p. 146).

For the 'hosted' respondents, it is important to acknowledge that a lack of contact with UNHCR is unlikely to be related to their 'refugee-ness' or otherwise. The circumstances in which Afghans live in host countries Iran and Afghanistan and the gradual and systematic reduction in support and assistance to Afghan refugees in Iran and Pakistan over many years will undoubtedly have had an impact on the capacity and/ or willingness of Afghans to seek UNHCR's assistance in host countries. Survey respondents, as IMAs granted protection in the second half of 2011 and calendar year 2012, would have been likely to have travelled prior to 2012, and so a point in time aspect needs to be taken into consideration.

Another key finding of the survey is that the overwhelming majority of irregular migrants surveyed were motivated by multiple factors. The public discourse about 'economic migrants' and 'genuine refugees' is limited and potentially unhelpful in light of the survey results, which show that a range of factors underpin movement to Australia, such as those related to protection, employment, education services, housing, health services, poverty, corruption, geography and family/community links. The most prominent factors related primarily to protection. This is unsurprising given that the survey population comprised people who travelled as IMAs and had been granted protection in Australia.

Problems facing respondents prior to their departure overwhelmingly related to protection issues. Non-protection problems, such as poverty, corruption, poor education facilities and unemployment were also highlighted by respondents, which is also unsurprising when broader human development issues facing people in some countries of origin are taken into account; an issue that is even more profound for those with marginalised status in host countries (United Nations Development Program [UNDP], 2013).

In terms of reasons for leaving their country of origin and the problems they faced prior to departure, 85 per cent of respondents indicated that both protection and non-protection issues were involved. A much smaller 9 per cent indicated that they had faced or left because of protection issues only. There was a very small proportion of respondents (3 per cent) who indicated that they did not face protection-related problems in their origin country and who indicated that they had left their country of origin for non-protection reasons only.

This would appear to indicate that broader quality of life issues, such as corruption, education services, health services, and lack of economic opportunity, are being considered during decision-making, and are among the factors potential migrants (and their families and others) take into account when assessing and reassessing migration options.

Reasons for leaving as well as reasons for choosing Australia included 'pull factors', most particularly Australia's perceived acceptance of refugees and treatment of asylum seekers. These two factors would appear to be part of decision-making processes as they relate to leaving and choosing a destination, and appeared to be more important than other 'pull' factors (e.g. Australia's economic prosperity). It may be that the distinction between decision-making as it relates to 'leaving' and 'destination' masks more complex realities, and that (potential) migrants and their families, are likely to be continually assessing and reassessing their migration options, and that these assessments involve a range of complex interrelated and perhaps conflicting factors that have to be carefully balanced within dynamic environments. That a high proportion of respondents indicated that their migration was 'triggered' by an event or situation resonates with this notion.

It is possible that Monsutti's analysis of Afghan migration as 'partially blurring the boundary between forced migration and voluntary migration' may have wider implications for other groups of people (Monsutti, 2008, p. 73). As the survey has shown, respondents with protection issues are more often than not involved in making decisions about whether to migrate and where to migrate, and their decision-making processes include as well a range of non-protection reasons. This also accords with Neumayer's citing of Efionayi-Mäder et al., that 'such a decision is likely to be the result of a multitude of complex and mutually nonexclusive factors, whose relative importance can differ across origin countries as well as across individuals from the same country of origin' (Neumayer, 2004, p. 163, citing Efionayi-Mäder et al., 2001).

The survey results also highlight the utility of conducting further research on decision-making of potential migrants who decide not to migrate, including in relation to those who may be facing protection issues. Adhikari's research on the impact of a range of factors on potential refugees' decision-making in Nepal highlights that individual decision-making, even in extreme conflict situations, is based on more than just the threat to one's life, and includes factors related to economic livelihoods and social networks (Adhikari, 2013).

Conclusions

As one of the first commissioned research projects undertaken as part of the Irregular Migration Research Program (see Preface and Introduction of this volume for information on the program), and the first quantitative survey of first-hand experiences of IMAs to Australia, the IMA survey provides an empirical evidence-base to assist in the development of improved understanding of decision-making of IMAs to Australia. It is an important addition to the small but growing evidence-base on migrant decision-making.

The IMA survey results offer insights into a range of areas in which further analysis and research activity would be valuable for creating a solid base of measurement and analysis to inform policy and program considerations. For example, in looking at the differences between how citizenship groups answer questions, future analysis of the final survey results can seek to identify the gaps in our current understanding of the reasons for these differences. This may in turn inform research activities that are tailored to specific citizenship groups.

The findings on the extent to which IMAs access official information and media reporting demonstrate the need for more research into communication networks at the different stages of the journey to Australia, and how information campaigns can be better targeted, including through friends and family in origin countries, to encourage people to not travel to Australia irregularly. Finally, greater understanding of the experiences of IMAs during the transit phase of the journey to Australia could have a significant bearing on bilateral arrangements between destination and transit countries, enabling a greater level of discussion about issues such as voluntary and involuntary returns than perhaps is currently enjoyed.

There is no doubt that as an evidence-base the IMA survey results will be useful and relevant in a number of research areas and in policy deliberations. Ideally, future qualitative research will supplement the survey results, including helping to explain some of the results, particularly as they relate to specific demographic groups.

Reference list

Adhikari, P. (2013). Conflict induced displacement, understanding the causes of flight. *American Journal of Political Science, 57*(1), 82–89. doi.org/10.1111/j.1540-5907.2012.00598.x

Bernabe-Ortiz, A., Curioso, W. H., Gonzales, M. A., Evangelista, W., Castagnetto, J. M., Carcamo, C. P., ... Holmes, K. K. (2008). Handheld computers for self-administered sensitive data collection: A comparative study in Peru. *BMC Medical Informatics and Decision Making, 8*(11), n. p. doi.org/10.1186/1472-6947-8-11

Bowling, A. (2005). Mode of questionnaire administration can have serious effects on data quality. *Journal of Public Health, 27*(3), 281–91. doi.org/10.1093/pubmed/fdi031

Brekke, J.-P., & Aarset, M. F. (2009). *Why Norway? Understanding asylum destinations*. Oslo: Institutt for Samfunnsforskning (Institute for Social Research).

Castles, S. (2013). The forces driving global migration. *Journal of Intercultural Studies, 34*(2), 122–40. doi.org/10.1080/07256868.201 3.781916

de Haas, H. (2010). *Migration transitions: a theoretical and empirical inquiry into the developmental drivers of international migration*. Oxford: International Migration Institute.

de Haas, H. (2011). *The determinants of international migration: conceptualizing policy, origin and destination effects*. Working Paper 32. Oxford: International Migration Institute.

Doraï, M. (2011). Iraqis in exile: Migratory networks as a coping strategy. *International Journal of Contemporary Iraqi Studies, 5*(2), 215–29. doi.org/10.1386/ijcis.5.2.215_1

Efionayi-Mäder, D., Chimienti, M., Dahinden, J., & Piguet, E. (2001). *Asyldestination Europa: eine Geographie der Asylbewegungen*. Zurich: Seismo-Verlag.

Fussell, E., & Massey, D. (2004). The limits of cumulative causation: international migration from Mexican urban areas. *Demography, 41*(1), 151–72. doi.org/10.1353/dem.2004.0003

Hamlin, R. (2012). International law and administrative insulation: A comparison of refugee status determination regimes in the United States, Canada and Australia. *Law & Social Inquiry, 37*(4), 933–68. doi.org/10.1111/j.1747-4469.2012.01292.x

Hatton, T. J. (2011). *Seeking asylum—Trends and policies in the OECD*. London: Centre for Economic Policy Research.

Havinga, T., & Böcker, A. (1999). Country of asylum by choice or by chance: Asylum seekers in Belgium, the Netherlands and the UK. *Journal of Ethnic and Migration Studies, 25*(1), 43–61. doi.org/10.108 0/1369183X.1999.9976671

Hox, J., Kef, S., & de Leeuw, E. (2003). Computer assisted self-interviewing tailored for special populations and topics. *Field Methods* 15(3), 223–51.

Jewkes, R., Sikweyiya, Y., Morrell, R., & Dunkle, K. (2009). *Understanding men's health and use of violence: Interface of rape and HIV in South Africa*. Pretoria: South African Medical Research Council.

Johansson, R. (1990). The refugee experience in Europe after World War II: Some theoretical and empirical considerations. In G. Rystad (Ed.), *The uprooted: Forced migration as international problem in the post-war era* (pp. 227–69). Lund: Lund University Press.

Jones, M. (2009). Refugee status determination: three challenges. *Forced Migration Review, 32*, n.p. Retrieved from www.fmreview.org/statelessness/jones.html.

Koser, K. (1997). Social networks and the asylum cycle: The case of the Iranians in the Netherlands. *The International Migration Review, 31*(3), 591–611.

Koser, K. (2008). Why migrant smuggling pays. *International Migration, 46*(2), 3–26. doi.org/10.1111/j.1468-2435.2008.00442.x

Koser, K. (2011). Why take the risk? Explaining migrant smuggling. In T. Modood, & Salt, J. (Eds), *Global migration, ethnicity and Britishness* (pp. 65–84). London: Palgrave. doi.org/10.1057/9780230307155_4

Koser, K., & McAuliffe, M. (2013). *Establishing an evidence-base for future policy development on irregular migration to Australia*. Irregular Migration Research Program, Occasional Paper Series 01. Canberra: Australian Department of Immigration and Citizenship. Retrieved from www.border.gov.au/ReportsandPublications/Documents/research/evidence-base-for-future-policy.pdf.

Koser, K., & Pinkerton, C. (2002). *The social networks of asylum seekers and the dissemination of information about the countries of asylum*. London: Research Development and Statistics Directorate, UK Home Office.

McAuliffe, M. (2013). *Seeking the views of irregular migrants: Survey background, rationale and methodology.* Irregular Migration Research Program, occasional paper series 04, Department of Immigration and Border Protection. Retrieved from www.border.gov.au/Reports andPublications/Documents/research/views-irregular-migrant-background-rationale-methodology.pdf.

Middleton, D. (2005). *Why asylum seekers seek refuge in particular destination countries: an exploration of key determinants.* Global Migration Perspectives no. 34. Global Commission on International Migration.

Monsutti, A. (2005). *War and migration: Social networks and economic strategies of the Hazaras of Afghanistan.* New York and London: Routledge.

Monsutti, A. (2008). Afghan migratory strategies and the three solutions to the refugee problem. *Refugee Survey Quarterly, 27*(1), 58–73. doi.org/10.1093/rsq/hdn007

Monsutti, A. (2010). The transnational turn in migration studies and the Afghan social networks. In Chatty, D., & Finlayson, B. (Eds), *Dispossession and displacement: Forced migration in the Middle East and North Africa.* Oxford and New York: Oxford University Press.

Neumayer, E. (2004). Asylum destination choice: What makes some West European countries more attractive than others? *European Union Politics, 5*(2), 155-80. doi.org/10.1177/1465116504042444

Robinson, V., & Segrott, J. (2002). *Understanding the decision making of asylum seekers.* Home Office research study 243. London: Home Office Research, Development and Statistics Directorate.

Sayer, R. A. (1992). *Method in social science: A realist approach* (2nd ed.). London: Routledge.

Seebregtsa, J. C., Zwarenstein, M., Mathews, C., Fairall, L., Flisher, A. J., Seebregtse, C., … Klepp, K. I. (2009). Handheld computers for survey and trial data collection in resource-poor settings: Development and evaluation of PDACT, a Palm Pilot interviewing system. *International Journal of Medical Informatics 78* (11), 721–31.

Spinks, H. (2013). *Destination anywhere? Factors affecting asylum seekers' choice of destination country*. Research paper no. 1, Parliamentary Library. Canberra: Australian Government.

Thielemann, E. (2006). The effectiveness of governments' attempts to control unwanted migration. In Parsons, C. A., & Smeeding, T. M. (Eds), *Immigration and the Transformation of Europe* (442–72). Cambridge: Cambridge University Press. doi.org/10.1017/cbo 9780511493577.017

Toshkov, D. (2012). The dynamic relationship between asylum applications and recognition rates in Europe (1987-2010). *European Union Politics, 15*(2), 192–214. doi.org/10.1177/1465116513511710

Tourangeau, R., & Smith, T. W. (1996). Asking sensitive questions: the impact of data collection mode, question format and question context. *Public Opinion Quarterly 60*(2), 275–304. doi.org/10.1086/297751

United Nations Development Program. (2013). *The Rise of the South: Human Progress in a Diverse World*. Human Development Report 2013. New York: Author.

United Nations High Commissioner for Refugees. (2013). *Displacement: The New 21st Century Challenge*. Global Trends 2012. Geneva: Author.

van Liempt, I., & Doomernik, J. (2006). Migrant's agency in the smuggling process: The perspectives of smuggled migrants in the Netherlands. *International Migration, 44*(4), 165–90. doi.org/10.1111/j.1468-2435.2006.00383.x

Zimmerman, K. (1996). European migration: Push and pull. *International Regional Science Review, 19*(1-2), 95–128. doi.org/10.1177/016001769601900211

6

Leaving family behind: Understanding the irregular migration of unaccompanied asylum-seeking minors

Ignacio Correa-Velez, Mariana Nardone
and Katharine Knoetze

Introduction

Unaccompanied asylum-seeking minors (UAMs) are a particularly vulnerable group that present considerable humanitarian, legal and policy challenges to many countries around the world. The United Nations High Commissioner for Refugees (UNHCR) defines an unaccompanied minor as 'a person who is under the age of eighteen years, unless, under the law applicable to the child, majority is attained earlier and who is separated from both parents and is not being cared for by an adult who by law or custom has responsibility to do so' (1997, p. 5).

Since 2006, approximately 113,000 asylum claims have been lodged by unaccompanied or separated children worldwide (UNHCR, 2013). According to the UNHCR, 'more than 25,300 individual asylum applications were lodged by UASC [unaccompanied or separated children] in 77 countries in 2013, far more than in previous years … [which] constituted about 4 per cent of the total number of asylum claims lodged in these 77 countries' (2014, p. 29). The main countries of origin of UAMs were South Sudan, Afghanistan and Somalia. Kenya, Sweden, Germany, Malaysia, UK and Norway reported the highest number of UAM claims. 'Available information indicates that more than 7,100 unaccompanied or separated children were recognised in 2013 as refugees or granted a complementary form of protection in 44 countries … Roughly two thirds of all decisions taken on UASC claims during the year led to the granting of refugee status or another form of protection' (UNHCR, 2014, p. 29). Accordingly, the recognition rate for UAMs seems to be higher than the overall total recognition rate, which was 44 per cent in 2013 (UNHCR, 2014).[1]

Between 2008 and 2012, a total of 1,832 UAMs arrived in Australia as irregular maritime arrivals (IMAs) (Expert Panel on Asylum Seekers, 2012). The proportion of UAMs arriving as IMAs relative to the overall number of asylum seekers increased from 4 per cent in 2008 to 11 per cent in 2012 (Expert Panel on Asylum Seekers, 2012). Despite the many risks faced by this vulnerable group of children, and also the challenges this population poses for the Australian Government's humanitarian, legislative and policy frameworks (Crock & Kenny, 2012), very limited research has been conducted in Australia to date (Barrie & Mendes, 2011).

In 2013, the Australian Department of Immigration and Border Protection (DIBP) commissioned a large-scale quantitative survey of 1,008 adult IMAs who were granted protection visas between July 2011 and December 2012. The survey has provided vital empirical evidence to better understand 'why and how people decide to leave their countries of origin and travel to Australia, including in relation to economic, family, protection and other reasons' (McAuliffe, 2013, p. 5). Importantly, the survey findings have highlighted the need to undertake further qualitative research to supplement the quantitative results, 'particularly as they relate to specific demographic groups' (McAuliffe, 2013, p. 30).

This chapter presents the findings of a qualitative study funded by the 2012–13 Irregular Migration Research Small Grants Programme. The study aimed to address the following research questions:

1. Why do UAMs leave their parents/guardians or other family members and engage in irregular maritime migration?

---

1   2013 global recognition rates are indicative as some states have not yet reported relevant data.

2. Who makes the choice of destination country and what factors influence this choice?

3. How do UAMs travel between source, transit and destination countries?

4. What are the experiences of UAMs in transit countries?

Current knowledge of the irregular migration of unaccompanied asylum-seeking minors

Although there is an emerging body of literature on the irregular migration of asylum seekers to Australia (McAuliffe, 2013; Koser & McAuliffe, 2013), little is known about UAMs in the Australian context. This section draws on what is known about three of the four main stages of the irregular migration process and highlights issues of particular interest for Australian research on UAMs: the decision to leave the country of origin, the choice of destination, and the transit countries.

The decision to leave

A recent quantitative survey of irregular migrant adults (mainly from Afghanistan, Iran, Pakistan and Sri Lanka) living in Australia on protection visas found that although protection-related factors were prominent, other factors such as employment, education services, housing, health services, poverty, corruption, geography and family/community links were also important drivers of irregular migration (McAuliffe, 2013). The available literature pinpoints a number of reasons for UAMs to seek asylum, including widespread poverty, economic hardship, political instability and poor educational prospects, along with trigger elements such as violent incidents, threats, or a parent's death (Mounge, 2010; Thomas, Nafees, & Bhugra, 2004).

Most recent irregular migration frameworks focus on macro-level (structural reasons to move) and meso-level (role of policies; intermediaries) explanations, but little is known about the micro-level of individual or family decision-making (Koser & McAuliffe, 2013). A study of 30 UAMs and 70 service providers in Scotland found that 'a community helping response' commonly involving an 'uncle' (not necessarily a close relative but a familiar person) was part of the migration decision-making process (Hopkins & Hill, 2008). Another study of Afghan UAMs in Europe showed that birth order and sex are important variables in determining who leaves; generally, it is the oldest son who makes the journey (Mounge, 2010). This study also found that in some cases minors make their own decision to leave (especially when they are already separated from their families).

The choice of destination

In the global context, growing evidence indicates that the choice of destination country for irregular migrants is influenced, among other aspects, by geography, finances, available travel routes, documentation and chance (Koser & McAuliffe, 2013; Spinks, 2013). Some of the factors that may influence asylum seekers to choose Australia as a destination country include: economic prosperity and the stability of Australia in comparison with other countries in the Asia–Pacific region; Australia is a signatory of the UN Refugee Convention (while many of the other countries in the region are not); and preexisting connections of asylum seekers with people already in Australia (Crock & Ghezelbash, 2010).

There is evidence from Europe that 'a global network of agents' is critical in determining the destination of children (Hopkins & Hill, 2008). Relationships with these agents are sometimes exploitative, abusive and traumatic for the UAMs (Hopkins & Hill, 2008). While international and Australian research has reported that in many cases asylum seekers have their destination chosen for them by people smugglers (Spinks, 2013), a 2009 study in Norway found that people smugglers do not have a significant power in questions of destination; the presence of social networks played a significant role, instead (Breke & Aarset, 2009).

There is contradictory evidence about the level of knowledge irregular migrants and asylum seekers have about the destination country, ranging from very little knowledge to well-informed (Koser & McAuliffe, 2013).

Transit countries

UAMs from Afghanistan frequently move to Iran and Pakistan with their families or on their own to live and work some years before they travel to Europe (Mounge, 2010). Pakistan and Iran continue to host a significant number of Afghan refugees. Reasons for secondary movement from countries of first asylum are related to lack of legal status which represents numerous risks to asylum seekers including risk of refoulement, harassment or arrest by police, lack of access to healthcare, education, housing and employment (Human Rights Watch, 2002), and lack of access to child protection services (Mounge, 2010).

Indonesia has traditionally been an essential transit country for UAMs travelling to Australia (Human Rights Watch, 2013). UAMs in Indonesia have no legal status, no work rights, limited access to education, and are subject to detention for long periods of time (Human Rights Watch, 2013).

There is evidence from Australia and internationally that a large number of IMAs pay people smugglers for one or more parts of the migration journey (Koser & McAuliffe, 2013). This journey can be very costly and often families incur debt or sell possessions in order to pay. Where these options are not available, the agreement with the smuggler is to pay in instalments (Mounge, 2010). The length of the journey depends on the way the payment is made: those who pay in instalments usually have longer journeys than those who pay in full at the outset (Mounge, 2010).

Afghan UAMs travelling to Europe have little understanding of the conditions of the journey (Mounge, 2010). Smugglers tend to separate groups of children travelling together, preventing them from making friendships that could threaten their authority (Mounge, 2010). While some boys have regular contact with their parents or relatives, for others, this contact depends on the smugglers (Mounge, 2010). The boat journey from Indonesia to Australia is very risky, overloaded, with no safety regulations, and with smugglers often failing to supply enough water, food and fuel (Human Rights Watch, 2013).

Methods

The research was a collaborative effort between the Queensland University of Technology (QUT) and the Queensland Program of Assistance to Survivors of Torture and Trauma. Full ethics approval was granted by the QUT Human Research Ethics Committee. Using a qualitative approach, a peer-interviewer model and a snowballing technique, semi-structured interviews were conducted with 17 participants who: (i) were living in Brisbane on a protection visa; (ii) had arrived in Australia over the past five years as IMAs; (iii) had arrived in Australia as UAMs (12–17 years of age at time of arrival); (iv) were aged 16 years or over at the time of the interview; and (v) had the capacity to provide informed consent to participate. Questions were informed by the objectives of the research and the current literature gaps, and were developed in consultation with DIBP.

Significant efforts were made to interview protection visa holders from both sexes (although most UAMs who have arrived in Australia as IMAs are males) and diverse ethnic backgrounds. However, all recruited participants were males and all but one were either born in Afghanistan or born elsewhere to Afghanistan-born parents. A number of female protection visa holders and other potential participants from Sri Lanka, Iran and Iraq were approached but declined to participate. Those who provided reasons for declining to participate indicated their reluctance to talk about past traumatic experiences. As shown in the literature, refusals by potential participants should be seen as a positive sign, because they are 'indicative of an ability to make a choice' (Molyneux, Kamuya, & Marsh, 2010, p. 25). All interviews with protection visa holders were conducted by peer interviewers who received training in research skills and the ethical conduct of research. Written notes only were taken during these interviews.

In addition, semi-structured interviews were conducted with eight nongovernment service providers working with UAMs in the Greater Brisbane area with the aim of obtaining multiple perspectives, uncovering deeper meaning in the data and enhancing the validity of the research (Patton, 2002). All interviews with service providers were conducted, audio recorded and transcribed by a senior research assistant.

Interview transcripts were entered into NVivo software (QSR, v.10) and analysed using a thematic analysis approach (Patton, 2002). A coding matrix was created using the first three stages of the irregular migration process as a broader thematic framework (i.e. decision to leave country of origin, choice of destination, and transit countries). This chapter focuses on protection visa holders' and service providers' perspectives and presents the key themes derived within each of the three stages of the irregular migration process.

Findings

Seventeen protection visa holders who had arrived in Australia as UAMs were interviewed. All were males. Fifteen respondents were born in Afghanistan, one was born in Pakistan from an Afghan background, and one was born in Iran. The majority of those born in Afghanistan or to Afghan parents were ethnic Hazara. Their average age at the time of the interview was 19 years, and they had been in Australia for 2.3 years, on average.

In addition, eight service providers (six females and two males) from five non-governmental organisations (NGOs) working with UAMs in the Greater Brisbane area were interviewed. Their average time as individuals working with refugees and asylum seekers at the time of the interview was 6 years. For one service provider, English was not their first language.

Stage 1: The decision to leave the country of origin

All protection visa holders stated that they had no other choice but to leave their country of origin. Their decision to leave as UAMs was prompted by discrimination (because of their ethnicity or religion), persecution, threat to their lives, or torture. All young people indicated that one of the main reasons to leave their country of origin (or the country they were living in) was the fear for their own life. In some cases (5 out of 17) the decision to leave was influenced by other family members or close friends being detained, missing or killed:

> [O]n my way to Kabul we were stopped by Taliban and held up for few hours. I was so scared as they threatened us to death. Few of us managed to escape but some of my friends are still reported missing ever since. After that incident, I went straight to Kabul City and stayed in a hotel. I contacted my mother and explained my encounter with Taliban, my mother was very frightened she said I am everything that she is left with and she would want to protect my life by any means possible. (PV11, 19 years old, male, Afghan-born, 1 year in Australia)[2]

> I have left Pakistan because it is not a safe country for people who are from Afghanistan. And it is very unsafe for Hazara people, because Hazara people are Shia and they hate Hazara Shia people. Because the enemies

---

2   For the purposes of this chapter, the acronym PV has been used to refer to protection visa holders.

we have in Pakistan, they kill us wherever they get us. And also most of the time in Pakistan they make bomb blasts to kill us and also do target killing in different areas of Pakistan. They want us to leave Pakistan or be killed there, no other options. (PV05, 18 years old, male, Afghan-born, 3 years in Australia)

Almost all service providers mentioned that there was 'no choice' for these young people but leaving their region of origin.[3] They indicated that the main protection reasons for the UAMs to leave their countries of origin were: political, religious or ethnic persecution, discrimination, arrest by the authorities or other organisations, and/or torture:

> I guess young people leave, unaccompanied minors leave their families either they are forced to leave. They are not given a choice. It is something that the parents are deciding for them and they are taking that decision on behalf of the family. So, war, persecution, discrimination, racism and violation of human rights, torture and kidnapping. My clients have spoken of, they have been abducted and held I guess within this like a cell or a place they don't know, they don't really have details about it, but it is a place where they don't know where it is. Sometimes that's done. They are covering over their head when they are taken there, so they don't know where they are, and tortured in those situations. (SP01)[4]

A number of young people (6 out of 17) mentioned that, in addition to protection reasons, they left their region of origin with the aspiration of getting a 'better life' or 'opportunities in life'. In this context, 'better life' was understood as being able to live free from persecution, feeling safe, and being able to access education and employment opportunities. Other non-protection reasons mentioned were: general insecurity/lack of safety/conflict, a pessimistic outlook for the future, widespread violence, looking forward to living a peaceful/free life, and deportation from a neighbouring host country:

> In Afghanistan there are many issues that have really made people's life very hard. It is very hard for people to live a good life or you can say a 'good quality life' in Afghanistan. Because Afghanistan is a country where no one can feel safe. Taliban can attack any one at any time, at anywhere. They are the real people who have control over the country. Most of the times they burn the schools. Because they do not want us,

---

3   Region of origin encompasses either 'country of birth' or 'neighbouring host country'.
4   For the purposes of this chapter, the acronym SP has been used to refer to service providers.

they do not want Hazara people to get education, to be healthy, to feel safe and live a happy life. (PV08, 19 years old, male, Afghan-born, 3 years in Australia)

I was not allowed to go to school and get education because I was an Afghan. So because of all these issues I had to leave Iran and travel to a country where I would feel safe, where there is right for human beings. And where I could get education. (PV09, 21 years old, male, Afghan-born, 4 years in Australia)

In addition to protection reasons, service providers also mentioned non-protection reasons for the children to leave, such as internal conflict, war or unsafety in their countries of origin, to get a 'better life', security, or to have education or employment opportunities to assist their families financially:

It is important to acknowledge that some of these young people have never lived in their country of origin. They might be born in the refugee camp, that isn't the country of origin, but they wanted to be safe, they wanted to get a better life, they wanted security, go to school, get education, employment, and get better health. (SP02)

I've had a few clients who didn't know why their parents put them in a boat. And obviously when they come here to tell their story is 'I don't know'. It's because they are so young and they've been, I am assuming for their own safety by their parents, they put them on a boat. (SP05)

According to the young people, the decision to leave the country of origin (or the host country they were living in) was either made by their parents (or close relatives), a joint decision between their family and themselves, their own decision, or a decision made together with friends. In many cases (14 out of 17), at least one parent or another member of the family was involved in the decision to leave. No participant stated that people smugglers influenced their decision to leave. Finding a people smuggler was 'easy' once the decision to leave was made:

My parents and brothers made the decision for me to leave Iran and I also did not want to stay there anymore. (PV09, 21 years old, male, Afghan-born, 4 years in Australia)

Both my mother and I decided that it was time for me to leave the country and save my life. (PV11, 19 years old, male, Afghan-born, 1 year in Australia)

My friends from school and I all five of us sat together and decided if we want to live a peaceful life we need to leave Afghanistan. Once this decision was made by us as individuals we then informed our families ... In Kabul is quite easy to find contact numbers of people who can arrange your travel from Afghanistan in return for some money. I got in touch with a man who agreed to plan my trip from Kabul to Indonesia. (PV12, 18 years old, male, Afghan-born, 1 year in Australia)

All service providers agreed that in most cases the family makes the decision for their children to leave (with no input from the children). In some situations (e.g. when their parents are dead or missing), the decision is made by their relatives (mostly uncles or aunts), while in a few cases, the decision is made by the children (when orphaned, or on their own choice to support their families back home). Some interviewees also mentioned the role that the community may play in the decision-making:

I don't think most of them approved many of the discussions, they have been told to leave. And a number of them said, their parents said 'You are leaving and you are going now'. (SP02)

I've had a few clients from Sri Lanka, they are from the same village. To keep the boys safe, what the village has done is to put all their money together to send these boys to Australia ... It's not that the families put their hand up and 'My boy', I think as a village they all decided who was going to go, which I don't know how they did. (SP05)

Protection visa holders frequently stated that they were the oldest male child of the family:

My family consists of my mother, 3 sisters and 2 brothers. My father has gone missing since about 6 years ago. I am the second child but the eldest son in the family. (PV13, 19 years old, male, Afghan-born, 2 years in Australia)

I made the decision that it was time for me to leave the country. I was the eldest son in the family and I felt very responsible towards my siblings. I decided to leave and make a better life for us in Australia. (PV15, 19 years old, male, Afghan-born, 2 years in Australia)

According to service providers, it was common for whole families to face protection issues (e.g. due to their ethnicity and/or religion) and consequently one member of the family was chosen to leave 'and rescue the others' (SP06). Almost all service providers agreed that the decision about which member of the family leaves is made on the basis of age and sex; the oldest male child in the family leaves. In some cases, other factors are taken into consideration by the families in order to get the best outcome, such as: strength, intelligence, maturity, courage, ability to learn English quickly, having some level of education, or on the basis that they are more likely to survive and succeed in Australia. Some service providers mentioned that, to a lesser extent, female asylum-seeking minors also seek to come to Australia after experiences of kidnapping and sexual assault in their country of origin, or when families living in unsafe conditions have a single female child or constitute an all-female family (in that case the oldest daughter would be chosen), or when they are the only survivors of the family:

> It is safety, certainly safety issues, for some of the families I worked for, at least one member of the family would survive, and so they would put all their finances and ensuring that member of the family got out alive. So the expectation on that child was so high to survive and succeed on behalf of the family. (SP07)

> [T]here was a situation where one of the boys had a twin brother and he wanted to come and I said: 'How did they choose out of you who was the person who was meant to come?' and he is like: 'Because I came first'. So literally is the oldest and he was bigger and he was sent. (SP01)

> We do have one, who recently turned 18, she was from Iran, Iranian background, but we don't have many females. And I've asked my clients 'Why do you think why girls don't come if it's not safe at home?' And they would say 'Because it's not safe for them on the boat'. They see them as either they would be targeted upon by males, and they also see it as males are stronger than females, they wouldn't be able to survive. (SP05)

Stage 2: The choice of destination

Young people and service providers were asked about the choice of destination country, the sources of information and the people involved in this choice, the presence of family or friends in Australia, and whether or not the choice was made prior to or after leaving their country of origin.

Ten out of 17 respondents had lived in neighbouring countries for at least a year (in most cases with their families) but left those countries because of safety concerns, discrimination, deportation or lack of rights and entitlements. For 6 out of 17 respondents, Australia became a choice after living in or being deported from neighbouring countries (Pakistan and/or Iran):

> Before coming to Australia I lived only in Pakistan no other countries. Because Pakistan and Iran are the countries where most of Hazara people go to when they abandon Afghanistan. But unfortunately in those countries too, we are targeted and killed every single day. (PV08, 19 years old, male, Afghan-born, 3 years in Australia)

> I had already attempted living in Pakistan or Iran but failed. I only considered Australia after that. (PV15, 19 years old, male, Afghan-born, 2 years in Australia)

Similarly, many service providers mentioned Pakistan or Iran as the most common neighbouring countries for people fleeing Afghanistan.

Some young people considered other destination countries such as USA, Canada, England, Denmark, Sweden and/or New Zealand before choosing Australia. Although most participants indicated they had little knowledge about Australia prior to leaving their countries of origin, they had heard that Australia was a safe, free and peaceful country that welcomes refugees. These general impressions were also mentioned as the main reasons for choosing Australia:

> I also considered Denmark and Sweden, but I decided to come to Australia as I found this to be the easiest to arrange for logistically, with a better chance of success and obtaining refugee protection. (PV17, 19 years old, male, Afghan-born, 2 years in Australia)

> Australia is a country where everyone wants to come to. And for people like us it is the country where we can live our life without being threatened to be killed or targeted by any religious, politician or any other group. (PV05, 18 years old, male, Afghan-born, 3 years in Australia)

All service providers agreed that young people have no or very little knowledge about Australia before leaving their region of origin. Some service providers stated that young people's families might have more information about Australia than the young people themselves. Many service providers agreed that safety and opportunities to study, to work, for family reunification, and for sending remittances back are the main reasons for choosing Australia.

All service providers agreed that young people do not consider staying in any of the countries of transit, mainly because of the lack of safety, rights and entitlements in those countries:

I don't think Indonesia is ever the destination, because there is no work rights, there is no education, there is no citizenship, they are nobodies. (SP08)

Minors had greater involvement in the choice of destination country than in the decision to leave their countries of origin. For 6 out of 17, choosing Australia was their own decision, for five the decision was made by their families (with no input from the minors), while for four the decision was shared between minors and their families. Importantly, for 8 out of 17 minors, the decision to choose Australia was somewhat influenced by friends and acquaintances. Only one young person indicated that a people smuggler directly influenced the decision to come to Australia:

After that day I decided that I must leave Pakistan and since I had heard a lot about Australia from my friends in Iran and Pakistan I decided to come to Australia. (PV15, 19 years old, male, Afghan-born, 2 years in Australia)

I contacted my mother from Kabul ... We discussed my options of survival and decided I should leave the country and go to a safe place. We had heard a lot from random people that Australia accepts refugees and many Afghans are travelling there and being accepted into the country. (PV11, 19 years old, male, Afghan-born, 1 year in Australia)

I did not have any direct contact with that person [people smuggler]. And he did influence the decision to go to Australia. (PV01, 19 years old, male, Pakistan-born, Afghan background, 3 years in Australia)

Service providers ascribed greater influence on the decision to choose Australia to people smugglers. One service provider also mentioned that the community ('the village' in the case of some UAMs from Sri Lanka) may play a role in the decision:

I think for a lot of the young people, I think it's the people smugglers that choose Australia. I don't think the family sit down and go 'OK, where are you going to go?' and sit with a map and map it out. I think the people smugglers are the ones that say 'Go to Australia, you get an easy ride'. (SP04)

Others in the village will decide to put money in together and also bring them, the village puts some money together and send them on a boat to come to Australia for a better life. (SP05)

None of the young people interviewed indicated they had family or relatives in Australia prior to arrival, and only two stated they had friends living already in the destination country:

> I had a friend in Melbourne who arrived a couple of years before me. I contacted him on Facebook from Indonesia. (PV13, 19 years old, male, Afghan-born, 2 years in Australia)

It is important to note, however, that this finding may be somewhat different if other cohorts of young people (e.g. other countries of origin or ethnicities) had been interviewed.

According to service providers, whether or not UAMs have family or relatives in Australia varies and is frequently related to minors' cultural/ethnic backgrounds:

> With the clients I'm working with at the moment, Hazara clients most of them have family members, either if it's a distant cousin, or an aunty, an uncle, they know someone. I haven't met a Hazara person that doesn't know someone in Australia, either because they've arrived 10 years beforehand or they arrived just last week. They all at least know someone in their community here in Australia. (SP05)

All young people indicated that the decision to come to Australia was made before leaving their country of origin (or a neighbouring host country). In some instances, the decision was prompted after being deported from a neighbouring host country:

> My auntie and her husband and myself sat together in their house in Kabul and explored my options. Together we reached the decision that I must leave Afghanistan, we knew that Pakistan is also infested with Taliban and therefore we decided that I should come to Australia. (PV13, 19 years old, male, Afghan-born, 2 years in Australia)

> I was deported from Iran and then I really did not have anywhere to call home and feel safe, and also because there is also problems in Afghanistan, especially the conflict. So I decided to come to Australia, live my life under the shadow of peace and call it home. (PV06, 18 years old, male, Afghan-born, 2 years in Australia)

Service providers agreed that the decision to come to Australia is frequently made before leaving their countries of origin or while in a neighbouring host country, although in some cases the decision is made in transit (Indonesia). One service provider highlighted differences according to ethnicity; while Hazaras and Sri Lankans make the decision in their countries of origin, Rohingyans are more likely to decide when they are in Indonesia:

> With Hazaras they've all decided in their own country, so before they started their travels they had Australia in their mind. With Sri Lankans, again I think it's their parents who put that, because they come straight from Sri Lanka, they don't have another country in the middle. I've had a few Burmese or the Rohingyan clients, who obviously went to Indonesia, and they were not too sure if they wanted to come to Australia or New Zealand, and they chose there ... It's a mixture of all, I guess. (SP05)

Stage 3: Transit countries

Regarding transit countries, respondents provided information about the ways in which UAMs leave their countries of origin and travel through transit countries, the difficulties experienced during their journey and how they cope with it, the assistance they receive, and how they look after themselves.

Almost all young people had direct or indirect contact with people smugglers (or their networks). Contact with people smugglers took place at airports, through phone calls, or through other asylum seekers. In order to leave their countries of origin, young people themselves, their families and/or friends contacted a people smuggler to arrange the journey. In a few cases, the arrangement with the smuggler was made for the journey from the region of origin to Indonesia. Once in Indonesia, it was up to the minor to find a smuggler to travel to Australia:

> I flew from Karachi to Bangkok in Thailand. It was 14 of us that were travelling in the same plane from Karachi to Bangkok. At Bangkok airport only 3 of us managed to pass through the passport check. The other 11 were detained at the airport and were later deported back to Pakistan. We were picked up by a taxi at the airport and took us to a hotel. The next day a taxi picked us up from the airport and drove us to the bus terminal. We went on a bus that drove us to Malaysia. We spent two nights in a hotel in Kuala Lumpur and on the third night we were picked up by a taxi from our hotel. The taxi took us to the seashore ... We boarded a small boat and after 2 hours we reached Indonesia. We spent one night in a big beach house and the next day we were left on our own to find our own way to Australia. (PV15, 19 years old, male, Afghan-born, 2 years in Australia)

> Yes, I met with the people smuggler who arranged my travel from Kabul to Indonesia … My house mates in Jakarta arranged the contact with the people smugglers in Indonesia and therefore I did not see them. (PV13, 19 years old, male, Afghan-born, 2 years in Australia)

All service providers agreed that people smugglers are contacted by the minors or family members to arrange the journey and that payments are made before departure, once they arrive in Australia, and/or throughout the journey. Some service providers pointed out that people smugglers are in regular contact with UAMs during the journey (i.e. to get them out of jail, find accommodation, keep them hidden, getting a boat):

> They are continually paying people to get them to that next point, or to get them out of jail, or to take them somewhere where they can go into hiding for a few weeks, or take them into a jungle. (SP01)

Young people used a variety of ways to travel from one place to another during their journey to Australia: cars, taxis, buses, motorcycles, planes, trains, boats. Some had to walk to cross borders or move inside transit countries. Many left their country of origin by plane using their valid passports. Subsequently, people smugglers at countries of transit provided them with false passports, and also SIM cards for mobile phones to keep in contact. In some cases, young people bought the SIM cards themselves to communicate with their families. Most young people were able to talk to their families back home by phone during the journey, although the frequency of these calls varied. Three young people did not have any contact with their families during the journey:

> I flew from Kabul to Delhi in India legally with my Afghan passport and spent 28 days in there. I was met at the Delhi airport and was given a fake passport. After 28 days in India, I flew to Malaysia using my new passport and stayed in the airport for 5 hours as transit and then flew to Bali. I was lucky that I made friends with a man in Delhi who was also coming to Australia. In Bali we had to get Indonesian visas on our passports and I was scared to death at that point, I thought that I will be caught out. Luckily we managed to get the visas and we flew to Jakarta. (PV13, 19 years old, male, Afghan-born, 2 years in Australia)

> I flew from Kabul to Dubai and was picked up by someone at the Dubai airport and was given a SIM card for my phone. I was taken to a room which I spent about a month in—there were other people that shared the room with me. I was only allowed to leave that room once per day to go to the bakery and purchase bread. After about a month, I received a phone call and it was arranged for me to be taken to the airport.

I boarded the plane and reached Malaysia, I was told as soon as I reach Malaysia I should tear up their visa at Kuala Lumpur airport and show them the Thailand visa that was also in my passport. Therefore I was able to reach Thailand by plane. (PV12, 18 years old, male, Afghan-born, 1 year in Australia)

According to service providers, Malaysia and Indonesia are the two main transit countries (other transit countries mentioned are United Arab Emirates, Thailand, and Bangladesh). Some service providers pointed out that in some cases minors have very limited contact with their families back home during the journey:

I've had a few clients who said that they had no contact at all when they came into Australia, so easily 8 months with no contact with family back home. I had others who had contact with them in Indonesia, and then that was it. It is only when they have money to be able to call back home that they would. Most of them were out of contact for the whole time, especially when they are hiding from the government in Indonesia, it's very hard for them, and in some cases I had clients say the family told them not to contact, because they thought the telephones were all bugged, so why risk it? Just get to Australia and call us when you are there. (SP05)

The journey through transit countries was commonly characterised by danger and unpredictability and by the need for young people to 'maintain a degree of invisibility' (SP08). Although the final boat voyage was seen by young people (10 out of 17) as the most logistically difficult part of the journey, respondents found 'leaving home' also difficult, and felt particularly vulnerable while hiding in the jungle, being away from their family, not knowing who to trust, not being able to speak the local language, feeling sick and unable to see a doctor, finding themselves hungry, thirsty and with no money, struggling to find accommodation, and fearful of being stopped by police and government officials. Six respondents mentioned that they had direct contact with government officials during their journey, but only one was detained while in transit:

I had a significant number of issues on the way, because I could not speak the language of the countries I had to go through. I did not have enough money to pay for the journey. I did not have any money even to get food and feed myself. I was always worried about being cheated by the smugglers, and being arrested by the government officials. And I was also very afraid of getting on the boat. Because I had never travelled by boat in my whole life before coming to Australia. (PV04, 19 years old, male, Afghan-born, 3 years in Australia)

> But being away from my family members and not being an adult to know what to do and what not to, was a hard thing for me to deal with. (PV05, 18 years old, male, Afghan-born, 3 years in Australia)

Service providers identified a number of issues faced by UAMs in their journeys through transit countries, including lack of food and water and poor sanitary conditions during the boat voyage or while in detention, fear of the boat sinking, adverse weather conditions, health issues and no access to healthcare services, lack of adequate shelter, lack of money, isolation and lack of information, separation from groups of other asylum seekers, fear of being robbed or detained, physical abuse, and fear of animals while hiding in the jungle.

Assistance during the journey sometimes came from people smugglers and/or locals who provided phones, food, clothing, information about places or how to find a boat and accommodation, and often from other asylum seekers they met along the way (e.g. by helping each other with money, companionship, finding a boat, or being introduced to people smugglers' assistants). However, the unpredictability of the journey meant that friendships were short lived. Only three participants indicated they already had family members or friends in Indonesia who provided assistance:

> There were some rare occasions where the people smugglers would provide me with a phone to contact my family and inform them of my whereabouts. In Indonesia, however, I purchased a mobile phone and communicated with my mother regularly. (PV11, 19 years old, male, Afghan-born, 1 year in Australia)

> But like others, I would meet new people make friends and then we were separated again. Because, during the journey, no one knows what is going to happen and when. So that is why it is very difficult to keep being together and stay with each other during the whole journey. (PV05, 18 years old, male, Afghan-born, 3 years in Australia)

> I had a friend who had been living in Indonesia for 2 years and were waiting for their refugee application to be processed. I made contacts with my friend … He provided me with accommodation. (PV15, 19 years old, male, Afghan-born, 2 years in Australia)

Support or assistance from locals, friends made along the way, extended family members, acquaintances and in some cases the assistance of people smugglers were also identified by service providers.

In addition to receiving support or assistance from other people, young people looked after themselves and increased their sense of safety by using strategies such as remaining positive and hopeful, being careful, staying healthy and praying:

> I tried to concentrate on the good future that I will have after all this journey is passed. I remained positive and knew that I have no way of turning back since my passport was valid only for a month. (PV14, 19 years old, male, Iran-born, 1 year in Australia)

> I was praying to God every day to look after me. I tried to follow the instructions of the guide person very closely at different stages of my journey, such as when we were crossing the Thai–Malay border. I was quite healthy and did not feel sick during the journey. I tried to eat well and take care of myself. (PV15, 19 years old, male, Afghan-born, 2 years in Australia)

Service providers also mentioned that remaining hopeful, building relationships, meeting locals and praying were important strategies used by UAMs during their journeys:

> I know they talked about praying a lot, lots on the boat, and that they've been in absolute fear. A lot of them don't know if they are going to survive the journey, and certainly they talked about the lack of food, being sick, lack of water, so I think the way they do look after themselves is through prayer. (SP04)

> I guess their own upbringing to be that strong to be able to survive, something like that and I guess street smart, if that makes sense? … A lot of them got together in groups of young men, young boys together, I think that helped a few, to build that relationship to other people in the same situation as them. (SP05)

The data shows young people's strong determination to reach Australia. Most participants indicated never considering staying in any of the countries en route to Australia (because they do not accept refugees or because of poor life conditions) or going back to their countries of origin during the journey because of concerns about their safety and security. Three participants also mentioned lack of money or validity of current passport as barriers to return. Only two respondents stated that they thought about going back when they saw the conditions of the boat or realised the dangers involved in the journey.

The data also shows the strong responsibility young people feel about the wellbeing of their family members back home. Fourteen respondents stated that their families wanted to come to Australia and join them through sponsorship. Seven young people also mentioned that their families back home expected them to provide financial support. For three respondents, their families were expecting them to get a good education and succeed in life:

> I really wanted to come to Australia, but on the way to Australia I had to go to Indonesia. And then I really liked being and living in Indonesia. Because Indonesia too is a war-free and peaceful country. But because they would not accept me stay there and would not give me any ID card so that is why I had no choice but to come to Australia. (PV01, 19 years old, male, Pakistan-born, Afghan background, 3 years in Australia)

> I could sense death with every wave that hit our boat and I knew this is a life or death journey but I also knew that going back was not an option since it would equate to death. (PV11, 19 years old, male, Afghan-born, 1 year in Australia)

> I was certain that I will reach Australia. I knew that even if I am caught and sent back I will attempt again and again until I reach Australia … My family's first and foremost request from me is to take my education seriously and pursue my dream of becoming someone great in life, someone who can make a difference. They also would like to come to Australia and expect me to assist with their sponsorship and if I am financially able to do so, provide them with some financial support. (PV12, 18 years old, male, Afghan-born, 1 year in Australia)

> They want me to sponsor them and save their life. (PV04, 19 years old, male, Afghan-born, 3 years in Australia)

According to most service providers, experiences of detention in transit countries do not influence onward movement (either to third countries or returning to their regions of origin). UAMs' strong determination to reach Australia was also highlighted by service providers, and this determination was influenced by families' expectations for the children to find safety, to join their children in Australia or to receive financial support from them:

> I think that it probably makes them more determined in regards to, they come on such a journey and I think it makes them more determined to be able to gain their education and to be able to get employment, so that the journey is worthwhile. Probably it makes them more determined. (SP04)

Conclusion

By interviewing protection visa holders who arrived in Australia as UAMs, as well as service providers working with this population group, this study provides valuable qualitative micro-level insights on the drivers, determinants and decision-making processes of irregular migration among UAMs arriving in Australia, in particular those born in Afghanistan. In light of the need for a better understanding about decision-making by irregular migrants (Koser & McAuliffe, 2013), this study complements the quantitative findings reported recently by the DIBP-commissioned survey with adult irregular migrants living in Australia (McAuliffe, 2013).

Similar to what was found in the DIBP survey (McAuliffe, 2013), young people's decisions to leave their country of origin were influenced by both protection and non-protection reasons (although the most prominent factors were primarily related to protection). This highlights the complexity of irregular migration and the danger of oversimplifying its root causes. The study has also shown that some UAMs actively participate in the decision-making process to leave their country of origin and in the choice of destination country.

Our research found that while service providers ascribed greater influence to people smugglers in choosing a destination country, young people did not attribute a major direct role to smugglers in their decision to leave or in their choice of destination. The DIBP's recent survey also found lesser involvement of smugglers in the final decision to travel to Australia (i.e. only 16 per cent of respondents were influenced by people smugglers) (McAuliffe, 2013). Similarly, a 2009 study of asylum seekers in Norway (Breke & Aarset, 2009) suggested that smugglers are central in facilitating travel but not in determining destinations. Further research is needed to investigate the potential indirect influence smugglers can have on asylum seekers' decision-making through other people in the community.

Among this group of protection visa holders who arrived in Australia as UAMs, a critical factor that influenced their choice of Australia as a destination country was not the presence of family or friends in Australia, but the information they received from friends and acquaintances in their region of origin. There is contradictory evidence on the level of knowledge irregular migrants and asylum seekers have on the destination countries prior to departure (Koser & McAuliffe, 2013). This group of UAMs had little knowledge about Australia before leaving their region of origin, and their limited knowledge was related to their reasons for leaving: a safe, free, peaceful and welcoming place for refugees.

Like the results of a study of unaccompanied Afghan children in Europe (Mounge, 2010), our research shows that many of the UAMs interviewed lived in a neighbouring host country (sometimes for several years) before they moved to Australia. In those countries, these young people commonly experienced discrimination, lack of rights and entitlements, and even persecution. In some instances, the decision to travel to Australia was prompted by being deported from their host countries.

As highlighted by Hopkins (2008), UAMs have a marginal position for multiple reasons: because they are children and asylum seekers, lacking the company of parents or another adult caregiver. Young people's stories describe a journey marked by unpredictability, vulnerability and the need to 'maintain a degree of invisibility'. Nevertheless, this research illustrates the resilience of the young people interviewed: they were highly resourceful, had a remarkable capacity to look after themselves, and showed a strong determination to reach Australia.

Since the aim of the research was to understand the micro-level drivers and determinants of irregular migration among UAMs arriving in Australia, the approach adopted here was qualitative. As stated by Yin (2010), 'the events and ideas emerging from qualitative research can represent the meanings given to real-life events by the people who live them, not the values, preconceptions, or meanings held by researchers' (p. 8). This study was based on a small sample of protection visa holders (mostly males from Afghanistan) and service providers. Therefore, the findings here cannot be extrapolated to other UAMs in Australia or elsewhere. Nevertheless, this research, along with the previous and current studies undertaken as part of DIBP's Irregular Migration Research Program, makes a significant contribution to addressing the evidence gaps and has the potential to inform policy deliberations.

In some instances, information given by service providers diverged from protection visa holders' statements. Patton (2002) cautions that triangulation does not aim to reach consistency across data sources. Our study has offered multiple perspectives which proved to be successful in uncovering deeper meaning, providing additional and complementary information and enhancing the validity of the research. In order to enrich our understanding of the complexity of UAMs' irregular migration, there is a need to include in future research the perspectives of female UAMs, young people from other ethnic backgrounds (e.g. Sri Lanka, Iran, Iraq), UAMs living in transit countries, as well as the perspectives of the family members left behind. Importantly, further research is needed to determine how UAMs can be better protected while living in host and transit countries.

Reference list

Barrie, L., & Mendes, P. (2011). The experiences of unaccompanied asylum-seeking children in and leaving the out-of-home care system in the UK and Australia: A critical review of the literature. *International Social Work, 54*(4), 485–503. doi.org/10.1177/0020872810389318

Breke, J., & Aarset, M. F. (2009). *Why Norway? Understanding asylum destinations.* Oslo: Institute for Social Research.

Crock, M., & Ghezelbash, D. (2010). Do loose lips bring ships? The role of policy, politics and human rights in managing unauthorised boat arrivals. *Griffith Law Review, 19*(2), 238–87. doi.org/10.1080/10383 441.2010.10854676

Crock, M., & Kenny, M. A. (2012). Rethinking the guardianship of refugee children after the Malaysian solution. *Sydney Law Review, 34*(3), 437–65.

Expert Panel on Asylum Seekers. (2012). *Report of the expert panel on asylum seekers.* Canberra: Australian Government.

Hopkins, P. (2008). Ethical issues in research with unaccompanied asylum-seeking children. *Children's Geographies, 6*(1), 37–48. doi.org/ 10.1080/14733280701791884

Hopkins, P. E., & Hill, M. (2008). Pre-flight experiences and migration stories: the accounts of unaccompanied asylum-seeking children. *Children's Geographies, 6*(3), 257–68. doi.org/ 10.1080/14733280802183981

Human Rights Watch. (2002). *'By invitation only': Australian asylum policy.* New York: Author.

Human Rights Watch. (2013). *Barely surviving: detention, abuse and neglect of migrant children in Indonesia.* New York: Author.

Koser, K., & McAuliffe, M. (2013). *Establishing evidence-base for future policy development on irregular migration to Australia.* Canberra: Australian Government, Department of Immigration and Citizenship.

McAuliffe, M. (2013). *Seeking the views of irregular migrants: Decision making, drivers and migration journeys.* Irregular Migration Research Program, Occasional Paper Series 05. Canberra: Australian Department of Immigration and Border Protection. Retrieved from www.border. gov.au/ReportsandPublications/Documents/research/views-irregular-migrant-decision-drivers-journey.pdf.

Molyneux, S., Kamuya, D., & Marsh, V. (2010). Community members employed on research projects face crucial, often under-recognized, ethical dilemmas. *American Journal of Bioethics, 10*(3), 24–26. doi.org/ 10.1080/15265161003708623

Mougne, C. (2010). *Trees only move in the wind: A study of unaccompanied Afghan children in Europe.* Policy Development and Evaluation Service report. Geneva: United Nations High Commissioner for Refugees.

Patton, M. Q. (2002). *Qualitative research and evaluation methods.* Thousand Oaks, California: Sage.

Spinks, H. (2013). *Destination anywhere? Factors affecting asylum seekers' choice of destination country.* Research paper no. 1, Parliamentary Library. Canberra: Australian Government.

Thomas, S., Nafees, B., & Bhugra, D. (2004). 'I was running away from death'—the pre-flight experiences of unaccompanied asylum seeking [sic] children in the UK. *Child: Care, Health & Development, 30*(2), 113–22. doi.org/10.1111/j.1365-2214.2003.00404.xh

United Nations High Commissioner for Refugees. (1997). *Guidelines on policies and procedures in dealing with unaccompanied children seeking asylum.* Geneva: Author.

United Nations High Commissioner for Refugees. (2013). *Displacement: The new 21st century challenge.* UNHCR global trends 2012. Geneva: Author.

United Nations High Commissioner for Refugees. (2014). *War's human cost*. UNHCR global trends 2013. Geneva: Author.

Yin, R. K. (2010). *Qualitative research from start to finish*. New York: Guilford Publications.

7

Indonesia as a transit country in irregular migration to Australia

Graeme Hugo, George Tan and Caven Jonathan Napitupulu

One important element in the growing complexity of international migration is the increasing role of countries of transit. Movement trajectories in contemporary migrations can extend over long periods of time and a number of intermediate locations before reaching a final destination. This is especially the case for asylum seekers and for irregular migration. In both of these cases, transit countries are increasingly significant; however, the bulk of migration research is focused on the destination, and to a lesser extent, the origin country.

Several Asian countries are playing increasingly significant roles as transit locations. This chapter focuses on one country, Indonesia, which, until the commencement of the Australian Government's military-led 'Operation Sovereign Borders', in September 2013,[1] functioned as a transit point for asylum seekers and irregular migrants seeking to land on Australia's northern shores.

---

1 The objective of Operation Sovereign Borders was primarily to deter IMAs from seeking asylum on Australian territories by intercepting and turning around suspected illegal entry vessels (SIEVs), and by denying resettlement in Australia by assessing asylum claims in a third country, resettling those found to be refugees in a third country.

This chapter is based largely on field studies undertaken in Indonesia between 2012 and 2014. The centrepiece was a survey of 119 intending irregular maritime arrivals (IMAs). These subjects were located in Indonesian detention centres or were living in Indonesian communities located in Medan, Tanjung, Pinang, Jakarta, Kupang and in Puncak, a former colonial hill station area located in the mountains to the south of Jakarta (Figure 7.1). A structured questionnaire was used, which asked questions about the IMAs' characteristics, their experience of migration, their motivations and intentions relating to moving to Australia. In addition, a substantial number of informant interviews were conducted in Indonesia with people involved in the migration process or interacting with transiting migrants.

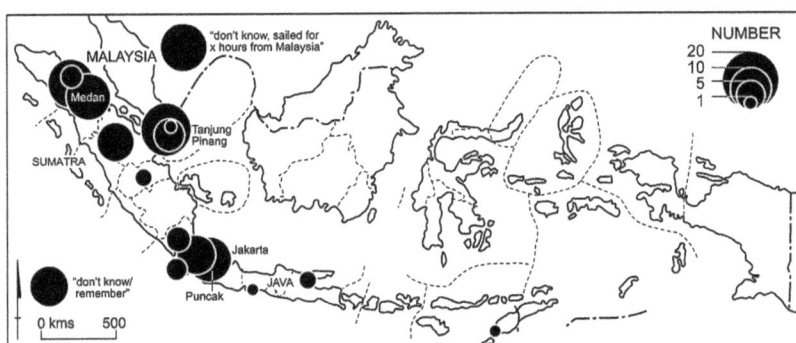

Figure 7.1: Intending asylum seekers in Indonesia: Arrival location and place of interview of respondents to survey
Source: Image produced by the Department of Geography, Environment and Population at the University of Adelaide, for this study.

The respondents to the survey were identified within detention centres, in accommodation provided by the International Organization for Migration (IOM), and in communities in several locations in Indonesia, Jakarta, Puncak and adjoining areas in West Java, Timor, northern Sumatra, Riau and South Sumatra. Once identified, they were approached and asked if they would agree to be interviewed. The agreement was difficult to get, given their precarious situation. The clandestine nature of irregular migration makes it challenging to survey this migrant group as it was not uncommon for research subjects to view researchers with some degree of suspicion and apprehension (e.g. United Nations Office on Drugs and Crime [UNODC], 2009, p. 5). As Düvell, Triandafyllidou, and Vollmer (2008, p. 7) note, the fears of a smuggled migrant that s/he will be identified upon participation in a study can be a research obstacle, as it is usually associated with fears of reprisal from smugglers and authorities, in the possible form of deportation or imprisonment. Accordingly, large numbers had to be approached to get the number of completed interviews obtained.

Transit migration in Asia

Transit migration can be seen as part of a global situation in which international migration has become more complex than the 'assimilation narrative' (Ley & Kobayashi, 2005) in which migration is seen as a one-off, more or less permanent, displacement from an origin to a single destination and the process of adjustment to that destination. There are now elements of coming and going between origin and destination, temporary and circular migration, migration to third, fourth and more countries and diaspora linkages between origins and destinations.

It is important to note the strong association of transit migration with two important forms of international migration in the contemporary world: forced migration (especially refugee and asylum seeker movement but also that associated with disasters); and irregular migration.

Most forced migrants are not able to move directly to a place of permanent resettlement due to the largely unplanned and unanticipated nature of the move and the sudden circumstances which precipitate the move. Accordingly, they often move to a temporary haven which Kunz (1973) describes as a 'midway to nowhere' situation to emphasise the precariousness, uncertainty and temporariness of their stay there.

Often migrants cannot move directly to their intended final destination because they lack the appropriate documentation or are not able to meet the entry requirements of that destination. This is especially the case when the destination is a nation belonging to the Organisation for Economic Co-operation and Development (OECD), with sophisticated border entry controls and highly controlled migration systems. Australia is such a nation, and a combination of its island geography, isolation, highly developed immigration bureaucracy and institutions and modern technologies of surveillance mean that it can control very effectively the number and characteristics of immigrants.

A country of transit can be a place where irregular migrants can arrange their entry to their intended destination, but it is also one of the places where they are at risk of repatriation.

The Indonesian context

Indonesia in many ways is a quintessential transit migration country in that it meets almost all the defining characteristics of a transit country. These include:

- Its intermediate geographical location between the Middle East, Africa and Asia on the one hand, and Australia on the other. It is comparable to Turkey and Russia, in that, for those countries, being located on the edges of Western Europe has meant that they have become important transit locations for irregular migrants from Asia and Africa and the Middle East intending to enter Europe.
- Its archipelago geography, comprising more than 3,000 islands. This presents virtually unlimited opportunities to enter Indonesia by boat without detection.
- Its strong historical linkages, involving centuries of population movement and settlement, with the main origin countries (South Asia and the Middle East) of many groups seeking to enter Australia and seek asylum.
- Its complex contemporary migration system, which not only involves important flows to the origins of asylum seekers and to other transit nations involved in their movement, but has seen the development of a substantial migration industry.
- A system of government in which corruption and bribery play a significant role, which opens up possibilities, not only for staying in Indonesia, but also for facilitating onward migration.

It is the world's fourth largest country by population, and despite recent rapid economic growth and fertility decline, it has a substantial labour surplus, especially of low-skilled, poorly educated workers. Accordingly, there has been significant emigration with the largest group being low-skilled temporary contract labour migrants.

The importance of Malaysia and the Middle East is especially important in creating migration corridors and linkages which have played a role in the contemporary movement of transit migrants with an intended destination of Australia. Malaysia and the Middle East are the origins of significant numbers of immigrants to Indonesia as well as the destination of emigrants. The importance of these migration flows in establishing corridors of movement along which asylum seekers and irregular migrants can move needs to be stressed. The connections which have been established between Indonesia and Malaysia are especially important. The Malaysia–Indonesia leg of the migration of IMAs intending to go to Australia is an important part of the migration process.

A key issue is that undocumented migration remains substantial, especially to Malaysia. While this process is complex, it has a number of elements which impinge on the movement of irregular migrants and asylum seekers using Indonesia as a transit nation with the intention of moving to Australia (Jones, 2000). Some of the major features are as follows:

- There are strong family, community and agent networks linking Malaysia and Indonesia, which facilitate migration.
- A strong 'industry' has developed, with multiple stakeholders at a range of levels ranging from the local to the international.
- There are a multiplicity of sea routes and coastal embarkation and disembarkation points in Malaysia and Indonesia.
- There is complicity of government officials in the irregular migration in both countries.
- Most of the movement, especially irregular migration, involves maritime journeys, much of it using erstwhile fishing boats, and there is substantial involvement of fishermen.

Indonesia as a transit country for Intending IMAs to Australia

Indonesia's function as a transit point for asylum seekers and irregular migrants who have Australia as an intended final destination is not new. Indonesia was an important transit point, along with Malaysia and other parts of Southeast and East Asia, for the wave of Indo Chinese boat people in the 1970s, 1980s and 1990s (Lander, 1996; Missbach, 2013).

Figure 7.2 presents results from a study by the Indonesian Directorate of Immigration of 40 Iraqi asylum seekers. This shows a pattern of initially flying to Kuala Lumpur in Malaysia and then moving to Indonesia through multiple channels.

The survey respondents' countries of origin are shown in Table 7.1. The bulk of respondents were from Afghanistan, Sri Lanka and Myanmar. Among these groups, only Sri Lankans have large numbers that sail directly from their homeland to Australia (Jayasuriya & McAuliffe, 2013; Hugo & Dissanayake, 2014).

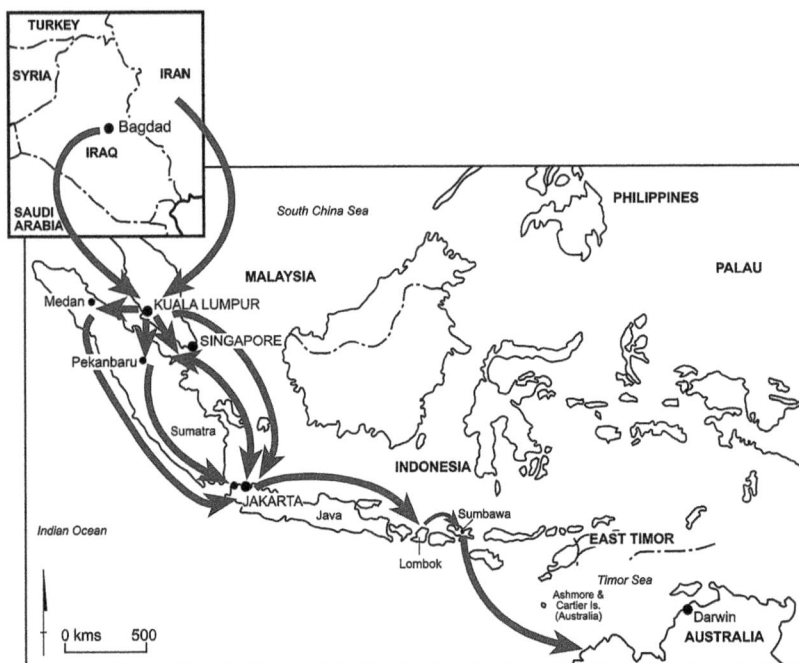

Figure 7.2: Trajectories of movement of 40 Iraqi asylum seekers, 2008

Source: Unpublished map supplied by Directorate General of Immigration, Jakarta, Indonesia. Reproduced with permission from Hugo and Napitupulu (2015, p. 224).

Table 7.1: Birthplace of survey respondents compared with IMAs in Australia, 2011–13

Birthplace	Survey	
	Number	%
Afghanistan	65	52.8
Sri Lanka	26	21.1
Myanmar	15	12.2
Iraq	7	5.7
Sudan	4	3.3
Iran	3	2.4
Palestine	2	1.6
Somalia	1	0.8
Total	123	100.0

Source: Transit migration survey (2010, 2012).

Note: The transit migration survey was conducted in 2010 and 2012 by C. J. Napitupulu for use in this study.

All of the asylum seekers surveyed flew initially to Malaysia as 'tourists', since Malaysia offers visas upon arrival to nationals of more than 60 countries, especially those with Islamic populations, in order to facilitate tourism (Missbach & Sinanu, 2011, p. 73). From Malaysia, they travel to Indonesia, which is the taking-off point for the final leg: a boat trip to Australia. These corridors of movement have become well established and a complex industry of interconnected agents has developed along the route to facilitate the migration from Malaysia to Indonesia. Many asylum seekers from Afghanistan, the most common origin, move initially to camps in Pakistan from where they negotiate with a people smuggler. Some asylum seekers travel directly to Indonesia, especially those like Iranians who could obtain a 30-day tourist visa on arrival. The removal of this visa has seen this direct flow to Indonesia dry up, and Iranians now travel via Kuala Lumpur.[2] Some asylum seekers also move initially to Thailand, which has long been a hub for trafficking in the Asia region (Skrobanek, Boonpakdi & Janthakeero, 1997). Many of the asylum seekers arriving initially in Malaysia then travel to Indonesia clandestinely by boat.

There is substantial boat traffic between Indonesia and Malaysia and an established migration industry linking them, with more than 2 million Indonesians working as international labour migrants in Malaysia, many of them undocumented (Hugo, 2011; Jones, 2000). In many cases, the people smugglers, who the asylum seekers negotiate with in their home country, only get them as far as Malaysia or Indonesia and it is then up to the asylum seekers to negotiate a passage to Australia with agents based in Malaysia, or especially Indonesia. The borders of Malaysia and Indonesia present little problem to asylum seekers as they seek to make their way to Australia. However, there are risks of detection and detention as well as experiencing exploitation at the hands of unscrupulous agents, police, officials and other groups in Malaysia and Indonesia.

The majority of survey respondents who transited in Indonesia entered illegally. Excluding respondents who unintentionally arrived, a significant 90.7 per cent (n=88) of respondents indicated that they entered illegally, compared with 9.3 per cent (n=9) of respondents who entered legally. As Table 7.2 shows, the main reason for entering Indonesia illegally (as indicated by 84.1 per cent of respondents) was because they were not able to travel legally.

---

2 This pattern may well change again, because in 2014 the Malaysian government removed access for Iranians to Visa on Arrival facilities.

Table 7.2: Reasons for entering Indonesia illegally

	Afghanistan (n=61)		Sri Lanka (n=6)		Myanmar (n=11)		Others (n=10)		Total (n=88)	
	No.	%	No.	%	No.	%	No.	%	No.	%
Formal means of travel were impossible/banned	52	85.2	3	50.0	11	100.0	8	80.0	74	84.1
Other	28	45.9	1	16.7	1	9.1	2	20.0	32	36.4
Proper entry would be rejected at the border	24	39.3	4	66.7	0	0.0	3	30.0	31	35.2
I didn't want to be sent back to my country	9	14.8	2	33.3	1	9.1	0	0.0	12	13.6
No time to get proper documents	8	13.1	1	16.7	0	0.0	0	0.0	9	10.2
I lost my genuine documents	0	0.0	1	16.7	0	0.0	0	0.0	1	1.1
Other	Afghanistan (n=11)		Sri Lanka (n=5)		Myanmar (n=5)		Others (n=4)		Total (n=25)	
	No.	%	No.	%	No.	%	No.	%	No.	%
I was following the arrangements made by my smuggler	14	50.0	0	0.0	0	0.0	2	100.0	16	50.0
My status in last country of residence was illegal— perpetuating the illegal nature of my journey	14	50.0	1	100.0	1	100.0	0	0.0	16	50.0
Common to enter illegally	-	-	-	-	-	-	-	-	-	-

Source: Transit migration survey (2010, 2012) (n=88).

Moreover, the shift towards illegality for those who began their journey legally usually occurred when entering or exiting Malaysia. Entering Indonesia illegally is also partly linked to the proportion of respondents who anticipated likely rejection by immigration authorities if they attempted to enter through formal channels (35.2 per cent). A visa restrictions index on the freedom of travel for citizens of each country (Henley & Partners, 2013) ranked Myanmar and Sri Lanka lowly on its index at 86 and 88 respectively (out of 93);[3] Afghanistan in particular was

---

3   There were only 93 rankings in the index because they included joint rankings.

ranked lowest in the world at 93. Further, these countries are exempt from obtaining the 30-day visa on arrival (VOA) which would make travelling to Indonesia an onerous if not impossible process. The hard line taken by the Indonesian Government was highlighted in 2013 when Iran had their access to the 30-day VOA privilege removed. Up to then, Iran was the only major source country for asylum seekers with access to the 30-day VOA (Brown, 2013).

Further clarification from respondents revealed that clandestine entry was to avoid deportation to their home country, as they did not have to risk being rejected by immigration officials at the airport. The role of smugglers is again noted, with a small number of respondents (n=16) indicating that they were only following their smuggler's instructions to enter Indonesia illegally; again, this seemed to be more prevalent for Afghan respondents. For some, that is, their illegal status continues throughout their journey, while others seek to enter undetected in order to avoid deportation back to their home countries if they were rejected at formal entry points. This latter appears to be quite an efficient strategy.

As shown in Figure 7.3, the majority of respondents (93.2 per cent) who deliberately entered Indonesia illegally did not encounter any border control or immigration authorities. This not only highlights the likely success of undocumented entry into Indonesia, but also perhaps is indicative of a less than efficient border control. Figure 7.4 shows the mode of transport used by respondents entering Indonesia. As anticipated, 86.6 per cent of all respondents entered Indonesia on a raft or boat, followed by 12.6 per cent who travelled by air.

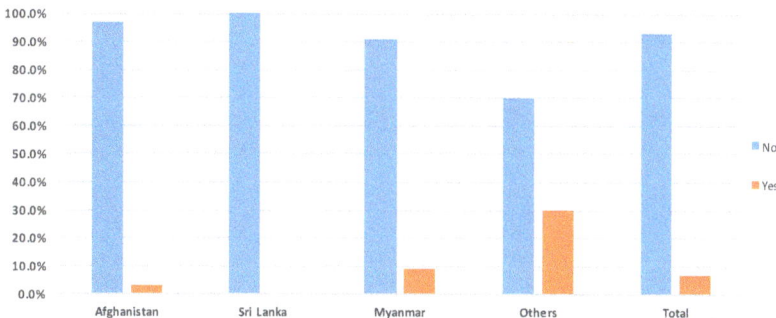

Figure 7.3: Encountering border control/immigration authorities when illegally entering Indonesia

Source: Transit migration survey (2010, 2012) (n=88).

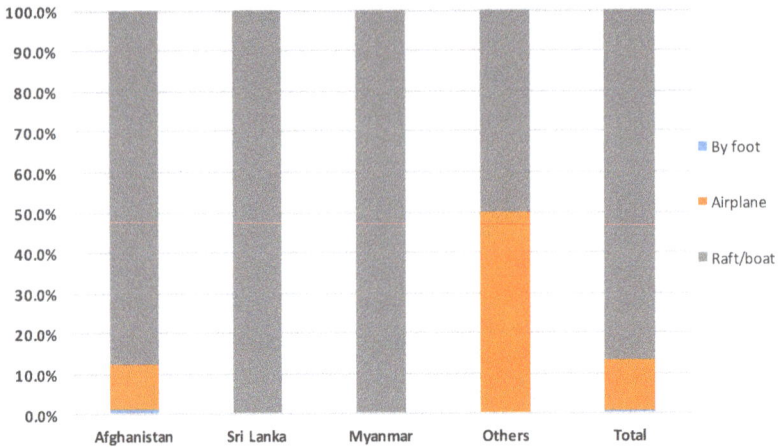

Figure 7.4: Mode of transport used to enter Indonesia
Source: Transit migration survey (2010, 2012) (n=119).

Sumatra plays a significant role in receiving asylum seekers: over half of respondents (57.7 per cent) indicated that they disembarked somewhere in Sumatra. Clearly, Sumatra's location is important: it is an island situated in Western Indonesia, of close proximity to Malaysia, and with the Strait of Malacca along its north-eastern shore separating it from the Malay Peninsula. This corridor of movement is well established and a complex industry of interconnected agents has developed to facilitate migration along this route. In addition to asylum seekers, illegal workers constitute another part of the irregular migration occurring in this region, with 200,000 to 300,000 Indonesians working in Malaysia estimated to have bypassed the regular migration channels in 2008 (Ford & Lyons, 2011, p. 109).

There are elements of corruption, with accounts of Malaysian people smugglers working together with the Indonesian navy to facilitate the return of undocumented Indonesian migrant workers (Ford & Lyons, 2013, pp. 216–17). Such examples contribute to the blurring of boundaries between legitimate and illegal practices which have led to the 'aspal' route, a greying of the illegal nature of labour migration of Indonesians to Singapore and Malaysia (Ford & Lyons, 2011). In this context, it is easy to see how smuggling operations can flourish in the Riau Islands and other locations along the north-eastern shores of Sumatra and how they are a magnet for asylum seekers using Indonesia as a transit point.

The role of the migration industry

It is important to acknowledge, however, that while it is possible to recognise some movements as being totally forced or voluntary, many migrations contain elements of both (Hugo, 1996). In the case of asylum seekers coming to Australia, for most respondents, the major reason impelling their migration was insecurity and fear of violence or war and conflict in the origin countries. But there were clearly also elements of choice involved in the decision-making process. Whether or not people move is clearly influenced by the social network of the potential movers and the extent to which they have family and friends in Australia. This is important in terms of both supply of information regarding the destination and assurance of support at the destination, as well as of the financing of the move itself. The nexus between the community in Australia and asylum seekers is important. Asylum seekers are in constant contact with their Australian contacts before and during the migration process, often using mobile phones.

However, it is crucial to recognise the pivotal role of the migration industry. Agents are a very important element in the asylum migration process. Very often, the agents are of the same nationality or ethnicity as the asylum seekers themselves. Almost all asylum seekers rely, to some extent, on people smugglers during at least some stage of the process, if not throughout the movement to Australia.

In most cases, it seems that people smugglers do not arrange the complete journey from the origin country to Australia, but rather one or more legs of the movement. The overall picture which emerges is not of an integrated international structure of tightly linked elements between origin and international destination, but one described by Missbach and Sinanu (2011, p. 66) as 'loose, temporary, acephalous networks', and by Içduygu and Toktas (2002, p. 46) as 'a loosely cast network consisting of hundreds of independent smaller units which cooperate along the way'.

Government officials and police in transit countries also play a role in the networks. Missbach and Sinanu (2011) point out that there is a contrast between Malaysia and Indonesia in this respect:

> Unlike in Malaysia, where asylum seekers face massive repression by the local police and immigration authorities even if they hold UNHCR documents, the Indonesian authorities normally accept these documents. (p. 74)

Throughout the corridors of movement, corrupt officials are a key element in the people smuggling process. The dangers that many asylum seekers face cannot be underestimated, and the personal tragedies that so frequently occur not only must be an important part of the narrative of asylum seekers, they must also (and they do) influence policy. It does need to be said also, however, that these corridors of movement do contain networks of support and communication which facilitate and support the migration.

In examining the role of the migration industry, it is crucial to recognise a number of its characteristics:

a. It did not arise in Indonesia in the 1990s purely to facilitate IMAs destined for Australia. It has a history extending over centuries.

b. The migration industry with Indonesia is very large and multilayered, from the involvement of international criminal organisations down to large cities with agents and local communities with subagents and sub-subagents.

c. There is a high level of complicity of government and government workers at all levels.

d. It is often linked to legal migration, with many agents being involved in both legal and illegal movement.

e. It is interlinked with family and regional networks.

f. It operates both for internal migration within Indonesia as well as for international movement.

g. It is extremely flexible, with workers in the industry able to diversify into other areas of activity if demand for their services in one area of migration should dry up. Accordingly, the industry can be very quick to respond to new opportunities and it cannot be killed off by destroying one avenue for undocumented migration (Munro, 2011).

h. The industry is embedded in local communities.

i. The industry has strong linkages with the fishing industry.

j. The migration industry has very strong, long historical connections with the Middle East and Malaysia, which have been utilised in facilitating the flow of intending IMAs.

k. In most cases, there is not a single agent; rather, migrants and intending migrants are passed through networks of agents at different points and often with new payments at each point.

l. Co-ethnics play a key role, and in the case of asylum seekers they are often working together with Indonesian colleagues. Some of the co-ethnics are unsuccessful former asylum seekers. The preexisting Arab community in Indonesia has been the anchor around which these co-ethnic agents have developed.

m. It is becoming increasingly professionalised.

The chains of migration-industry connections reaching to the areas which intending IMAs come from or pass through is an important element in understanding the movement of asylum seekers and irregular migrants. The connection with Malaysia is of particular importance, since most intending IMAs initially come to Kuala Lumpur. The migration industry has 'seeped into' and penetrated state institutes in both Malaysia and Indonesia.

Life in transit

There are around 10,000 asylum seekers and refugees currently in Indonesia registered with the United Nations High Commissioner for Refugees (UNHCR) and IOM.[4] Table 7.3 lists the ratings of respondents on their living conditions in Indonesia. As shown below, more respondents rated living conditions to be bad or very bad (a combined 60.5 per cent of respondents), than good or very good (about one fifth of respondents, 21.9 per cent).

Respondents were also asked to indicate if they had any contact with Indonesian locals. As Figure 7.5 illustrates, two thirds of respondents (67.2 per cent) did not socialise with any local Indonesians. This was followed by 18.5 per cent of respondents who socialised on occasion, and 14.3 per cent who socialised on a regular basis.

---

4   This was as of February 2014. There have subsequently been significant changes with the International Labor Organization (ILO) and IOM detaining, for the first time, more than 2,000 asylum seekers and refugees. Nearly one in four detainees is a child (416 total, 216 of them unaccompanied). This is leading to crowding of several of the centres and some violence. The total number of refugees and asylum seekers registered with the UNHCR is the lowest since March 2013: 9,547, after 2,385 have abandoned their claim for asylum.

Table 7.3: Negative experiences/abuses experienced by respondents

	Afghanistan (n=65)		Sri Lanka (n=26)		Myanmar (n=12)		Others (n=16)		Total (n=119)	
Freedom of communication totally denied	25	38.5%	12	46.2%	2	16.7%	5	31.2%	44	37.0%
Freedom of movement totally denied	20	30.8%	13	50.0%	1	8.3%	4	25.0%	38	31.9%
None	23	35.4%	1	3.8%	3	25.0%	8	50.0%	35	29.4%
Freedom of movement partially denied	12	18.5%	10	38.5%	5	41.7%	2	12.5%	29	24.4%
Freedom of communication partially denied	14	21.5%	9	34.6%	3	25.0%	2	12.5%	28	23.5%
Verbal/psychological abuse	12	18.5%	5	19.2%	1	8.3%	2	12.5%	20	16.8%
Physical abuse	12	18.5%	2	7.7%	3	25.0%	2	12.5%	19	16.0%
Money and personal possessions were 'confiscated'	13	20.0%	3	11.5%	2	16.7%	1	6.2%	19	16.0%
Was searched roughly	8	12.3%	2	7.7%	1	8.3%	3	18.8%	14	11.8%
Imprisonment without charges	5	7.7%	5	19.2%	-	-	-	-	10	8.4%
Asked for bribes to be treated well	3	4.6%	2	7.7%	-	-	-	-	5	4.2%
Documents were seized without permission	2	3.1%	1	3.8%	-	-	1	6.2%	4	3.4%
Forced to engage in activities against will	1	1.5%	-	-	-	-	-	-	1	0.8%
Work without wages	1	1.5%	-	-	-	-	-	-	1	0.8%
I was not paid accordingly for work	1	1.5%	-	-	-	-	-	-	1	0.8%

Source: Transit migration survey (2010, 2012) (n=119).

By and large, the majority of asylum seekers are quite isolated from local Indonesians. However, the social networks of asylum seekers evolve with the progression of their migration. Other migrants and detainees were cited as major sources of information by respondents, which illustrates how asylum seekers establish useful social networks with other migrants and asylum seekers. Moreover, their travel companions from one transit point to the next usually comprised of newly acquainted fellow asylum seekers who can be valuable sources of information, which again underlines how information gathering and sharing can improve in transit as asylum seekers learn en route.

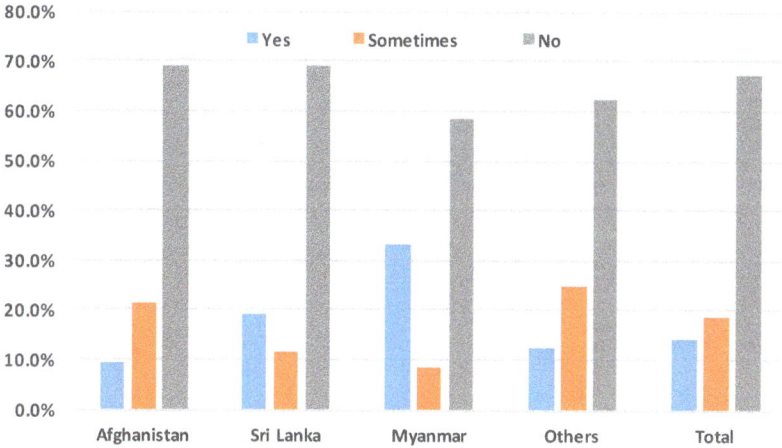

Figure 7.5: Socialising with local Indonesians
Source: Transit migration survey (2010, 2012) (n=119).

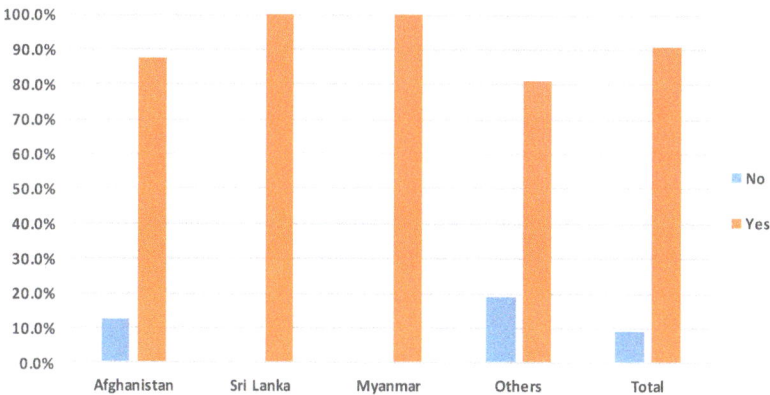

Figure 7.6: Have you applied for asylum in Indonesia?
Source: Transit migration survey (2010, 2012) (n=119).

Respondents were also asked to indicate what their status was in Indonesia and if they intended to irregularly onward migrate to Australia. As Figure 7.6 shows, the majority of respondents (90.8 per cent, n=108) had applied for asylum in Indonesia. Of this proportion, only three respondents had their applications rejected, while the remainder were approved or still pending. This proportion of respondents were then asked to state the reasons which would motivate them to irregularly onward migrate despite their asylum claims being approved or awaiting determination. As Table 7.4 shows, the majority of respondents (86.7 per cent) indicated that they did not intend to irregularly onward migrate to Australia and were adamant that they would wait to be resettled. However, it is suspected that most of this group of respondents were likely to have impressed this on the field researcher for fear of any recourse that might jeopardise their asylum applications.

Table 7.4: Reasons for irregularly migrating to Australia

	Afghanistan (n=55)		Sri Lanka (n=25)		Myanmar (n=12)		Others (n=13)		Total (n=105)	
Don't intend to escape	45	81.8%	24	96.0%	12	100.0%	10	76.9%	91	86.7%
Long wait for status determination	8	14.5%	0	0.0%	0	0.0%	1	7.7%	9	8.6%
Other	6	10.9%	0	0.0%	0	0.0%	2	15.4%	8	7.6%
Long wait for resettlement	3	5.5%	1	4.0%	0	0.0%	1	7.7%	5	4.8%
Want to go to a specific country of asylum	4	7.3%	0	0.0%	0	0.0%	1	7.7%	5	4.8%
Other	Afghanistan (n=6)		Sri Lanka (n=0)		Myanmar (n=0)		Others (n=2)		Total (n=8)	
Poor conditions in detention centre (bad treatment/ stressful)	5	83.3%	-	-	-	-	1	50.0%	6	75.0%
Registered so as to be safe and I wouldn't be harassed by authorities	1	16.7%	-	-	-	-	1	50.0%	2	25.0%

Source: Transit migration survey (2010, 2012) (n=105).

Nonetheless, it is worth examining the reasons that would motivate these respondents to further their illegal migration to Australia. As anticipated, a small number of respondents stated that a long wait for the determination of their asylum status (n=9) and/or a long wait for resettlement (n=5) would be a catalyst to irregularly onward migrate to Australia. Refugee status determination has been characterised as a period fraught with uncertainty, frustration and anxiety. Lengthy processing times, empty promises and perceived unresponsiveness of officials were mentioned. Asylum seekers feel trapped in a state of limbo whereby children are deprived of an education and adults denied gainful employment (Taylor & Rafferty-Brown, 2010a, pp. 157–59; 2010b, pp. 561, 573). The indefinite nature of this process has been argued as a driving force behind those who elect to irregularly onward migrate to Australia as they 'are acting out of a strongly felt need to end this limbo, even at the risk of death' (Taylor & Rafferty-Brown, 2010b, p. 561).

A small number of respondents (n=5) also indicated that they were only interested in a specific country of asylum, which at this stage is Australia. Indonesia was a desirable location to apply for asylum, as its UNHCR division was perceived to have faster processing times in terms of status determination and the resettlement of refugees. Respondents who indicated that they only wanted to seek refuge in Australia were motivated by opportunities to receive an education, train or upgrade their skills and find employment. Additionally, some respondents also reflected that, through family reunification, they would, in the future, apply for their family members to join them in Australia.

Under other reasons, poor conditions in detention centres were likely to encourage some respondents (n=6) to irregularly onward migrate to Australia. Conversely, a very small number (n=2) indicated that Australia was their primary destination and that registering with UNHCR was simply to obtain their attestation for safety reasons and avoid harassment from the Indonesian authorities.

Respondents were also asked to state their sources of financial support whilst in Indonesia. Given that asylum seekers and refugees do not have any rights to employment in Indonesia, it is unsurprising to see in Table 7.5 that none of the respondents had a full-time job, and only a small minority (n=2) had a part-time job.

As expected, the majority (83.2 per cent) were reliant on support from UNHCR/IOM. Over half of respondents (55.5 per cent) also indicated that they had some money in hand and a small number relied on remittances from family and friends overseas (n=16) and from non-governmental organisations (NGOs) (n=5). However, despite the lack of employment or income, respondents underlined the importance of sending remittances back to their home country, as illustrated in Figure 7.7.

Table 7.5: Source of financial support in Indonesia

	Afghanistan (n=65)		Sri Lanka (n=26)		Myanmar (n=12)		Others (n=16)		Total (n=119)	
Full-time job	-	-	-	-	-	-	-	-	-	-
UNHCR/IOM	51	78.5%	25	96.2%	12	100.0%	11	68.8%	99	83.2%
Money in hand	49	75.4%	4	15.4%	5	41.7%	8	50.0%	66	55.5%
Family and friends abroad	11	16.9%	3	11.5%	-	-	2	12.5%	16	13.4%
Other NGOs	4	6.2%	1	3.8%	-	-	-	-	5	4.2%
Part-time job	-	-	-	-	1	8.3%	1	6.2%	2	1.7%

Source: Transit migration survey (2010, 2012) (n=119).

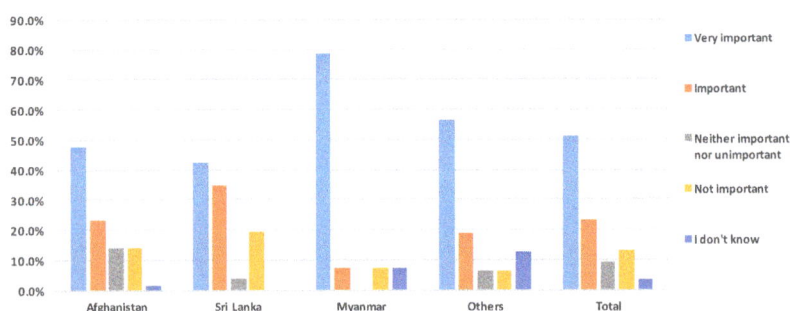

Figure 7.7: Importance of sending remittances to family back in home country

Source: Transit migration survey (2010, 2012) (n=121).

Just over half of respondents (51.2 per cent) indicated that it was very important for them to send remittances back to their respective home countries, and a further 23.1 per cent felt that it was important to do so. Less than one tenth (9.1 per cent) stated that it was neither important nor unimportant to do so. This reflects the pressure of financially supporting their families at home and repaying debts incurred in funding their migration, which fuels the likelihood of irregular onward migration to Australia.

Respondents were asked what reasons would encourage them to remain in Indonesia, if the Indonesian Government permitted permanent resettlement. Table 7.6 shows one fifth of respondents (20.2 per cent) indicated that they were motivated to further their journey and had no desire to remain in Indonesia. Conversely, 40.3 per cent of respondents indicated that friendly Indonesian locals were a positive factor for remaining in Indonesia. Although seeking protection was the underlying factor behind the selection of Australia as their final destination, economic reasons were also important in their decision-making process. As much as the main reasons for transiting in Indonesia were to flee from conflict and to live in peace, it does not necessarily mean that economic reasons were not relevant.

Table 7.6: Reasons encouraging settlement in Indonesia

	Afghanistan (n=65)		Sri Lanka (n=26)		Myanmar (n=12)		Others (n=16)		Total (n=119)	
Friendly locals	22	33.8%	15	57.7%	6	50.0%	5	31.2%	48	40.3%
It is a peaceful country	24	36.9%	12	46.2%	7	58.3%	4	25.0%	47	39.5%
No particular reason	23	35.4%	4	15.4%	-	-	4	25.0%	31	26.1%
I don't want to stay in Indonesia	11	16.9%	3	11.5%	4	33.3%	6	37.5%	24	20.2%
Lack of money to continue my trip	-	-	4	15.4%	5	41.7%	-	-	9	7.6%
Other	5	7.7%	-	-	3	25.0%	1	6.2%	9	7.6%
Low cost of living	2	3.1%	4	15.4%	1	8.3%	1	6.2%	8	6.7%
Too tired to continue my journey	2	3.1%	3	11.5%	2	16.7%	-	-	7	5.9%
I was/am well adjusted	1	1.5%	3	11.5%	1	8.3%	-	-	5	4.2%
A good job	0	0.0%	2	7.7%	3	25.0%	0	0.0%	5	4.2%
Other	Afghanistan (n=5)		Sri Lanka (n=3)		Myanmar (n=0)		Others (n=1)		Total (n=9)	
Marriage to a local	2	3.1%	1	3.8%	0	0.0%	0	0.0%	3	2.5%
Indonesia allows refugees to live in the community	3	60.0%	2	66.7%	-	-	1	100.0%	6	66.7%
Indonesia is an Islamic country	2	40.0%	1	33.3%	-	-	-	-	3	33.3%

Source: Transit migration survey (2010, 2012) (n=119).

Next steps of transiting migrants

Analysing preferred destinations for resettlement sheds light on the decision-making process of asylum seekers and assists in understanding or deconstructing the labels of genuine asylum seekers or economic migrants attached to this particular group of migrants. Respondents who applied for asylum in Indonesia (n=108) were asked to state the countries which they would like to be resettled in, and Figure 7.8 indicates their first, second and third choices.

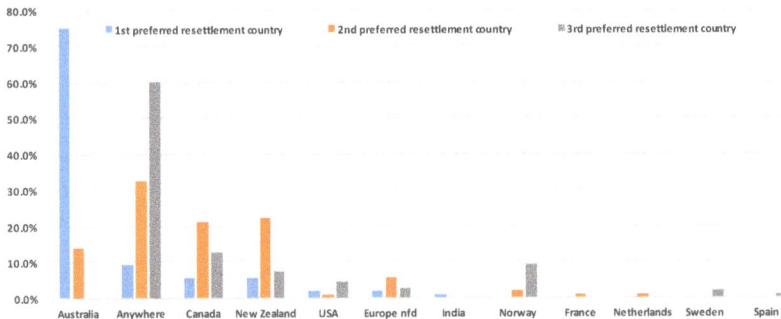

Figure 7.8: Preferred countries of resettlement
Source: Transit migration survey (2010, 2012) (n=108).
Note: 'nfd' means 'not further defined'.

A strong desire to be resettled in Australia was displayed by three quarters of respondents (75.0 per cent) indicating Australia as their first choice, while nearly one tenth (9.3 per cent) indicated that they would be happy to be resettled anywhere in the world. Remaining respondents stated Canada (5.6 per cent), New Zealand (5.6 per cent), USA (1.9 per cent) and Europe. Not further defined (1.9 per cent) and India (0.9 per cent) were the other preferred first choices. This finding is not surprising, given that all of the respondents were knowingly en route to Australia and had committed to Australia as their final destination. It is fair to assume that most respondents, at this near-final stage of their migration (i.e. transit in Indonesia), would nominate Australia as their preferred location. However, if respondents were asked this question before they commenced their journey, or at the early stages of their migration, Australia might not be as prominent. Nonetheless, beyond Australia as the most preferred destination, the willingness to be resettled in any country (as reflected in their second and third choices), and the fact that only a small proportion of respondents had second and third choices, suggests that attempts to dichotomise genuine from nongenuine refugees are perhaps too simplistic.

Respondents reflected mixed reasons for leaving their respective home countries and for choosing Australia as a destination. While reasons relating to protection and escape from conflict and persecution can overlap with factors associated with employment, education or simply the opportunity to lead a better life, it would appear that for many respondents, the principal characteristic of a preferred resettlement country is to seek protection.

> Any country that can guarantee freedom. (SL05TP1)

> Any country, even Indonesia. (SL04TP1)

> Canada, Australia, New Zealand. They are the same [in terms of safety, freedom and opportunities]. (AF03TP2)

> Anywhere that I can get education and freedom. (AF10TP2)

Onward migration from Indonesia

Figure 7.9 shows that a small number of Afghan and Sri Lankan respondents have attempted this journey more than once. Irregular migration is a very costly affair, and Myanmese respondents are probably the least likely to be able to afford multiple attempts. Overall, however, it is evident that most respondents (95.9 per cent) have only attempted to make their way to Australia once.

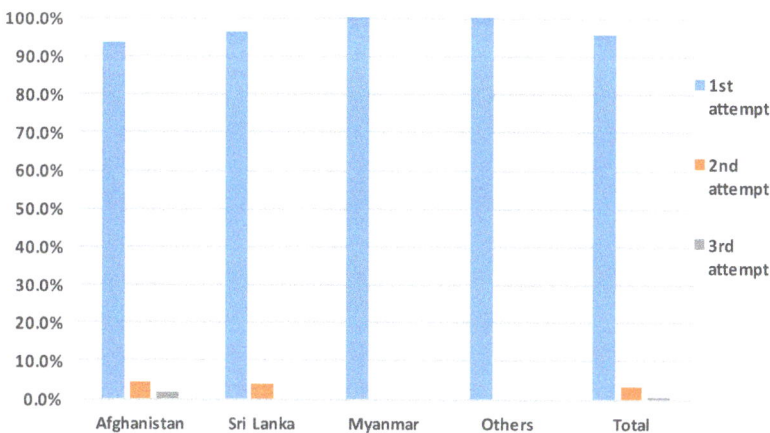

Figure 7.9: Number of attempts to Australia
Source: Transit migration survey (2010, 2012) (n=121).

When it comes to making arrangements for the journey from Indonesia to Australia, it is clear that smugglers have a crucial role, as Table 7.7 shows. One third of respondents (32.8 per cent) engaged the services of smugglers, with 16.8 per cent of all respondents transiting in Indonesia engaging with a local smuggler only, 14.3 per cent engaging with their previous smuggler and local smuggler (i.e. same network) and a small number (1.7 per cent, n=2) who used a smuggler based outside of Indonesia along with a local smuggler.

It would seem that almost two thirds of respondents (64.7 per cent) made arrangements for the journey to Australia while transiting in Indonesia. Smugglers and individual operators based in Indonesia are significant in the final leg of an asylum seeker's journey to Australia. The sample size does warrant caution, and while the findings are certainly not conclusive, they do suggest that while transnational smuggling networks can be quite efficient in getting asylum seekers to Indonesia, asylum seekers have to be resourceful in negotiating the final leg of their passage to Australia with smugglers based in Indonesia.

Table 7.7: Stakeholders assisting with migration to Australia by nationality

	Afghanistan (n=65)		Sri Lanka (n=26)		Myanmar (n=12)		Others (n=16)		Total (n=119)	
Previous and local agent	11	16.9%	1	3.8%	-	-	5	31.2%	17	14.3%
Myself	-	-	-	-	-	-	1	6.3%	1	0.8%
Family/relative/ friend migrating with me	-	-	-	-	-	-	-	-	-	-
Family/relative/ friend in Australia	-	-	-	-	-	-	-	-	-	-
Family/relative/ friend abroad	-	-	-	-	-	-	-	-	-	-
Family/relative/ friend in Indonesia	-	-	-	-	-	-	-	-	-	-
Family/relative/ friend at home	-	-	-	-	-	-	-	-	-	-
Smuggler in Australia	-	-	-	-	-	-	-	-	-	-
Smuggler abroad and local smuggler	2	3.1%	-	-	-	-	-	-	2	1.7%

	Afghanistan (n=65)		Sri Lanka (n=26)		Myanmar (n=12)		Others (n=16)		Total (n=119)	
A local smuggler only	17	29.2%	1	3.8%	-	-	2	12.5%	20	16.8%
Smuggler at home	-	-	-	-	-	-	-	-	-	-
A smuggler (unknown location)	-	-	-	-	-	-	-	-	-	-
I don't know	-	-	-	-	-	-	-	-	-	-
Haven't arranged anything due to detention	33	50.8%	24	92.3%	12	100.0%	8	50.0%	77	64.7%
Was resettled by UNHCR	2	3.10%	-	-	-	-	-	-	2	1.70%

Source: Transit migration survey (2010, 2012) (n=121).

Independent units, individuals, and local service providers are crucial. As Figure 7.10 shows, half of respondents (n=20) who managed to make arrangements to travel to Australia engaged the services of an Indonesian local (i.e. local service provider) to assist with some aspect of their journey.

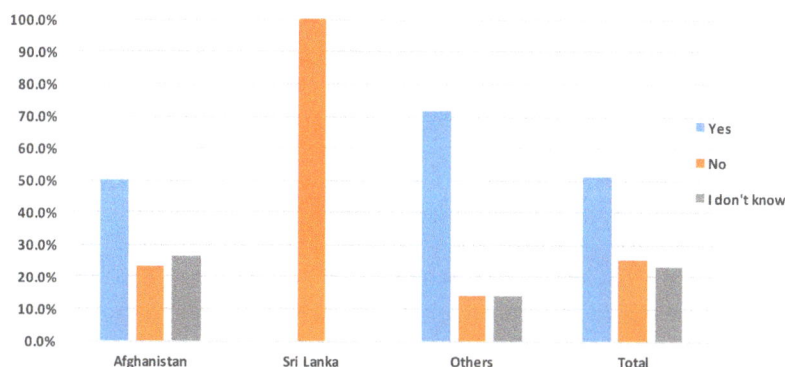

Figure 7.10: Intending IMAs to Australia: Use of an Indonesian local to arrange passage

Source: Transit migration survey (2010, 2012) (n=40).

At a mean cost of USD5,364, the Indonesian–Australian leg is evidently the most expensive part of their journey, when considering that the mean cost of respondents' overall migration to Australia is USD10,310. Asylum seekers usually have a 'contract' or an agreement of sorts with smugglers in case their migration to Australia was unsuccessful, as indicated by the majority (70 per cent, n=28) of respondents who used a smuggler (see Table 7.8).

Table 7.8: Contract or agreement with smuggler for failed migration to Australia

	Afghanistan (n=30)		Sri Lanka (n=2)		Others (n=8)		Total (n=40)	
Yes	21	70.0%	2	100.0%	5	62.5%	28	70.0%
No	9	30.0%	0	0.0%	3	37.5%	12	30.0%
	Afghanistan (n=21)		Sri Lanka (n=2)		Others (n=5)		Total (n=28)	
Work in Australia	-	-	-	-	-	-	-	-
Full or partial return of money for failed migration	1	4.8%	0	0.0%	2	40.0%	3	10.7%
Payment upon successful migration	3	14.3%	0	0.0%	0	0.0%	3	10.7%
Down payment and finalisation upon success	8	38.1%	2	100.0%	1	20.0%	11	39.3%
Payment managed by third party based on outcome	11	52.4%	0	0.0%	0	0.0%	11	39.3%
Agent will attempt to resend the migrant between 1-3 more times	12	57.1%	0	0.0%	3	60.0%	15	53.6%

Source: Transit migration survey (2010, 2012) (n=40).

Respondents were also asked how long they had to wait in Indonesia before embarking on their journey to Australia. As Table 7.9 shows, more than half (a combined 42.5 per cent [n=17]) of respondents, excluding 'I don't know' results, transited in Indonesia for 4 weeks or less, compared with a combined 30 per cent (n=12) who transited for a longer duration, ranging from 4 upwards towards 24 weeks. Overall, the waiting times in Indonesia are similar to those in previous transit countries like Malaysia and Thailand, with most respondents spending less than a month before continuing their migration to the next destination.

Table 7.9: Duration spent in Indonesia before departing for Australia

	Afghanistan (n=30)		Sri Lanka (n=2)		Others (n=8)		Total (n=40)	
Less than 1 week	4	13.3%	-	-	1	12.5%	5	12.5%
1 to < 2 weeks	3	10.0%	-	-	2	25.0%	5	12.5%
2 to < 4 weeks	6	20.0%	-	-	1	12.5%	7	17.5%
4 to < 8 weeks	3	10.0%	1	50.0%	-	-	4	10.0%
8 to < 16 weeks	4	13.3%	-	-	2	25.0%	6	15.0%
16 to < 24 weeks	1	3.3%	-	-	1	12.5%	2	5.0%
I don't know	9	30.0%	1	50.0%	1	12.5%	11	27.5%

Source: Transit migration survey (2010, 2012) (n=40).

In general, the majority of the embarkation locations stated by respondents in Table 7.10 tended to be around East Java and the Lesser Sunda Islands in South Eastern Indonesia, evidently favoured launching points due to their close proximity to Australia.

Table 7.10: Location from which respondents departed for Australia

Location of departure	Province	Frequency	Per cent
I don't know	-	15	37.5%
Unspecified hours of drive from Jakarta	-	5	12.5%
Kupang	East Nusa Tenggara	5	12.5%
Surabaya	East Java	3	7.5%
Lombok	West Nusa Tenggara	3	7.5%
Jakarta	Jakarta	3	7.5%
Mataram	Central Java	2	5%
Unspecified hours of drive from Bogor	-	1	2.5%
Sumbawa Island	West Nusa Tenggara	1	2.5%
Cilacap	Central Java	1	2.5%
Bali	Bali	1	2.5%

Source: Transit migration survey (2010, 2012) (n=40).

Respondents were asked if they had any intentions to return to their home countries after resettlement in Australia. As Figure 7.11 shows, only a small number of respondents (10.5 per cent, n=9) intended to return to their home country, compared with 41.0 per cent who did not. This indicates that there is a possibility that some refugees, even after resettlement in Australia, would voluntarily return to their home countries in the future.

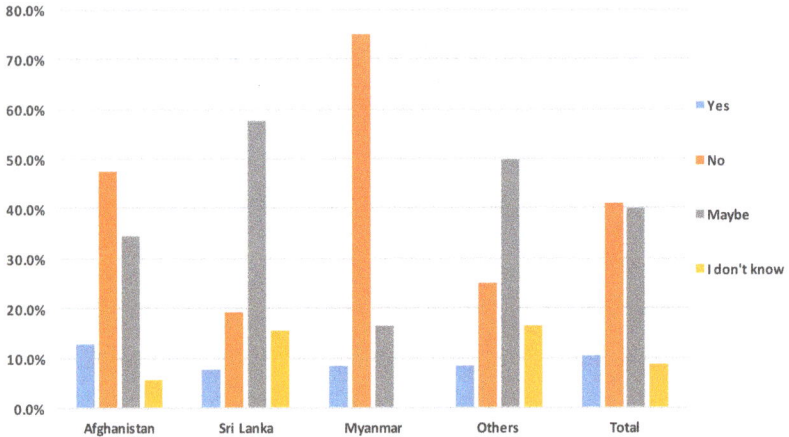

Figure 7.11: Intention to return to home country after resettlement
Source: Transit migration survey (2010, 2012) (n=105).

Some 85.1 per cent of respondents (n=103) in Figure 7.12 below who indicated that in spite of negative experiences they have had with irregularly migrating, they would still have migrated even if they knew of the difficulties before leaving their home countries.

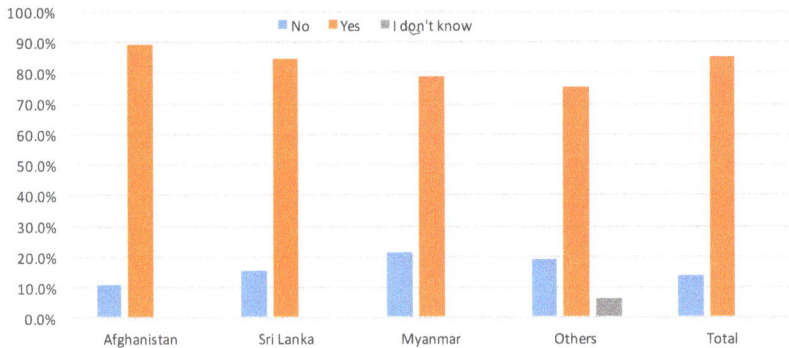

Figure 7.12: Would they still have migrated if they had known of the difficulties of irregular migration?
Source: Transit migration survey (2010, 2012) (n=121).

Conclusion

The study found that the majority of respondents would enter Indonesia illegally, often by boat. There were a variety of reasons for this, but the main factor was simply their inability to travel legally. Their migration status might have been legal from the beginning of their journey, but shifted towards illegality in Thailand or Malaysia. For some, entering illegally was a strategy to avoid detection at official ports or channels, so as to eliminate the possibility of deportation to their home countries. The porous borders of Indonesia are further underlined, as the majority of asylum seekers who entered illegally were able to do so undetected. Moreover, respondents indicated that the Riau Islands and parts of Sumatra were their landing points—areas where Indonesian labour migrants are also smuggled to and from Malaysia and Singapore, underscoring the challenges in addressing the arrival of asylum seekers in Indonesia.

Life in Indonesia as indicated by respondents is generally poor. Although respondents had access to services, the quality of education and housing was poor. The majority of respondents were also quite isolated and did not socialise with Indonesians. Asylum seekers might be open to settling in Indonesia; however, poor living conditions, indefinite processing and resettlement times and negative experiences can drive asylum seekers to onward migrate to Australia.

While smugglers play a significant role, their networks seem to be weaker in Indonesia. Respondents transiting through Thailand and Malaysia often used the same smuggling network, whereby the smuggler used to travel from their last transit point to Malaysia would arrange for another smuggler in Malaysia to assist with the migration. However, there were fewer respondents who used the same network of agents in Indonesia. This is not only indicative of weaker transnational smuggling networks in Indonesia, but also underlines the importance of independent smugglers as well as independent units or local service providers assisting with other aspects of the migration.

The concept of transit migration is problematic, conceptually and politically, but it refers to a phenomenon of increasing significance in the Asian region where migration is both a cause and effect of rapid economic growth. However, in several countries in the region, governance issues, lack of institutional and human capacity, excessive rent taking and transaction costs dilute migration's potential positive developmental impacts, and in this context, as this study has shown, irregular migration and transiting is likely to increase in scale and impact.

Reference list

Brown, H. (2013). Indonesia to change visa requirements for Iranians entering the country following request from PM Kevin Rudd. Retrieved from ABC News: www.abc.net.au/news/2013-07-18/indonesia-to-change-visa-requirements-for-iranians/4829434.

Düvell, F., Triandafyllidou, A., & Vollmer, B. (2008). Ethical issues in irregular migration research. Cladestino Project. Retrieved from www.compas.ox.ac.uk/media/PR-2008-Clandestino_Ethics.pdf.

Ford, M., & Lyons, L. (2011). Travelling the Aspal route: Grey labour migration through an Indonesian border town. In Aspinall, E., & van Klinken, G. (Eds), *The state and illegality in Indonesia* (pp. 107–122). Leiden: Kitlv Press.

Ford, M., & Lyons, L. (2013). Outsourcing border security: NGO involvement in the monitoring, processing and assistance of Indonesian nationals returning illegally by sea. *Contemporary Southeast Asia, 35*(2), 215–34. doi.org/10.1355/cs35-2d

Henley & Partners. (2013). *The Henley & Partners Visa Restriction Index 2013*. Jersey: Author.

Hugo, G. J. (1996). Environmental concerns and international migration. *International Migration Review, 30*(1), 105–31. doi.org/10.2307/2547462

Hugo, G. J. (2011). *Economic, social and civic contributions of first and second generation humanitarian entrants*. Canberra: Department of Immigration and Citizenship.

Hugo, G. J., & Dissanayake, L. (2014). *The process of Sri Lankan migration to Australia focusing on irregular migrants seeking asylum— stage 1*. First draft of a report presented to the collaborative research program on the international movement of the people, Department of Immigration and Border Protection and Crawford School of Public Policy. Canberra: The Australian National University.

Hugo, G. J., & Napitupulu, C. J. (2015). Boats, borders, and ballot boxes: Asylum seekers on Australia's northern shore. In van der Velde, M., & van Naerssen, T. (Eds), *Mobility and migration choices: Thresholds to crossing borders* (pp. 213–34). London: Routledge.

Içduygu, A., & Toktas, S. (2002). How do smuggling and trafficking operate via irregular border crossings in the Middle East? Evidence from fieldwork in Turkey. *International Migration, 40*(6), 25–54. doi.org/10.1111/1468-2435.00222

Jayasuriya, D., & McAuliffe, M. (2013). *Placing recent Sri Lankan maritime arrivals in a broader migration context*. Irregular Migration Research Program, occasional paper series 02. Canberra: Department of Immigration and Border Protection. Retrieved from www.border. gov.au/ReportsandPublications/Documents/research/placing-recent-sri-lankan-maritime-arrivals-broader-migration-context.pdf.

Jones, S. (2000). *Making money off migrants*. Hong Kong: Asia 2000 Limited.

Kunz, E. F. (1973). The refugee in flight: Kinetic models and forms of displacement. *International Migration Review, 7*(2), 125–46. doi.org/10.2307/3002424

Lander, B. (1996, 1 June). Indonesia: Far from paradise. *Refugees Magazine, 104*. Retrieved from www.unhcr.org/publications/refugeemag/3b558c2a4/refugees-magazine-issue-104-unhcrs-world-indonesia-far-paradise.html.

Ley, D., & Kobayashi, A. (2005). Back to Hong Kong: Return migration or transnational sojourn? *Global Networks, 5*(2), 111–27. doi.org/10.1111/j.1471-0374.2005.00110.x

Missbach, A. (2013). Waiting on the islands of 'stuckedness': Managing asylum seekers in island detention camps in Indonesia from the late 1970s to the Early 2000s. *ASEAS—Austrian Journal of South-East Asian Studies, 6*(2), 281–306.

Missbach, A., & Sinanu, F. (2011). 'The scum of the earth?' Foreign people smugglers and their local counterparts in Indonesia. *Journal of Current Southeast Asian Affairs, 30*(4), 57–87.

Munro, P. (2011). People smuggling and the resilience of criminal networks in Indonesia. *Journal of Policing, Intelligence and Counter Terrorism, 6*(1), 40–50.

Skrobanek, S., Boonpakdi, N., & Janthakeero, C. (1997). *The traffic in women: Human realities of the international sex trade.* London and New York: Zed Books.

Taylor, S., & Rafferty-Brown, B. (2010a). Difficult journeys: Accessing refugee protection in Indonesia. *Monash University Law Review, 36*(3), 138–61.

Taylor, S., & Rafferty-Brown, B. (2010b). Waiting for life to begin: The plight of asylum seekers caught by Australia's Indonesian solution. *International Journal of Refugee Law, 22*(4), 558–92. doi.org/10.1093/ijrl/eeq034

United Nations High Commissioner for Refugees. (2014). *UNHCR Indonesia—Fact Sheet, March 2014.* Retrieved April 5, 2014 from www.unhcr.org/50001bda9.pdf.

United Nations Office on Drugs and Crime. (2009). *Smuggling of migrants from India to Europe and in particular to UK: A study on Tamil Nadu.* New Delhi: Author. Retrieved from www.unodc.org/documents/human-trafficking/Smuggling_of_Migrants_from_India.pdf.

8

The process of Sri Lankan migration to Australia focusing on irregular migrants seeking asylum

Graeme Hugo and Lakshman Dissanayake

Introduction

Sri Lanka is one of the contemporary world's major emigration nations. The United Nations (2013) has shown that there were 1.25 million Sri Lankan–born persons living outside of their country of birth, equivalent to 5.9 per cent of the current Sri Lankan resident population. Australia is one of the important destination countries, with an estimated 106,280 Sri Lankan–born residents in 2013 (Australian Bureau of Statistics, 2013). While Australia has only 7.9 per cent of the overseas Sri Lankan population, it is an important part of the Sri Lankan diaspora. Not only has the Sri Lankan presence in Australia been established for a long period (Weerasooria, 1988), but as well it comprises predominantly permanent settlers who have maintained important linkages with their homeland.

Sri Lankan immigrants are the 13th largest overseas-born group in Australia and their movement to Australia has a long history. It has become increasingly complex, with movement in both directions and increasing levels of both permanent and non-permanent migration. This complexity increased in 2012–13, with the sudden influx of over 6,000 Sri Lankan irregular maritime arrivals (IMAs) seeking asylum, and with the repatriation of significant numbers. This study adopts a multisite, mixed-method approach to analysing this mobility within the broader context of all Sri Lankan migration to Australia. By collecting, analysing and interpreting quantitative and qualitative information from origin, transit and destination countries, the study seeks to understand the nature and drivers of the process of irregular movement from Sri Lanka to Australia. It investigates the characteristics of the movers and the decision-making processes that underlie irregular migration, selecting a destination and whether or not to return. It examines how individual, family and contextual factors influence the migration as well as the role of social networks and the Sri Lankan diaspora. The findings are related to migration theory and their implications for understanding irregular migration more generally and Australian IMA policy are discussed.

Methods and data

In Sri Lanka, we collected existing research and secondary data sources and carried out key informant interviews with the Sri Lanka Police, Immigration and Emigration Officials and Criminal Investigation Department staff, since they deal directly with the Sri Lankan irregular maritime migrants who are captured at the Sri Lankan border, as well as with those who are sent back by the Australian authorities after disqualifying them for asylum status. The main secondary data sources that the current study used for its analysis are:

- the Sri Lanka Population Census 2012 (5 per cent sample);
- data from the Department of Immigration and Emigration;
- data from the Sri Lanka Bureau of Foreign Employment;
- airport statistics;
- data from the Criminal Investigation Department on IMAs;
- data from a few regional police stations; and
- data and information from various media reports.

In addition, two people smugglers, four facilitators and 17 IMAs were interviewed to gather information about the process of irregular migration to Australia.

The Australian secondary data used here is of two types. The first is the quinquennial population census, which is a high quality total count of the population in each year that ends with a one or a six. Sri Lankans can be identified by their place of birth, their ancestry or the language they speak at home. Here, we mainly use the birthplace information. Extensive use is also made of data collected at the Australian borders about all persons arriving and departing.

Sri Lanka—A quintessential emigration country

Sri Lanka's geographical position has had a significant impact on population movement into and out of the country over the years. At the latest census of 2012, the total population of Sri Lanka was estimated to be 20,277,597. Sri Lanka is a multiethnic country, comprising 75 per cent Sinhalese, 11 per cent Sri Lankan Tamils, 4 per cent Indian Tamils and 9 per cent Moors (and less than 1 per cent of various other ethnicities such as Burgher and Malays). The Sinhalese population is substantially distributed over the southern and western parts of Sri Lanka, while Muslims dominate the eastern region and most Sri Lankan Tamils live in the northern part of the island. A substantial proportion of Tamils live in the Colombo district, where the commercial capital is located.

The post-independence era has been significantly marked by the conflict between Sinhalese and Tamils, and these tensions still have an enormous impact on political and economic development as well as migration patterns in Sri Lanka. Sri Lanka experienced a series of sociopolitical disturbances over around 30 years, which reduced growth and discouraged investment, destroyed human and physical capital, redirected natural resources to non-productive uses, and caused a dramatic deterioration in the quality of life—not only in communities in the north and east, but across all communities on the entire island. Impacts of the 30-year war, which ended in 2009, loom large when considering contemporary events in Sri Lanka. This is also the case when examining the movement of IMAs to Australia, particularly as the majority came from the war-affected northern and eastern parts of the island.

Sri Lanka is a significant emigration nation with the United Nations (2013) showing that the number of Sri Lankan–born living in other countries increased from 0.8 to 1.3 million between 2000 and 2013, the equivalent of roughly 5–6 per cent of the resident population. Figure 8.1 shows the distribution of these migrants. Jayasuriya and McAuliffe (2013, pp. 6–7) explain that migration outflows of Sri Lankans can be categorised into five groups:

- temporary workers (skilled, semi-skilled and unskilled)
- skilled settlers
- students
- asylum seekers
- tourists, including pilgrims to Nepal and India.

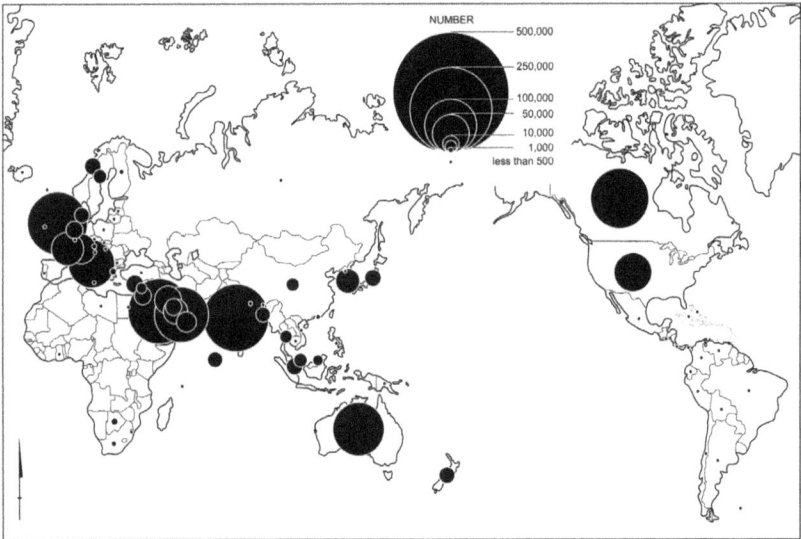

Figure 8.1: Countries of residence of the Sri Lankan diaspora, 2013
Source: United Nations (2013).

Since several of these flows are temporary or circular, not all are captured in United Nations' estimates of the numbers of Sri Lankan–born persons resident outside of Sri Lanka. Contract labour migration of low-skilled workers, especially female domestic workers to the Middle East and to a lesser extent Southeast and East Asia, has increased, as Figure 8.2 shows.

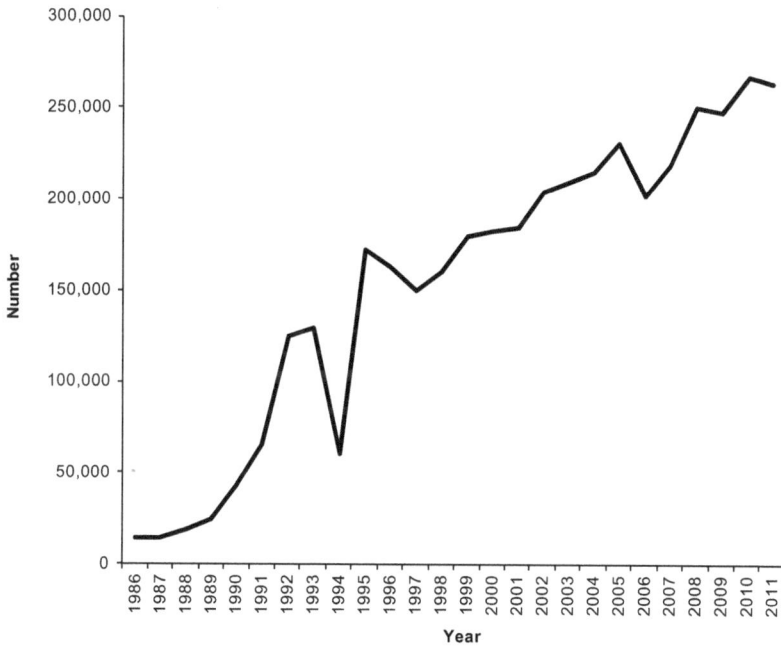

Figure 8.2: Sri Lanka: Departures for foreign employment, 1986–2011
Source: Sri Lanka Bureau of Foreign Employment.

Irregular migration has been an important element in Sri Lankan emigration for several decades. It is difficult to estimate the size of this outflow because it occurs outside of the formal migration system. There has also been an outflow of refugees and asylum seekers, mostly associated with civil conflict involving Tamils in the north and east of the country. India has been the main destination, but as Jayasuriya and McAuliffe (2013, p. 15) point out, people have also travelled within Sri Lanka, as well as to Australia, the UK, France, Switzerland, Canada, Germany, Japan and a number of other European, North American and Asian countries.

Links between Sri Lanka and its diaspora have become increasingly important. A major dimension of this has been the sending of remittances to Sri Lanka by expatriates overseas on a permanent or temporary basis. Remittances make up 10 per cent of the national gross domestic product (GDP). While the Middle East is the most important source of remittances, Australia is also a significant source. This reflects the fact that the Australian Sri Lankan community is a tightly knit one, maintaining strong links with the homeland (Weerasooria, 1988). It is important to note that there are also high levels of internal migration within Sri Lanka. At the 2012 population census, almost a fifth of Sri Lankans (19 per cent, or 3.86 million) were living in a district other than the one in which they were born.

There is some evidence in Sri Lanka of a strong link between internal migration and international migration (Hugo, 2015; King, Skeldon, & Vullnetari, 2008). Internal migration, especially rural–urban movement, can be the first stage of a subsequent international migration (Cornelius, 1992; del Rey Poveda, 2007, pp. 291–92; King, 1976, pp. 70–72; Lozano-Ascencio, Roberts, & Bean, 1999; Skeldon, 2006, pp. 22–24; Zabin & Hughes, 1995). Nevertheless, direct migration from rural areas to international destinations also occurs in international labour migration flows (Cornelius, 1992, pp. 162–63; Lozano-Ascencio et al., 1999, p. 140; Zabin & Hughes, 1995). Emigration may also be preceded by more than one internal move in multistep migration, perhaps starting from a small village, migrating to a provincial town and then on to the national capital before proceeding with an international move (Lozano-Ascencio et al., 1999). This suggests that it is imperative to study both the internal as well as international migration dynamics in order to understand the environment in which IMAs make decisions to migrate to Australia.

The effects of remittances and the obvious wealth of returning migrants has sent a strong signal to many Sri Lankans, especially young people, that migration offers an avenue to income-related success. The culture of migration is important to factor in any strategy addressing irregular migration to Australia.

Sri Lankan migration to Australia

There is a long history of migration from Sri Lanka to Australia extending over most of the period of European settlement. Table 8.1 summarises the major historical waves of Sri Lankan settlement migration to Australia. The Sri Lankan community in Australia is currently the sixth largest in the Sri Lankan diaspora, but Table 8.2 shows that it is only relatively recently that it has assumed a significant size.

Table 8.1: Major historical trends in Sri Lankan migration to Australia

Period	Description	Ethnicity of settlers	Location of settlement
Up to 1870s	Small-scale individual movement between British colonies	Sinhalese	NSW, Victoria
1870s–1900	Flows of contract workers for sugar plantations, permanent settlers	Sinhalese	North Queensland, NT, North Western Australia
1870s–1900	Small-scale individual movement to goldfields		Victoria, NSW
1900–50	Limited family migration	Sinhalese	Northern Australia
1950–80	Migration of descendants of European settlers, Colombo Plan students	Burghers	Victoria, capital cities
1980s–Present	Skilled and family migration, refugees	Tamils, Sinhalese	Victoria, capital cities
2012–13	Asylum seekers	Tamils	Victoria (on bridging visas) and detention centres

Source: Authors' own research.

Table 8.2: Growth of the Sri Lankan–born population in Australia, 1901–2011

Year	Population	% Growth per annum
1901	609	
1911	611	0.03
1921	637	0.42
1933	638	0.01
1954	1,961	5.49
1961	3,433	8.33
1966	5,562	10.13
1971	9,018	10.15
1976	14,761	10.36
1981	17,900	3.93
1986	23,600	5.68
1991	40,400	11.35
1996	46,984	3.07
2001	53,461	2.62
2006	62,257	3.09
2011	86,412	6.78
2013	106,280	3.21

Source: Data derived from Australian censuses, 1901 to 2011.

Note: The 1947 census population has been excluded because Sri Lanka and India were recorded together in that year. Growth between 2011 and 2013 is of the estimated resident population.

The pattern of settlement migration since 1960 is shown in Figure 8.3 and it indicates that in the modern era there has been considerable annual variation in the flow of Sri Lankan permanent migrants to Australia. The final peak was in recent years and coincided with the end of the Civil War and an unprecedented increase in Australian skilled immigration associated with the mining boom (Hugo, 2014).

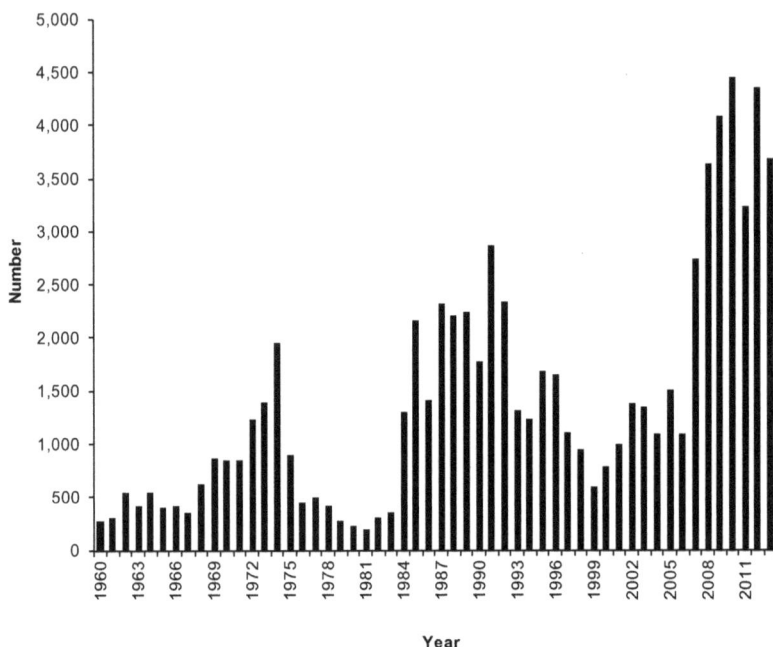

Figure 8.3: Settler arrivals from Sri Lanka to Australia, 1959–60 to 2012–13

Source: Department of Immigration and Multicultural and Indigenous Affairs, *Australian Immigration: Consolidated Statistics*, various issues; Department of Immigration and Border Protection (DIBP), unpublished data.

Note: Settler arrivals from 2006–07 onwards are by country of birth.

One of the defining characteristics of permanent immigration to Australia since the mid-1990s has been the increasing focus of immigrant selection on skill and a reduction in family migration (Hugo, 1999). This has been the case in Sri Lankan immigration to Australia. Figure 8.4 shows how skilled migration has increasingly dominated Sri Lankan immigration in recent years.

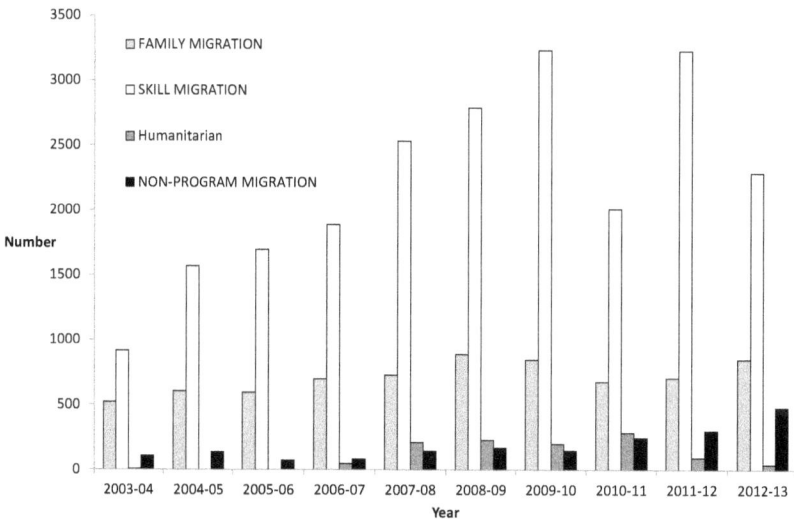

Figure 8.4: Australia: Sri Lankan–born by visa category, 2003–04 to 2012–13

Source: DIBP, unpublished data.

Particular attention in recent years has focused on asylum seeker and refugee migration to Australia from Sri Lanka. Figure 8.4[1] shows that refugee migration has been a small but significant factor. In terms of refugee movement, Table 8.3 shows the numbers of refugees from Sri Lanka settled in Australia over the last decade or so, and the dominance of onshore settlers who arrived initially as asylum seekers.

Table 8.3: Australia: Humanitarian settlers from Sri Lanka

Year	Onshore	Offshore	Year	Onshore	Offshore
2000–01	170	100	2007–08	370	210
2001–02	115	55	2008–09	400	230
2002–03	60	35	2009–10	505	200
2003–04	25	5	2010–11	355	285
2004–05	34		2011–12	410	90
2005–06	215		2012–13	320	41
2006–07	275	50			

Source: DIBP, unpublished data.

---

1   Nonprogram migration arrivals consist mainly of New Zealand citizens arriving under the Trans-Tasman travel arrangement and a small group of other nonprogram arrivals (children born to Australian citizens overseas, residents of Cocos Islands, Norfolk Island and persons granted Australian citizenship overseas).

The mid-1990s saw the introduction of a skilled temporary worker visa (subclass 457) (Khoo, McDonald, & Hugo, 2009), as well as student and working holiday maker visas. This produced a paradigmatic shift in Australian migration (Hugo, 1999) and has reshaped Sri Lankan migration to Australia. Accordingly, Figure 8.5 shows how long-term arrivals[2] have a strikingly different pattern to the permanent migration flows in Figure 8.3. There has been a remarkably steep increase in the temporary immigrant inflow from Sri Lanka. It is clear that, to some extent, temporary migration is being used by some highly skilled Sri Lankans who hitherto would have used the permanent migration avenue to Australia. It has also led to new migrant flows.

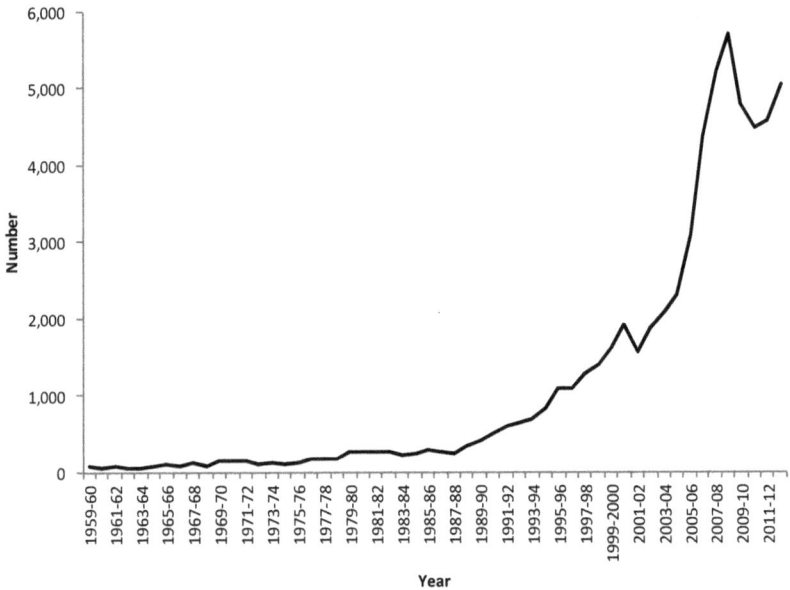

Figure 8.5: Long-term arrivals from Sri Lanka to Australia, 1959–60 to 2012–13

Source: Department of Immigration and Multicultural and Indigenous Affairs, *Australian Immigration: Consolidated Statistics*, various issues; DIBP, unpublished data.

Jayasuriya and McAuliffe (2013, p. 9) point out that a degree from an Organisation for Economic Co-operation and Development (OECD) university is highly valued in Sri Lanka, and show that Australia is the

---

2   Persons entering Australia on a temporary residence visa intending to leave but only after spending more than one year in Australia.

destination for the largest number of student migrants leaving Sri Lanka. Australia has been an important destination for students since the Colombo Plan in the 1960s. There has been a significant increase in the number of student visa holders from Sri Lanka in Australia, from 1,201 in 2002 to 7,555 in 2009. Australia is the destination of over a third of Sri Lankan students going overseas, but Sri Lanka is only the 13th largest supplier of overseas students to Australia.

Temporary skilled migrant workers (subclass 457 visa holders) are also an increasingly important part of the migration flow from Sri Lanka to Australia. The 457 program is entirely demand driven, while the number of permanent immigrants is capped by government. The 457 program is available only to highly skilled workers. Sri Lanka is the fifth largest Asian source of 457 migrants to Australia. As is the case with students, many 457s from Sri Lanka apply for, and are granted, permanent residence in Australia. Temporary migration, like permanent migration, from Sri Lanka to Australia is selective of the highly skilled.

An important dimension of change in Australian international migration over the last 15 years has been the increasing proportion of permanent settlers each year who are persons already in Australia who entered earlier under some form of temporary residence visa. Over a quarter (27.8 per cent) of the 52,791 Sri Lankans who settled permanently in Australia over this period were already in Australia as a temporary resident before applying successfully for permanent residence. There is, therefore, a pattern of Sri Lankans travelling to Australia as a student or skilled temporary worker and, upon completion of their studies or work contract, taking up permanent residence. This has become a common pattern among students in Australia from Asia. In 2011–12, some 30,978 former students applied for, and obtained, permanent residence in Australia.

Moreover, it is apparent that different waves of migrants from Sri Lanka to Australia have been dominated by different ethnic groups. In the late nineteenth century it was mainly Sinhalese. In the early post–World War II decades it was mainly Burghers, and in the latest wave (after the mid-1980s) it was Tamils.

Table 8.4 shows that the Australian Tamil population is predominantly from Sri Lanka. and that it has doubled in the 2006–11 intercensal period.

Table 8.4: Persons in Australia indicating their ancestry was Tamil by birthplace, 2006 and 2011

Birthplace	Tamil				
	2006		2011		% change
	No.	%	No.	%	
Sri Lanka	5,158	64.1	11,630	63.7	125.9
Australia	1,312	16.3	2,811	15.4	114.3
Malaysia and Singapore	515	6.4	1,014	5.6	96.9
India	505	6.3	1,293	7.1	156.0
Other	558	6.9	1,503	8.2	169.4
Total	8,048	100.0	18,251	100.0	126.8

Source: Data derived from Australian censuses, 1901 to 2011.

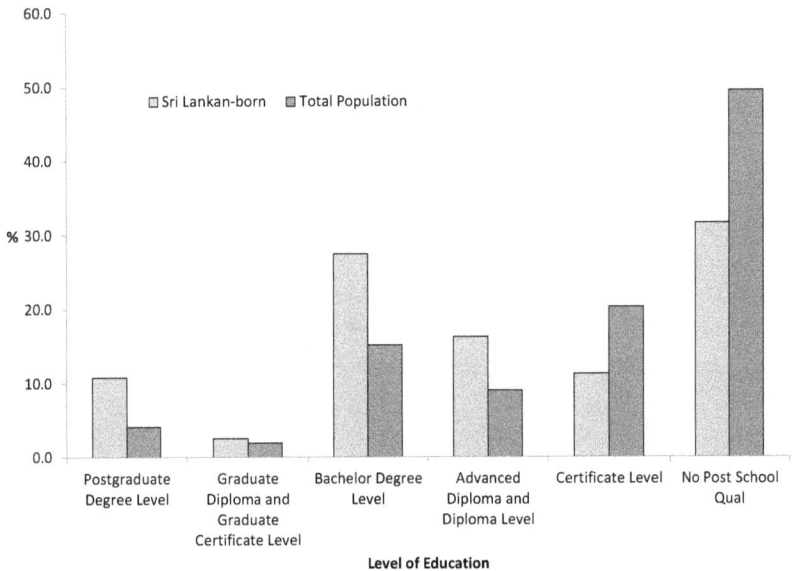

Figure 8.6: Level of post-school qualification of total Australian and Sri Lankan–born population, 2011

Source: Data derived from Australian censuses, 1901 to 2011.

Policy-imposed selectivity is evident when we examine the educational qualifications of the Australian Sri Lankan–born population. Figure 8.6 shows that 30.6 per cent of the Sri Lankan–born population aged 15 years and over in Australia did not have a post-school qualification compared with 52.5 per cent of the total Australian population. However, the difference is most dramatic for those with a University degree or higher qualification, since more than 30 per cent of the Sri Lankan–born are at this level compared with 15 per cent of the total Australian adult population. For higher degrees it is 10.8 compared with 4.1 per cent. This points to a very high level of educational selectivity in the permanent migration from Sri Lanka to Australia.

Thus far, our focus has been on the flows of Sri Lankans moving to Australia as well as the characteristics of the Sri Lankan population in Australia. It is also important to appreciate that there are reciprocal and circular flows between Australia and Sri Lanka. Indeed, it has been argued that it is more appropriate to view Asian–Australian migration as a complex interactive system rather than a unidirectional permanent relocation of populations (Hugo, 2008a, 2008b). This certainly applies to the migration relationship between Australia and Sri Lanka. It is important to establish the extent and nature of these reciprocal movements, since they can influence development in Sri Lanka.

The flow from Australia to Sri Lanka, like the permanent flow in the other direction, is highly skilled. Revealingly, managers and professionals make up 65 per cent of all departures. It is clear that in the flow from Australia to Sri Lanka, the dominant group are those in the economically active age groups and their children. Hence, their potential to have a positive impact on development in Sri Lanka is considerable.

Permanent return migration is not the only form of movement that Sri Lankan expatriates in Australia have with their homeland. In fact, Sri Lankans overseas can keep a significant investment in their homeland by frequently visiting and maintaining economic links with institutions and individuals in Sri Lanka. Table 8.5 identifies three types of Sri Lankan–born individuals who indicated they are moving in and out of Australia on a temporary (either long-term or short-term) basis. This table shows three categories of Sri Lankan–born persons according to their residential status and time periods: new settlers 1998–2006; visitors 1998–2006; and Australian residents who settled prior to 1998.

Table 8.5: Number of Sri Lankan–born individual persons travelling in and out of Australia temporarily by resident status, 1998–2006

Sri Lankan–born persons' resident status	Number moves into Australia	Travelling out of Australia
New settlers 1998–2006	13,279	272
Visitors 1998–2006	22,355	15,814
Australian residents who settled prior to 1998	24,021	24,320

Source: DIBP, unpublished data.

What is apparent, then, is that many Sri Lankan–born people settling in Australia have made several temporary moves out of Australia since arriving.

Refugee migration

Since the mid-1980s Sri Lanka has been a significant source of both asylum seekers and refugees as is shown in Figure 8.7.

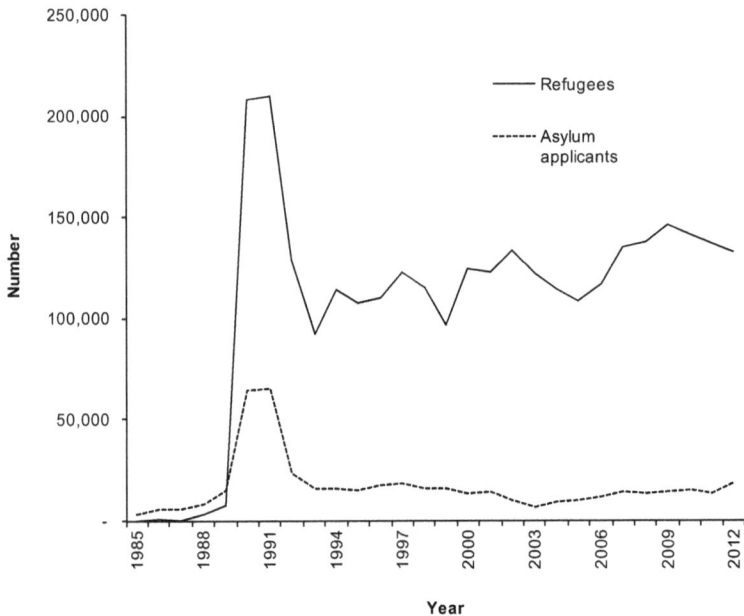

Figure 8.7: Refugees and asylum applicants from Sri Lanka, 1985–2012
Source: UNHCR Statistics.

Most have been Tamils who have been displaced as a result of the civil conflict. As Jayasuriya and McAuliffe (2013, p. 15) point out:

> India has historically been, and continues to be, the main host country of Sri Lankan refugees. At the end of 2012 it hosted some 67,165 Sri Lankan (predominantly Tamil) refugees.... However, estimates of the number of Sri Lankans with pending asylum claims in Tamil Nadu vary considerably between organisations, from around 100,000 to 200,000.

While India has been the main destination, Sri Lankans have also applied for asylum in a number of OECD and Asian countries. A recent United Nations Office on Drugs and Crime (UNODC) study (2013, p. 28) has shown that in the 1980s, 1990s and early 2000s, the main destinations were Germany, France, UK, Canada and Switzerland.

Figure 8.8 demonstrates that in recent years there have been some significant changes, with the largest numbers now being in France, and Malaysia and Australia becoming increasingly significant. Table 8.6 reveals that France and Australia have received the largest number of asylum applications up to the first half of 2013, with Australia experiencing a sharp increase in 2012.

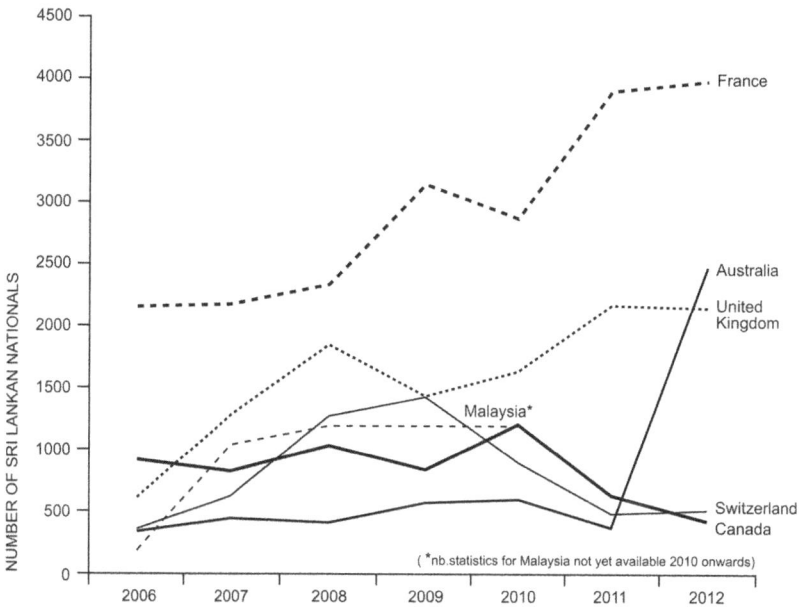

Figure 8.8: Asylum claims, Sri Lankan nationals, six most important countries, 2006–12

Source: UNODC (2013, p. 29).

Table 8.6: Sri Lankan global asylum applications, 2012 and 2014

Country	2012	2014
France	6,890	3,700
Australia	2,427	1,194
UK	3,162	2,645
Malaysia	709	1,752
Switzerland	1,177	1,277
Germany	481	534
Indonesia	360	238
Canada	428	196
Japan	461	755

Source: United Nations High Commissioner for Refugees (UNHCR) population statistics, extracted 13 January, 2014.

Note: UNHCR data does not include all IMAs to Australia, only those who were able to lodge an asylum claim following the lifting of a statutory bar.

There are more than 100,000 ethnic Tamil Sri Lankans in the southern Indian state of Tamil Nadu, including 68,000 in 112 government-run camps and 32,000 outside camps (IRIN, 2012). It is important to note that India, which has been the host for the majority of war refugees, shows a clear downward trend in the numbers of Tamil Sri Lankans because, as has been reported, an increasing number of refugees are returning home, both spontaneously and with the help of the UNHCR (Refugees return by ferry, 2011).

The migration industry in Sri Lanka

Overseas migration became an industry with the opening up of the Sri Lankan economy during the late 1970s. Prior to that, migrating overseas was an individual affair and there was little third-party involvement in Sri Lanka. Overseas migration was mainly for higher education and employment. As Sri Lanka began to encourage labour migration to Middle Eastern countries, a 'migration industry' was built. It initially started with a few unauthorised migration agents in Colombo. It expanded to include both authorised and unauthorised agents not only for sending unskilled and semi-skilled labour migrants overseas but also for skilled migration to immigration-encouraging countries such as Australia, New Zealand and Canada.

The government created a Foreign Employment Unit in the Department of Labour in 1976 in order to find employment overseas, organise and monitor migration as well as maintain migration records (Korale, 1983). In 1980, the Foreign Employment Act No. 32 allowed private agencies to take care of some of the governmental functions and responsibilities of managing overseas labour employment but with governmental control (Gamburd, 2000). Figure 8.9 shows that the number of licensed agencies has grown significantly over the years.

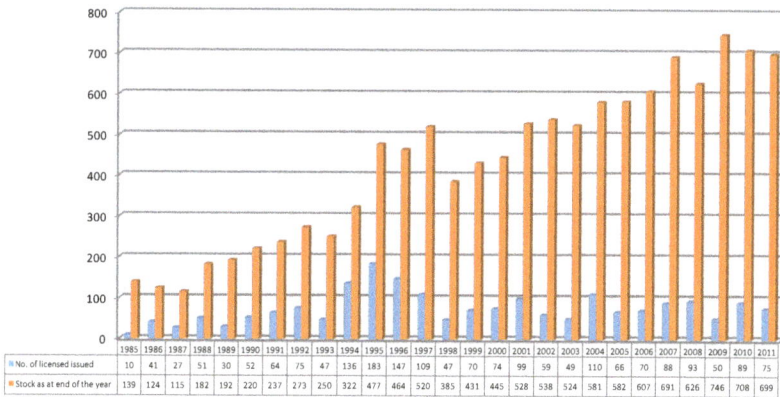

Figure 8.9: Number of licensed agencies, 1985–2011

Source: Sri Lanka Bureau of Foreign Employment (2011).

Note: Blue bars show the new licences issued each year for the newly established agencies.

A substantial institutional framework has developed in Sri Lanka to govern labour migration. The Sri Lankan Foreign Employment Agency Ltd was set up in 1996 for directing youth into foreign employment. This agency functions under the Ministry of External Affairs and manages the recruitment for employment overseas.

Departures for foreign employment have grown between 2006 and 2011 in almost all the districts, but the volume of departures is relatively low for the northern districts of Sri Lanka, as depicted in Figure 8.10. Potential migrants did not have the opportunity to leave the northern districts during the war period in order to be involved in the process of labour migration since almost all of the licensed agencies are located outside the Northern Province, and mainly in Colombo and Kurunegala districts.

Although a coherent framework for governing labour migration is in place in Sri Lanka, a substantial proportion of migrants prefer to take up informal channels to organise their migration (Eelens, 1995; Gamburd,

2000, 2005; Gunatilleke, 1998; Shaw, 2008; Ukwatte, 2010). Shaw (2008)[3] observed that about one third of migrants organised their migration through informal contacts.

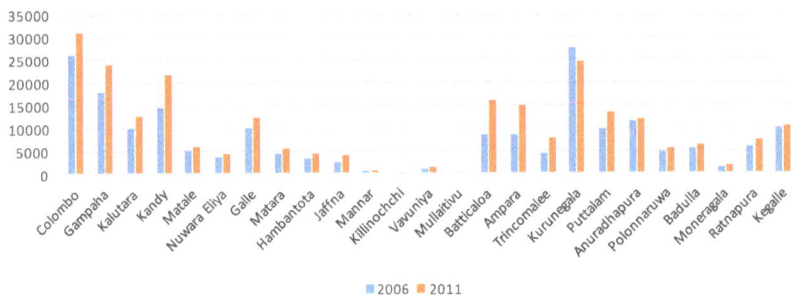

Figure 8.10: Departure for foreign employment by district, 2006 and 2011
Source: Sri Lanka Bureau of Foreign Employment, various reports.

The Sri Lanka Bureau of Foreign Employment reports that only 75.5 per cent of the departures in 2008 were from licensed agencies (Sri Lanka Bureau of Foreign Employment, 2009, p. 5). Many studies have reported that numerous illegal recruitments continue,[4] although the number of licensed agencies has increased (Dias & Jayasundera, 2004; Eelens & Speckmann, 1990).

Boat migration or IMAs is not a phenomenon that has been specifically developed for Australia. The smuggling of people overseas from Sri Lanka by boat was booming a decade ago (Brown, 2012). Although Australia became the preferred destination of smuggled migrants in 2012–13, Italy has in the past been one of the major destinations. IMAs to Italy changed significantly in 2002 for two reasons. First, the Italian Parliament sanctioned a new immigration law known as the Bossi-Fini law that allowed for regularisation of those already living in Italy, as well as devising a mechanism for the processing of new immigrants with offices all over the country and severe border controls (Totah, 2003). The second was a consequence of the Asia–Europe Meeting (ASEM) Ministerial Conference on Cooperation for the Management of Migratory Flows between Europe and Asia, which paved the way for the Italian

---

3   Shaw's paper is based on fieldwork conducted in 2006 in Kurunegala district, a rural agrarian region about 70 kilometres northeast of Colombo. A mix of quantitative and qualitative techniques has been employed. The primary survey instrument was a structured questionnaire, administered to individuals responsible for household finances in 153 remittance-receiving households in which the migrant had been abroad for six months or more at the time of the survey.
4   'Illegal recruitments' means the recruitment of labour by nonlicensed recruiters.

Government to establish bilateral agreements with sending countries to help curb illegal migratory flows by offering them special quotas for immigrants and readmission priorities in exchange for their cooperation. Most importantly, the agreement supported externalising the policing of the Italian border by cooperating logistically and financially with local law enforcement agencies to stop IMAs at the point of departure.

International migration has increased significantly in Asia during the past two decades (Hugo & Young, 2008). Although there have been some initiatives to improve governance and cooperation in relation to international migration, undocumented movement remains a major challenge (Abella, 2008; Colford, 2013). The International Organization for Migration (2010) has estimated that there are 20 to 30 million migrants worldwide without proper documentation.

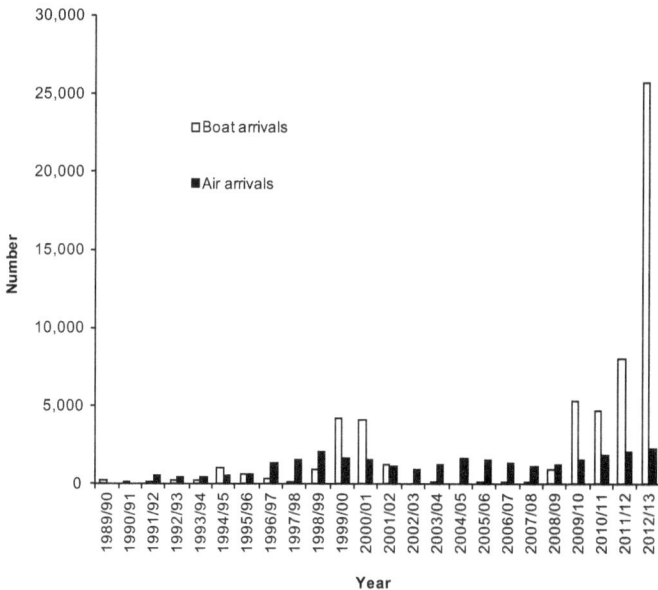

Figure 8.11: Unauthorised arrivals to Australia, 1989–90 to 2012–13

Source: Department of Immigration and Multicultural and Indigenous Affairs (2002, 2004, 2005); Department of Immigration and Citizenship, *Annual Report*, various issues; Phillips and Spinks (2013).

Persons who arrive in Australia without a visa, most of whom ultimately apply for asylum, arrive by sea and air, and the numbers are shown in Figure 8.11. Sri Lankans were an important part of this upswing in IMAs. In 2008 there were just over 200 IMAs from Sri Lanka, but in 2012 there were over 6,400.

Jayasuriya and McAuliffe (2013, p. 19) note that there has been an increase in the number of asylum seekers repatriated to Sri Lanka: between July 2012 and May 2013, 162 voluntary and 965 involuntary returns were undertaken. At the Sri Lanka end, data obtained from the Katunayake Airport shows nonvoluntary returnees by special charter flights in 2012–13 were 1,265 compared with 56 voluntary returnees by commercial flights, as depicted in Figure 8.12. All the voluntary returnees were males, while 6.2 per cent of the nonvoluntary migrants were females.

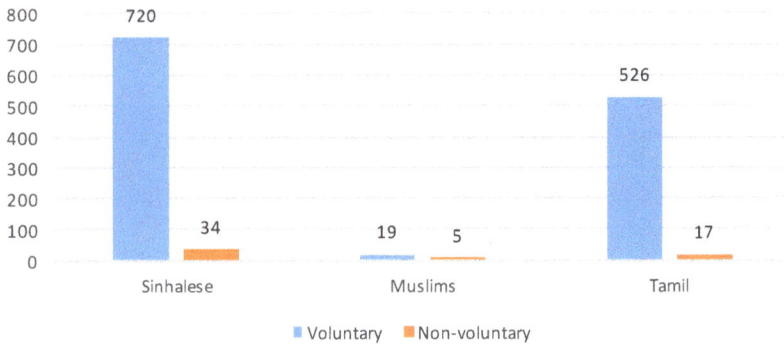

Figure 8.12: Number of voluntary and nonvoluntary returnees from Australia, 2012–13

Source: Data obtained from various annual reports – Bandaranaike Airport. Retrieved from www.airport.lk/aasl/business_info/annual_reports.php.

In recent years, it was not only Tamils who were involved with boat migration, but Sinhalese as well. There were no Sinhalese IMAs in 2011 but their number suddenly jumped to 13 per cent in 2012 (Jayasuriya & McAuliffe, 2013). This suggests that the reasons for boat migration are not related only to factors linked with 'protection'. Table 8.7 shows that interdictions were on a substantial scale. Moreover, they were at a high level at the time of peak IMA arrivals from Sri Lanka in Australia.

Table 8.7: Sri Lankan irregular migrants detected by the Sri Lankan authorities, 2009–12

Item	2009	2010	2011	2012	Total
Total number of vessels detected	8	3	3	67	81
Total number of passengers arrested	182	10	115	3,139	3,446
Total number of facilitators arrested	35	19	12	304	370

Source: Criminal Investigation Department, Sri Lanka. Data collected by the authors.

Most of the IMAs originated from the Northern and Eastern provinces, which were conflict-affected districts for more than two decades. In 2012, the Eastern districts of Trincomalee and Batticalo and the Northern district of Vavuniya dominated the irregular maritime migration, but a completely different pattern of migration was observed for 2013, as shown in Figure 8.13.

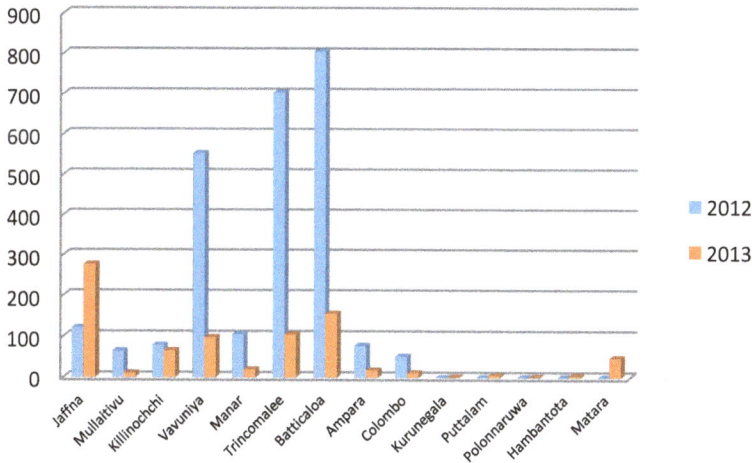

Figure 8.13: District of origin of irregular maritime migrants, 2012 and 2013
Source: Criminal Investigation Department, Sri Lanka. Data collected by the authors.

The Northern district of Jaffna has produced many irregular maritime migrants, while other districts both in the Northern as well as Eastern provinces have a smaller number of migrants. The most important feature of the differences between 2012 and 2013 was the substantial decline of irregular maritime migration in all the districts except Jaffna.

Figure 8.14 shows that of those who attempted to depart for Australia by boat between January 2012 and October 2013, the majority were Tamil. These people were arrested while attempting to depart or before crossing the Sri Lankan sea border. If 'protection factors' are the reason for illegal maritime migration, as indicated by some authors (Howie, 2013; Kanagasabapathipillai, 2013), involvement of a large number Sinhalese and a significant number of Muslim migrants raises questions as to what the reasons are behind their migration. Many who have investigated 'boat migration' suggest that an economic motive was also a main reason (Waduge, 2013; Karunaratne, 2013; Kariyakarawana, 2013; Saravanathan, 2013).

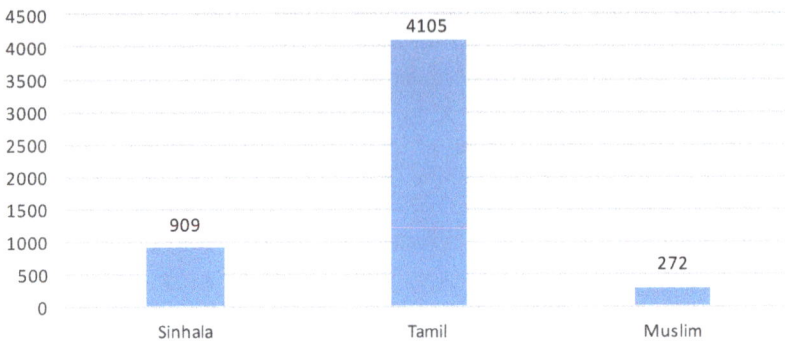

Figure 8.14: Number of people captured while departing to Australia by ethnicity, January 2012 to October 2013

Source: Criminal Investigation Department, Sri Lanka. Data collected by the authors.

It is interesting to note that all ventures in 2013 involved children, compared with less than half (22) of the 56 attempts in 2012. The majority of the latter occurred towards the end of 2012.

Irregular maritime migrants interviewed were either unemployed or worked in low-paid, informal-sector occupations. They worked as fishermen, drivers, farmers or labourers. Most of the illegal migrants were the eldest child of their family, who took on the responsibility of supporting the family including younger siblings who are still schooling. The majority of them do not own any property, and others only owned their house. Therefore, the migrants generally come from very poor families.

The Sri Lankan community in Australia plays a significant role in the migration of Sri Lankans to Australia—both documented and undocumented. This role involves the supply of information, both detailed and general, in terms of the economic and social opportunities in Australia. The community also helps to fund migration, and in some cases community members act as sponsors.

There appears to be some mismatch between the fact that most of the IMAs detected either in Sri Lanka or Australia tend to have middle to low education and low status occupations while the Sri Lankan population in Australia tends to have higher levels of education and occupational status.

The role of family in Australia and in other countries in influencing the decision to migrate was evident in the comments from a repatriated respondent. A 27-year-old Tamil man from Trincomalee explained to us that:

I am still unemployed because I have studied up to GCE (O. L.) but was not successful. My family still supports me because my brother is in England and the sister live in Canada. I can communicate in English to some extent. I also have some relatives living in Australia. I am very much frustrated because only I have this low standard of living in Sri Lanka. For this reasons I decided to migrate to Australia by boat because one of my friends who went to Australia by boat suggested me that it saves time and money. Although the bad memories of war are over, there are many jobless youth so I was expecting better opportunities in Australia.

The intending IMAs that were intercepted by the Anti-Human Smuggling Unit of Sri Lanka's Criminal Investigation Department were overwhelmingly young, and the majority came from the Northern and Eastern regions, so they are Tamils. They have a strong network in Australia because of the relatives and friends who live there and receive encouragement to travel to Australia by illegal means to avoid the immigration screening.

The study of IMAs who have been successful in gaining protection (McAuliffe, 2013) showed in the case of Sri Lankans that more than 15 per cent had relatives, more than 10 per cent had friends, friends of relatives or friends of friends, and a little less than 5 per cent had fellow ethnic members in Australia prior to their departure.

Regional disparities in development in Sri Lanka have led people to migrate locally or internationally looking for better income opportunities. The government is now making a significant attempt to develop war-torn Northern and Eastern districts. It is important to stress that Sri Lankan people have become very mobile locally as well as internationally. The major reason for such movement is to find better employment, whether locally or overseas. Moreover, illegal migration to overseas countries to look for employment opportunities is not a new phenomenon. Sri Lanka already had a network of agents able to organise this illegal movement. In addition, we have seen a mass flow of refugees to India, by boat, during the war years. Therefore, 'boat' migration to overseas destinations involving risks is not a recent phenomenon for the low socioeconomic portion of the Sri Lankan community, irrespective of their ethnicity. Moreover, the idea that migration—especially international migration— is the key to prosperity has become a norm in Sri Lanka.

Conclusion

Sri Lanka has become, in many ways, a major emigrant society over recent decades. There are a number of elements to this. First, the country has a substantial diaspora. In 2013 the United Nations indicated there were 1,245,187 Sri Lankan–born persons living in other countries, equivalent to 5.9 per cent of the Sri Lankan resident population. Second, remittances now account for 10.1 per cent of GDP (World Bank, 2014). Third, a strong local culture of migration has developed, whereby internal and international migration is seen as a normal way for Sri Lankans to seek to improve their economic situation or respond to crisis.

Sri Lanka has initiated several livelihood development programs under its policy known as Mahinda Chinthanaya.[5] But these programs need to be accelerated and better accommodate the most vulnerable and disadvantaged communities, especially in the northern and eastern parts of the country, where the majority of the IMAs originated. This study has found that most of the IMAs are less-educated and low-skilled people from these areas. It is important to enhance their vocational skills according to the jobs demanded by the labour market in Sri Lanka without making a mismatch between education or skills with the available employment opportunities. In this regard, preparing a livelihood development plan specifically designed for the Northern Province—by identifying, with the participation of local communities, the livelihood requirements of individuals as well as communities—seems beneficial.

One of the few generalisations which has emerged from research on irregular and undocumented migration is that it often occurs because there are no regular or documented channels available for potential migrants, so that they are left with no alternative but to move irregularly. It follows that the most successful measures to prevent irregular migration involve the creation of legal channels that make irregular migration unnecessary. Usually, this is considered in terms of creating those channels along

---

5   Mahinda Chinthanaya, which is the Sri Lankan Government's policy agenda, strongly emphasises that public spending should be pro-poor, pro-growth and pro-regional. In this context, rural–urban imbalances in access to transport, electricity, quality drinking water, education and health are being attended with more resources being allocated to supplement regular programs through regionally focused development initiatives: Uthuru Wasanthaya, Negenahira Navodaya, Rajarata Navodaya, Wayamba Pubuduwa, Pubudamu Wellassa, Kandurata Udanaya, Sabaragamu Arunalokaya and Ran Aruna. Furthermore, public investment is expected to promote growth and value-creation opportunities. In addition, spending on social security will be encouraged through community participation.

the same corridors of what is currently irregular migration. However, a somewhat different initiative is suggested here, noting that the major areas of origin of IMAs who have attempted to move to Australia have a number of key characteristics:

- Low levels of education and skill, so that few people are eligible for skilled migration, permanent or temporary, to OECD nations.
- No readily available channels for contract labour migration to the Middle East and Southeast Asia, because of a lack of agents and an insecure situation which has prevented recruiters and other parts of the migration industry to operate in those parts of the country.

Accordingly, it is suggested that steps be taken by the Sri Lankan Government to create legal alternatives to IMA migration to Australia by setting up the full infrastructure to recruit, process etc. international labour migrants in the region for the Middle East and Southeast Asia. This would also involve providing training facilitators for local people, to fit the needs of employers in the Middle East and Southeast Asia.

A major policy implication of this report is that, rather than try to prevent migration from the 'hot spots' from which IMAs have left, we seek to facilitate legal migration through regular channels to the Middle East and Southeast Asia. This builds on the considerable infrastructure and experience that already exists in other parts of Sri Lanka. It builds on the culture of migration in the area, but channels it into other more secure pathways to legal movement overseas.

Reference list

Abella, M. I. (2008, 25–28 March). *Challenges to governance of labour migration in Asia–Pacific.* Paper presented at PECC-ABAC conference on demographic change and international labour mobility in the Asia–Pacific Region: Implications for business and cooperation, Seoul, Korea.

Australian Bureau of Statistics. (2013). *Migration Australia—2011–12 and 2012–13.* Catalogue No. 3412.0. Canberra: Author.

Brown, B. (2012). Undocumented Sri Lankan migration to Italy: Its rise and fall. Retrieved from groundviews.org/2012/08/02/the-rise-and-fall-of-sri-lankan-undocumented-migration-to-italy/.

Colford, P. (2013, 2 April). 'Illegal immigrant' no more. Retrieved from Associated Press: blog.ap.org/2013/04/02/illegal-immigrant-no-more.

Cornelius, W. A. (1992). From sojourners to settlers: The changing profile of Mexican immigration to the United States. In Bustamante, J. A., Reynolds, C. W. and Hinojosa-Ojeda, R. (Eds), *US-Mexico relations: Labor market interdependence*. Stanford: Stanford University Press.

del Rey Poveda, A. (2007). Determinants and consequences of internal and international migration: the case of rural populations in the south of Veracruz, Mexico. *Demographic Research, 16*(10): 287–314.

Department of Immigration and Border Protection (DIBP). Overseas arrivals and departures statistics, unpublished data.

Department of Immigration and Citizenship. *Annual report*, various issues. Canberra: Australian Government Publishing Services.

Department of Immigration and Multicultural and Indigenous Affairs. *Australian immigration: Consolidated statistics*, various issues. Canberra: Australian Government Publishing Services.

Department of Immigration and Multicultural and Indigenous Affairs. (2002). *Unauthorised arrivals by air and sea*. Fact sheet 74. Canberra: Australian Government Publishing Services.

Department of Immigration and Multicultural and Indigenous Affairs. (2004). *Unauthorised arrivals by air and sea*. Fact sheet 74. Canberra: Author.

Department of Immigration and Multicultural and Indigenous Affairs. (2005). *Managing the border: Immigration compliance 2004–05 edition*. Canberra: Australian Government Publishing Services.

Dias, M., & Jayasundara, R. (2004). *Sri Lanka: Good practices to prevent women migrant workers from going into exploitative forms of labour*. GENPROM working paper No. 9. Series on Women and Migration. Geneva: Gender Promotion Program, International Labour Organization.

Eelens, F. (1995). Migration of Sri Lankan women to Western Asia. In *International migration policies and the status of female migrants: Proceedings of the United Nations Expert Group meeting on international migration policies and the status of female migrants, San Miniato, Italy, 28-31 March 1990, Issue 126* (pp. 267–77). Geneva: United Nations.

Eelens, F., & Speckmann, J. D. (1990). Recruitment of labour migrants for the Middle East: The Sri Lankan case. *International Migration Review, 24*(2), 297–322. doi.org/10.2307/2546553

Gamburd, M. R. (2000). *The kitchen spoon's handle: Transnationalism and Sri Lanka's migrant housemaids.* New York: Cornell University Press.

Gamburd, M. R. (2005). Lentils there, lentils here! Sri Lankan domestic labour in the Middle East. In Huang, S., Yeoh, B. S. A., & Rahman, N. A. (Eds), *Asian Women as Transnational Domestic Workers*, (pp. 92–114). Singapore: Marshall Cavendish Academic.

Gunatilleke, G. (1998). The role of networks and community structures in international migration from Sri Lanka. In Appleyard, R. (Ed.), *Emigration dynamics in developing countries*. Volume II: South Asia (pp. 71–112). Surrey: Ashgate.

Howie, E. (2013). Sri Lankan boat migration to Australia: Motivations and dilemmas. *Economic and Political Weekly, 48*(35), 97–104.

Hugo, G. J. (1999). A new paradigm of international migration in Australia. *New Zealand Population Review, 25*(1–2), 1–39.

Hugo, G. J. (2008a). In and out of Australia: Rethinking Indian and Chinese skilled migration to Australia. *Asian Population Studies 4*(3), 267–91. doi.org/10.1080/17441730802496508

Hugo, G. J. (2008b). Quantifying transnationalism: Asian migration to Australia. In Stojanov, R., & Novosak, J. (Eds), *Migration, development and environment: Migration processes from the perspective of environmental change and development approach at the beginning of the 21st Century* (pp. 172–208). Newcastle: Cambridge Scholars Publishing.

Hugo, G. J. (2014). Sri Lankan migration to Australia. *Sri Lanka Journal of Population Studies 14*, 1–32.

Hugo, G. J. (2015). The Sri Lankan population in Australia. In Dissanayake, L., & Ukwatta, S. (Eds), *Population and development* (pp. 15–38). Colombo: Department of Demography, University of Colombo.

Hugo, G., & Young, S. (Eds). (2008). *Labour mobility in the Asia–Pacific region*. Singapore: Institute of Southeast Asian Studies.

IRIN. (2012, 4 September). Refugees in India reluctant to return. Retrieved from www.irinnews.org/report/96233/sri-lanka-refugees-in-india-reluctant-to-return.

International Organization for Migration. (2010). *World migration report 2010: The future of migration—Building capacities for change*. Geneva: Author.

Jayasuriya, D., & McAuliffe, M. (2013). *Placing recent Sri Lankan maritime arrivals in a broader migration context*. Irregular Migration Research Program Occasional Paper Series 02. Canberra: Department of Immigration and Border Protection.

Kanagasabapathipillai, D. (2013, 22 August). The Illegal Boat Ride to Australia. *Ceylon Today*. Retrieved from passionparade.blogspot.com/2013/08/.

Kariyakarawana, K. (2013, 1 September). Sri Lanka—Australia to check illegal migrants. *Sunday Observer*. Retrieved from archives.sunday observer.lk/2013/09/01/sec03.asp.

Karunaratne, C. (2013, 18 December). Sri Lankans and irregular migration: A journey to die for? *Daily Mirror*. Retrieved from www.dailymirror.lk/business/features/40380-sri-lankans-and-irregular-migration-a-journey-to-die-for.html.

Khoo, S., McDonald, P., & Hugo, G. J. (2009). Skilled temporary migration from Asia–Pacific countries to Australia. *Asian and Pacific Migration Journal, 18*(2), 255–81. doi.org/10.1177/011719680901800204

King, R. (1976). The evolution of international labour migration movements concerning the EEC. *Tijdschrift voor Economische en Sociale Geografie, 67*(2), 66–82.

King, R., Skeldon, R., & Vullnetari, J. (2008). *Internal and international migration: Bridging the theoretical divide.* Sussex Centre for Migration Research, University of Sussex, UK. Retrieved from eprints.soton. ac.uk/377323/.

King, R., Skeldon, R., & Vullnetari, J. (2012). *Internal and international migration: Bridging the theoretical divide.* Sussex Centre for Migration Research, University of Sussex, UK. Retrieved from www.imi.ox.ac. uk/pdfs/russell-king-ron-skeldon-and-julie-vullnetari-internal-and-international-migration-bridging-the-theoretical-divide.

Korale, R. B. M. (1983). *Migration for employment to the Middle East: Its demographic and socioeconomic effects in Sri Lanka.* Colombo: Ministry of Plan Implementation.

Lozano-Ascencio, F., Roberts, B., & Bean, F. (1999). The interconnections of internal and international migration: The case of the United States and Mexico. In Pries, L. (Ed.), *Migration and transnational social spaces,* (pp. 138–61). Aldershot: Ashgate.

McAuliffe, M. (2013). *Seeking the views of irregular migrants: Decision making, drivers and migration journeys.* Irregular Migration Research Program, Occasional Paper Series 05. Canberra: Department of Immigration and Border Protection.

Phillips, J., & Spinks, H. (2013). *Boat arrivals in Australia since 1976.* Parliamentary library research paper. Canberra: Parliament of Australia. Retrieved from www.aph.gov.au/About_Parliament/Parliamentary_ Departments/Parliamentary_Library/pubs/rp/rp1314/BoatArrivals.

Refugees return by ferry. (2011, 13 October). *Daily FT.* Retrieved from www.ft.lk/article/51807/Refugees-return-by-ferry.

Sarvananthan, M. (2013). Causes of 'boat migration' to Australia from Sri Lanka: A rejoinder to Emily Howie. *Ground Views for Journalism.* Retrieved from groundviews.org/2013/09/08/causes-of-boat-migration-to-australia-from-sri-lanka-a-rejoinder-to-emily-howie/.

Shaw, J. (2008). Sri Lanka country study. In Shaw, J., & Eversole, R. (Eds), *Leveraging remittances with microfinance: Synthesis report and country studies* (pp. 153–94). Melbourne: AusAID Research Reports.

Skeldon, R. (2006). Interlinkages between internal and international migration and development in the Asian region. *Population, Space and Place, 12*(1), 15–30.

Sri Lanka Bureau of Foreign Employment. (2009). *Annual statistical report of foreign employment.* Colombo: Author.

Sri Lanka Bureau of Foreign Employment. (2011). *Annual statistical report of foreign employment.* Colombo: Author.

Totah, M. (2003). Comment—Fortress Italy: Racial politics and the new immigration amendment in Italy. *Fordham International Law Journal, 26*(5), 1438.

Ukwatte, S. (2010). *Economic and social impact of the migration of Sri Lankan transitional domestic workers on families and children left behind* (unpublished PhD thesis). University of Adelaide, Adelaide.

United Nations. (2013). *Trends in international migrant stock: The 2013 revision.* New York: Author.

United Nations High Commissioner for Refugees. (2003). Sri Lanka. In *UNHCR global appeal* (pp. 207–11). Geneva: Author. Retrieved from www.unhcr.org/3ddceb71a.pdf.

United Nations Office on Drugs and Crime. (2013). *Strategic assessment report on migrant smuggling from Sri Lanka.* Report produced by Regional Office for Southeast Asia and the Pacific, United Nations Office on Drugs and Crime.

Waduge, S. D. (2013, 23 July). Point of view boat smuggling mafia Sri Lanka's Tamil 'refugees' or economic migrants? *The Island.* Retrieved from www.srilankaguardian.org/2013_07_22_archive.html.

Weerasooria, W. S. (1988). *Links between Sri Lanka and Australia.* Colombo: Government Press.

World Bank. (2014, 11 April). *Migration and remittances: Recent developments and outlook.* Migration and Development Brief 22. Washington DC: Author.

Zabin, C., & Hughes, S. (1995). Economic integration and labour flows: stage migration in farm labour markets in Mexico and the United States. *International Migration Review, 29*(2): 395–422.

9

Applications for asylum in the developed world: Modelling asylum claims by origin and destination

Tim Hatton and Joseph Moloney

Introduction

Every year, hundreds of thousands of people apply for asylum, seeking sanctuary in the stable, safe and secure countries of the developed world. Most of them come from poor and middle-income countries in the grip of civil wars or international conflicts, where minorities are persecuted, or in which human rights abuses are commonplace. Those who manage to reach developed countries are a small minority of all who flee across national borders or who seek refuge elsewhere within their own country. Over the last 30 years, the number of asylum applications lodged in developed countries has soared and this has led to intense political controversy and what might be described as a policy backlash. Against this background, there has been examination of the motivations of asylum seekers and the effects of economic incentives and asylum policies on application rates.

In Australia, as elsewhere, asylum policy has been widely debated. Yet there is little quantitative analysis that places the Australian experience in a comparative context. This chapter provides an econometric analysis of the ebb and flow of asylum applications to Australia together with

18 other developed countries. Besides helping to identify the common factors that drive the application rates, this approach allows us to assess how and to what degree the Australian experience differs from that of other countries. One of the key issues is the deterrent effects of asylum policies, in particular the policy differences between countries. In order to assess these effects, we derive a quantitative index representing diverse elements of asylum policy and use this in our empirical analysis.

The approach followed here draws heavily on previous analysis by Hatton (2009, 2011) in terms of methodology and research design. It also draws on a wider literature on the determinants of international migration and a smaller literature that focuses specifically on modelling asylum applications. In the next section, we outline the trends in asylum applications to Australia in comparison with other developed countries. This is followed by a short survey of quantitative analysis of refugee movements and asylum applications. We then present a brief outline of the asylum policies in Australia and elsewhere, particularly in Europe. Our index of asylum policies in 19 Organisation for Economic Co-operation and Development (OECD) countries is then explained, before presenting fixed effects regression estimates of annual data on asylum applications by origin and destination. We then estimate the effects of asylum policies and explore differences between Australia and the other 18 destinations. Finally, we evaluate the effects of a few key variables and conclude with a brief discussion.

Comparative trends in asylum applications

The total number of asylum claims has fluctuated over the last two decades. Figure 9.1 shows total annual applications to what the United Nations High Commissioner for Refugees (UNHCR) defines as 'industrialized countries'. These are applications by asylum seekers who arrived spontaneously. They almost always applied for asylum within the destination country or at its border, having arrived by any mode of arrival (boat, air or by land). The total number of applications made in these countries peaked at over 850,000 in 1992; after some decline it reached a second peak of more than 600,000 between 2000 and 2002. Total applications declined to their lowest point of 300,000 in 2006 before rising again to 600,000 in 2013.

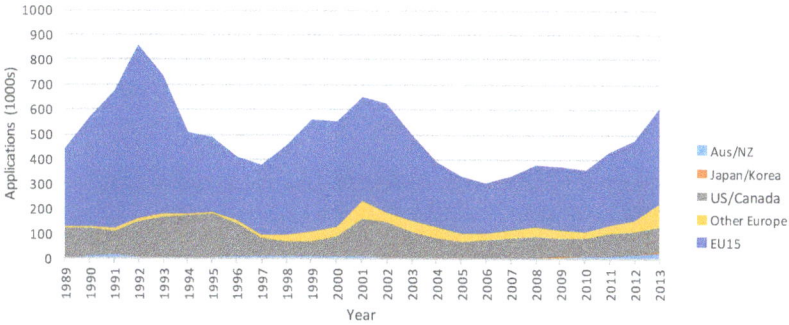

Figure 9.1: Asylum applications to 38 countries by region of asylum, 1989–2013

Sources: 1989–2000 from UNHCR, *Statistical yearbook* (2001), Table C1; 2001–13 from UNHCR, *Asylum levels and trends in industrialized countries* (2005; 2009; 2013), Table 1.

Note: The EU-15 is the pre-2004 membership: Austria, Belgium, Denmark, Finland, France, Germany, Greece, Ireland, Italy, Luxembourg, the Netherlands, Portugal, Spain, Sweden and the UK.

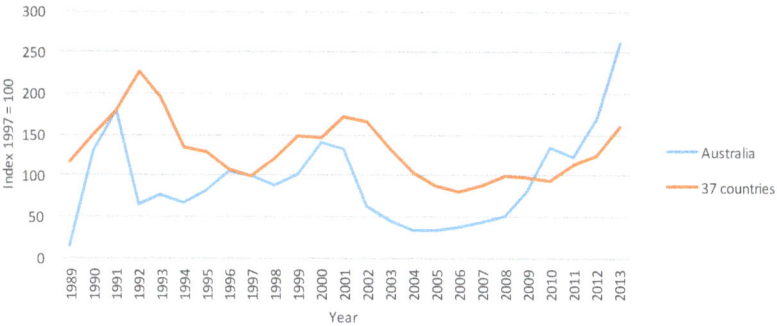

Figure 9.2: Asylum applications to Australia and 37 industrialised countries (1997 = 100)

Sources: As Figure 9.1.

Figure 9.1 also shows that the overwhelming majority claimed asylum in Europe. More than half of all applications in Europe were lodged in Germany (28 per cent), the UK (12 per cent) and France (11 per cent). It is difficult to see in Figure 9.1 how fluctuations in applications to Oceania compare with Europe and North America. Over the whole period the number of spontaneous applications (or onshore applications) in Australia amounted to 2 per cent of the 38-country total. Figure 9.2 displays an index of asylum applications to Australia, where 1997=100, comparing this with the total for the other 37 countries. Over much of the period, fluctuations in asylum applications to Australia are largely mirrored by

229

the number of applications received elsewhere. However, applications to Australia gradually increased after 1992, while the total for the 37 other countries fell. And after 2001, Australian applications fell faster to the middle of the decade and then increased more steeply to 2013.

Table 9.1: Asylum applications to Australia and 18 other destination countries (total), 2004–12

Applications to Australia, 2004–12				Applications to 18 other countries, 2004–12			
Top 40 origin countries				Top 40 origin countries			
China	18,157	Nigeria	524	Serbia	277,554	Algeria	47,590
Afghanistan	8,046	Thailand	455	Russia	222,424	India	47,056
India	6,539	P N Guinea	448	Iraq	193,980	Colombia	41,550
Sri Lanka	6,263	Libya	442	China	183,977	C. d'Ivoire	33,973
Iran	5,701	Syria	409	Afghanistan	159,695	Zimbabwe	32,247
Pakistan	4,664	Palestinian	402	Somalia	126,462	Ethiopia	31,389
Iraq	3,395	Serbia	392	Turkey	112,404	Bosnia	30,415
Malaysia	2,940	Ethiopia	384	Nigeria	108,295	El Salvador	30,193
Indonesia	2,867	Colombia	376	Iran	101,003	Sudan	29,491
Fiji	2,574	Tonga	350	Sri Lanka	89,311	Azerbaijan	28,666
Egypt	2,185	Jordan	325	Pakistan	87,964	Albania	28,557
Bangladesh	2,014	Mongolia	322	D.R. Congo	85,277	Cameroon	26,245
Lebanon	1,906	Kenya	305	Eritrea	84,487	Mauritania	24,314
Zimbabwe	1,745	Albania	252	Mexico	74,434	Guatemala	22,677
Nepal	1,637	Russia	240	Haiti	72,917	Vietnam	22,469
Korea	1,231	El Salvador	236	Armenia	61,122	Mongolia	21,903
Philippines	894	Ghana	235	Syria	60,174	Moldova	21,776
Turkey	873	S. Africa	198	Georgia	58,898	Ukraine	20,656
Vietnam	816	Israel	174	Bangladesh	53,465	Congo	20,152
Myanmar	684	Ukraine	152	Guinea	48,914	Angola	20,104
% of total	86.3	% of total	7.6	% of total	66.7	% of total	17.1

Source: UNHCR (2014). Has since been replaced online by UNHCR population statistics, retrieved from popstats.unhcr.org/en/asylum_seekers.

Notes: Serbia includes Montenegro, Kosovo and Macedonia; Sudan includes South Sudan. Stateless and unknown citizenships are included in total but not listed.

Part of the difference in the trends may be due to asylum policies and economic performance in Australia as compared with other destinations. But it may also be due to differences in the origin-country composition due to Australia's unique location. To examine the origin-country composition of applications, we focus on 19 major destination countries, which are also those used for the econometric analysis presented below.[1] Table 9.1 shows the origin-country composition of total applications from 2004 to 2012 for Australia and for the aggregate of 18 other destination countries. Over this period, total applications to Australia numbered 87,000, as compared with 3.4 million for the other 18 destination countries. Five of the top 10 countries of origin are the same for Australia as for the 18-country total, and this is likely to account for some of the similarity in the year-to-year movements. Not surprisingly, origin countries in the Asia–Pacific region are much more prominent for applications to Australia than for the other countries.

Analysing refugee and asylum seeker movements

A number of studies have used econometric analysis to explain the number of refugees emanating from a wide range of origin countries, focusing on the origin-country causes of displacement. In a pioneering paper, Schmeidl (1997) analysed the stock of refugees from over 100 countries during the 1970s. She found that the most significant variables were those representing armed conflict, especially genocide and politicide. These variables overshadowed others such as political rights, civil liberties and ethnic tensions. Intervening factors (those that facilitate or impede flight) appeared less important than has sometimes been suggested. Analysing changes over time in the stock of refugees, Davenport, Moore, and Poe (2003) and Moore and Shellman (2004) largely confirmed these findings. Subsequent research has elaborated on these themes. Moore and Shellman (2007) focus on the direction of refugee flights, finding that refugees move to places that are free of conflict, where incomes are higher and where the costs of transit are lower. Melander and Öberg (2006) analyse the persistence in displacements, arguing that the flows tend to decrease when those most able or willing to move have left. They also found that outflows are reduced by regime transition in the origin country but increased by regime collapse.

---

1   These are: Australia, Austria, Belgium, Canada, the Czech Republic, Denmark, France, Germany, Hungary, Ireland, Italy, the Netherlands, Norway, Poland, Spain, Sweden, the UK and the US.

A major theme emerging from these studies is that refugee flights can be understood as depending on the balance between the costs and benefits of leaving as compared with those of staying. This also helps to explain the distinction between cross-border flight and internal displacement. Moore and Shellman (2006) find that civil war, dissident terror and government violence increases the number of refugees relative to the number of internally displaced. This is also consistent with the finding that the wider the spread of violence, the more likely it will generate refugees (Melander & Öberg, 2007). A second generation of studies analyses displacement at the local level. Adhikari (2012) finds that migration from districts in Nepal depends positively on violence and opportunity but negatively on the solidarity of local networks. Studies of Columbia also highlight the individual- and community-level complexities in the choice of whether to leave and where to go (Engel & Ibáñez, 2007; Steele, 2009). Analysing individual-level data for four other Latin American countries, Alvarado and Massey (2010) find that emigration was less likely for those with higher wealth and education but more likely for those with family in the US. These studies serve as a reminder that (a) conditions in origin countries are heterogeneous and may not be well captured by country-wide aggregates, and (b) that some variables may influence both the costs and the benefits of flight.

Several studies have analysed panel data on asylum applications to countries in the developed world. Neumayer (2004) took as the dependent variable the shares for each destination of applicants from each origin country over the years 1982–99. This method nets out common origin-country effects. He found significant positive effects for the level and growth rate of gross domestic product (GDP) per capita in the destination, but a negative influence for the presence of right-wing populist governments. Bilateral links were also found to be highly significant, in the form either of the stock of migrants from the origin country, or deeper drivers such as colonial links, common language and distance. The only policy variable used was the overall recognition rate for the destination. The effect was positive, as expected, but small. Using a similar estimating framework, Thielemann (2006) analysed asylum applications to 20 destination countries for 1985–99. He found that a country's unemployment rate negatively influenced its share of asylum applications, while its foreign-born population had a positive effect. He also used an index of policy, made up of five components, which overall had a negative effect. Examining the individual components of policy, he found that the impact of refugee integration policies was weak compared with the effects of variables representing refugee status-determination procedures.[2]

Using panel data for 14 destinations for the years 1981–99 and disaggregating applications by origin continent, Hatton (2004) found that relative income, destination unemployment and the cumulative stock of applications were important influences. A composite index of asylum policy toughness based on 11 components gave a significant negative coefficient. This implies that the tightening of policy that occurred over the two decades to 1999 reduced asylum claims in the EU by about 150,000. Hatton (2009) examined the effects of policy on asylum flows from 56 origin countries to 19 destination countries from 1997 to 2009. The overall effect of the round of policy tightening between 2001 and 2006 was to reduce annual asylum applications to these 19 countries by 108,000, or about one third of the total decrease.

Focusing on Australia, Hatton and Lim (2005) made an econometric assessment of asylum applications to Australia together with six other countries: New Zealand, Canada, the US, the UK, France and Germany. They found that the destination country's unemployment rate had no significant effect. The change in Australian asylum policies in 2001 had a larger negative effect than was found for major policy packages in other countries, such as the UK in 2003 and Germany in 2002. Hatton and Lim argued that this was partly because the policy package itself was tougher both in terms of the scope of the changes and their enforcement. It was also partly due to the publicity that was generated, both nationally and internationally, by the Tampa incident. This may have produced a reputation effect that was not reversed by the subsequent easing of policy until the change of government in 2008 (Crock & Ghezelbash, 2010; Hatton, 2011, Ch. 9).

Other studies have focused on individual countries and on specific policies. Controlling for a variety of origin-country variables, Rotte, Vogler, and Zimmermann (1997) found that German policy reform of 1987 and the revision of the Basic Law in 1993 both had large negative effects (see also Vogler & Rotte, 2000). For Switzerland, Holzer, Schneider, and Widmer (2000a, 2000b) also found that policy reform in 1990 had a significant negative effect on applications.

---

2   See also Thielemann (2004) and Neumayer (2005).

While the studies of European countries have focused on changes in the criteria for asylum and the refugee status determination procedures, another line of enquiry examines the effects of border controls on irregular migration, particularly along the US border with Mexico. Such studies have typically found that greater effort and expenditure on border control had discernible but fairly modest effects on the number of apprehensions and by inference the number of crossings (see for example Hanson & Spilimbergo, 1999; Orrenius, 2006; Cornelius & Salehyan, 2007; Bohn & Pugatch, 2013). Other studies have assessed the impact of visa policies. Cziaka and Hobolth (2014) found that imposing visa requirements reduced asylum applications from an origin to a destination by around half—a similar effect to that found by Neumayer (2010) for all migration. Overall, these studies suggest that policy effects are likely to differ both across countries and between types of policy.

Asylum policy in Australia and other developed countries

Asylum policy in Australia is governed internationally by the 1951 Refugee Convention and in domestic legislation by the *Migration Act 1958* and subsequent acts and amendments. Australia has long operated a refugee settlement program, under which refugees are resettled from refugee populations in the Middle East, Asia and Africa. Since 1991, the quota for the Humanitarian Programme has fluctuated between 12,000 and 20,000 per annum. Spontaneous asylum seekers arriving by sea and by air (the onshore program) were few in number until the 1980s. The policy of mandatory detention for unauthorised boat arrivals (included in the *Migration Act 1958*) was increasingly enforced and extended to all unlawful arrivals in the *Migration Reform Act 1992*. From 1996–97 onwards, onshore grants of asylum were included in the overall target, so that they would effectively reduce the number accepted through the offshore program. A surge of arrivals led to the creation in 1999 of three-year temporary protection visas (TPVs), with much-reduced rights for unauthorised arrivals who qualified for protection.[3] The introduction

---

3   TPVs provided the right to work and to certain benefits, including Medicare, but they did not confer the right to re-enter Australia once having left, or the right to family reunification. TPV holders were eligible to apply for permanent protection after 30 months, a status that could only be granted if the need for protection was ongoing.

of TPVs was followed by legislation that imposed sanctions on people smugglers and provided for the boarding, search and detention of ships suspected of carrying unauthorised asylum seekers.[4]

Dramatic events followed in September 2001 with the arrival off Christmas Island of a Norwegian freighter the MV Tampa, which had taken on board 433 asylum seekers when their vessel the KM Palapa 1 had got into distress in the open seas. The Tampa was initially refused permission to land the asylum seekers, and there followed a week-long standoff until an agreement was reached by which a third of the passengers were taken to New Zealand and the remainder to Nauru, the latter in exchange for financial support from the Australian Government. A month later, the Australian Government passed six new bills into law. The first two involved the excision of Christmas Island, Ashmore Reef and some other small islands from Australian territory for the purposes of establishing claims to asylum in Australia, and they provided for such arrivals to be processed offshore in Nauru and Papua New Guinea. Applicants who had spent at least seven days in a 'safe' country while in transit were denied eligibility for a permanent protection visa. Another act significantly narrowed the definition of a refugee used in the procedure for determining status.[5] Further measures included harsher penalties for people smuggling offences and limitation of the grounds for judicial review of status determination decisions.

2001 witnessed a severe tightening of asylum policy, although some of the elements were later relaxed, including softening of TPV policy in 2004, and in 2005, time limits were introduced on the processing of asylum claims. In 2007, offshore processing on Nauru and Manus Island was terminated by the incoming government. The detention regime was partially and gradually relaxed, and from 2009, it was used only as a last resort. A further step came in 2008 with the abolition of TPVs so that all those granted protection received permanent visas. Taken together, these measures represent a substantial reversal of the key elements of the 2001 policy framework.[6]

---

4   Summaries of policy development and timelines are provided by York (2003), Karlsen, Phillips, and Koleth (2010) and Phillips and Spinks (2013).

5   In particular by restricting the interpretation of 'persecution' and of 'particular social groups' membership of which could give rise to a claim for protection.

6   Asylum seekers arriving in Christmas Island or other excised places were only permitted to enter the status determination procedure at the discretion of the Minister and they faced restricted rights of review or appeal.

Unauthorised boat arrivals resumed in 2009 and rose steeply thereafter. In 2010, processing was suspended for boat arrivals from Afghanistan and Sri Lanka, origin countries for a majority of arrivals at Christmas Island. In August 2011, a plan to transfer asylum seekers to Malaysia for processing was rejected by the High Court. In late 2011, some of the unauthorised arrivals were issued with bridging visas and released into community centres. In response to the mounting numbers, the government appointed an Expert Panel on Asylum Seekers, which reported in August 2012. It recommended offshore processing centres on Nauru and Manus Island be reopened. The new government of 2013 embarked on a policy to toughen border controls and to 'push back the boats', to reintroduce TPVs along the lines of the 1999 model, and to introduce a fast track status determination procedure. With this, the policy stance largely reverted to that of 2001.[7]

Since the late 1990s, asylum policies in Europe and North America have been influenced by two developments. The first relates to the broader issue of the securitisation of migration, following the 9/11 attacks. The USA PATRIOT Act, for example, dramatically increased the number of border control agents. An act of May 2002 further strengthened border controls by establishing an integrated database system for arrivals and departures linked to fingerprinting and biometric monitoring. Canada also tightened its border security and an act of 2001 introduced reforms that included detention of asylum seekers without documents.

The second development related to asylum policies in the EU, stemming from the Treaty of Amsterdam (effective 1999), which shifted asylum policies from the level of intergovernmental cooperation to that of community integration.[8] It marked the beginning of the establishment by stages of a common European asylum system (CEAS). The so-called Dublin II Regulation embodied a new mechanism for determining the state responsible for an asylum claim and providing for transfers. The Qualification Directive established a common set of criteria to be used in the refugee status determination procedure, and the Asylum Procedures Directive covered issues such as the treatment of manifestly unfounded claims, rights to interviews, to legal assistance and to appeals as well as common rules for granting subsidiary protection.

---

7   In some respects, such as offshore processing, recent policies go further than 2001. For example, those on Nauru and Manus Island have no right to resettlement in Australia, even if they are recognised as refugees (see Warbrooke, 2014). On the other hand, families with children who would otherwise be in detention in Australia are now released on bridging visas.

8   Further details on policy developments in Europe are provided in Hatton (2011, Ch. 6, 2012).

While the first stage of the CEAS fell far short of complete harmonisation, it did create some convergence in policy and practice (Thielemann & El-Enany, 2009). The second stage of the CEAS involved deeper cooperation in several areas, in particular the establishment in 2003 of the European Dactyloscopy (EURODAC) fingerprint database of asylum applicants, and in 2005 of the European Agency for the Management of Operational Coordination at the External Borders of the Member States of the European Union (Frontex), to strengthen the EU's external border. These initiatives were carried forward under the third stage of the CEAS from 2009, which also saw, among other things, the establishment of the European Asylum Support Office to support and promote further harmonisation and policy integration.

Despite EU harmonisation, the trends in policy differed widely among individual EU countries. One reason was that most EU regulations set minimum standards that were, initially at least, not binding on most countries. This left room for a considerable tightening of policy from the early 2000s at the national level. The Netherlands, for example, introduced a range of new border controls in 1998 and an act of 2001 restricted the scope of subsidiary protection and limited the right to appeal. A number of EU countries further tightened the processing of manifestly unfounded claims. But not all policy changes were restrictive. For example, a number of countries introduced proactive integration policies, and some, such as Finland in 2006 and Germany in 2007, expanded eligibility for employment.

A quantitative index of asylum policies

A number of attempts have been made to represent asylum policy in one or more quantitative indicators or in the form of a composite index (for a review, see Czaika & de Haas, 2013). Here, we apply a revised and updated version of the policy index used previously by Hatton (2009, 2011). The index includes 15 indicators of asylum policy, divided into three groups. The first group relates to policies that limit access to the destination country's asylum procedures, mainly by preventing potential asylum seekers from reaching the territory. The second relates to the status determination procedure and is intended to capture the likelihood that an applicant gains some form of residency status. The third relates to welfare conditions during and immediately after processing.

Access policies	*Processing polices*	*Welfare policies*
Visa requirements	Definition of a refugee	Permission to work
Border control/security	Humanitarian category	Access to welfare benefits
Trafficking regulations	Manifestly unfounded claims	Detention policy
Carrier sanctions	Expedited procedures	Deportation policy
Application outside country	Scope for appeals	Family reunification

The idea is to capture changes in a country's laws, regulations or practice under each of the 15 categories. These are intended to reflect 'major' changes in policy, i.e. those that amount to significant changes in the conditions facing a substantial share of asylum seekers. In each of the 15 categories, the index increases by one unit when policy becomes significantly tougher, i.e. less advantageous to asylum seekers. If policy becomes significantly more favourable towards asylum seekers, then the index decreases by one unit. As far as can be ascertained, the change is dated as the quarter that it took effect rather than when it was announced or when the legislation was first passed. Inevitably, the policy index developed here is a crude representation of policy developments in Australia and overseas. It takes no account of the differences in the scope and restrictiveness of specific Australian policies in comparison with those of other countries and neither does it account for differences in the way that policy is enforced.

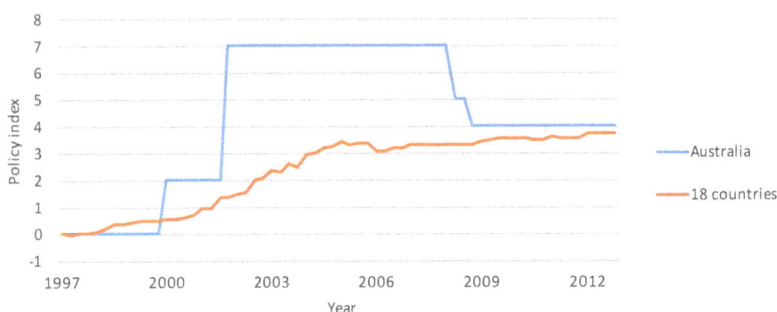

Figure 9.3: Composite policy index, Australia and 18-country average
Source: Authors' calculations, see text.

This 15-component quarterly index starts at zero for each component in the first quarter of 1997 and runs to the last quarter of 2012. Figure 9.3 shows the composite index for Australia compared with the unweighted average for the 18 other countries in the dataset. In keeping with the qualitative account of policy, it shows the steep increase in policy toughness from 1999 to 2001 followed by a partial reversal in 2008–09. The average index for 18 countries shows a fairly steep increase between 2000 and 2006, followed by a levelling off. However, this is an average of very diverse trajectories across different countries. Over the period as a whole there was a dramatic tightening of policy in the UK and Denmark and to a lesser extent Norway, Ireland, Switzerland and the Netherlands. By contrast, policy eased in Sweden and the Czech Republic and was little changed in Poland, Spain, Canada and Germany (see Hatton & Moloney, 2015).

Econometric analysis of asylum applications by origin and destination

We create an annual dataset of asylum applications from 48 origin countries to the 19 OECD destinations. The origin countries are those that feature in the top 40 of asylum applications to the 18 destination countries over the period 2004–12, as listed in Table 9.1 (right-hand panel). In addition, we include any others that appear in the top 20 origin countries for applications to Australia (left-hand column of Table 9.1) over the same period (excluding Myanmar which we are forced to drop for lack of key explanatory variables). The data on the number of first instance asylum applications from each origin to each destination are taken from the UNHCR's online database. These are supplemented from the UNHCR's annual report, *Asylum levels and trends in industrialized countries*, in order to extend the series back to 1997. The origin and destination countries included in the analysis are listed in Hatton and Moloney (2015). The particular origin–destination dyads that are included for analysis are those that involve at least 300 applications over the 16 years included in our analysis, 1997–2012. This avoids cases in which there are a large number of dyad-years where the number of applications is zero. This leaves us with 626 origin–destination country pairs out of a possible 48×19=912. We also lose some observations in cases where we are unable to obtain the data for the full period, notably for the years 1997–99, so that the average number of observations per dyad is 15.4.

Apart from the policy index, the other explanatory variables have been widely used in other studies. To capture terror and human rights abuses in origin countries we use the political terror scale, an index ranging from 1 (no terror) to 5 (high terror). We also use the indexes provided by Freedom House, one for civil liberties and one for political rights. These are on a scale of 1 (complete freedom) to 7 (freedom highly restricted). We also include a variable to capture the wars (usually civil wars) that are a prominent feature of many origin countries. Here we use the Uppsala Conflict Data Program (UCDP) index of battle deaths (best estimate), in thousands. For both origin and destination countries, we capture overall living standards with real GDP per capita from the Penn World Tables. The employment situation in destination countries is represented by the OECD harmonised unemployment rate.

We include a measure of the stock of immigrants from each origin country living at each destination. This is the bilateral migrant stock in 2000–01, and it includes only adults aged 25 and over. This is aimed at capturing the diaspora network effect that is well known in the migration literature. In order to reflect previously established communities, we use observations from near the beginning of the period of analysis. While this captures the assistance and encouragement of relatives, often working though family reunification systems and deepening migration corridors, it also reflects deeper fundamentals such as colonial and historic links, and language and cultural affinities. Finally, we also include the distance between the national capitals of each origin and destination pair. The sources of all the variables are listed in Hatton and Moloney (2015).

Table 9.2 shows the results of regressions with fixed effects by origin country. The dependent variable is the log of the number of applications from an origin to a destination (plus one to account for zeros). The first column of Table 9.2 includes a dummy variable for each year but no destination country dummies. Not surprisingly, the diaspora effect is highly significant. Given that origin-country fixed effects are included, this reflects differences in the migrant stock across destinations. As both the dependent variable and the migrant stock are in logs, the coefficient implies that a 10 per cent increase in the stock would increase the flow of asylum applications by 2.7 per cent. The effect of log distance between country capitals is negative and significant, even in the presence of the migrant stock. The result is as would be expected if the cost and difficulty of reaching a destination increases with distance, and it may also reflect the existence of alternatives nearer to the origin country. Every 10 per cent increase in distance reduces applications by more than 5 per cent.

Table 9.2: Asylum applications, origin and destination effects, 1997–2012 (Dependent variable: log asylum applications from origin to destination)

	(1)	(2)	(3)	(4)
Political terror scale	0.214** (4.44)	0.214** (4.48)	0.221** (4.55)	0.200* (1.98)
Civil liberties (Freedom House index)	0.285** (4.81)	0.285** (4.93)	0.290** (4.76)	0.291** (4.70)
Political rights (Freedom House index)	−0.044 (1.07)	−0.044 (1.06)	−0.049 (1.18)	−0.049 (1.18)
Civil war battle deaths (000s)	0.011 (0.64)	0.012 (0.76)	0.010 (0.62)	0.010 (0.60)
Log origin country real GDP per capita	−0.486** (2.19)	−0.517** (2.35)	−0.526** (2.26)	−0.524** (2.25)
Log migrant stock in 2000–01 from origin at destination	0.270** (13.74)	0.226** (8.54)		
Log distance from origin to destination	−0.582** (4.41)	−0.777** (4.07)		
Log destination country GDP per capita	−0.404* (1.82)	0.178 (0.35)	0.082 (0.16)	0.082 (0.16)
Unemployment rate at destination	−0.043** (3.80)	−0.025** (2.22)	−0.025** (2.29)	−0.028* (1.85)
Political terror scale* distance from origin to destination				0.015 (0.26)
Unemployment rate at destination* distance				0.002 (0.19)
Fixed effects (number of FE)	Origin (48)	Origin (48)	Origin*Dest (626)	Origin*Dest (626)
Destination dummies	No	Yes	No	No
Year dummies	Yes	Yes	Yes	Yes
R² within	0.28	0.40	0.11	0.12
No. of obs.	9,610	9,610	9,610	9,610

Note: 'z' statistics are in parentheses; significance at 5 and 10 per cent denoted by ** and * respectively. Constant terms and coefficients on destination dummies and year dummies are not reported.

The coefficients on the migrant stock and distance change very little when destination dummies are added in column (2). But one effect of this is to change the coefficient on log destination GDP from negative to positive, although it remains insignificant. The destination dummies are not shown but it is worth noting that, conditional on the other variables, applications to Australia are about half the average for the other 18 countries. The third column includes origin-by-destination fixed effects, and so the migrant stock and distance, which take only one value for each dyad, drop out. Nevertheless, there is very little change in the other coefficients between columns (1) and (3). Not surprisingly, a large share of these dyad-specific effects is captured in columns (1) and (2) by the migrant stock and distance, and this accounts for the lower R-squared in column (3).

One of the most important origin-country effects is the political terror scale, where an increase of one point on the five-point scale increases asylum applications by about 20 per cent. Of the two Freedom House indexes, only that for civil liberties is significant, in contrast to some previous findings. An increase of one point on the scale (a deterioration in civil liberties) increases asylum applications by nearly 30 per cent. The lack of significance of political rights may reflect the fact that this can potentially cut in both directions: political repression may increase the incentive to leave but at the same time reduce the ability to do so. War deaths provide little additional explanatory power, which may seem surprising in light of large numbers fleeing from civil wars. But these effects are accounted for by the variables that represent human rights abuses and lack of civil liberties. Interestingly, the log of origin-country GDP per capita gives a significant negative coefficient, indicating that the richer (or the less poor) the country, the lower are asylum applications even though poverty may also constrain the ability to migrate. The coefficient implies that a 10 per cent increase in origin-country GDP per capita reduces asylum applications by around 5 per cent.

Although the effect of destination GDP per capita is weak, the destination unemployment rate has a negative effect, as expected. As Australia avoided the recession that began with the global financial crisis (GFC), this could account for the relative rise in applications from 2008. An increase in the unemployment rate in a destination country from, say, 5 to 10 per cent would reduce asylum applications to that country by 12.5 per cent. Although the unemployment rate rose more in other countries than in Australia from 2008 to 2010, this divergence in unemployment rates would account for at most a 5 per cent relative increase in asylum applications to Australia.

It is possible that the effects of 'push' and 'pull' on the number of applications would be attenuated by the cost and difficulty of reaching a destination. One way to test this is to interact some of the key variables with the log of distance. For example, an eruption of human rights abuses could induce refugees to seek the nearest destination. Column (4) in Table 9.2 adds an interaction between the log of distance and the political terror scale. The coefficient is not negative or significant as the hypothesis would suggest, although the main effect is weakened. A similar argument might be made for destination country effects: the more remote from the origin country the weaker the 'pull' effects would be. But although the interaction between distance and the unemployment rate at destination country is positive, as expected, it is small and insignificant. Other interactions, not reported here, produced similarly insignificant results.

The effects of policy

We add to the basic model the policy indexes discussed earlier. It should be recalled that there is no dyadic dimension to this: for a given destination, our index of policy is the same towards applicants from all origin countries. The first column of Table 9.3 shows that the asylum policy index has a strong negative effect. This is consistent with the results of other studies, which typically found that tougher policies have deterrent effects on the flow of applications that are significantly negative but often modest in magnitude. The coefficient implies that a one-point increase in the overall index reduces asylum applications by around 5 per cent. Column (2) of Table 9.3 includes each of the three components of the index separately. Two of the three have strong negative effects. These are policies on access to territory and more restrictive processing of applications. An increase of one point on one of these indices reduces asylum claims by around 10 per cent. By contrast, the index for 'welfare', which is a rather heterogeneous collection of reception conditions and rights, seems to have no negative effect and perhaps a marginally positive effect. In this respect, the results are consistent those reported previously in Hatton (2009).

A widely used measure of the stance of asylum policy is the recognition rate. The measure used here is the share of all first instance claims that resulted in a positive outcome, either full convention status or acceptance on humanitarian grounds. This is the overall rate for the destination country, so it is not a dyadic variable. One of the pitfalls of using the recognition rate is that it is an outcome variable: it depends not only on policy but also on the merits of the applications considered. In particular, tougher processing rules may deter those with weaker claims, so that the coefficient on the recognition rate could go either way. In order to avoid possible endogeneity, column (3) of Table 9.3 includes the recognition rate lagged one year. As this represents the refugee status determination procedure, the policy index for processing is omitted. The coefficient is only significant at the 10 per cent level and it suggests a modest effect on applications—an increase of 10 percentage points in the recognition rate raises applications by 1.4 per cent. When the processing index is also included, the latter remains strongly significant, suggesting that the index is a better representation of policy than the recognition rate.

Table 9.3: Asylum applications and policy effects, 1997–2012 (Dependent variable: log asylum applications from origin to destination)

	(1)	(2)	(3)	(4)
Political terror scale	0.221** (4.53)	0.221** (4.57)	0.220** (4.55)	0.159** (2.64)
Civil liberties (Freedom House index)	0.289** (4.74)	0.292** (4.80)	0.290** (4.80)	0.206** (2.09)
Political rights (Freedom House index)	−0.050 (1.21)	−0.049 (1.19)	−0.050 (1.20)	0.019 (0.40)
Civil war battle deaths (000s)	0.010 (0.62)	0.010 (0.64)	0.010 (0.63)	0.009** (3.21)
Log origin country real GDP per capita	−0.533** (2.26)	−0.542** (2.32)	−0.540** (2.32)	−0.941** (3.87)
Log destination country GDP per capita	0.066 (0.12)	−0.122 (0.23)	−0.130 (0.25)	0.421 (0.93)
Unemployment rate at destination	−0.024** (2.14)	−0.024** (2.19)	−0.021* (1.90)	−0.024* (1.79)
Asylum policy index overall	−0.046** (4.03)			
Policy on access		−0.115** (4.12)	−0.130** (3.54)	−0.142** (4.34)
Policy on processing		−0.100** (6.45)		
Policy on welfare		0.049* (1.76)	−0.002 (0.24)	−0.011 (0.46)
Recognition rate (lagged)			0.143* (1.74)	0.099 (0.95)
Visitor visa required				−0.193 (1.63)
Fixed effects (number of FE)	Origin*Dest (626)	Origin*Dest (626)	Origin*Dest (626)	Origin*Dest (626)
Year dummies	Yes	Yes	Yes	Yes
R^2 within	0.12	0.13	0.12	0.15
No. of obs.	9,610	9,610	9,610	5,662

Note: 'z' statistics are in parentheses; significance at 5 and 10 per cent denoted by ** and * respectively. Constant terms and coefficients on year dummies are not reported.

One important issue raised in the literature is the effect of visa requirements, as noted above. The requirement for a visitor visa can be used as a screening device to reduce the number of claims from those entering the destination country from origin countries that are likely to produce asylum applications. The data on visa policy is limited, but Hobolth provides a dataset on visa requirements from each origin country to each destination. Unfortunately, the dataset starts only in 2001 (later for some destinations), and it omits Australia, Canada and Ireland. This reduces the number of available observations by more than 40 per cent. But an even greater limitation is that for 98 per cent of available observations, a visa is required and there are very few within-dyad changes (only 36). The result of adding the dummy variable for visa required is shown in column (4) of Table 9.3, and it gives a negative but insignificant coefficient. The order of magnitude—a reduction of about 20 per cent when a visa is required—is rather smaller than that obtained in other studies (Hatton, 2004; Czaika & Hobolth, 2013).

Of course, the policy effects in Table 9.3 are an average across all destination countries, where a one-point tightening in policy could mean different things. It is worth asking if the policy effects observed here adequately capture the effects of the sharp changes in Australian asylum policies. On one hand, the policy shifts in Australia were more dramatic than elsewhere, and might therefore be expected to have larger effects. But on the other hand, asylum seekers heading for Australia have fewer alternative destinations than those heading for Europe, and as a result the deterrent effect of policies for Australia would be weaker.

In the first column of Table 9.4 we include two dummies for key periods in asylum policy, one for 2002 onwards and another for 2008 onwards. Not surprisingly, the 2002 dummy is large and negative. This is on top of the average policy effect, so the restrictive policies introduced in late 2001 had larger effects than would have been expected based on the experience of other countries. The easing of policy from 2008 had the opposite effect, but its magnitude is not fully offsetting. It should be remembered, however, that our data stops in 2012, and so it does not include the surge of applications in 2013. It is worth noting, however, that these are large effects: a cut of around half in the numbers after 2001, and an increase of around a third from 2008. Column (2) of Table 9.4 shows that the results are similar when the three components of the policy index are entered separately, although the 2008 dummy is no longer significant.

Table 9.4: Asylum applications and policy effects, 1997–2012
(Dependent variable: log asylum applications from origin to destination)

	(1)	(2)	(3)	(4)
Political terror scale	0.222** (4.56)	0.222** (4.59)	0.223** (4.55)	0.222** (4.58)
Civil liberties (Freedom House index)	0.287** (4.70)	0.292** (4.75)	0.287** (4.70)	0.289** (4.76)
Political rights (Freedom House index)	–0.049 (1.18)	–0.048 (0.64)	–0.049 (0.63)	–0.049 (1.16)
Civil war battle deaths (000s)	0.010 (0.63)	0.010 (0.64)	0.010 (0.63)	0.010 (0.64)
Log origin country real GDP per capita	–0.537** (2.32)	–0.545** (2.33)	–0.537** (2.27)	–0.545** (2.33)
Log destination country GDP per capita	0.020 (0.04)	–0.145 (0.28)	0.028 (0.05)	–0.141 (0.27)
Unemployment rate at destination	–0.026** (2.25)	–0.026** (2.30)	–0.026** (2.35)	–0.026** (2.35)
Asylum policy index overall	–0.039** (3.24)		–0.040** (3.54)	
Policy on access		–0.099** (2.76)		–0.100** (2.80)
Policy on processing		–0.094** (5.79)		–0.095** (5.92)
Policy on welfare		0.054* (1.88)		0.053* (1.89)
Dummy: Australia from 2002	–0.513** (3.84)	–0.457** (2.99)		
Dummy: Australia from 2008	0.384** (2.03)	0.300* (1.76)		
Policy index overall* Australia dummy			–0.075** (3.40)	
Policy on access* Australia dummy				–0.097 (0.83)
Policy on processing* Australia dummy				–0.095 (1.25)
Fixed effects (number of FE)	Origin*Dest (626)	Origin*Dest (626)	Origin*Dest (626)	Origin*Dest (626)
Year dummies	Yes	Yes	Yes	Yes
R^2 within	0.12	0.13	0.13	0.13
No. of obs.	9610	9610	9610	9610

Note: 'z' statistics are in parentheses; significance at 5 and 10 per cent denoted by ** and * respectively. Constant terms and coefficients on year dummies are not reported.

Columns (3) and (4) investigate the issue of whether these shifts reflect stronger policy effects in Australia than in other destination countries. In column (3), the overall policy index is interacted with a dummy variable for Australia. The significant negative coefficient supports the idea that Australian policies had stronger effects than the average of other countries. Column (4) adds interactions for the two most important policy components, access and processing. Here, both interactions are negative, implying effects that are twice as large as the average for the other countries, but neither is significant, probably due to multicollinearity.

Counterfactual analysis

It is worth briefly illustrating what the regression results imply for individual countries in the dataset. We first look at the effects of changes in terror and civil liberties on the number of applications from certain origin countries. The method is to predict the change in applications to all destination countries over a period that is accounted for by the political terror scale and the Freedom House index of civil liberties in a particular origin country. The coefficients used in the prediction are from column (2) of Table 9.4. The predicted percentage changes in applications from 2000 to 2006 and from 2006 to 2012 are reported in Table 9.5. These countries are the top 20 origins of asylum applications to Australia (listed in the left-hand column of Table 9.1), with the addition of Syria and exception of Myanmar. However, the prediction is for the change in applications to all 19 destination countries, not just Australia.

Table 9.5: Predicted change in asylum applications due to political terror and civil liberties (percentage)

Country	2000–06	2006–12	Country	2000–06	2006–12
China	−9.2	0.6	Egypt	31.2	−16.8
Afghanistan	43.4	10.0	Bangladesh	29.5	−8.1
India	−7.9	13.2	Lebanon	−24.3	1.2
Sri Lanka	12.9	−17.2	Zimbabwe	78.2	−9.1
Iran	12.2	1.0	Nepal	27.3	−26.6
Pakistan	12.4	26.2	Korea	−8.0	1.4
Iraq	−24.8	−19.2	Philippines	0.2	0.8
Malaysia	−14.4	3.2	Turkey	−43.6	21.0
Indonesia	−39.9	0.6	Vietnam	−18.9	15.5
Fiji	−13.3	2.5	Syria	−23.9	112.3

Source: Authors' calculations, based on column (2) of Table 9.4.

Not surprisingly, the patterns are very different across origin countries. From 2000 to 2006, the number of applications from Afghanistan is predicted to increase by 43.4 per cent, and those from Zimbabwe by 78.2 per cent, solely due to the rise in terror and the decrease in civil liberties. On the other hand, these two variables predict substantial decreases in applications from Indonesia and Turkey. Over the period 2006 to 2012, there are again some negative and some positive predictions, notably the dramatic increase in predicted applications from Syria. As the scale and timing of these events varies widely between origin countries, their effects on total applications to any given destination are to some degree offsetting, and the overall impact is muted. For applications to Australia from the origin countries in our database, the overall effects of changes in terror and civil liberties is to decrease asylum applications by 9.1 per cent from 2000 to 2006 and to increase them by 6.5 per cent from 2006 to 2012.

The effects of asylum policies can be assessed by applying the same method to destination countries. The predictions in Table 9.6 are based on changes in policy on access and policy on the processing of asylum claims. For Australia, prediction (1) is based on the two policy indexes only. Based on those coefficients, the tightening of policy in the early 2000s is predicted to have reduced asylum claims by 28.7 per cent between 2000 and 2006, while the easing of policy at the end of the decade increased applications by an estimated 19.4 per cent. If, in addition, we include the effects of the dummy variables for 2002 onwards and 2008 onwards (prediction 2), the effects are greater than 50 per cent in both directions.

Table 9.6: Predicted change in asylum applications due to policy on access and processing (percentage)

Country	2000–06	2006–12	Country	2000–06	2006–12
Australia (1)	−28.7	19.4	Ireland	−14.1	1.8
Australia (2)	−53.6	59.6	Italy	−11.5	2.9
Austria	−27.7	−2.0	Netherlands	−27.1	1.4
Belgium	−8.7	0.9	Norway	−9.1	−12.2
Canada	−13.5	−8.1	Poland	3.5	−4.9
Czech Rep	−5.1	1.8	Spain	−9.5	3.0
Denmark	−26.5	5.8	Sweden	33.3	4.0
France	−16.8	11.2	Switzerland	−9.0	−18.0
Germany	−1.5	0.7	UK	−43.4	−8.5
Hungary	−6.1	−0.9	US	−8.5	−11.5

Source: Authors' calculations, based on column (2) of Table 9.4.

There is considerable diversity in the effects of policy in other countries. Table 9.6 shows that the severe tightening of policy in the UK between 2000 and 2006 predicts a reduction in applications of 43.4 per cent, while the tightening in Austria, Denmark and the Netherlands predict reductions of more than 20 per cent. By contrast, the easing of policy in Sweden is predicted to increase applications by a third. In 2006–12, applications in France are predicted to increase by 11.2 per cent, while declines of more than 10 per cent are predicted for Norway, Switzerland and the US, although the magnitude and variation in policy effects is less than for 2000–06. For the 18 countries excluding Australia, the predicted policy effect was to reduce applications overall by 11.5 per cent in 2000–06 and by 2.2 per cent in 2006–12.

Discussion

Consistent with our expectations, we find that terror, oppression and human rights abuse are the most powerful drivers of asylum applications from origin countries. Among the measures of origin-country political and social conditions, the political terror scale has a strong positive effect, while lack of civil liberties also has a positive effect. Origin country GDP per capita has a negative effect on the number of asylum claims, while destination country unemployment rates also have negative effects. Differences in unemployment trends since the recession account for only a small part of the relative increase in applications to Australia. Finally, destination country policy has a negative deterrent effect, but only through access and processing policies, not through welfare policies. These policies have significant deterrent effects, but they do not fully capture the impact of shifts in Australian policy after 2001 and again after 2007.

While the results obtained here are fairly robust, they come with several caveats. One is that we model flows as depending on conditions only in the origin and destination countries. This does not account for the effects of conditions in third countries, and particularly in transit countries. Although our approach sidesteps the heterogeneity across origin and destination country pairs, it may still be vulnerable to biases arising from within-pair endogeneity. Second, there is a great deal of heterogeneity in the circumstances that lead to asylum claims, which cannot be captured in aggregate-level analysis. As a result, we explain only a small proportion of the year-to-year variation in individual origin-to-destination streams.

The indicators that we use to explain migration flows are measured at the country level and do not capture within-country differences in the forces that drive asylum applications, for example between regions or ethnic groups. And third, for reasons outlined above, our policy index is inevitably a crude representation of the often subtle shifts in asylum policies.

Reference list

Adhikari, P. (2012). The plight of the forgotten ones: Civil war and forced migration. *International Studies Quarterly, 56*(3), 590–606. doi.org/10.1111/j.1468-2478.2011.00712.x

Alvarado, S. E., & Massey, D. S. (2010). In search of peace: Structural adjustment, violence, and international migration. *Annals of the American Academy of Political and Social Science, 630*(1), 137–61. doi.org/10.1177/0002716210368107

Bohn, S., & Pugatch, T. (2013). *US border enforcement and Mexican immigrant location choice.* Institute for the Study of Labor (IZA) discussion paper 7846. Bonn: IZA.

Cornelius, W. A., & Salehyan, I. (2007). Does border enforcement deter unauthorized immigration? The case of Mexican migration to the United States of America. *Regulation and Governance, 1*(2), 139–53. doi.org/10.1111/j.1748-5991.2007.00007.x

Crock, M., & Ghezelbash, D. (2010). Do loose lips bring ships? The role of policy, politics and human rights in managing unauthorised boat arrivals. *Griffith Law Review, 19*(2), 238–87. doi.org/10.1080/10383 441.2010.10854676

Czaika, M., & de Haas, H. (2013). The effectiveness of immigration policies. *Population and Development Review, 39*(3), 487–508. doi.org/10.1111/j.1728-4457.2013.00613.x

Czaika, M., & Hobolth, M. (2014). *Deflection into irregularity? The (un) intended effects of restrictive asylum and visa policies.* Working paper 84. Oxford: International Migration Institute.

Davenport, C. A., Moore, W. H., & Poe, S. C. (2003). Sometimes you just have to leave: Domestic threats and forced migration, 1964–1989. *International Interactions, 29*(1), 27–55. doi.org/10.1080/03050620304597

Engel, S., & Ibáñez, A. M. (2007). Displacement due to violence in Colombia: A household-level analysis. *Economic Development and Cultural Change, 55*(2), 335–65. doi.org/10.1086/508712

Hanson, G. H., & Spilimbergo, A. (1999). Illegal immigration, border enforcement, and relative wages: Evidence from apprehensions at the US–Mexico border. *American Economic Review, 89*(5), 1337–57. doi.org/10.1257/aer.89.5.1337

Hatton, T. J. (2004). Seeking asylum in Europe. *Economic Policy, 19*(38), 5–62. doi.org/10.1111/j.1468-0327.2004.00118.x

Hatton, T. J. (2009). The rise and fall of asylum: What happened and why. *Economic Journal, 119*(535), F183–F213. doi.org/10.1111/j.1468-0297.2008.02228.x

Hatton, T. J. (2011). *Seeking asylum: Trends and policies in the OECD.* London: Centre for Economic Policy Research.

Hatton, T. J. (2012). *Asylum policy in the EU: The case for deeper integration.* The Australian National University, Centre for Economic Policy Research working paper 660. Canberra: Centre for Economic Policy Research.

Hatton, T. J. and Lim, A. (2005), Australian Asylum Policy: The Tampa Effect. *Agenda, 12*, 115–30.

Hatton, T. J., & Moloney, J. (2015). *Applications for asylum in the developed world: Modelling asylum claims by origin and destination.* Centre for Economic Policy Research discussion paper 10678. London: Centre for Economic Policy Research.

Holzer, T., Schneider, G., & Widmer, T. (2000a). Discriminating decentralization: Federalism and the handling of asylum applications in Switzerland, 1988–1996. *Journal of Conflict Resolution, 44*(2), 250–76. doi.org/10.1177/0022002700044002005

Holzer, T., Schneider, G., & Widmer, T. (2000b). The impact of legislative deterrence measures on the number of asylum seekers in Switzerland. *International Migration Review, 34*(4), 1182–216. doi.org/10.2307/2675979

Karlsen, E., Phillips, J., & Koleth, E. (2010). Seeking asylum: Australia's humanitarian response to a global challenge. Parliamentary library. Canberra: Parliament of Australia. Retrieved from library.bsl.org.au/jspui/bitstream/1/3915/1/Seeking%20asyllum%20Australias%20humanitarian%20response%20to%20global%20challenge.pdf.

Melander, E., & Öberg, M. (2006). Time to go? Duration dependence in forced migration. *International Interactions, 32*(2), 129–152. doi.org/10.1080/03050620600574873

Melander, E., & Öberg, M. (2007). The threat of violence and forced migration: Geographical scope trumps intensity of fighting. *Civil Wars, 9*(2), 156–73. doi.org/10.1080/13698240701207310

Moore, W. H., & Shellman, S. M. (2004). Fear of persecution: Forced migration, 1952–1995. *Journal of Conflict Resolution, 48*(5), 727–53. doi.org/10.1177/0022002704267767

Moore, W. H., & Shellman S. M. (2007). Whither will they go? A global study of refugees' destinations, 1965–1995. *International Studies Quarterly, 51*(4), 811–34. doi.org/10.1111/j.1468-2478.2007.00478.x

Neumayer, E. (2004). Asylum destination choice: What makes some West European countries more attractive than others? *European Union Politics, 5*(2), 155–80. doi.org/10.1177/1465116504042444

Neumayer, E. (2005). Bogus refugees? The determinants of asylum migration to Western Europe. *International Studies Quarterly, 49*(3), 389–409. doi.org/10.1111/j.1468-2478.2005.00370.x

Neumayer, E. (2010). Visa restrictions and bilateral travel. *Professional Geographer, 62*(2), 171–81. doi.org/10.1080/00330121003600835

Orrenius, P. M. (2006). The effect of US border enforcement on the crossing behavior of Mexican migrants. In Durand, J., & Massey, D. S. (Eds), *Crossing the border: Research from the Mexican migration project* (pp. 281–98). New York: Russel Sage.

Phillips, J., & Spinks, H. (2013). *Boat arrivals in Australia since 1976*. Parliamentary library research paper. Canberra: Parliament of Australia. Retrieved from www.aph.gov.au/About_Parliament/Parliamentary_ Departments/Parliamentary_Library/pubs/rp/rp1314/BoatArrivals.

Rotte, R., Vogler, M., & Zimmermann, K. F. (1997). South–North refugee migration: Lessons for development cooperation. *Review of Development Economics, 1*(1), 99–115. doi.org/10.1111/1467-9361.00008

Schmeidl, S. (1997). Exploring the causes of forced migration: A pooled time series analysis. *Social Science Quarterly, 78*(2), 284–308.

Steele, A. (2009). Seeking safety: Avoiding displacement and choosing destinations in civil wars. *Journal of Peace Research, 46*(3), 419–29. doi.org/10.1177/0022343309102660

Thielemann, E. R. (2004). Why asylum policy harmonisation undermines refugee burden-sharing. *European Journal of Migration and Law, 6*(1), 47–64. doi.org/10.1163/1571816041518769

Thielemann, E. (2006). The effectiveness of governments' attempts to control unwanted migration. In Parsons, C. A., & Smeeding, T. M. (Eds), *Immigration and the transformation of Europe* (pp. 473–80). Cambridge: Cambridge University Press. doi.org/10.1017/CBO 9780511493577.017

Thielemann, E., & El-Enany, N. (2009). *Beyond fortress Europe? How European cooperation strengthens refugee protection*. Unpublished paper. London School of Economics.

United Nations High Commissioner for Refugees. (2001). *Statistical yearbook for 2001*. Geneva: Author.

United Nations High Commissioner for Refugees. (2014). Statistical online population database, accessed 16 October, 2014. Has since been replaced online by UNHCR population statistics, retrieved from popstats.unhcr.org/en/asylum_seekers.

United Nations High Commissioner for Refugees. (Various years). *Asylum levels and trends in industrialized countries*. Geneva: Author.

Vogler, M., & Rotte, R. (2000). The effects of development on migration: Theoretical issues and new empirical evidence. *Journal of Population Economics 13*(3), 485–508. doi.org/10.1007/s001480050148

Warbrooke, A. (2014). Australia's 'Pacific solution': Issues for the Pacific Islands. *Asia and the Pacific Policy Studies, 1*(2), 337–48. doi.org/10.1002/app5.32

York, B. (2003). *Australia and refugees, 1901–2002: An annotated chronology based on official sources.* Parliamentary library. Canberra: Parliament of Australia. Retrieved from www.aph.gov.au/binaries/library/pubs/online/03chr02.pdf.

10

Assisted voluntary return and reintegration of migrants: A comparative approach

Khalid Koser and Katie Kuschminder

Sustainable voluntary return of migrants back to their origin countries is an important aspect of comprehensive migration management. It is widely recognised as the preferred mode of return and its take-up is a key issue in return management. It should ensure that the rights and dignity of the migrants involved are respected.

Both origin and destination countries support a wide range of policies and programs intended to facilitate sustainable voluntary return. Program criteria and conditions vary significantly, and it is not clear which settings are the most effective in enabling return, or promoting sustainable return and reintegration. A lack of accessible data and consensus on how to define and measure program effectiveness makes it more difficult to assess the impact of assisted voluntary return (Paasche, 2014). Program impact also varies across different types of migrants.

This chapter presents a summary of the findings of a comparative study that explored the factors influencing the decision to return, including the role played by return policy interventions. The study also aimed to enhance understanding of the concept of sustainable return, how to measure it, and how to promote it. The full report of the study is available on the International Organization for Migration (IOM) website.[1]

The overall aim of this research is to inform policies and programs for assisting the voluntary return and reintegration of migrants, including irregular migrants and unsuccessful asylum seekers. Three specific objectives support this aim: analysis of the migrant return decision; development of a framework for defining and measuring sustainable return; and an assessment of what factors determine reintegration and sustainable return.

This chapter is in five main sections. The next section summarises the methodological approach. The following section considers the factors influencing the decision to return, further testing a model developed in an earlier study. The third main section develops a new definition of 'sustainable return', and a return and reintegration index, which is subsequently tested. We then consider the factors that promote reintegration and sustainable return. The final section summarises the key policy implications arising from the study, with appropriate warnings concerning wider applicability.

Methodology

This study included three primary sources of data collection. First, a comprehensive literature and policy review was conducted on assisted voluntary return and reintegration and sustainable return. Second, an analysis was conducted of data on returns from the various destination countries, and of IOM-assisted voluntary return data for the selected origin countries. Finally, primary data were collected through interviews with migrants and returnees in destination, transit and origin countries, as well as with key stakeholders wherever possible to gain further information on the context of assisted voluntary return. This chapter mainly draws on this primary data.

Research was conducted in four destination countries (Australia, the Netherlands, Switzerland and the UK), eight origin countries (Afghanistan, Bangladesh, Ethiopia, Iraq, Pakistan, Sri Lanka, Sudan and

---

1   For the full report, see Koser and Kuschminder (2015).

Vietnam) and three transit countries (Indonesia, Greece and Turkey). These study countries were selected in consultation with the Department of Immigration and Border Protection and IOM, and for various reasons, including their relevance in terms of priority migration flows to Australia, the scale of asylum and return flows, and the variety of assistance policies and programs.

A semi-structured interview questionnaire was used with migrants and returnees. A separate questionnaire was used in the origin countries and destination countries, and a slightly modified version of the destination country questionnaire was used in the transit countries. All of the questionnaires followed a life-cycle approach and, wherever possible, had the same questions to ensure comparability.

Recruitment of participants depended on the country context. In each destination country, the Department assisted the research team by seeking the cooperation of the appropriate government authority. Through this participation, the government in each destination country connected the research team with appropriate individuals or organisations for arranging and completing interviews. In each country, this worked slightly differently. In the origin countries, all participants were recruited by the IOM, and the vast majority of interviews took place at the IOM office. For the transit countries, as a result of each country's unique context, participants were selected in different ways. In Indonesia, all participants were refugees or asylum seekers living in IOM-provided accommodation in various locations in Jakarta, and the interviews were arranged by the IOM. In Turkey, the majority of interviews took place at a removal centre in Istanbul, and the remainder at the IOM office. In Greece, the majority of interviews took place at the IOM office in Athens.

Understanding the decision to return

The model shown in Figure 10.1 was used in this study for the purposes of research design and subsequent analysis of the return decision-making process, and was developed in an earlier study by Black et al. (2004). It conceives the individual return decision as being influenced by: 'structural' conditions (conditions in the origin and destination country); individual conditions including individual attributes and social relations;

and policy interventions. The model also recognises the significance of information about conditions in origin and transit countries, and about policies, which may vary significantly between individuals and groups.

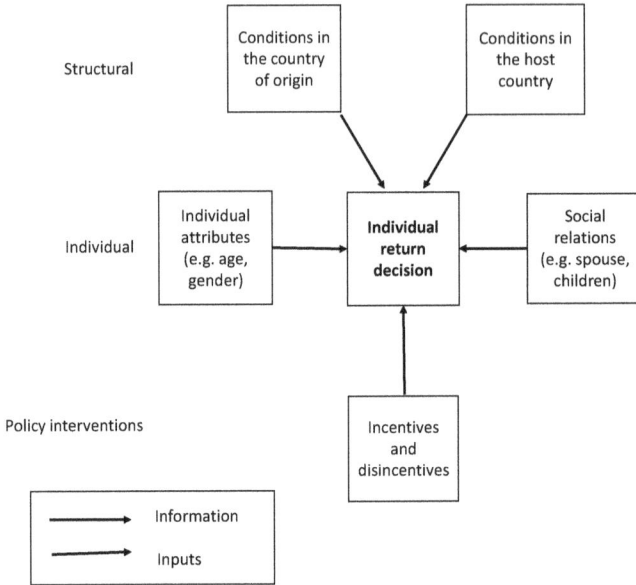

Figure 10.1: Factors determining the decision to return
Source: Black et al. (2004), p.13.

Conditions in the country of origin

As very few respondents in any origin, transit or destination country identified conditions in the origin country as influential in their decision whether to return, the total number of responses is very small, and not suitable for detailed analysis. There was only one item within the broad category of conditions in the origin country not cited as relevant by any respondent at all, and that was a sense of political commitment or desire to help rebuild the country of origin.

Conditions in the country of destination

Across all the respondents, conditions in the destination country significantly outweighed any others as factors identified as influencing the return decision. For 80 respondents across all the countries surveyed (almost 30 per cent of the respondents), not having the right to work or experiencing difficulty in finding employment was cited as important. The second most cited (by 40 respondents or 14.7 per cent) was a negative decision on an asylum request. Ranked sequentially after employment and asylum status were financial factors (35 individuals or 12.8 per cent); a lack of security and discrimination (14 individuals or 5.1 per cent); the expiry of a work or student permit (10 individuals or 3.7 per cent); a lack of access to social services (seven individuals or 2.6 per cent); and that the respondent was 'tired of being in a detention centre' (four individuals or 1.5 per cent).

Given the prevailing discourse in many migrant destination countries that access to social services is an important magnet for asylum seekers and other migrants, it is interesting that no respondent interviewed in any destination country cited lack of access to these services as a factor influencing their return decision. It is not clear from the data whether this was not much of an issue because most respondents legally had access to social services, had found alternative access, or simply had not required these services by the time of the survey, but the conclusion stands that, for the vast majority, access to social services was not apparently a 'make or break' issue in considering whether or not to stay in the destination country.

Individual factors

Of the five categories identified in Figure 10.1 (conditions in origin countries, conditions in destination countries, individual factors, social factors and policy interventions), individual factors were the second most cited category influencing the return decision, by just over one third of respondents. Of the specific variables covered within this category, of most concern was that people were 'tired of living as undocumented', followed by 'I felt I had no other choice', 'inability to meet migration aspirations', 'psychological problems', and the importance of 'dignity of return as a normal passenger'.

This last variable was only cited by a total of three respondents. Yet it is often assumed that one of the reasons rejected asylum seekers and irregular migrants subscribe to organised return programs is to avoid the indignity (and potential subsequent reintegration challenges) of deportation.

The data on age show no obvious trends. The majority in each age category in both transit and destination countries had decided to return, with the exception of people aged 40+ in transit countries (of whom five had decided to return and eight not to). Turning to data on sex, this study covered significantly more men than women. Of the 42 men interviewed in destination countries, 64 per cent had decided to return, 19 per cent had decided not to return, and 17 per cent were undecided. Among the 11 women interviewed, six had decided to return, three had decided not to return, and two were undecided. In transit countries, overall almost twice as many participants had decided to return as the number who had decided not to return. However, more women had decided not to return than to return.

No clear patterns emerged concerning marital status. In both destination and transit countries, more respondents, both married and unmarried, had decided to return rather than not to return, although the differentials varied quite widely (for example, in transit countries almost as many married people had decided not to return as the number of married people who had decided to return). There is also no clear pattern when it comes to children. In both transit and destination countries more people, whether or not they had children, had decided to return than those who had decided not to return.

The correlations between return intentions and whether or not the respondent migrated alone are more interesting. The significant majority of those who had migrated alone to destination countries had decided to return, whereas a small majority of those who had migrated alone to transit countries had decided not to return. More of those who had not migrated alone to destination countries had decided not to return than those who had decided to return, whereas it was the opposite in transit countries.

Social factors

Factors broadly categorised as 'social factors' were cited third most often among all the categories of factors identified in the model in Figure 10.1. By far the most important was a desire to rejoin family members at home, cited 57 times. As a single factor, this is the second most cited across the entire study, following the difficulty of finding work under the 'conditions in destination country' category. Here is a strong reminder that migration, and return migration, are as much social processes as they are economic and political processes.

Another social factor was changes in family circumstances (cited 26 times). It is unclear whether this refers to changes in circumstances among family in the destination country or the origin country, but it seems more likely to be in the latter. Nostalgia about the origin country and its way of life was cited nine times.

Perhaps the most surprising results in this category were that problems of integration and the shame of return ranked at the bottom of the variables. Many of the challenges of integration, for example to do with legal status and finding a job, are covered elsewhere in the survey and data. However, the specific factor of 'integration' could have been expected to figure more highly here.

Another way that social factors intersect with the return decision-making process is where other family members are involved in making the decision. Only 15 per cent of the respondents in this study had made the decision to migrate alone.

Reporting on their decisions after they had already returned home, respondents in origin countries named family members back at home as the most important influence in decision-making (38 per cent). Family members in the origin country were also most involved in the decision whether to return for those interviewed in destination countries (33 per cent) and transit countries (72 per cent). The particularly high response in this category for the latter group was presumably because so few had family members in the transit country to consult, whereas for those who had made it to their destination, family members there were also significantly involved in the decision. These findings illustrate the importance of policy interventions being considered not just at the individual migrant level, but also in the wider family context.

Finally, 13 per cent of respondents in transit and destination countries reported that both government authorities and the IOM were involved in the decision. Among respondents interviewed in destination countries, 22 per cent reported that government authorities had been involved in the decision, compared with only 5 per cent referencing the IOM.

Policy interventions

It is not clear from this study if policy interventions play an important role in the decision whether to return. As an entire category, this was only the fourth most important of the five categories considered in the survey: cited by only about one fifth of the respondents. Equally, the variables considered here overlap and probably combine to influence the return decision. It is also worth reiterating that aspects of the return decision may be beyond direct policy intervention, for example regarding certain individual and social characteristics. The most important specific factor cited, 26 times, was the possibility to benefit from voluntary return programs, closely followed by compliance with the law to leave voluntarily.

Information

As well as having assistance programs in place, it is equally important that their intended beneficiaries know about them, understand who they apply to, what they offer, and under what circumstances. Migrants' knowledge about immigration policy in particular may often be subject to rumour and speculation. To begin to explore whether or not there is an information gap around assistance for return, respondents in origin and destination countries were asked what they knew about assistance programs and how they knew about them.

Across all four destination countries surveyed, 47 respondents had heard of assistance programs and only seven had not. It is somewhat surprising that any respondents had not come across these programs, as they were identified by the IOM, other return service agencies, or the government.

It is worth separately considering information dissemination in transit countries—a significant gap in existing research that this study can at least start to fill. In the transit countries, 45 respondents (75 per cent) knew something about return programs. Of these, 14 reported receiving the information from friends and family in the transit country; eight from the IOM; and the remainder from government authorities, a non-governmental organisation (NGO), friends or family in a destination country, and friends or family in the origin country, in that order.

Conclusions

Based on the model of return decision-making presented above, this section has drawn on data from respondents across the origin, transit and destination countries to try to understand the decision to return. Overall respondents ranked the five main categories of factors influencing the return decision as follows: by far most important were conditions in the country of destination, followed in order by individual factors, social factors, policy interventions and lastly conditions in the origin country. As discussed, this ranking is striking and in contrast to most other studies on return, in particular the positions of the final two categories.

Within these broad categories, the following specific variables were found to be most significant for the respondents in making their decisions: the difficulty of finding employment/no right to work; tired of living as an undocumented migrant; a desire to reunify with family at home; the opportunity to benefit from voluntary return programs; and job prospects at home.

Discerning policy implications from this analysis is challenging, not just because of the limitations of the methodology, but also because in reality the categories and variables distinguished here intersect and influence each other. Even though it may not be possible to highlight specific policy interventions, a number of wider policy implications emerge. First, the results suggest that neither 'sticks' nor 'carrots' alone work as policy interventions, and instead a judicious mix may be most effective. Second, there may be certain aspects of the return process that are largely beyond the influence of policy interventions, for example some of the social and cultural factors that may influence attitudes towards return and towards women. Finally, there is a reality check: assisted voluntary return–related policy interventions were not considered by most participants as a fundamental reason for their decision, and some said they did not even know about return programs and other assistance programs.

Defining and measuring sustainable return

Drawing on an extensive literature review and consolidating key elements of various existing definitions, this study defines 'sustainable return' as when: 'The individual has reintegrated into the economic, social and cultural processes of the country of origin and feels that they are in an environment of safety and security upon return.'

This definition assumes that reintegration is a necessary precondition for meaningful sustainable return. It adopts a comprehensive perspective on reintegration across the dimensions of economic, sociocultural and political-security processes. This definition also highlights that the returnee must perceive they are in conditions of safety and security upon return (Black & Gent, 2006).

According to this definition, sustainable return is achieved by: economic reintegration whereby an individual is able to sustain a livelihood and is not in a situation of economic vulnerability; social and cultural reintegration whereby the returnee is actively incorporated into the receiving society, for example at the local community level; and political-security reintegration whereby the returnee feels they have access to safety and justice upon return.

Measuring sustainable return

Using the definition and building on the measures established above, a return and reintegration index was created, combining the three dimensions of economic, sociocultural and safety/security criteria. As return and reintegration cannot be measured by one variable, an index is useful because it allows all the variables of interest to be combined to create a single measure.

The methodology used to develop the index follows that developed by Roelen and Gassman (2012)—based on work by Alkire and Santos (2010) and Alkire and Foster (2011)—to create a multidimensional child wellbeing index. The methodology consists of three simple steps and is replicable for the case of developing a multidimensional return and reintegration index.

The three steps were:

- First a threshold was identified for each return and reintegration measure detailed above to assess if each returnee was reintegrated according to that variable. For example, on the measure 'employment', an individual was assessed as reintegrated if they were employed. Individual variable reintegration rates were then determined by counting the number of returnees who met the threshold requirement. This is a basic measure—for example it cannot gauge how long the returnee has been employed or the conditions of employment—but it provides a benchmark for understanding sustainability.

- Second, return and reintegration rates were determined for each dimension. The dimension 'reintegration' rates reflect the number of returnees who have achieved a sufficient level of reintegration across the dimension variables. Each variable was given an equal weight within the dimension. A returnee was considered reintegrated if the weighted indicator for the dimension was equal to or above 0.6. This means that returnees had to meet a level of reintegration of at least three of the five variables in each dimension to be considered reintegrated. There are a number of assumptions in this step, regarding the weighting of variables and the 'cut-off' point for reintegration, which can be adjusted for further research.

- The third step was to create an overall return and reintegration index by aggregating the reintegration rates across the three dimensions. Each dimension was equally rated at one third of the total index. An individual was therefore considered to be reintegrated if they exceed the 60 per cent threshold across all three dimensions. Once again these arbitrary weightings and thresholds may be adjusted as necessary in future.

Applying the return and reintegration index

In the economic dimension of the return and reintegration index, 56 per cent of returns in the sample may be considered reintegrated in three out of five of the economic dimension indicators. Within this dimension, returnees were most vulnerable on the number of income sources in the household, as 35 per cent of returnees' households did not have more than one income source. Seventy per cent of returnees were employed, and this does include self-employment or part-time employment. Fifty-seven per cent of returnees currently had no debt. Of the 43 per cent of returnees who were currently in debt, 45 per cent had incurred the debt for their original migration. Costs of migration were cited as high as USD12,000, which is generally a much larger sum than return allowances offered. Similarly, 57 per cent of returnees currently owned land or their house. Finally, in terms of self-perception, 53 per cent of returnees perceived that they were currently struggling economically.

On the sociocultural dimension, 64 per cent of returnees were reintegrated. Within this dimension, returnees were most likely to participate in local events (79 per cent), but least likely to be a member in an organisation (21 per cent). Organisations in the survey included informal groups such as funeral or savings associations, which were quite common in several of the study countries, suggesting that the returnees had low levels of participation relative to the rest of the population. The majority of returnees identified themselves as having networks they could rely on for support (69.7 per cent) and having transnational networks (66.9 per cent). It is concerning that 41 per cent of returnees expressed that they were generally dissatisfied or very dissatisfied with their life in the past month.

Overall, returnees showed the highest levels of reintegration in the safety and security dimension, at 71 per cent. The majority of returnees reported feeling safe in their home (79.2 per cent) and in their community (69 per cent). Further, the majority had not experienced personal harassment since return (78.6 per cent) and felt they could access justice if their rights were violated (60.8 per cent).

On the whole, 37 per cent of returnees were reintegrated based on the index. There were significant variations in the degree of reintegration across the eight origin countries covered by this study. Returnees to Vietnam and Pakistan were more likely to be reintegrated. Returnees to Vietnam in this study had all returned from the UK and were a particular migrant group: the group interviewed from Vietnam tended to be better off economically compared with others in their local communities. In Pakistan, it appears that the reintegration assistance was meaningful in establishing employment in that country.

Returnees to Iraq were the least likely to be reintegrated on return. Afghanistan, Ethiopia and Sri Lanka also had very low percentages of returnees who were reintegrated. Similarly to Iraq, Afghans reported low levels of reintegration in the safety and security dimension, which is unsurprising given the current instability in Afghanistan. Ethiopians, Bangladeshis and Sri Lankans reported the lowest levels of economic reintegration.

Conclusions

This section has provided the basis of the analytical framework for measuring sustainable return through the return and reintegration index. The index highlights the multidimensional nature of reintegration and the importance of the three dimensions of economic reintegration, sociocultural reintegration, and safety/security. The interplay between these dimensions determines if an individual is reintegrated or not. It is evident that participants in the different origin countries had varying levels of reintegration, with returnees to Iraq being the least likely to be reintegrated and returnees to Vietnam and Pakistan the most likely to be reintegrated.

Promoting reintegration and sustainable return

This section explores the factors that influence sustainable return, drawing on the return and reintegration index presented above. Building from the literature review, the following categories of factors will be examined:

- individual factors
- the migration cycle, including experiences prior to migration and in the destination country
- structural factors during return including the community of return and attitudes from locals
- the role of assisted voluntary return programming.

It is important to note that these factors may overlap, and separating them out into categories is, to an extent, artificial. At the same time, this separation is helpful for analysis, and potentially also for targeting policy interventions to promote reintegration and sustainable return.

Individual factors

The literature review found no systemic evidence on the impact of individual factors such as age, sex and education levels on reintegration and sustainable return. However, in one study comparing Bosnia and Kosovo, it was found that young men were more likely to be able to find employment upon return (Black et al., 2004).

Similarly, in this study's sample there was no significant relationship either between age or sex and reintegration, as measured by the aggregate return and reintegration index. Individuals in their 30s were the most likely to be reintegrated, and individuals over 50 or between 17 and 29 years of age were the least likely to be reintegrated. Although the total numbers are small, it may also be noteworthy that only 24 per cent of female returnees were reintegrated, compared with 40 per cent of male returnees (still less than half). This is in line with the conclusions of other studies that reintegration is a gendered process, often more difficult for women than men (Wong, 2013).

A noteworthy relationship was found between education and reintegration. Those with no primary education, or only with primary education, were reintegrated less than those with a secondary education who, in turn, were reintegrated less than those with a tertiary education. On one hand, those educated to a tertiary level may be expected to be more likely to find employment upon return. On the other hand, however, still only 52 per cent of those with tertiary education were reintegrated, and it may be that the most educated are the most likely not to find work commensurate with their skills and training.

Experiences prior to migration

As uncovered by the literature review, an individual's situation prior to their migration can have a significant impact on their potential to be reintegrated upon return. In general, for example, earlier studies have indicated that those who are well off prior to migration (for example, in terms of personal security, employment and financial resources) have a higher likelihood of also being well off on return.

In contrast, this study's findings indicated no significant relationship between reintegration and either employment prior to migration or an individual's self-perception of their standard of living prior to migration. For both those who were and those who were not working prior to migration, around 40 per cent were reintegrated and 60 per cent were not. In regard to standard of living prior to migration, however, a higher percentage of those who were comfortable prior to migration were reintegrated (46 per cent), compared with those who reported struggling prior to migration (27.9 per cent).

The study found instead that social and political-security experiences prior to migration were significant factors in determining likelihood of reintegration. Twenty-two per cent of participants stated that they did not have a sense of belonging to the community prior to migration. This group was found to be significantly less likely to be reintegrated, compared with those who did have a sense of belonging prior to migration (42 per cent).

It is also not surprising that individuals who reported experiencing threats to their personal security prior to their migration were also significantly less likely to be reintegrated (27.1 per cent), compared with those who had not apparently experienced threats prior to migration (47.9 per cent). Also, unsurprisingly, those who had reported experiencing threats prior to migration were particularly less reintegrated on the safety-security dimension of the return and reintegration index, at 60 per cent reintegrated, compared with 86 per cent of those who had not cited experienced threats prior to migration.

Experiences in the destination country

Participants had returned from a total of 25 different countries of destination; the four most common countries were Norway (32), UK (27), Greece (25) and Belgium (14). There is a clustering effect of return from Greece being primarily to Pakistan and Bangladesh, and 56 per cent of returnees from the UK went home to Vietnam.

According to the data in this study, returnees from the UK were significantly more likely to be reintegrated (60.9 per cent), whereas returnees from Belgium were significantly less likely to be reintegrated (21.4 per cent). The situation of the UK, however, must be interpreted with caution. As indicated, all returnees in the sample in Vietnam had returned from the UK, and this represented a highly specific migration stream. When excluding Vietnam from the sample, there were 12 remaining participants who returned from the UK. Only one of these participants was reintegrated upon return. For all the other destination countries, around one third of returnees were reintegrated according to the return and reintegration index. This could not be defined as success.

The study also examined the relationship between the living situation in the destination country, employment, time spent in the destination country and reintegration. The living situation on arrival comparison indicates that individuals in asylum reception centres were significantly less likely to be reintegrated. Only 21 per cent of this group could be described as reintegrated, according to the index. Although the sample size for detention centres is very small, it is striking that those respondents who had spent time in asylum centres were even less likely to be reintegrated than those in detention centres.

The majority of returnees were not legally entitled to work while in the destination country; however, 41 per cent had worked informally at some point during their stay. On the whole, there was no clear relationship between working or not working in the destination country and reintegration. Interestingly, those who had worked informally were better reintegrated than those who had worked legally (47.2 per cent compared to 28.6 per cent).

Finally, it might be expected that reintegration would become more unlikely when migrants had been away for a longer period of time. Indeed, participants who had been abroad for over 10 years were the least likely to be reintegrated, although this was not statistically significant. There was, however, little variation in the correlation between duration abroad and reintegration for other time periods—ranging between 33 and 47 per cent for all other time periods. A recent study has argued that duration abroad itself is not significant in returnee reintegration; rather, it is the experiences abroad that matter more (Kuschminder, 2014).

Community of return

Within the broad range of conditions in the country of origin, the community level was an especially important factor in reintegration. Individuals who returned to the same community where they lived before they left were significantly more likely to be reintegrated, compared with individuals who returned to a different community than the one they left: 44.9 per cent compared with 19.5 per cent. This has potentially important implications for policy, suggesting a correlation between community of return and reintegration, and highlighting the risks of return where access to the community of origin is not yet feasible. There are at least two potential reasons to explain this. First, people only return to the same community when they do not feel their safety and security will be violated in that community, therefore already suggesting a higher level of reintegration within this dimension. Second, people return to the same community when they have existing networks or support services within that community, which would also suggest higher levels of reintegration in the sociocultural dimension. In addition, individuals who returned to an urban community were more likely to be reintegrated than those who returned to a rural community.

Conclusions

This section has examined the relationship between different variables pertaining to the circumstances and experiences of the returnees and their migration cycle, and reintegration as measured by the return and reintegration index. Several factors were assessed to have a significant relationship with reintegration. These included having a sense of belonging in the community prior to migration, the reason for migration, the country of destination, residing in an asylum reception centre and returning or not returning to the same community on return.

Policy implications

In drawing initial policy implications, a number of reservations are worth flagging: The first concerns the research topic itself. The decision to return, reintegration, and the sustainability of return all often depend on highly individual characteristics and experiences, many of which defy accurate measurement or prediction. In part, therefore, the value of this research has been to identify areas where policy is unlikely to make a difference. At the same time, however, it does allow at least for preliminary conclusions about where policy interventions can be effective.

A second reservation concerns the research process. While every effort was made to ensure a degree of trust between interviewer and respondent, there can be no guarantee of the accuracy of the responses provided by respondents. In part, this reflects the sensitive and sometimes vulnerable situation in which some respondents found themselves. It also reflects the nature of the research, which in some cases depended on participants' recall up to a year after making certain decisions and taking actions as well as requiring responses to hypothetical questions, from which final actions may diverge significantly.

A related consideration concerns access to evidence and data. Various aspects of return programs have been monitored and evaluated in several of the study countries, including by governments and relevant organisations. However, this information was not always easily accessible, and neither was it collated in a single location. In several origin countries the tracking of returnees is not systematic or thorough enough to answer important questions regarding reintegration and sustainable return. This has implications for the management, analysis, and publication of data and evidence by government authorities and international organisations.

Fourth, a key gap in this study is determining the role of assisted voluntary return and reintegration packages in the overall reintegration process. All participants in this study had received reintegration assistance, and therefore the study was not able to compare their experiences with those of other assisted voluntary returnees who did not receive reintegration assistance. Neither could it systematically compare the relevance or differential outcomes of different types of assistance packages. This has direct implications for program management and assisted voluntary return policy design, and should be explored in further research.

A final reservation concerns the wider applicability of these findings. None can be considered representative of the nationality groups or countries surveyed, let alone of migrants or returnees more generally. The purpose of focusing on a semi-structured interview approach was therefore to identify and explore relevant issues rather than provide firm conclusions.

Bearing in mind these reservations, while also recognising the uniquely comprehensive and comparative nature of the study, the findings of the study have implications for policy in three main areas: influencing the decision to return, measuring sustainability, and promoting sustainable return and reintegration.

Influencing the decision to return

- Conditions in their origin countries were generally not an important influence on the respondents' decisions on whether to return. This is likely to reflect the fact that nearly half of respondents migrated for broadly economic reasons, and would likely differ among asylum seekers and refugees.

- Conditions in destination countries may strongly influence the decision to return. For many respondents, an inability to work and insecure legal status in particular were important incentives to return, although rarely in isolation from other individual and social factors.

- Other key factors influencing the decision to return are largely beyond the scope of direct policy interventions. For example, the desire to reunite with family members at home, or a change of family circumstances there, were also important factors in the return decision. Family members were also often involved in the decision-making process.

- Policy interventions are not considered a major influence on the decision whether to return.

- Enabling policy interventions can influence the decision to return as much as restrictive policies. For many respondents, the opportunity to benefit from voluntary return programs, and the chance to wind up their affairs before departure, facilitated their return decision.

- More could be done to disseminate information on return programs, especially in transit countries. In contrast to destination countries, where most respondents knew about return programs and from multiple sources, in transit countries almost half had not even heard of return programs. Equally, it is important not to raise the expectations of migrants, many of whom may not be eligible for limited return assistance programs.

- There is a fine line between facilitating return and encouraging it. Any policy intervention in this area should be designed to allow potential returnees to make their own decisions, rather than encouraging them towards any particular option.

Measuring sustainability

- Measuring sustainability depends on how it is defined. The definition proposed in this study is that 'The individual has reintegrated into the economic, social and cultural processes of the country of origin and feels that they are in an environment of safety and security upon return'.

- It is possible to develop an index for measuring reintegration. The index developed in this study distinguishes economic, sociocultural, and political-security dimensions, and sets reintegration thresholds across each to gauge individual reintegration rates. The variables and the thresholds can be adjusted for future studies.

- To measure sustainability for individual returnees, it is important to set up an adequate sample frame at an early stage of a return program. It was not possible in any of the origin countries to obtain a representative sample of returnees from which to gain a generalised view of the sustainability of return for individuals.

- A system to measure reintegration and the sustainability of return could be put in place as part of any future voluntary assisted return program.

- Ongoing monitoring of sustainability is possible, but involves trade-offs in terms of costs. In particular, the in-depth interviews that would be required to properly gauge sustainability take time, and are challenging from a logistical perspective.

- Remigration is not a valid proxy for measuring sustainability.

Promoting sustainable return and reintegration

- Many of the factors influencing the sustainability of return appear beyond the influence of direct policy intervention. These include premigration experiences such as level of education and social belonging, and individual characteristic such as sex.

- Living conditions in the destination country are significantly correlated with sustainable return and reintegration. This was particularly the case in this sample for returnees who had spent significant periods in asylum or detention centres, very few of whom were subsequently reintegrated.

- The ability to work in the country of destination does not clearly correlate with sustainable return or reintegration.

- The ability to return to the community in which respondents lived before migration promoted sustainable return and reintegration. This was particularly the case where the community was in an urban area.

- The reason for initial migration significantly correlates with reintegration. Individuals who migrated for political-security reasons were less likely to be reintegrated than those who migrated for economic reasons. This suggests that, although migration motivations are frequently mixed, the distinctions are still important when examining the reintegration process.

- The factors that influence return may also impact on its sustainability and reintegration, but sometimes in opposing directions. In particular, a negative decision on asylum was a strong determinant for return, but also a strong indicator for a lack of reintegration after return.

Reference list

Alkire, S., & Foster, J. (2011). Counting and multidimensional poverty measurement. *Journal of Public Economics 95*(7–8), 476–97. doi.org/10.1016/j.jpubeco.2010.11.006

Alkire, S., & Santos, M. E. (2010). *Acute multidimensional poverty: A new index for developing countries.* Oxford Poverty and Human Development Initiative working paper No. 38. Oxford: Department of International Development, University of Oxford.

Black, R., & Gent, S. (2006). Sustainable return in post-conflict contexts. *International Migration, 44*(3), 15–38. doi.org/10.1111/j.1468-2435.2006.00370.x

Black, R., Koser, K., Monk, K., Atfield, G., D'Onofrio, L., & Tiemoko, R. (2004). *Understanding voluntary return.* Home Office Report 50/04. London: Home Office.

Koser, K., & Kuschminder, K. (2015). *Comparative research on the assisted voluntary return and reintegration of migrants.* Geneva: International Organization for Migration. Retrieved from www.iom.int/files/live/sites/iom/files/What-We-Do/docs/AVRR-Research-final.pdf.

Kuschminder, K. (2014). *Female return migration and reintegration strategies in Ethiopia* (unpublished PhD dissertation). Maastricht Graduate School of Governance, Germany.

Paasche, E. (2014). *Why assisted return programmes must be evaluated. Insights from the project 'Possibilities and realities of return migration'.* Peace Research Institute, policy brief No. 5. Oslo: Peace Research Institute.

Roelen, K., & Gassman, F. (2012). *Child well-being in Kazakhstan.* Atana, Kazakhstan: United Nations Children's Fund.

Wong, M. (2013). Navigating return: The gendered geographies of skilled return migration to Ghana. *Global Networks, 14*(4), 438–57. doi.org/10.1111/glob.12041

11

Media and migration: Comparative analysis of print and online media reporting on migrants and migration in selected countries

Marie McAuliffe, Warren Weeks and Khalid Koser[1]

By its very nature, international migration is transnational. The movement of people across borders necessarily relates to more than one state, and given the increase in scale and diversity of international migration over recent decades, nearly all countries in the modern era are affected by international migration (Castles, de Haas, & Miller, 2014). Some countries, including some of those within the scope of this project, are affected by migration significantly, both positively and at times negatively. Immigration has become a first order public policy issue in many countries in the world.

It is unsurprising, then, that the topic of international migration is often included in public opinion surveys, although arguably the political significance of migration often outweighs its numerical significance. Analysis of print and online media in the UK, for example, has shown that the substantial political interest in this complex public policy topic can be put in a somewhat different perspective by examining overall

---

1   The authors are grateful for research assistance from Simone Gangell and Adam Palmer in the preparation of this chapter.

media coverage by themes. Content analysis undertaken as part of this study found that migration-related media coverage in the UK accounted for around 2–3 per cent of total coverage compared to, for example, sport (24–30 per cent), the economy (19–20 per cent), science/health (8–10 per cent) and climate change (1–2 per cent).

How migrants and migration are covered in the media matters for at least three reasons. First, although the chain of causality and the distinctions between causes and consequence is complex, there is a general acceptance that the media can influence, and be influenced by, popular opinion and political agendas. Thus, media coverage may be a barometer for political and public attitudes towards migration, and in turn shape these attitudes. Second, media coverage is likely to influence the perceptions of migrants themselves in society, for example, regarding to what extent they perceive migrants to be widely accepted or excluded, to be fairly represented, or to be scapegoated. Third, it is possible, given global access to much media, that media coverage may also influence the decision-making of migrants considering whether to move to particular destination countries.

Against this backdrop, the purpose of this research is to analyse in more depth how the media covers migrants and migration. More specifically, the purpose of this research is to compare media discourses on migrants and migration in selected countries by examining thematic content, contextual framing and the extent of polarisation of messages communicated via print and online media over two six-month periods.

Research questions and scope

The objective of the media and migration research project was to create baseline analyses of media coverage of migration and migrants in 13 selected countries for two six-month study periods on:

- the thematic content of print and online media messages;
- the extent to which that coverage was favourable, unfavourable or neutral;
- the high-level contextual framing in which migration messages were reported.

We analysed media messaging within two sets of print and online media pieces for the 13 selected countries during two six-month periods (1 October, 2013 to 31 March, 2014; and 1 April, 2014 to 30 September, 2014), which are referred to as Phase I and Phase II throughout this chapter. The 13 countries in scope have been categorised as either 'very high human development (HD)' countries or 'other HD' countries.[2] This has been done for several reasons. First, one of the key findings from Phase I of the project was that characterising countries as either 'destination' or 'origin' countries for migration purposes was found to be overly simplistic given the range of migration issues they may face. Pakistan, for example, is a significant destination and origin country as well as a transit country and the world's largest host country of refugees. It could be argued that at least one of the additional countries included in this phase (Thailand) is perhaps more of a transit country for irregular migration than a destination or origin country, further complicating a destination–origin typology. Second, the application of the Human Development Index (HDI) has been chosen because it incorporates a number of elements, including Gross National Income (GNI) per capita at purchasing power parity (PPP), life expectancy and mean and expected years of schooling, so is more than just an economic indicator. In addition, the HDI is reasonably long-standing, widely accepted and UN-supported. Third, the HDI has been found to correlate with international migration flows (Kandemir, 2012), and so it is arguably one of the least worst bases from which to develop a dichotomous categorisation to analyse media and migration coverage in multiple countries. That said, any and all such categorisations are generally applied only to ensure high-level analysis is as accessible and digestible as possible. Individual country reports are also provided, to supplement the high-level analysis.

The six 'very high HD' countries in scope are Australia, Canada, the Netherlands, Norway, Switzerland, and the UK. The seven 'other HD' countries are Afghanistan, Bangladesh, Malaysia, Pakistan, Sri Lanka, Thailand and Vietnam. Within these two types, a mix of countries was included, both from a geographic perspective and from a migration perspective (e.g. regular/irregular migration, asylum–refugee/labour/student migration). The three countries that were added for Phase II were Australia, Malaysia and Thailand, which were considered to be of particular interest to the Research Program.

---

2   These categories are based on United Nations Development Programme (2014).

Table 11.1: Human Development Index rankings and groupings of selected countries in scope, 2014

Country	Ranking (187 countries)	HDI group
Norway	1	Very high HD
Australia	2	Very high HD
Switzerland	3	Very high HD
Netherlands	4	Very high HD
Canada	8	Very high HD
United Kingdom	14	Very high HD
Malaysia	62	High HD
Sri Lanka	73	High HD
Thailand	89	High HD
Vietnam	121	Medium HD
Bangladesh	142	Medium HD
Pakistan	146	Low HD
Afghanistan	169	Low HD

Source: United Nations Development Programme (2014).

Content from both print and online sources was obtained from commercial media content suppliers or the publishers' archives. Broadcast media content was generally outside the scope of the project, partly because of the prohibitive cost involved in sourcing such material retrospectively. The exclusion of broadcast material necessarily poses limitations on the analysis. This limitation is potentially more of an issue for some of the non-industrialised country analyses, given literacy and access issues within those countries. Radio broadcasting, for example, is a particularly important form of media in Afghanistan, with its patchy literacy, poor infrastructure and low incomes levels.

Advances in journalism and digital media, however, have led to the converging of news organisations, where news is more commonly published across a multitude of media platforms (Quandt & Singer, 2009; Erdal, 2009). Research has also indicated that there are no significant differences in news coverage across the different platforms; rather, the main differences are between the types of news organisations and in particular the extent to which they use emotive language (Semetko & Valenburg, 2000; Keith, Schwalbe, & Silcock, 2010).

Social media was also generally outside the scope of this project, primarily due to feasibility. Including broadcast and social media messages would have enabled a more complete comparative analysis. However, while broadcast media is a widely accepted form of mass media in all countries, and could have been included (if feasible cost-wise), including social media would arguably have posed methodological concerns. The extent of social media coverage remains highly variable (Kohut et al., 2012; International Telecommunication Union, 2013), with substantial differences within and between countries. This is less so for print and online media coverage. As a result, comparative analysis of messaging in print and online media was considered the most reasonable approach. Further research on broadcast media would likely shed new light on aspects of the portrayal of migration in the media, but the initial findings from this study of online and print media are still relevant for both very high HD and less developed countries. With growing use of social media in some locations, this is an area that would benefit from targeted mixed methods research in the future.

It is important to note the very different contexts in which media reporting and messaging operates, including in relation to economic, political, social and security-related regulatory environments. These potential differences can include linguistic/sociocultural tendencies towards expression, such that the same story is likely to be expressed using more emotive language in Italy than in Germany, for example. In addition, the results are likely to reflect differences in the proportion of opinion-based coverage versus traditional fact-based journalism. For example, the UK media continues to publish higher proportions of pieces containing opinion compared to media in many other countries.

Of particular relevance to this project was the extent to which the media is free to report news and current affairs. Reporters Without Borders (Reporters Sans Frontiéres, RSF) publishes an annual *World press freedom index* that measures the level of freedom of information in 180 countries and ranks them accordingly. Final scores for each country range from 0 to 180 (with 0 representing the greatest degree of press freedom of the countries evaluated and 180 representing the lowest) and are based on measurements of plurality, media independence, environment and self-censorship, legislative framework, transparency, infrastructure and the level of violence against reporters during the study period.

Table 11.2 shows the 2014 ranking for each country in scope as well as their corresponding ranking by RSF as either 'good situation', 'satisfactory situation', 'noticeable problems', 'difficult situation' or 'very serious situation'.

Table 11.2: World press freedom index ratings and rankings, 2014

Country	Ranking (of 180 countries)	Rating
Netherlands	2	Good situation
Norway	3	Good situation
Switzerland	15	Good situation
Canada	18	Good situation
Australia	28	Good situation
United Kingdom	33	Satisfactory situation
Afghanistan	128	Difficult situation
Thailand	130	Difficult situation
Bangladesh	146	Difficult situation
Malaysia	147	Difficult situation
Pakistan	158	Difficult situation
Sri Lanka	165	Very serious situation
Vietnam	174	Very serious situation

Source: Reporters Without Borders (2014).

Along with issues associated with press freedom, the results of the research need to be viewed within a range of other contexts, including economic, political, security and social—all of which are intrinsically linked to human displacement and migration. These different contexts feed into migration-related articles in the media.

Research method

The methodology for this project relied on a combination of qualitative content analysis of media articles in representative country-specific sample sets and quantitative modelling. The content analysis was undertaken by multilingual analysts working in both the original (published) language and English. The quantitative component involved the application of a sophisticated human cognitive modelling method able to deal with very large volumes of media articles.

It was important to begin with the most complete media dataset possible—within the cost, time and feasibility limitations—so that a reasonably precise, sizeable and representative sample of topic-specific media articles for each country could be developed. Refining the country samples involved a 'top-down' analytical approach based on iteratively designing, testing and fine-tuning search strings based on human analysis. The first stage involved multilingual analysts examining media material in its published language—English, Bengali, Dutch, Farsi, French, German, Malay, Dari, Norwegian, Thai, Urdu, Vietnamese, Sinhalese or Tamil—before being interpreted and stored in English for further analysis.

The methodology also relied on substantial quality assurance and data verification processes throughout the data collection, sorting and analysis phases. A detailed discussion of the methodology is contained in McAuliffe and Weeks (2015).

No allowance was made for significant in-country events, such as general, local or regional elections, which inevitably affected the analysis. The main reason for this limitation was the significant methodological complication required to account for a multitude of in-country events that may affect results, such as elections, economic/financial shocks, natural disasters or terrorist events. In addition, the creation of time series data is assisted by maintaining a consistent approach across all study periods, including as more countries are added to the scope.

A series of country-specific datasets capturing migration-specific themes published in the media during the two six-month research periods was produced. The focal piece country datasets ranged in size from 20,000 pieces (Australia) to 500 (Bangladesh), while the country datasets used for in-depth analysis ranged in size from 1,400 pieces (Switzerland and Canada) to 500 (Bangladesh).

It is important to note the potential for seasonal effects during the two six-month study periods. For example, there was a tendency in very high HD countries for coverage on migration-related issues overall to drop during the Christmas/New Year period. Likewise, the volume of reporting of irregular maritime migration is related to activity, which can involve 'sailing seasons' in some parts of the world (McAuliffe & Mence, 2014), and reporting of overseas student issues can be related to seasonal student application, acceptance and/or departure times. To overcome some of the potential seasonal effects, future phases would be best undertaken on an annual basis.

Analytical framework

The country-specific in-depth analysis sets were analysed to determine thematic content, the tone of the media messaging (favourable–neutral–unfavourable), and how messages were contextually framed (humanitarian, sociocultural, economic and/or security). This analytical framework has been replicated from Phase I, and is discussed in detail in McAuliffe and Weeks (2015). By way of a summary, the three analytical frames employed are:

- examination of thematic content under headings that emerged from multiple rounds of analysis in Phase I: 'asylum seekers and refugees', 'emigration and emigrants', 'immigration and immigrants', 'irregular migration', 'migrant accommodation (including detention)', 'overseas students', 'overseas workers' and 'people smuggling and trafficking';

- analysis of message tone as either favourable, unfavourable or neutral, with fact-based reporting being generally neutral and messages containing opinion being generally assessed as 'favourable' or 'unfavourable';

- analysis of message context using a contextual-associative typology that comprised 'sociocultural', 'economic', 'humanitarian' and 'security' contexts.

Key findings are reported by variables including study period, country, theme, 'favourability', and contextual framing. This can sometimes result in small subsamples being analysed. To ensure the veracity of the research, findings based on subsamples of less than 50 messages (very high HD countries) and 30 messages (other HD countries) are not reported. It is also important to note that quantitative analysis is based on messages rather than articles.

Key findings

The key findings of the research presented in this paper focus primarily on comparative analysis across the two study periods. From the two phases of research, it is becoming clearer that the media discussion on migration in very high HD countries tends to contain more in-depth analysis compared to other HD countries, which was more likely to have been driven by specific events and so tended to be more sporadic.

Taking into account all print and online messages on migration and migrants in all countries, it is evident that there was a small but noticeable shift in message tone between Phases I and II toward a more balanced overall coverage. Favourable messages increased marginally and unfavourable coverage decreased. Despite the slight shift, reporting in Phase II was again largely assessed as being neutral. However, where it was not neutral, reporting was more likely to be unfavourable than favourable. Some themes were more likely to be reported unfavourably (e.g. 'people smuggling and trafficking' in all countries, 'irregular migration' in other HD countries and 'immigration and immigrants' in very high HD countries).

One striking finding of the research was that messaging on migration and migrants in print and online media was predominantly depicted through a 'humanitarian' lens. 'Humanitarian' framing dominated in all countries in scope across Phase II—a change from Phase I, which saw some very high HD countries experience more 'economic' framing. Media reporting tended to be framed in a border/national security context where it related to irregular migration or people smuggling and trafficking.

Each country had its own particular set of migration issues being discussed in print and online media, and it was slightly clearer from the comparisons between the two phases that these migration issues can be linked to a range of broader discussions, including those associated with factors such as political cycles and processes. The changes in Switzerland and the UK's reporting, for example, would appear to be related to elections/referendums.

Key findings and comparisons—very high HD countries

The key findings from the analysis of the very high HD country datasets highlight a range of similarities and some differences across the selected group as well as some changes between the phases.

Consistent with Phase I findings, there was a reasonable level of convergence found in very high HD countries of media coverage on migration that does not exist to the same extent for other HD countries studied. This possibly reflects similarities in terms of their migration circumstances and issues.

The volume of migration-specific print and online messaging increased in Phase II for all countries, which appears to be due in part to the heightened coverage of 'asylum seekers and refugees' and/or 'irregular migration'.

Taking into account all print and online messages on migration and migrants in the very high HD countries,[3] it is evident that there was a small but noticeable shift in message tone between Phases I and II toward more balanced coverage. While neutral coverage remained the same, favourable messages increased marginally and unfavourable coverage decreased. Notwithstanding the small but positive shift, coverage of migration in print and online media remained more polarised than in other HD countries, with less neutral reporting and more unfavourable reporting.

The limited extent of favourable messaging on migration across all very high HD countries is one of the starker findings. Unfavourable coverage significantly outweighed favourable messages. Very high rates of unfavourable messaging were experienced consistently for coverage on 'people smuggling and trafficking', followed by 'irregular migration'.

In terms of contextual framing of all messages, there were noticeable shifts between the two phases, with increases in 'humanitarian' framing and reductions in 'economic' and 'security' framing. This was almost certainly related to the increase in coverage on 'asylum seekers and refugees' (both proportionally and numerically) during Phase II.

Thematic content in print and online media in very high HD countries

All media messages from the country-specific datasets were analysed against a number of themes. A single print or online article may contain more than one message, and each message may relate to more than one theme. Analysing the datasets in this way allows for all messages to be accounted for in thematic terms.

As shown in Figure 11.1, the volume of migration-specific print and online messaging increased in Phase II for all countries. While the increases may be related to seasonal effects, they are clearly due in part to the heightened

---

3   Involved analysis of more than 77,000 individual messages from 7,500 articles reported between 1 October, 2013 and 30 September, 2014 in Australia, Canada, the Netherlands, Norway, Switzerland and the UK.

coverage of 'asylum seekers and refugees' and/or 'irregular migration', which increased in both actual and proportional terms in all countries between the two study periods.

The increase was related to ongoing coverage of mass displacement in key parts of the world, such as Syria, as well as the large maritime flows of asylum seekers and refugees in the Mediterranean Sea and Italy's Mare Nostrum operational response. Some countries, such as Switzerland, also saw increased coverage of integration of asylum seekers and refugees.

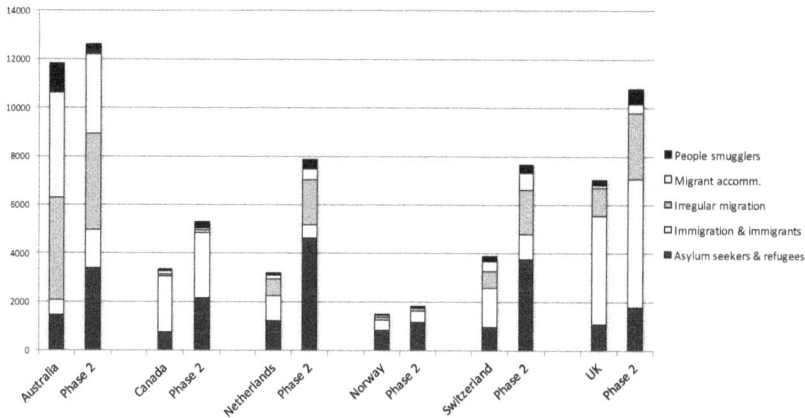

Figure 11.1: Thematic coverage of migration in print and online media in selected very high HD countries by volume—key migration themes: Phase I and II

Notes: Messages: Australia (n=24,428), Canada (n=8,629), Netherlands (n=11,023), Norway (n=3,327), Switzerland (n=11,538), UK (n=17,840). Articles: Australia (n=13,256), Canada (n=5,640), Netherlands (n=4,337), Norway (n=1,364), Switzerland (n=4,875), UK (n=8,360).

When the messaging is analysed on a proportional basis, as illustrated in Figure 11.2, one of the first things to note is that countries experienced quite distinctive media coverage of migration themes. Outside of the theme 'people smugglers' (which was uniformly low in proportional terms, at 10 per cent or less in all countries), there was variation of themes proportionally in all six very high HD countries. Australia was the only country that experienced significant coverage of migrant accommodation, which was related largely to asylum seeker processing centres in Papua New Guinea and Nauru. Canada and the UK appeared to have a more generalised media discussion, largely focused on the broad theme of 'immigration and immigrants', while Norway's media coverage in both phases was dominated by the 'asylum seekers and refugees' theme.

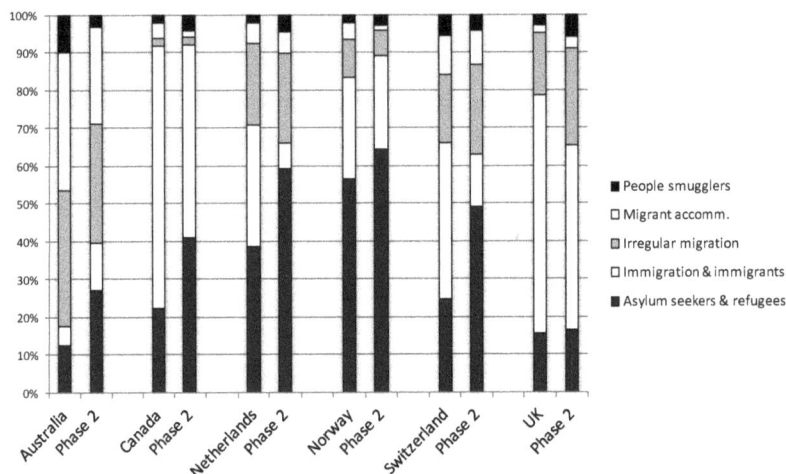

Figure 11.2: Thematic coverage of migration in print and online media in selected very high HD countries by proportion—key migration themes: Phase I and II

Notes: Messages: Australia (n=24,428), Canada (n=8,629), Netherlands (n=11,023), Norway (n=3,327), Switzerland (n=11,538), UK (n=17,840). Articles: Australia (n=13,256), Canada (n=5,640), Netherlands (n=4,337), Norway (n=1,364), Switzerland (n=4,875), UK (n=8,360).

The other striking aspect of the data is that between the two study periods, thematic coverage was reasonably consistent proportionally. As shown in Figure 11.2, this was particularly noticeable for the UK, Norway and to a lesser extent Canada, with all showing little variation.

Several countries experienced significantly reduced coverage of the theme 'immigration and immigrants', most notably the Netherlands and Switzerland. In Switzerland's case, this related to the February 2014 national referendum 'against mass immigration', reporting of which was included in the 'immigration and immigrants' theme during Phase I. A 30 November, 2014 Swiss national referendum on limiting immigration was rejected, and coverage in the lead-up to the vote almost certainly occurred outside the Phase II study period (which ended on 30 September).

In the UK …

'Immigration and immigrants' was the most prominent theme across the 12-month period, accounting for 45 per cent of all local focal stories. It was most prominent in Phase I of the study, when more than half of all coverage focused on this issue. It was again the dominant theme for the second study period, accounting for around half of all focal stories.

The late-February, 2014 release of figures showing a rise of more than 30 per cent in net migration, to 212,000 over the year to September 2013, was seen in many quarters as evidence the government had failed to meet its pledge to bring net migration to below 100,000. In late July, calls for tougher restrictions on migrant benefits became more prominent after Prime Minister David Cameron proposed new policies.

Extent of polarisation of print and online media content in very high HD countries

Much has been written about the polarisation, and the perceived increasing polarisation, of the public discourse on migration in destination countries (International Organization for Migration [IOM], 2011a; Koser, 2012; Koser, 2014). The discourse has variously been described as 'toxic', 'unbalanced' and 'extreme' (IOM, 2011a; Koser, 2012).

To a significant extent, this research supports those views and findings. However, as was the case with Phase I, this phase has again found that there is considerable variation in the extent of polarisation when examined by specific themes. In addition, there is also variability between countries. More importantly, however, when all messages related to migration and migrants are aggregated across all very high HD countries, an interesting picture emerges. It is evident that there was a small but noticeable shift between Phases I and II for the better in terms of overall balance. Overall, and as can be seen from Figure 11.3, neutral coverage remained the same (40 per cent) while favourable coverage increased (from 14 per cent to 17per cent) and unfavourable coverage decreased (from 46 per cent to 43 per cent). It would appear that no specific events or circumstances drove this change—it is more likely that a combination of changes in overall message volume in some countries (e.g. Switzerland and the Netherlands), together with variations in thematic content, appears to have overall had a combined effect. It will be interesting to examine this high-level indicator in future phases, particularly as it tends to blunt the more event-based changes, and has the ability to provide a useful overall barometer on print and online media coverage of migration and migrants.

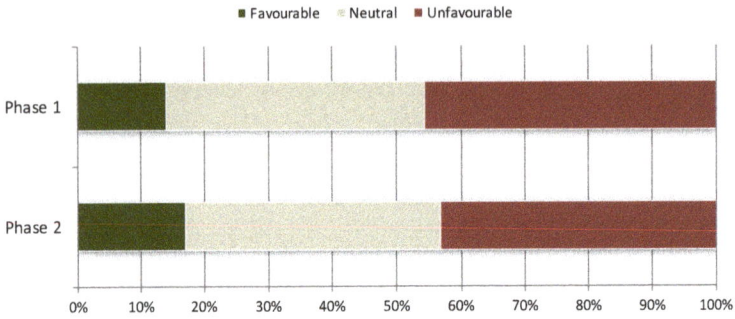

Figure 11.3: Favourable–neutral–unfavourable coverage of migration in print and online media in selected very high HD countries combined— all migration themes: Phase I and II

Notes: Messages: Phase 1 (n=31,064), Phase II (n=46,552). Articles: Phase 1 (n=16,226), Phase II (n=22,189).

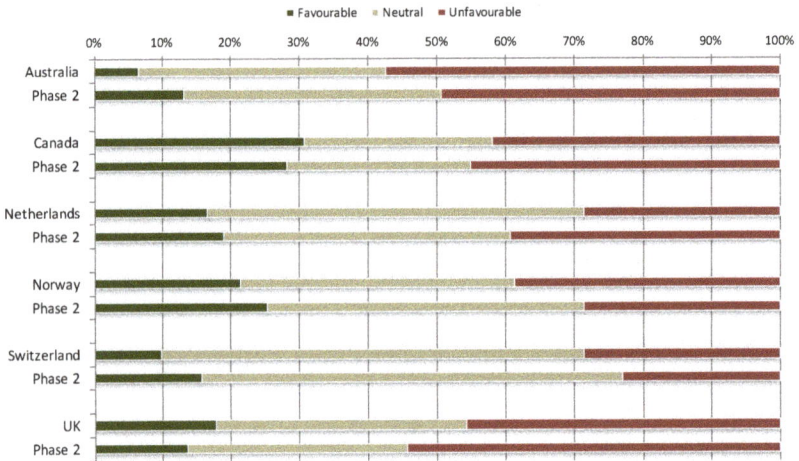

Figure 11.4: Favourable–neutral–unfavourable coverage of migration in print and online media in selected very high HD countries by country— all migration themes: Phase I and II

Notes: Messages: Australia (n=24,428), Canada (n=8,751), Netherlands (n=11,080), Norway (n=3,345), Switzerland (n=11,628), UK (n=18,385). Articles: Australia (n=13,256), Canada (n=5,738), Netherlands (n=4,364), Norway (n=1,371), Switzerland (n=4,940), UK (n=8,745).

Despite the shift toward slightly more balanced coverage between the two phases, it is clear from both Figures 11.3 and 11.4 that there is less favourable messaging than unfavourable messaging on migration and migrants in print and online media across all selected very high HD countries. This is one of the more striking findings, including because it holds true for both study periods. In all countries for both phases, unfavourable messages significantly outweighed favourable messages. Figure 11.5 also shows that for both study periods, Australia and the UK had the highest proportion of unfavourable messaging of migration issues (ranging between 46 and 57 per cent). Australia also experienced the lowest favourable coverage of all countries.

In Switzerland …

In December 2013, the media landscape was dominated by four stories: the Swiss People's Party (SVP) initiative to cut mass immigration, conditions in the Lampedusa Island refugee camps, irregular immigrants arriving in the Spanish enclaves of Morocco and debates in the UK about migrant worker access to benefits.

The SVP initiative remained a prominent story in January, with a focus on seasonal workers, the economy and social welfare. There was also discussion relating to Swiss support for Syrian refugees. Coverage spiked in February 2014, as the SVP initiative against mass migration was accepted by referendum. Much of this coverage consisted of short bulletin-type reports.

Canada again experienced the most polarised coverage, with the lowest neutral coverage (27 per cent), the highest favourable coverage (28 per cent) and the third highest unfavourable coverage (45 per cent). Switzerland, on the other hand, again experienced the least polarised coverage of aggregate migration messaging, with the highest neutral coverage (61 per cent). Switzerland and Norway both experienced shifts in tone of coverage, with slightly higher proportions of favourable messaging and slightly lower proportions of unfavourable messaging between the two study periods.

Overall, the consistency between the results for the two study periods is notable, particularly for the proportions of favourable messaging. The consistency occurred despite the changes in overall volume (Figure 11.1) and applied to both Switzerland and the UK, whose citizens went to the polls in or very near Phase I. It would be very interesting to examine the proportions of favourable messaging over time. In relation to specific themes—the most prominent being 'immigration and immigrants', 'irregular migration' and 'asylum seekers and refugees'— there was noticeable variability among the very high HD countries and compared with the aggregate results for all migration content.

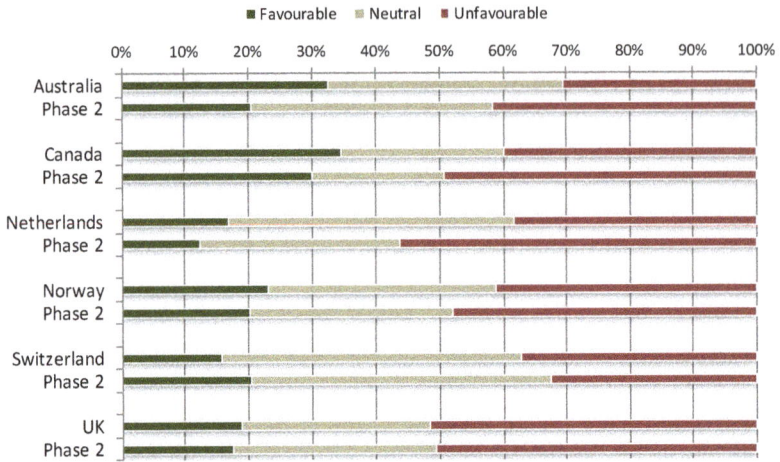

Figure 11.5: Favourable–neutral–unfavourable coverage of migration in print and online media in selected very high HD countries—immigration and immigrants theme: Phase I and II

Notes: Messages: Australia (n=2,188), Canada (n=5,017), Netherlands (n=1,543), Norway (n=853), Switzerland (n=2,660), UK (n=9,720). Articles: Australia (n=996), Canada (n=2,555), Netherlands (n=676), Norway (n=313), Switzerland (n=980), UK (n=3,920).

The UK and the Netherlands experienced the highest proportion of unfavourable coverage on 'immigration and immigrants', as shown in Figure 11.6, with Canada again having had the highest proportion of favourable coverage, as well as the most polarised coverage. As with the aggregate results, all countries experienced more unfavourable than favourable coverage.

It is also interesting to note that despite 'immigration and immigrants' being the least polarised theme across the five countries, it was again the most polarised theme within the Swiss context. That said, there was a slightly positive shift in Switzerland in Phase II, which ended just prior to the November 2014 failed referendum on reducing immigration quotas. The Netherlands, on the other hand, witnessed a shift between the two phases, which appears to have been related to discussion of the potential links between migration and social disharmony as well as the employment market. In Australia, 'immigration and immigrants' received the highest proportions of favourable messaging of all themes, notwithstanding the drop in Phase II.

Media on 'irregular migration' showed increased unfavourable messaging across most very high HD countries. Australia, Canada and the UK all had more than half of all messaging on 'irregular migration' as being unfavourable, which was in contrast to the mainland European countries. It is, however, important to note that Canada and Norway experienced very low volumes of coverage on this theme. Australia recorded no favourable messaging on 'irregular migration', noting that proportions of favourable messaging were very low for Phase II across all countries.

There was also noticeable variability between Phase I and II in most of the countries (Australia, Canada, Norway and the UK), with Switzerland and the Netherlands remaining fairly constant. Australia was the only country that experienced a discernible positive shift in coverage tone, becoming more positive in Phase II, which is likely to be related to the much-reduced volume and tempo of coverage associated with irregular maritime arrivals (IMAs)—no IMAs reached Australia during Phase II. In contrast, Canada, Norway and the UK's coverage contained much higher proportions of unfavourable coverage.

In Australia …

During the 12-month period from October 2013 to September 2014, Australia's media outlets published the second largest volume of material, second only to the UK. The Australian public received a constant background hum of migration-related messages. From this ocean of material, coverage of particular events would periodically rise, attain prominence for a time, then recede, to be replaced by the next hot item. Messages, in the form of both news and opinion relating to migration events, often appeared in media outlets across the country—their audience footprints enlarged by syndication across online media networks.

In the context of Australian reporting of issues associated with IMAs, the related themes of 'irregular migration', 'migrant accommodation' (including detention), 'asylum seekers and refugees' and 'people smuggling and trafficking' together accounted for 93 per cent of all coverage.

In contrast to 'irregular migration', the theme 'asylum seekers and refugees' received more favourable messaging in most countries, with positive shifts occurring in Switzerland, Canada and Norway (as shown in Figure 11.7). Interestingly, Australia experienced the lowest levels of unfavourable messaging on this theme, which was in stark contrast to messaging on 'irregular migration'.

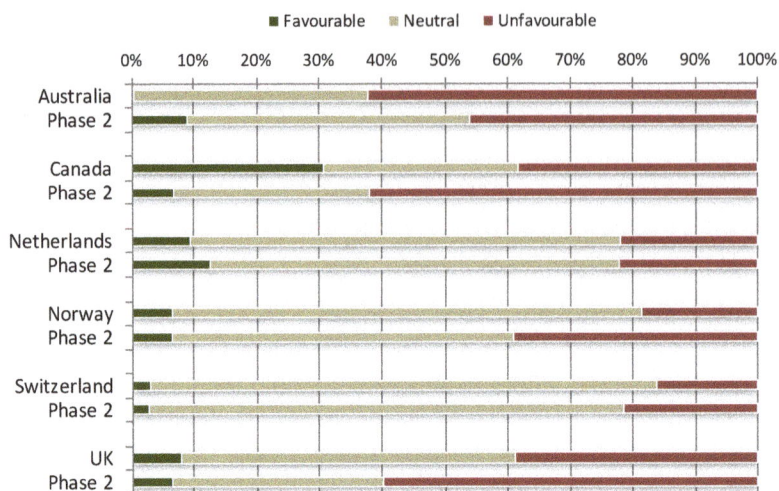

Figure 11.6: Favourable–neutral–unfavourable coverage of migration in print and online media in selected very high HD countries—irregular migration theme: Phase I and II

Notes: Messages: Australia (n=8,210), Canada (n=181), Netherlands (n=2,566), Norway (n=273), Switzerland (n=2,498), UK (n=3,925). Articles: Australia (n=4,350), Canada (n=148), Netherlands (n=793), Norway (n=137), Switzerland (n=1,108), UK (n=1,800).

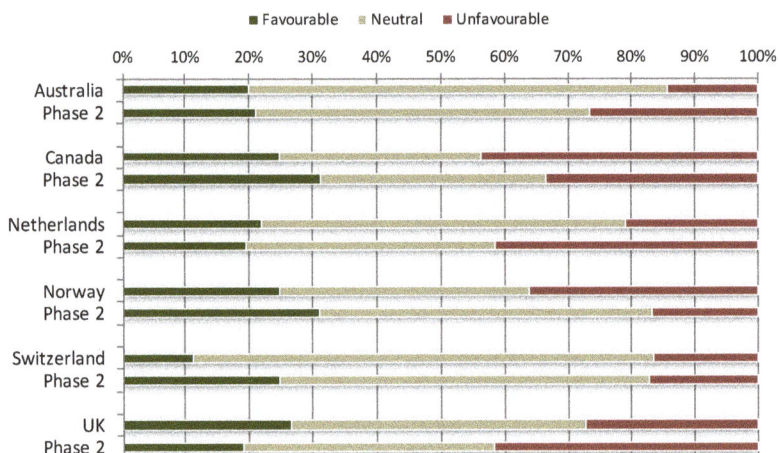

Figure 11.7: Favourable–neutral–unfavourable coverage of migration in print and online media in selected very high HD countries—asylum seekers and refugees theme: Phase I and II

Notes: Messages: Australia (n=4,850), Canada (n=2,913), Netherlands (n=5,871), Norway (n=2,021), Switzerland (n=4,718), UK (n=2,880). Articles: Australia (n=2,860), Canada (n=2,637), Netherlands (n=2,516), Norway (n=785), Switzerland (n=1,808), UK (n=1,700).

The Netherlands saw a notable increase in unfavourable messaging on this theme. This related largely to criticism of the government's handling of asylum seeker and refugee issues, including refugee intake numbers, accommodation and child pardon policies.

Overall, and as was seen during Phase I, there are substantial differences between countries on the extent of polarisation of media messaging on migration and migrants. Switzerland again exhibited a more nuanced discussion of migration and migrants as well as a much less polarised discussion. Canada's print and online media messaging was generally the most polarised overall; however, Australia and the UK experienced very high proportions of unfavourable messaging (and low or no favourable messaging) on specific themes. Overall, Australia experienced the most unbalanced overall discussion on migration and migrants in both phases.

Framing of the media discourse in very high HD countries

As well as grouping messages into thematic sets to facilitate the quantitative assessment of media across the countries in this study, we also analysed media content according to a contextual-associative typology. This enabled critical examination and reporting on the overall context in which various propositions and/or themes were couched.

Overall, and as shown in Figure 11.8, the research found that migration coverage in Phase II was more likely to have been discussed in a 'humanitarian' context in all countries, with very high proportions across all countries (ranging from 57 per cent in the UK to 74 per cent in the Netherlands). This appears to correlate to the increase in the 'asylum seekers and refugees' theme across all countries (see Figure 11.1). In contrast, the 'security' context dropped or remained the same across all countries, although was still noticeably larger proportionally in Australia compared to elsewhere (at 17 per cent). The 'economic' framing also dropped in most countries but most dramatically in the UK (from 53 per cent to 20 per cent).

At the aggregate level, and taking into account all media messages from all six very high HD country datasets, the variability between countries apparent in Phase I was not found in Phase II. All very high HD countries experienced notable uniformity in the framing of all media messaging in Phase II, which may be related to the increase in proportional and actual terms of coverage of 'asylum seekers and refugees'.

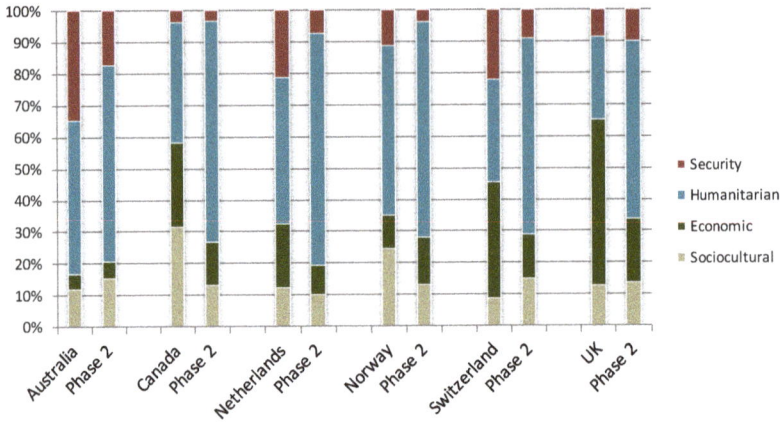

Figure 11.8: Framing of migration messages in print and online media in selected very high HD countries—all migration themes, October 2013 to March 2014

Notes: Messages: Australia (n=23,739), Canada (n=8,397), Netherlands (n=10,895), Norway (n=3,249), Switzerland (n=11,313), UK (n=17,715).

In the UK and Switzerland, it does appear that migration was part of broader economic and political discussions during Phase I, particularly in the lead-up to the UK local elections (May 2014) and the Swiss referendum on immigration quotas (February 2014). Both countries experienced substantial reductions in the 'economic' framing of messaging in Phase II, and so were more in line with the other countries.

In Norway …

The 'asylum seeker and refugee' theme captured the greatest share of coverage, accounting for 57 per cent of all the messages tracked.

This was also the only theme for which favourable commentary outstripped the unfavourable – although this only happened in the latter part of the study, as negative issues covered in the first half faded, to be replaced by greater coverage of Norway's involvement in United Nations High Commissioner for Refugees (UNHCR) programs. While many news pieces addressed global issues such as the plight of Syrian refugees and those in other pockets of unrest and strife throughout the world, the Norwegian press often brought the discussion back to the impact this is having on the numbers of people seeking refuge and asylum in the EU and, by extension, Norway.

Notwithstanding the uniformity of message-framing at the aggregate level with all migration messaging taken into account, there were differences both between countries and between phases, when specific themes were analysed. As shown in Figure 11.10, the framing of media messages on 'immigration and immigrants' appeared to be quite different in the six very high HD countries. Australia and Canada were the only countries that had messaging framed in a security context, although Australia's messaging was predominantly framed in a sociocultural context (60 per cent) and Canada's was framed mainly in a humanitarian context (61 per cent).

Economic framing was still high in Switzerland, although this had come down since Phase I—a reduction in economic framing of this theme was experienced across all six countries to a greater or lesser degree but most noticeably in the UK (79 to 38 per cent). While this reduction may be related to a postelection period of 'normalisation', it is interesting that the economic framing of this theme reduced across all countries. It may be that solid economic growth and a greater sense of economic stability is underpinning the change in these countries. It may also be possible that messaging related to 'immigration and immigrants' was affected by the substantial increase in the humanitarian framing of the 'asylum seekers and refugees' theme.

In the Netherlands …
'Asylum seekers and refugees' was the most prominent theme during the study periods. There was an increase in unfavourable commentary in Phase II. This was driven by discussion of contentious issues, including the need for a 'rejection quota' for unsuccessful asylum seekers and limits on the extent to which asylum seekers should have access to health care. There was also a greater focus on asylum seeker processing and deportation in the second phase, which again served to increase the proportion of unfavourable messaging on asylum seekers and refugees. News of the arrival of asylum seekers from Eritrea and Syria also fed into these discussions.

Australia—which experienced a relatively small proportional coverage of the theme 'immigration and immigrants' in both phases—had a discussion on the topic that was more likely to have been framed in the sociocultural and security contexts compared with the other countries. This would appear to be related to the messaging in print and online media on the integration of Muslim migrants in Australia, a topic that appeared to be dominated by unfavourable messaging.

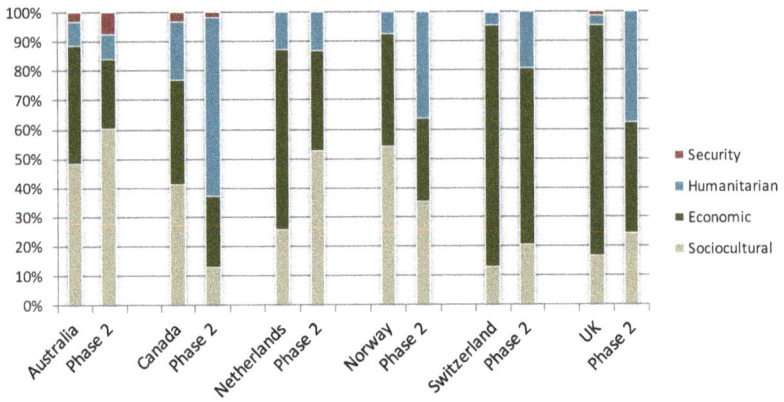

Figure 11.9: Framing of migration messages in print and online media in selected very high HD countries—immigration and immigrants theme: Phase I and II

Notes: Messages: Australia (n=2,185), Canada (n=4,738), Netherlands (n=1,488), Norway (n=813), Switzerland (n=2,630), UK (n=9,440).

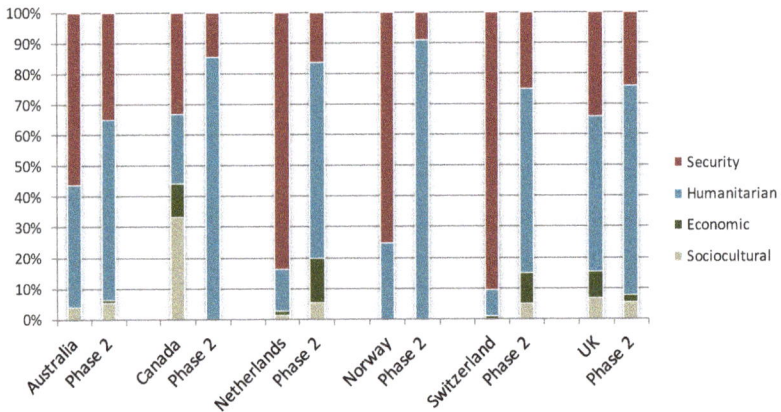

Figure 11.10: Framing of migration messages in print and online media in selected very high HD countries—irregular migration theme: Phase I and II

Notes: Messages: Australia (n=7,908), Canada (n=166), Netherlands (n=2,548), Norway (n=269), Switzerland (n=2,498), UK (n=3,825).

As shown in Figure 11.10, a very different picture emerges of reporting of the theme 'irregular migration', with the framing of media messaging in Switzerland, Norway and the Netherlands having shifted from a predominantly security-related framing to a humanitarian framing, and bringing them more in line with the UK. The security framing of the Phase

I messaging appeared to have been related to discussion of border security within Europe and irregular maritime migration across the Mediterranean Sea, from North Africa in particular. It is difficult to fully account for the evening-out of the message contexts, which now appear to be much more consistent across all countries. As with other themes, Australia's messaging had a slightly higher proportion framed in a security context.

Analysis of the 'asylum seekers and refugees' theme shows that the messaging was predominantly framed in the humanitarian context, although all three contexts were present in all countries. Norway saw a slight shift in framing of the theme, with an increase in 'economic' framing, while Australia's sociocultural framing in Phase I dropped markedly to become similar to levels in the other countries.

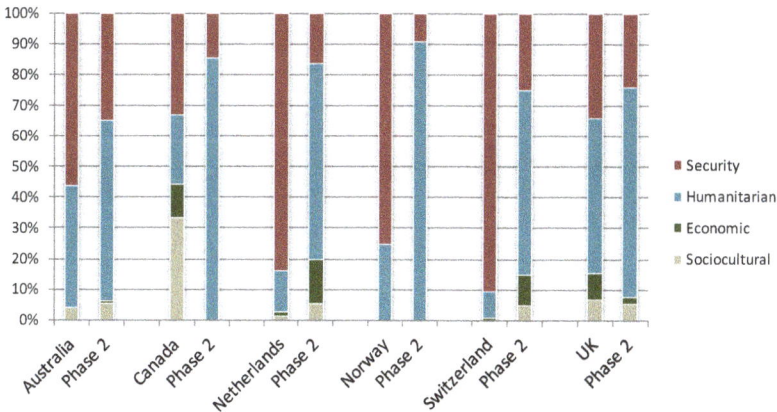

Figure 11.11: Framing of migration messages in print and online media in selected very high HD countries—asylum seekers and refugees theme: Phase I and II

Notes: Messages: Australia (n=4,679), Canada (n=2,854), Netherlands (n=5,803), Norway (n=1,970), Switzerland (n=4,620), UK (n=2,795).

Key findings and differences between other HD countries

There has been very little research on the media coverage of migration issues in countries that are not the very high HD migration destination or receiving countries. Countries that have been rated as having lower HD, but particularly those with low HD, have not tended to have been included in research on this topic. As discussed in McAuliffe and Weeks

(2015), there would appear to be several reasons for this. First, it can be very difficult to access and collect media articles from some countries. Second, the need for multilingual analysts with native language skills and an appreciation of current social and cultural environments poses challenges. Third, and particularly in relation to comparative analysis, ensuring consistency across different country analyses can be difficult.

This project attempts to fill some of this research gap. In doing so, and taking into account the findings of Phase I, the seven 'other' HD countries have been grouped to facilitate comparative analysis: Afghanistan (low HD), Bangladesh (medium HD), Malaysia (high HD), Pakistan (low HD), Sri Lanka (high HD), Thailand (high HD) and Vietnam (medium HD). We have moved away from categorising the countries in scope as 'origin' countries.

The key findings rely on smaller country-specific datasets compared with those compiled for very high HD countries. This was partly related to significant differences in media volumes and to difficulties with collection. Nevertheless, a comparative analysis produced some interesting findings:

- Consistent with Phase I findings, there remains a diversity of coverage by theme as well as tone and context across the seven other HD countries.

- The inclusion of Malaysia and Thailand highlighted the very different volumes of media, with Malaysia's volume being very high, which is likely to be related to infrastructure and access, but also to the nature of the topics covered in those countries—Malaysia and Thailand's coverage tended to reflect their status as migration 'receiving' countries.

- Taking into account all print and online messages on migration and migrants in the other HD countries,[4] it is evident that there was a small but noticeable shift in message tone between Phases I and II, toward a more balanced coverage overall. While neutral coverage decreased slightly, favourable messages increased and unfavourable coverage decreased marginally.

---

4   Involved analysis of more than 28,000 individual messages from 6,000 articles reported between 1 October 2013 and 30 September 2014 in Afghanistan, Bangladesh, Malaysia, Pakistan, Sri Lanka, Thailand and Vietnam.

- Overall, coverage of migration in print and online media tended to be less polarised in other HD countries than in very high HD countries, with more neutral reporting and less unfavourable reporting in origin countries. That said, reporting was more likely to be unfavourable than favourable, which is consistent with very high HD countries.

- Most media reporting on migration in both phases was framed in a humanitarian context, far outstripping economic, sociocultural and security contexts.

- Perhaps partly due to issues related to press freedom—as discussed above—the focus on migration in print and online media related primarily to the multitude of aspects associated with the rights and treatment of citizens.

- Reporting in a security context was evident in both phases in relation to people smuggling and, to a lesser extent, irregular migration.

Thematic content in print and online media in other HD countries

All media messages from the country-specific datasets were analysed against a number of themes. As noted in the previous section, a single print or online article may contain more than one message, and each message may relate to more than one theme. Analysing the datasets in this way allows for all messages to be described in thematic terms.

As shown in Figure 11.12, the volume of migration-specific print and online messaging was relatively similar in Phases I and II for all countries except Thailand and Vietnam, which experienced significant increases in the second phase. While the increases may be related to seasonal effects (as discussed above), they are clearly due in part to the heightened coverage of 'irregular migration' in Thailand and 'overseas workers' in Vietnam.

As with the very high HD countries, the volume of migration-related print and online media messaging varied substantially between the two countries. Malaysia's volume is akin to that of Canada and far exceeds all of the other countries in this group—a result that reflects the maturity and size of its media industry, as well as the focus on migration in public discourse.

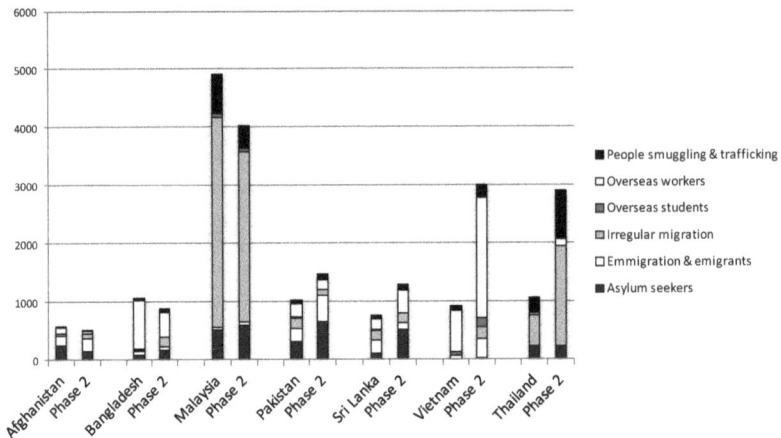

Figure 11.12: Thematic coverage of migration in print and online media in selected other HD countries by volume—key migration themes: Phase I and II

Notes: Messages: Afghanistan (n=1,100), Bangladesh (n=1,961), Malaysia (n=8,936), Pakistan (n=2,522), Sri Lanka (n=2,041), Thailand (n=3,964), Vietnam (n=3,945). Articles: Afghanistan (n=703), Bangladesh (n=1,027), Malaysia (n=3,716), Pakistan (n=1,654), Sri Lanka (n=1,317), Thailand (n=1,870), Vietnam (n=1,725).

In terms of thematic messaging analysed proportionally, and as shown in Figure 11.13, there was considerable variation in the thematic content between the countries. It is likely that the differences between the other HD countries reflect the very different national discussions that occurred during the study periods. Further, the substantial differences, and the nature of some of the thematic messaging, reflect the current state of migration more broadly within each country. Consistent with migration flows from Vietnam and Bangladesh, for example, 'overseas workers' dominated the print and online media messages in both phases. Reporting on Phase I findings noted that the results from Sri Lanka were somewhat at odds with the long history of regular labour migration flows from Sri Lanka; however, Phase II saw this theme become more prominent in Sri Lanka, with a reduction in both 'irregular migration' and 'emigration and emigrants'.

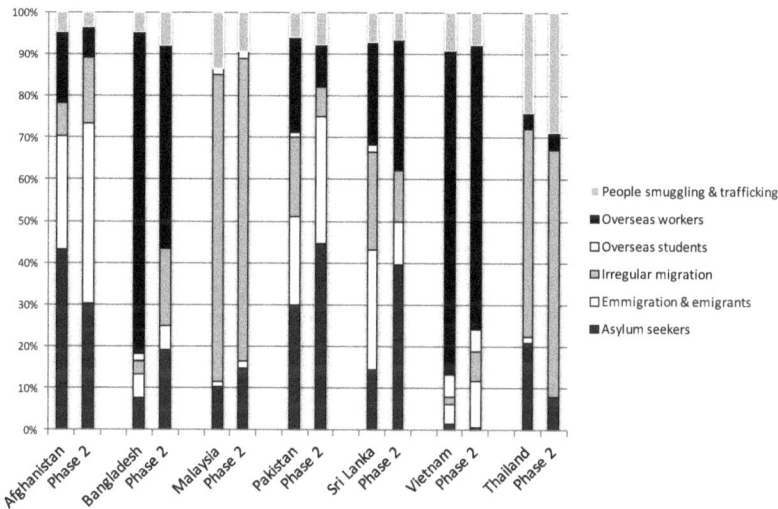

Figure 11.13: Thematic coverage of migration in print and online media in selected other HD countries by proportion—key migration themes: Phase I and II

Notes: Messages: Afghanistan (n=1,100), Bangladesh (n=1,961), Malaysia (n=8,936), Pakistan (n=2,522), Sri Lanka (n=2,041), Thailand (n=3,964), Vietnam (n=3,945). Articles: Afghanistan (n=703), Bangladesh (n=1,027), Malaysia (n=3,716), Pakistan (n=1,654), Sri Lanka (n=1,317), Thailand (n=1,870), Vietnam (n=1,725).

It is interesting to note the dominance of the media messaging on 'irregular migration' in Malaysia and Thailand, which is far greater proportionally than any of the other countries, including the very high HD countries. This appears to reflect the current migration issues facing those countries. In Malaysia, for example, there are estimated to be up to two million irregular migrants residing in the country, many working in the unregulated economy (McAuliffe & Mence, 2014). In Thailand, the very high proportional messaging on 'irregular migration' was related mainly to the Thai Government's crackdown of illegal migrant workers from Cambodia, Myanmar and Laos in early 2014, which preceded its migrant worker registration scheme (from June 2014). The scheme was reported as resulting in the registration and legalisation of more than one million former illegal migrants.

The amount of messaging on 'asylum seekers and refugees' increased in the majority of countries in Phase II, with slight reductions experienced in only Afghanistan and Thailand. Unlike coverage of this theme in very high HD countries, examination of the articles related to 'asylum seekers and refugees' indicates that these tend to be on local issues rather than the more general material on refugee crisis situations (e.g. Syria) and Mediterranean Sea asylum seeker movements. For example, in Pakistan the focus was on Afghan refugees and repatriation, while in Sri Lanka the discussion revolved around Pakistani asylum seekers in Sri Lanka as well as on Sri Lankan asylum seekers attempting to reach Australia. Bangladesh, on the other hand, witnessed a discussion on this theme that was dominated by Rohingya-related issues.

In Sri Lanka ...

Throughout the year-long study period, the Sri Lankan print and online media showed substantial interest in those citizens choosing to leave Sri Lanka. It explored these departures from a number of different perspectives. The message theme of 'asylum seekers and refugees' often dealt not just with those entering Sri Lanka, but also with Sri Lankans seeking refuge outside the country. 'Emigration and emigrants' addressed the matter of citizens leaving through proper channels, while 'irregular migration' messages related to both irregular arrivals into Sri Lanka, and, to some extent, news of citizens accused of irregularly migrating to other countries.

Extent of polarisation of print and online media content in other HD countries

Consistent with the findings for very high HD countries, when all messages related to migration and migrants are aggregated across all other HD countries, it is evident that there was a small but noticeable positive shift between Phases I and II toward more balanced coverage overall. Overall, and as can be seen from Figure 11.14, favourable coverage increased (from 11 per cent to 17 per cent), while unfavourable coverage decreased (from 49 per cent to 46 per cent), as did neutral coverage (39 per cent to 36 per cent). It would appear that no specific events or circumstances drove this change—it is more likely that a combination of changes in overall message volume in some countries, together with variations in thematic content, appear to have overall had a combined effect. It will be interesting to examine this high-level indicator in future phases, particularly as it tends to blunt the more event-based changes, and has the ability to provide a useful overall barometer on print and online media coverage of migration and migrants. This summary result is based on analysis of over 28,000 individual messages from more than 6,000 articles.

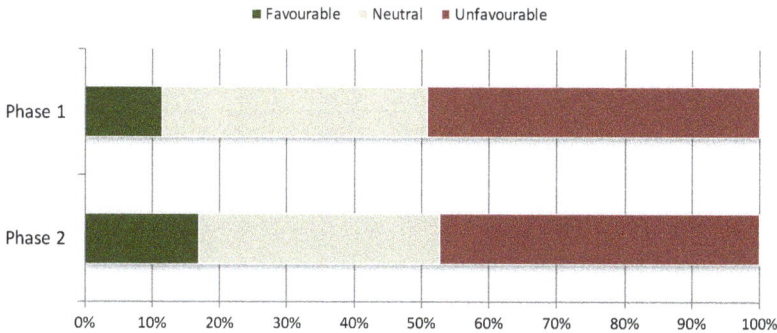

Figure 11.14: Favourable–neutral–unfavourable coverage of migration in print and online media in selected other HD countries combined—all migration themes: Phase I and II

Notes: Messages: Phase 1 (n=12,040), Phase II (n=16,349). Articles: Phase 1 (n=6,035), Phase II (n=8,010).

In Thailand ...

The 'immigration and immigrants' theme generated the highest level of favourable messages, with commentary pointing to the economic benefits (legitimate) foreign workers bring to the country. Unfavourable messages relating to this theme appeared more in a sociocultural context, with reports suggesting links between immigrants and criminal activity.

The 'asylum seekers and refugee' theme was another in which Thailand's media was similar to its neighbour, Malaysia. Media in each country focused on the plight of Rohingya refugees, while also presenting news relating to the Australian Government's asylum seeker policy. Favourable messages were driven by support for the plight of Rohingya living in Thailand, while unfavourable messages highlighted the difficulties faced by asylum seekers suffering with deportation or detention.

While not overly prominent in terms of absolute message numbers, the 'overseas workers' theme attracted a reasonably high level of favourable commentary (33 per cent). Government support of Thai workers was a leading positive message, while unfavourable commentary (25 per cent) appeared largely in connection with stories about the hardships faced by Thai workers, internationally.

As was the case with very high HD countries, the research found considerable variability in the tone of the media coverage of migration between other HD countries. Figure 11.15 shows that higher proportions of unfavourable messaging were experienced in all countries except Malaysia and Thailand, which remained at high levels. Malaysia experienced the highest levels of unfavourable messaging (57 per cent) and the lowest levels of favourable (10 per cent), very closely echoing the results for Australia (49 per cent unfavourable; 13 per cent favourable).

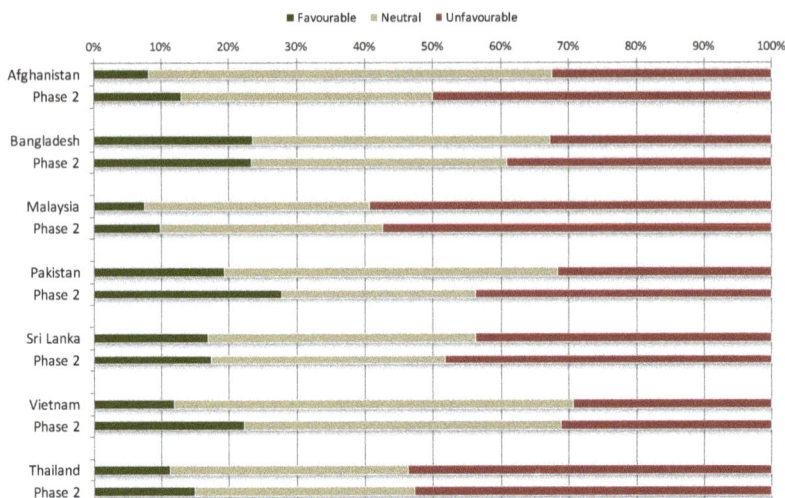

Figure 11.15: Favourable–neutral–unfavourable coverage of migration in print and online media in selected other HD countries—key migration themes: Phase I and II

Notes: Messages: Afghanistan (n=1,124), Bangladesh (n=2,028), Malaysia (n=11,128), Pakistan (n=2,656), Sri Lanka (n=2,142), Thailand (n=4,730), Vietnam (n=4,581). Articles: Afghanistan (n=721), Bangladesh (n=1,070), Malaysia (n=4,804), Pakistan (n=1,766), Sri Lanka (n=1,393), Thailand (n=2,338), Vietnam (n=1,953).

The proportions of neutral media coverage between the two phases dropped in all countries except Malaysia, where it remained the same. The print and online messaging in Afghanistan and Pakistan became noticeably more polarised in the second phase, with both unfavourable and favourable messaging increasing. This was in a context of otherwise fairly consistent results between the two phases and across almost all countries.

Not surprisingly, the two countries with the highest proportional and actual messaging on irregular migration (Malaysia and Thailand) experienced the highest proportions of unfavourable messaging and low levels of favourable, when all themes are taken into account. These results accord with the findings for Australia, which shared these key characteristics related to thematic messaging and the tone of the overall messaging. In all three countries, there would seem to be an emphasis on linking irregular migration to the success or otherwise of government policy and practice in managing immigration.

In Pakistan …

The 'asylum seekers and refugees' theme accounted a third of all messages, and was the most prominent issue across the entire study period. While overall unfavourable messages still outnumbered favourable ones, the second phase of the study saw an improvement in tone with the announcement of monetary aid from foreign nations, including the US and Japan, and support from the UN. Pakistan was also praised for the magnanimity with which it receives refugees.

Unfavourable messages related to the suffering of refugees in the country's camps and their inadequate accommodation. We also saw significant frustration expressed about the level of ongoing support needed for refuges, and, concurrently, concerns about potential links between terrorists and refugees, while the large economic and social burden placed on countries hosting refugees was also noted.

As shown in Figure 11.16, the theme 'overseas workers' received a reasonable amount of favourable media coverage in most origin countries during the study period, with a significant increase having occurred in Pakistan. Consistent with the findings for Phase I, the two countries in which the theme dominated (Bangladesh and Vietnam) did not have the highest proportions of favourable coverage, although they both increased in Phase II. One of the starker findings is that all countries experienced polarisation of messaging on this theme—lower levels or much lower levels of neutral reporting occurred in Phase II.

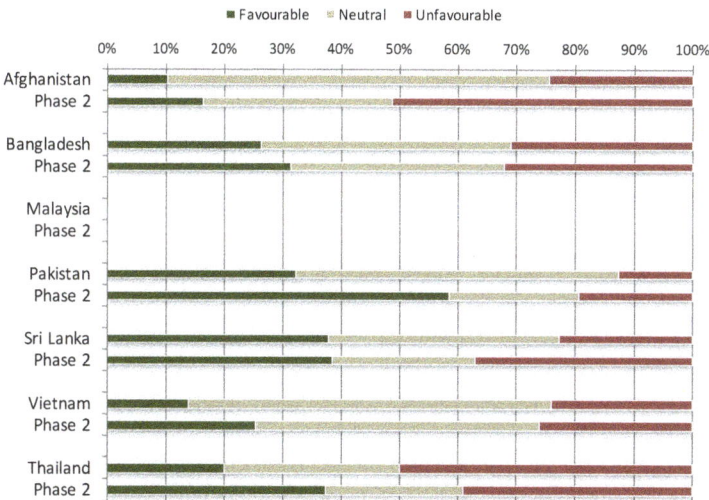

Figure 11.16: Favourable–neutral–unfavourable coverage of migration in print and online media in selected other HD countries—overseas workers theme: Phase I and II

Notes: Messages: Afghanistan (n=135), Bangladesh (n=1,257), Malaysia (n=8), Pakistan (n=390), Sri Lanka (n=585), Thailand (n=158), Vietnam (n=2,785). Articles: Afghanistan (n=89), Bangladesh (n=589), Malaysia (n=8), Pakistan (n=276), Sri Lanka (n=314), Thailand (n=74), Vietnam (n=1,074).

In Bangladesh …

Print and online media was highly focused on the 'overseas workers' theme, typically addressing the hardships confronting these people. Over half of all messages reported during the one-year study period were on this theme. The prominence of stories and messages on the plight of overseas workers aligned with the often-reported link between the health of the Bangladeshi economy and the remittances flowing from its foreign workers.

A long way back in terms of its prominence was the second-most reported theme of 'asylum seekers and refugees' (15 per cent). The standout issue discussed here was Rohingya refugees in Bangladesh and Myanmar, which became more prominent in Phase II.

In contrast to the tone of the media messaging on 'overseas workers', the coverage of 'irregular migration' was once again extremely unfavourable, although there were some changes evident in Pakistan and Vietnam. As was found in Phase I, the tone of the coverage of this theme was the second most unfavourable of all of the thematic coverage across all very high HD and other HD country datasets—second only to 'people smuggling and trafficking', which received extremely unfavourable commentary in all countries.

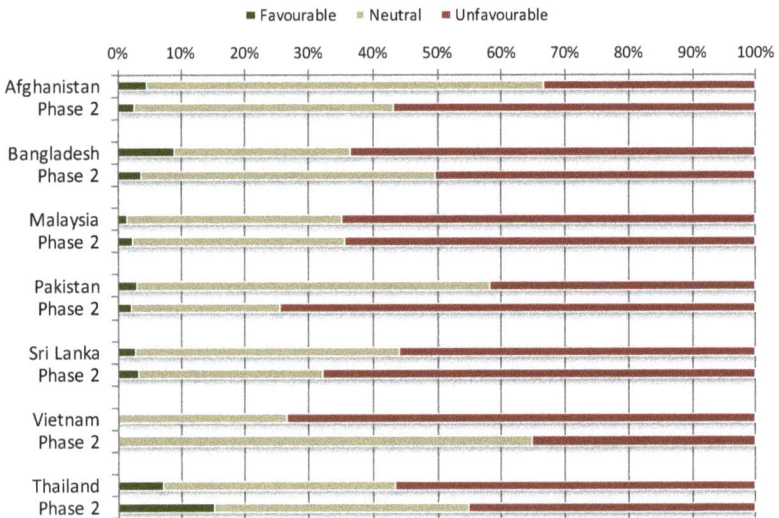

Figure 11.17: Favourable–neutral–unfavourable coverage of migration in print and online media in selected other HD countries—irregular migration theme: Phases I and II

Notes: Messages: Afghanistan (n=126), Bangladesh (n=205), Malaysia (n=6,516), Pakistan (n=298), Sri Lanka (n=338), Thailand (n=2,234), Vietnam (n=225). Articles: Afghanistan (n=83), Bangladesh (n=129), Malaysia (n=2,544), Pakistan (n=220), Sri Lanka (n=227), Thailand (n=992), Vietnam (n=126).

Interestingly, the tone of the messaging on irregular migration in other HD countries tended to be much more unfavourable (35 per cent to 75 per cent) compared with very high HD countries. This reflected the focus on the dangers to potential irregular migrants, deportations of irregular migrants back to the other HD country as well as commentary on the dangers posed by irregular migrants from elsewhere. It should be noted, however, that the volume of messaging on 'irregular migration' was reasonably low, with only Malaysia and Thailand experiencing substantial volumes (see Figure 11.12).

In Vietnam …

Print and online media on migration issues in Vietnam was similar in many respects to that of other countries ranked lower on the HDI. It had a strong focus on the opportunities and challenges faced by citizens working in foreign countries, and the valuable contribution these workers make to the Vietnamese economy through the flow of remittances. Discussion surrounding inbound migration in the Vietnamese press was limited and was largely driven by specific events.

This event-driven media surrounding inbound migration produced something of shift when comparing the two phases in this study period. In the first phase of the study, press articles relating to 'overseas workers' made up the lion's share of coverage (68 per cent), while coverage relevant to 'immigration and immigrants' was insignificant. In the second phase, tensions caused by the development of a Chinese oil rig in Vietnamese waters led to anti-China protests that targeted industrial zones housing large numbers of Chinese workers. The subsequent media interest in these events saw the 'immigration and immigrants' theme jump to a 15 per cent share of coverage across the April–September 2014 period.

Framing of the media discourse in other HD countries

The first striking result of the research is the dominance of the 'humanitarian' framing in all other HD countries across both phases. Messaging on migration and migrants in print and online media coverage is being predominantly depicted through a 'humanitarian' lens. Other framing is present and in some countries not insubstantial—24 per cent 'security' in Malaysia, 25 per cent 'economic' in Bangladesh—but all countries' messaging is predominantly framed in a 'humanitarian' context, regardless of the differences in substance and complexity of national migration issues.

The second key finding is the noticeable degree of uniformity between the two phases. All countries experienced similar results in the two phases, with moderate changes largely being limited to increases in 'humanitarian' framing in Afghanistan, Pakistan and Sri Lanka (with concomitant decreases largely in 'sociocultural' framing). While it is difficult to anticipate the results of future phases, it would be useful to have this trend finding confirmed (or otherwise) through further research.

In Malaysia …

The Malaysian press was most focused on the inflow of immigrants, with the most prominent area of discussion being 'irregular migration'. This theme accounted for 53 per cent of the messages studied across the 12-month study period, and its significance in the study set points to the high importance of this issue to the Malaysian nation. Very large numbers of people enter the country to work each year, and the management of this human flow was shown through the media to be a daunting task for policymakers and administrators alike.

With two thirds of 'irregular migration' messages being critical of people entering Malaysia through unlawful channels, and half of all messages unsupportive of legal 'immigration and immigrants', it's no surprise that the most prominent themes were represented in a largely unfavourable tone.

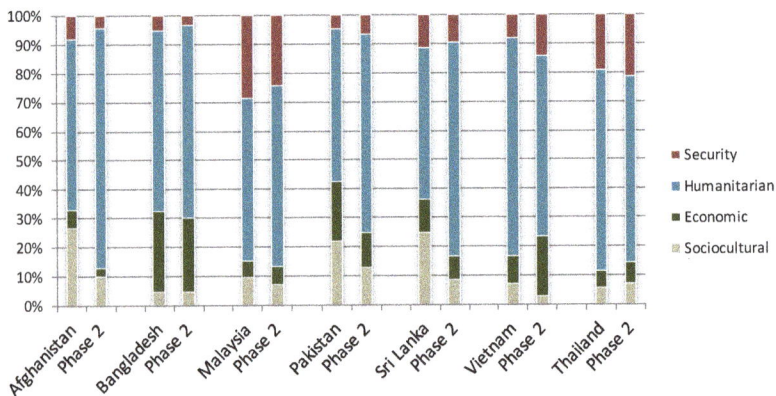

Figure 11.18: Framing of migration messages in print and online media in selected other HD countries—all migration themes: Phases I and II

Messages: Afghanistan (n=1,018), Bangladesh (n=1,995), Malaysia (n=11,128), Pakistan (n=2,612), Sri Lanka (n=1,603), Thailand (n=4,730), Vietnam (n=4,497).

The two countries that experienced the highest proportions of 'security' framing (Malaysia and Thailand) have arguably the highest numbers of irregular labour migrants who are not asylum seekers or refugees in their communities (International Federation for Human Rights [FIDH] & Suara Rakyat Malaysia [Suaram], 2008; IOM, 2011b). While acknowledging that this is difficult to state categorically, given the lack of hard data on migrant flows and stocks, the little we do know seems to be consistent with the overall results.

Consistent with Phase I, the discussion of 'overseas workers' was more likely to have been framed in an economic context compared with the overall migration discussion, with an exception being Thailand. In Thailand, there was not much coverage of this theme either in volume or proportional terms, but the little that was reported was framed in a humanitarian context, indicating perhaps less of a reliance on remittances in this country.

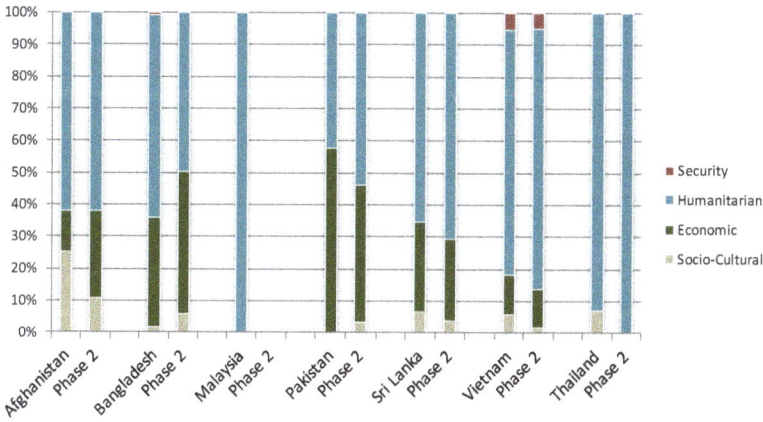

Figure 11.19: Framing of migration messages in print and online media in selected other HD countries—overseas workers theme: Phases I and II
Messages: Afghanistan (n=138), Bangladesh (n=1,255), Malaysia (n=8), Pakistan (n=424), Sri Lanka (n=414), Thailand (n=158), Vietnam (n=2,718).

In other HD countries, as was the case in very high HD countries, discussion on 'irregular migration' saw a greater proportion of messages framed in a security context, with little or no economic framing. While there was uniformity across the two phases for most countries, Vietnam was an exception: security framing jumped from 23 per cent in Phase I to 96 per cent in Phase II. There appear to be two main reasons for this. First, the volume of messaging in Vietnam in both phases was small. Second, the coverage was mainly associated with event-driven reporting of Chinese irregular labour migrants and security-related incidents (including shootings) and threats.

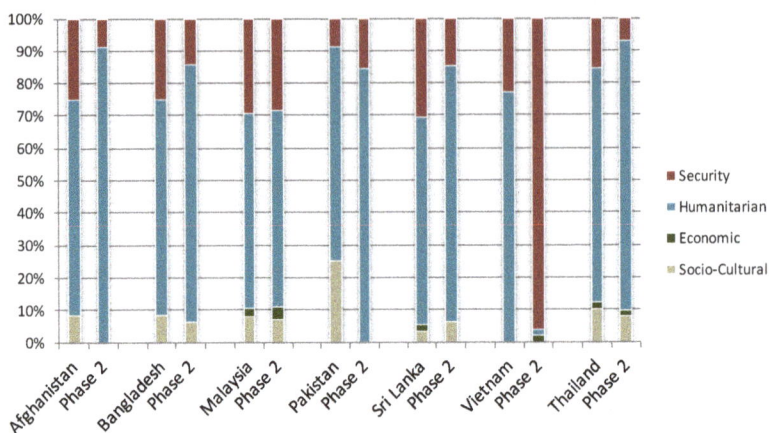

Figure 11.20: Framing of migration messages in print and online media in selected other HD countries—irregular migration theme: Phases I and II

Messages: Afghanistan (n=112), Bangladesh (n=201), Malaysia (n=6,516), Pakistan (n=284), Sri Lanka (n=243), Thailand (n=2,234), Vietnam (n=226).

Implications for policymakers

The media is often accused of generalising—usually negatively—about migrants and migration, for example by scaling up individual misdemeanours to entire populations, or failing to tell good news as well as bad news stories. One of the implications of the preceding analysis is that those who criticise the media in this way are in turn generalising. It is clear that media coverage of migrants and migration is dynamic and quite sophisticated, and varies significantly between countries as well as within countries over time. This noted, a number of initial implications for policymakers can be suggested from this research.

First, and given the significance of media coverage on migrants and migration noted in the Introduction, it is important to promote a fair and reasonable portrayal of migrants in the media, and as this analysis has illustrated this is often still not the case. At a national level, promoting and protecting the freedom of the press is paramount. At the corporate level, there are implications, for example concerning safeguarding editorial independence from commercial interests. At the level of individual media outlets, providing internship or employment opportunities for journalists with a migrant background has been suggested as one way to increase a better understanding and more objective coverage of this and indeed other cross-cultural issues. There are powerful reasons to support these sorts of policies beyond just potential migration outcomes.

A second policy area that can be informed by this and subsequent analysis is the design and dissemination of information on migration policies and programs to settled migrants as much as to potential migrants. It is likely that media content and comment has more influence on migrant decisions than many official sources of information, for example because the former may be more trusted and more easily accessible. Understanding how the media shapes its coverage of migration, as this analysis has begun to, has important implications for trying to predict and perhaps direct its influence.

In this regard, one of the key contributions made by the research is the application of a consistent methodology to a selected number of countries to develop a measurable set of indices, which can be monitored over time. This can be appealing for policymakers, as it offers the opportunity to compare media discourses about migration in other countries, including other HD countries. Detecting changes and shifts over time, in a solid and measurable manner, enables policymakers to consider a range of options, including for communications activities, with the benefit of evidence.

Conclusions

The purpose of this research has been to compare migration discourses in selected countries by examining thematic content, contextual framing, and the extent of polarisation of messages communicated via print and online media over two six-month periods. It is the second phase of a research collaboration between the Department of Immigration and Border Protection and Cubit Media Research, designed to inform migration policymakers and practitioners by drawing on expertise built up in the private sector on large-scale quantitative media analytics.

This project involved large-scale quantitative research that relied on a combination of multilingual human analyses and a human cognitive modelling software system. This developed a unique evidence-base, albeit covering two finite periods and with certain limitations. The research has highlighted, with a reasonable level of confidence, the nature of the migration discussions occurring within the media in the selected countries, as well as the relative 'space' devoted to different migration topics.

Overall, the evidence this research provides adds to the existing body of work on migration and the media. However, it could be argued that a more pressing longer-term benefit will only be realised through analyses of trends stemming from additional research phases. Discerning changes over time has the potential to uncover trends that are likely to have implications for policymakers and migration practitioners internationally.

Reference list

Castles, S., de Haas, H., & Miller, M. (2014). *The age of migration: International population movements in the modern world* (5th ed.). Hampshire: Palgrave Macmillan.

Erdal, I. J. (2009). Repurposing of content multi-platform news production. *Journalism Practice, 3*(2), 178–95. doi.org/10.1080/17512780802681223

International Federation for Human Rights, & Suara Rakyat Malaysia. (2008). *Undocumented migrants and refugees in Malaysia: Raids, detention and discrimination.* Report 489/2. Paris: International Federation for Human Rights. Retrieved from www.fidh.org/IMG/pdf/MalaisieCONJ489eng.pdf.

International Organization for Migration. (2011a). *World Migration Report 2011—Communicating Effectively about Migration.* Geneva: Author.

International Organization for Migration. (2011b). *Thailand Migration Report 2011 – Migration for Development in Thailand: Overview and Tools for Policymakers.* Bangkok: Author.

International Telecommunication Union. (2013). *Measuring the Information Society.* Geneva: Author.

Kandemir, O. (2012). Human development and international migration. *Procedia: Social and Behavioral Sciences, 62,* 446–51. doi.org/10.1016/j.sbspro.2012.09.073

Keith, S., Schwalbe, C. B., & Silcock, B. W. (2010). Comparing war images across media platforms: Methodological challenges. *Media, War & Conflict, 3*(1), 87–98. doi.org/10.1177/1750635210353676

Kohut, A., Wike, R., Bell, J., Horowitz, J. M., Simmons, K., Stokes, B., Poushter, J., Barker, C., & Gross, E. M. (2012). *Social networking popular across the globe: Arab publics most likely to express political views online*. Retrieved from Pew Research Centre: www.pewglobal. org/files/2012/12/Pew-Global-Attitudes-Project-Technology-Report-FINAL-December-12-2012.pdf.

Koser, K. (2012, 15 August). *Securitizing migration: A good or bad idea?* (International Relations and Security Network, Zurich, Interviewers) [audio recording]. Retrieved from www.video.ethz.ch/campus/isn/ e64b372e-c59e-4fbb-a091-6bfe68d9a17f.html.

Koser, K. (2014, 5 June). *Cities and the case for migration*. Keynote address to the 2014 Cities of Migration Conference, Berlin.

McAuliffe, M., & Mence, V. (2014). *Global irregular maritime migration: Current and future challenges*. Irregular Migration Research Program, occasional paper series 05. Canberra: Australian Department of Immigration and Border Protection. Retrieved from www.border. gov.au/ReportsandPublications/Documents/research/global-irregular-maritime-migration.pdf.

McAuliffe, M., & Weeks, W. (2015). *Media and migration: Comparative analysis of print and online media reporting on migrants and migration in selected origin and destination countries*. Irregular Migration Research Program, occasional paper series 13. Canberra: Australian Department of Immigration and Border Protection. Retrieved from www.border.gov. au/ReportsandPublications/Documents/research/media-migration.pdf.

Quandt, T., & Singer, J. B. (2009). Convergence and cross-platform content production. In Wahl-Jorgensen, K., & Hanitzsch, T. (Eds), *The Handbook for Journalism Studies* (pp. 130–44). New York: Free Press.

Reporters Without Borders. (2014). *World Press Freedom Index 2014*. Retrieved from rsf.org/en/world-press-freedom-index-2014.

Semetko, H. A., & Valkenburg, P. M. (2000). Framing European politics: A content analysis of press and television news. *Journal of Communication, 50*(2), 93–109. doi.org/10.1111/j.1460-2466.2000. tb02843.x

United Nations Development Programme. (2014). *Human development report 2014*. Geneva: Author. Retrieved from hdr.undp.org/en/2014-report.

12

Environmentally related international migration: Policy challenges

Victoria Mence and Alex Parrinder

Policy deliberations on environmentally related migration[1] have encountered a number of substantial challenges. The potential scale of environmentally related migration across borders both currently and in the future is unknown. Further research is required on the relationship between environmental factors and international migration to better understand what lies ahead and the implications this might have for Australia's policies to manage both regular and irregular migration. Challenges at the international, regional and national levels for policymakers involve understanding environmental impacts on human movement and the possible increase in the volume of international migration, including irregular migration, that may follow. In addition, the potential for environmental and climate change displacement to impact on states' viability (or parts thereof) and the ability of migrants to return is very difficult to quantify. From an Australian perspective, there is a perception that many of the challenges relate to the issues faced by Pacific Island nations, although there are implications for environmentally related movement in the broader Asia–Pacific region.

---

1   In this chapter the term 'environmentally related migration' is used to refer to the range of issues relevant to the relationship between the environment, climate change and migration.

It is widely recognised that there have been significant problems relating to historical research on environmentally related migration including because of the contentious and politicised context in which the knowledge base has developed. One effect of this schism is a dearth of empirical research and robust evidence on key concerns and a lack of clarity around international and national normative frameworks regarding environmentally related migration. The difficulties involved in conceptualising and defining the complexities of environmentally related migration are central to the challenge of increasing the knowledge base and engaging in effective policy deliberations and the formulation of policy responses.

The purpose of this chapter is to provide background on the key issues relating to environmentally related migration, including the debate on connections between migration and environmental stress; the development of global, regional and national-level policy responses (including policy considerations relevant to Australia); and priorities for further research. The second section below summarises the literature on this topic. The third section briefly discusses some of the key challenges for policymakers. The fourth section summarises potential future policy responses, noting examples of relevant measures that have been implemented in Australia and internationally.

While highlighting the challenges for policymakers that arise from the contested body of empirical research on environmentally related migration, it is beyond the scope of this chapter to draw conclusions on the evidence on the migration impacts of environmental factors.

Literature overview

One of the most striking features of the literature on the environment–migration nexus is that the issues have ignited intense interest and controversy across a range of academic disciplines. There is also keen interest among the public and the media, which is often characterised by heated debate. This is not surprising given that issues around migration, such as asylum seekers, refugees, forced migrants and irregular migration are all highly contested, as are the issues of environmental degradation and climate change.

Another feature of the literature is the enormous volume of information available from a diverse research community. In addition to numerous academic papers, there is an abundant array of reports and papers by governments, international agencies and non-governmental organisations (NGOs) (Gemenne, 2011).

Current thinking and research on the environment–migration nexus is to a large extent a product of the historical controversies that have characterised the development of research over the past two decades. Dun and Gemenne provide a useful analysis of the disciplinary divide within academia that has shaped the contested nature of much of the research. Prior to the focus on the interconnections between the environment and migration, the fields of study relating to migration and the environment evolved within very different branches of learning. Research on the environment was located in the natural sciences, and migration within the domain of the humanities and social sciences. 'Just as most classical theories on migration tend[ed] to ignore the environment as a driver of migration, most theories on environmental governance ignore[d] migration flows' (Dun & Gemenne, 2008). Both areas of research are relatively new and both have evolved in the context of growing economic, political and social tensions.

The polemic nature of the debate has its origins in the response to initial research by environmental scholars in the 1980s that linked environmental stress and migration in the context of a limited understanding of refugee and migration epistemological frameworks. From these beginnings, research and theories on environmentally related migration evolved within two distinctive clusters of disciplinary approaches. One group included authors who based their research approaches primarily from an environmental, disaster or conflict disciplinary perspective. The other group included scholars primarily from refugee and migration disciplinary backgrounds who challenged the definitional and theoretical assumptions that underpinned this research.

Until recently much of the literature relating to the environment–migration nexus concentrated on a number of controversial themes that surfaced in the 1980s. The most prominent included:

- the way migrants, thought to be migrating in response to environmental pressures, were described and defined;

- the strength of the evidence used to support estimates of existing examples of environmentally related migration, and the speculative nature of the predictions made about future migration flows;
- whether a direct link can be made between environmental factors and migration or more complex causalities apply.

Definitions, terminology and typologies

One of the most important and determinative debates in the literature has been about definitions and terminology. As Castles noted, poorly conceived definitions have implications beyond the research community as 'definitions are crucial in guiding policies of governments and international agencies' (Castles, 2002, p. 9).

'Environmental refugee' was a term commonly used in the context of environmentally related migration research and, in spite of some serious problems identified relating to its use, the term is still widely used. 'Environmental refugee' as a term first gained currency in the 1980s. A number of mainly environmental researchers and commentators maintained that a significant proportion of the forced migrant population were migrating because of environmental factors. Further, it was suggested that this category of forced migrants was a hidden problem and involved people who needed protection and should be referred to as 'environmental refugees' (El-Hinnawi, 1985; Jacobson, 1988).

Without further definition, linking concepts relating to the 'environment' and 'refugees' to describe a particular group of forced migrants was regarded by many scholars as conceptually misleading and legally meaningless (Kibreab, 1997; McGregor, 1993). As Zetter and others noted, the concept of 'refugee' has a clear legal meaning and historical weight anchored in the Refugee Convention, which remains confined to the criteria outlined in its original formulation (Castles, 2002; Suhrke, 1992; Zetter, 2007).

Attempting to expand the definition to define a particular category of forced migrant, a concept that in itself is still evolving, risked undermining refugee protection by inflating the numbers and thus providing states with further reasons to step away from asylum obligations (Black, 2001; Dun & Gemenne, 2008; Kibreab, 1997). Further, the term 'environmental refugee' also invoked some inherent assumptions about environmentally related migration, including the idea that the environment was the principal factor driving forced migration, and that the migration was cross-border, neither of which had been verified or supported by sound empirical evidence (Castles, 2002; Findlay & Geddes, 2011; Kibreab, 1997; McGregor, 1993).

The challenge of identifying meaningful definitions and categorisations for migrants, especially those in crisis, was central to discussions at the recent 2013 United Nations High-Level Dialogue on Migration and Development. The term 'migrants in crisis' was used in an attempt to 'straddle traditional categories and distinctions'. The aim was to capture the complexity of mixed migration populations that can include workers, as well as asylum seekers and refugees, migrating because of political, conflict related crises and/or natural disasters (Koser, 2013).

Estimates and predictions

The use of the term 'environmental refugee' in the context of forced migration received widespread attention and prompted further research in the 1990s that made some ominous predictions about future environmentally related migration flows. These predictions have had an ongoing influence in the discussion.

One of the most prominent and prolific writers on this theme was Myers (Morrissey, 2012). In 1993, while acknowledging that some of the analysis was 'speculative' and 'essentially exploratory', Myers claimed that, based on the most conservative calculations of what he called 'this refugee problem', the movement of people 'would …be of an altogether unprecedented scale' with an estimated 150 million environmental refugees by 2050 (Myers, 2001; Myers, 1997; Myers & Kent, 1995; Myers, 1993, p. 752). In subsequent papers this figure rose to 200 million, a figure Myers was still predicting in 2005 (Myers, 2005). Some advocacy publications went much further with one predicting up to one billion people displaced by the end of the 21st century (Christian Aid, 2007). In 1993, a report by the United Nations High Commissioner for Refugees (UNHCR) stated that 'it is entirely possible that the impact of environmental degradation and resource depletion on population movement may be even more important than these authors suggest' (UNHCR, 1993, p. 5). The predictions were widely accepted and were central to a body of literature that used the predictions to highlight the risks and the dangers of not acting on climate change.

Early critical responses to the scale of migration predicted were highly sceptical of the way the figures had been calculated. Critics argued that the figures did not take account of the role of personal agency in decisions to migrate, the ability of populations to adapt to changing conditions, nor the range of other political, economic and social factors at play (Lonergan, 1998; McGregor, 1993; Surhke, 1992).

A number of authors have suggested that there has been little appetite for reassessing the validity of the high estimates and predictions because the sheer scale of the migration predicted has successfully raised the profile of climate change and its potential consequences (Black, 2001; Castles, 2011; Crisp, 1999; Morrissey, 2009). The uncritical use of Myers' figures by international organisations, advocate groups and the media has also reinforced and influenced political and public discourse on the issues (Morrissey, 2009). However, in 2008, UNHCR warned that inflated figures were not helpful, rather they 'evoked fantasies of uncontrollable waves of migration that risk stoking xenophobic reactions' (A question of climate refugees, 2011, para. 7).

Estimates are important, but need to be based on more robust and rigorous empirical evidence. Further, research needs to be location and context specific and to take account of the multiple responses going on (Leighton, 2011). 'Mapping and monitoring potential environmental "hotspots" and changing regional conditions, and tracking migration trends, offer a more fruitful and evidence-based route for policy development' (Boano, Zetter, & Morris, 2008).

Mono-causality versus multiple causality

Until recently, one of the most contentious disagreements in the literature related to the assumption that there were direct links between environmental factors and international migration flows. In the view of some critics, predictions were often based on a simple process of subtracting current populations living in problem areas to calculate migration flows (Black, 2001).

Those critical of attempts to draw direct correlations have long argued that the causes of migration are highly complex, involving a range of political, economic and social factors that may influence responses to environmental stress. The strength of family, social, cultural and ethnic networks, the effectiveness of state responses to disasters and the level of poverty and wealth all appeared to influence coping strategies and migration decisions. Further, all of these variables are likely to vary over time and space (Black, 2001; Castles, 2011).

An additional level of complexity lies in the complicated variations involved in environmentally related migration, including: internal versus cross-border; short- or long-distance; temporary or permanent; rapid- or slow-onset events, that is, forced migration as a result of an environmental catastrophe or migrants who move voluntarily in the context of environmental stress and those who leave as opposed to those who stay (Bates, 2002; Hugo, 1996; Suhrke, 1993).

There has been a growing consensus in recent literature on the environment–migration nexus that multiple causality is a crucial consideration. There is a sense in more recent literature that some of the controversies that have characterised the debate are abating. 'Although the debate still goes on, the disciplinary divide is gradually being overcome: environmental scientists tend to be more cautious while migration specialists do recognise the role of the natural environment in migration dynamics. On the whole, most scholars now dismiss the apocalyptic predictions that used to influence debates' (Piguet, 2011, p. 4). Further, there is recognition in more recent literature by migration theorists that environmentally related migration is an issue that demands greater attention.

It is significant that reference is made many times in recent literature to how much is yet unknown about the interconnections between environmental factors and migration by both migration and environment researchers (Brown, 2008; Castles, 2011; Kniveton, Schmidt-Verkerk, Smith, & Black, 2008; Koser, 1996; Martin, 2010). This is especially true in relation to 'the circumstances in which international migration may result from climate change' (Martin, 2010).

It is evident that a more considered approach is starting to inform the discourse at a national and international governance level, as reflected in the more recent global discussions on related issues. There is also a growing recognition that an interdisciplinary approach, based on robust empirical research, is essential to support practical and realistic policy development by governments in particular. An important challenge ahead is to better negotiate the narrative in the public arena. Publications by academics containing apocalyptic themes, especially in relation to security issues, continue to have influence.

323

Challenges for policymakers

There is broad agreement that most environmentally related migration is expected to be internal (International Organization for Migration [IOM], 2013; McAdam, 2012; Martin, 2010; Newland, 2011). Nonetheless, discussions of the implications of environmentally related migration for Australia often focus on the possibility of international migration from Pacific Island nations, and the challenges Australia may face in addressing such flows through its current policy settings. If significant international migration flows do eventuate, Martin (2010, p. 3) has argued that 'the immigration policies of most destination countries are not conducive to receiving large numbers of environmental migrants, unless they enter through already existing admission categories'. Martin has summarised common parameters of immigration programs, highlighting that labour migration is usually based on the needs of the receiving country and that family migration is usually restricted to immediate relatives, as well as noting that admissions are sometimes based on point systems. Martin (2010) has also noted that humanitarian admissions are generally limited to people who fit the Refugee Convention definition, and that those admitted under resettlement programs are screened overseas.

In addition to migration policy, the complexities of environmentally related migration invoke a range of other policy fields, including international development, humanitarian assistance, the environment and climate change. Government agencies in these areas have particular responsibilities in relation to different stages of environmentally related migration: contributing to global climate change mitigation; supporting adaptation and resilience of affected communities to environmental events; contributing to humanitarian and disaster relief efforts; managing the movement of people across international borders; and supporting return, resettlement and reintegration following events (Martin, 2010). These responsibilities overlap, leading some commentators to argue that existing policy fields can be relied upon to address the challenges of environmentally related migration (Piguet, Pécoud, & de Guchteneire, 2011). Warner (2010), however, has argued that institutional and policy 'silos' limit the effectiveness of existing responses, which underscores the need for strong communication and coordination between policymakers in relevant fields if more effective responses are to be developed (Appave, 2012; Boano et al., 2008; Warner, 2010).

Approaches to adaptation (which is usually considered a matter of international development policy) and migration have been discussed in the literature in this context. It has been suggested that not only can adaptation function as a way to reduce migration, but that migration can also function as an adaptation strategy that may significantly increase the resilience of communities to environmental and climate change impacts (Hugo, 2010; Newland, 2011; Transatlantic Study Team on Climate-Induced Migration, 2010). It is also worth noting the increasing role of diasporas in enabling a range of adaptation strategies, including beyond the provision of remittances. Such connections demonstrate the potential for effective coordination between policymakers in relevant fields. In arguing that mobilisation of resources for adaptation may be contentious, White (2011) has suggested that a key challenge lies in balancing the use of reliable research to help mobilise support for adaptation and development strategies without igniting security fears.

Conceptualisation and definition

Definitions are important for policy development, as they allow rights and obligations to be identified. As Dun and Gemenne (2008) have argued, '[w]ithout a precise definition, practitioners and policymakers are not easily able to establish plans and make targeted progress' (p. 10). Many commentators have considered the challenge of defining environmentally-related migration to be complicated by 'the lack of good information and analysis about the circumstances in which international migration may result from climate change' (Martin, 2010, p. 2).

In the absence of a clear definition, McAdam (2012) has neatly summarised a range of considerations that responses to environmentally related migration will depend on: '(a) whether such movement is perceived as voluntary or involuntary; (b) the nature of the trigger (a rapid-onset disaster versus a slow-onset process); (c) whether international borders are crossed; (d) the extent to which there are political incentives to characterise something as linked to climate change or not; and (e) whether movement is driven or aggravated by human factors, such as discrimination' (p. 17).

A number of commentators have argued that effective policy responses need to recognise the multiple causality of migrant decision-making processes and take into account the social, economic, cultural and political factors involved (Black, 2001; Castles, 2011; Hugo, 2010; Zetter, 2010). Findlay and Geddes (2011) have emphasised the need for policymakers to appreciate the existing local context and to understand that 'those affected by environmental change are not simply passive populations onto which externally defined practices need to be imposed to protect them from "risk"' (p. 153). They have suggested the value of a policy approach that involves local populations as 'purposive actors' in addressing the challenges posed by the environment–migration nexus (Findlay & Geddes, 2011).

These considerations apply in cases where migration is perceived as voluntary as well as cases where it is perceived as forced, which Hugo (2010) has described as extremes along a continuum where, in reality, different levels of force operate in different circumstances. The nature of an environmental event—whether it is regarded as a rapid-onset (e.g. tsunami, flooding) or slow-onset (e.g. desertification, 'sinking islands') process—and its impact in the particular circumstances also have implications for policy responses.

It has been suggested that 'climate change impacts' should be distinguished from other environmental factors. Climate change processes have been argued to be connected to broader issues of human vulnerability that affect populations (e.g. rapid-onset environmental disasters, conflict), acting as a 'threat multiplier' that increases the likelihood of migration (Collinson, 2010; Kirsh-Wood, Korrebord, & Linde, 2008). Conversely, others have suggested that vulnerability can be aggravated in a very different way (e.g. reduced livelihoods, increased poverty), and that climate change processes thus act to reduce people's ability to migrate (Geddes & Somerville, 2013). Nevertheless, Zetter has argued that 'the interrelatedness of climate change, general changes in environmental conditions and socioeconomic factors which underpin decisions to migrate' makes it difficult to develop policy responses in relation to migration that is related specifically to climate change (Zetter, 2010).

Noting the disparate array of scenarios in which environmentally related migration may occur, McAdam (2011) has argued that 'it is not yet clear whether a universally applicable definition of those displaced by climate change is necessary or desirable' (p. 4).

Future policy: What is possible?

A range of policy responses to environmentally related migration have been proposed at both the international and national levels. At the international level, policy responses (proposed and/or current) include frameworks based on refugee protection, complementary protection, a new international instrument, protection of internally displaced people, and regionally based responses. Unsurprisingly, none of these has successfully overcome the fundamental difficulty of conceptualising environmentally-related migration in order to address the range of circumstances in which it might occur.

Notwithstanding the challenges that exist in the international arena, a number of countries have implemented domestic laws and policies regarding environmentally related migration. These measures also have limited applicability, and none would appear to effectively address migration induced by slow-onset processes. A summary of the national-level responses is provided below.

Refugee framework

Proposals to expand the Refugee Convention to protect people who move across borders due to environmental and climate change factors have been discussed extensively at the international level. The Office of UNHCR does not support revision of the Refugee Convention, and has argued that 'refugee' is a legal term with a settled meaning centred on persecution. People whose movement is related to environmental factors would not normally qualify as refugees, although some could fall within UNHCR's mandate (e.g. where conflict is involved, where governments persecute those affected by withholding assistance, or where statelessness is a concern). According to UNHCR, the terms 'environmental refugee' and 'climate refugee' have no basis in international law and their use could confuse environmental factors with persecution, potentially undermining refugee protection standards (UNHCR, 2009).

Other critiques of this approach have noted that refugee protection applies only to people who have already crossed international borders, while most environmentally related migration is expected to be internal. The term 'refugee' has also been seen to imply forced movement (Zetter, 2010), which may apply in particular circumstances of rapid-onset environmental disasters, but becomes much less clear in cases where people are considered to be migrating voluntarily in anticipation of slow-onset environmental or climate change impacts (Hugo, 2010).

Complementary protection framework

It has been suggested that nonrefoulement obligations under international human rights law might provide another avenue for protecting those affected by environmental and climate change factors (McAdam, 2012; European Commission [EC], 2013). This is envisaged primarily under the right to life (where relevant issues may be standard of living, means of subsistence, survival and protection of life, which could be affected by environmental factors) and the prohibition against torture and cruel, inhuman and degrading treatment or punishment (where return to socioeconomic deprivation, including that caused by humanitarian disasters, could constitute inhuman and degrading treatment) (United Nations General Assembly [UNGA], 1966). However, it is unclear in practice whether such claims can be relied upon: the harm faced must be found to be sufficiently severe and 'imminent'. As with refugee protection, this may imply forced movement, while migration in anticipation of slow-onset environmental or climate change impacts is more likely to be regarded as voluntary. Complementary protection has therefore been argued to be inadequate for addressing the complexities of environmentally related migration (McAdam, 2012).

New international instrument

A number of models for a new international instrument have also been proposed, including a stand-alone convention, a protocol to the United Nations Framework Convention on Climate Change (UNFCCC) and regional agreements under an international framework agreement (Biermann & Boas, 2010; Docherty & Giannini, 2009; Hodgkinson, Burton, Anderson, & Young, 2010). These proposals have significant variations in approach and detail (Appave, 2012), reflecting the difficulties involved in conceptualising environmentally related migration. There has been no common agreement among the proposals on how to define the individuals (and groups) their instruments seek to protect, including in relation to use of the term 'refugee'. Nor has there been a common approach to the applicability of the proposed instruments in relation to forced and/or voluntary movement, internal and/or cross-border movement, and rapid-onset and/or slow-onset environmental events (including how the interaction between environmental events and climate change is understood and whether climate change factors should be the specific focus).

Kälin and Schrepfer (2012) have argued that, in the present context, negotiating such an instrument is likely to be difficult because of the 'largely incompatible interests of potential countries of origin and countries of destination' (p. 70). Further, if not appropriately targeted, McAdam and Saul (2010) have suggested that a new instrument could actually 'encourage general migration, abusive claims and people smuggling'.

Guiding Principles on Internal Displacement

People displaced internally have been argued to be better protected by international norms (including human rights) than those who move internationally, as exemplified by governments having widely adopted the nonbinding Guiding Principles on Internal Displacement (Appave, 2012; Koser, 2011; Leighton, 2010). It has been argued that policymakers could usefully apply the Guiding Principles to situations of environmentally-related migration across borders. The Guiding Principles include in their scope 'persons or groups of persons who have been forced or obliged to flee or leave their homes or places of habitual residence, in particular as a result of or in order to avoid the effects of … natural or human-made disasters' (United Nations Commission on Human Rights, 1998).

However, the requirement that people are forced or obliged to move creates a lack of clarity once more about whether slow-onset processes are covered (Zetter, 2010), particularly as economic motivations for movement, which can be related to the impacts of climate change on livelihood and economic opportunities, were deliberately excluded from the text (Koser, 2011). Further, as the Guiding Principles are nonbinding, if they are not implemented effectively in national laws and policies they may not provide any actual guarantees to displaced people (Koser, 2011).

Regional responses

In view of the range of scenarios in which environmentally related migration may occur, McAdam (2011) has argued that localised or regional approaches may provide better responses than generic international normative frameworks. Regional discussions may provide an avenue for policymakers to consider the different contexts in which environmentally-related migration may pose challenges and opportunities. For example, the specific nature of the threat posed to low-lying Pacific Island nations by rising sea levels and the priorities of affected populations have been prominent features of Pacific regional discussions for a number of years. Importantly, the Pacific Islands Forum developed and endorsed the Niue Declaration on Climate Change in 2008 (Pacific Islands Forum Secretariat, 2008). On a more practical level, affected states in the Pacific are taking action on possible scenarios ranging from internal displacement to nonviability. For example, a recent decision by Kiribati to purchase an island in Fiji, while officially described as a response to food security, has been interpreted by some commentators in terms of environmentally-related migration.

Also in a regional context, McAdam (2012) has discussed the potential utility of existing regional instruments, such as the Organization of African Unity Convention Governing the Specific Aspects of Refugee Problems in Africa and the Cartagena Declaration on Refugees in Latin America. Both define refugees more broadly than the Refugee Convention, and include people who have moved because of events that have disturbed public order. McAdam (2012) has argued that under both instruments it is likely that attributing movement to 'climate change' would be difficult, and that protection seems to be limited to people who have already moved in response to an actual threat, therefore limiting coverage of people moving in anticipation of future environmental impacts.

While the European Union (EU) is a supranational body, with a different character from other regional bodies, it is relevant here to note the EU Temporary Protection Directive, which establishes temporary protection in cases of 'mass influx' of displaced persons. The Directive does not mention environmental factors explicitly, but the open definition of 'mass influx' is argued to provide flexibility (EC, 2013). However, invoking the Directive would require agreement by a majority of EU member states and it is considered unlikely that it would cover environmental migrants travelling as a result of slow-onset processes (Koser, 2012). Nonetheless, acknowledging that environmentally related migration may pose increasing challenges in the future, the EC has published a working document, *Climate change, environmental degradation, and migration*, which provides an overview of the EU perspective on the complexities involved in addressing the issues, and outlines the need for increased knowledge, dialogue and cooperation in order to build policy (EC, 2013).

National-level policy settings

Several countries have developed domestic laws and policies on environmentally related migration, although this has been limited and the implementation of such policies is, in some cases, untested.

Complementary forms of protection for people unable to return to their country of origin are provided for in Sweden's Aliens Act ('because of an environmental disaster')[2] and Finland's Aliens Act ('as a result of an environmental catastrophe').[3] Finland's Act also provides for temporary protection where 'there has been a massive displacement of people … as a result of an armed conflict, some other violent situation or an environmental disaster'.[4] As none of these provisions has yet been tested, their operation is unclear.

In the US, legislation allows for Temporary Protected Status (TPS) to be granted to people who are 'temporarily unable to return to their home country because of … an environmental disaster' (Martin, 2010, p. 3). TPS only applies to people already in the US at the time of a disaster (not to those fleeing an event), and the designation of nationals to whom it applies is discretionary (Koser, 2012; Martin, 2010).

A summary of national-level policy responses is in Table 12.1.

Table 12.1: Overview: National-level policies relevant to environmentally related migration

Country	Response	Comments
Finland	Aliens Act provides for complementary protection for people unable to return to their country of origin 'as a result of an environmental catastrophe'.[1] Aliens Act provides for temporary protection where 'there has been a massive displacement of people … as a result of an armed conflict, some other violent situation or an environmental disaster'.[2]	As these provisions have not yet been tested, their operation is unclear.

2   Aliens Act (2005:716) [Sweden], Chapter 4, Section 2.
3   Aliens Act (301/2004, amendments up to 458/2009 included) [Finland], Section 88a(1).
4   Aliens Act (301/2004, amendments up to 458/2009 included) [Finland], Section 109.

Country	Response	Comments
Sweden	Aliens Act provides for complementary protection for people unable to return to their country of origin 'because of an environmental disaster'.[3]	As this provision has not yet been tested, its operation is unclear.
US	Legislation allows for Temporary Protected Status (TPS) to be granted to people who are 'temporarily unable to return to their home country because of ... an environmental disaster'.[4]	TPS only applies to people already in the US at the time of a disaster (not to those fleeing an event). The designation of nationals to whom TPS applies is discretionary.[5]
Australia	Seasonal Worker Program (SWP) introduced in 2012 allows Australian businesses to recruit workers from Pacific states.	The SWP is designed to meet Australian workforce needs and contribute to poverty reduction and economic development in Pacific countries. It is not designed to address climate change adaptation.
New Zealand	Pacific Access Category (PAC) allows a number of Pacific Islanders to immigrate to New Zealand each year.	The PAC is based on employment— it is not designed to address climate change adaptation.[6]
EU (supranational)	Temporary Protection Directive establishes temporary protection in cases of 'mass influx' of displaced persons.	The Directive does not mention environmental factors explicitly, but the open definition of 'mass influx' is argued to provide flexibility.[7] Invoking the Directive would require agreement by a majority of EU member states. It has been considered unlikely that the Directive would cover migrants travelling as a result of slow-onset environmental processes.[8]

Source: (1) Finland, Aliens Act (301/2004, amendments up to 458/2009 included), Section 88a; (2) Finland, Aliens Act (301/2004, amendments up to 458/2009 included), Section 109; (3) Sweden, Aliens Act (2005:716), Chapter 4, Section 2; (4) Quoted in Martin (2010), p. 3; (5) Koser (2012), p. 10; (6) Martin (2010), p. 3; (7) EC (2013), p. 19; (8) Koser (2012), p. 10.

In the Australian context, there have been a number of instances in which migration-related operational responses have been put into effect following sudden-onset environmental disasters (e.g. the 2004 Indian Ocean tsunami), similar to the US's TPS policy approach. While Australia's responses have not been formalised via legislation, a similar approach is able to be applied, allowing people in Australia to remain following natural disasters on a case-by-case basis.

In Australia, an attempt to directly address the issue of 'climate refugees' came in the form of the Migration (Climate Refugees) Amendment Bill, introduced by the Greens in 2007. The Bill sought to amend the Migration Act to include a 'climate change refugee' visa class for 'a person who has been displaced as a result of a climate change induced environmental disaster'.[5] This approach raised the difficulties involved in identifying an environmental event as being induced by climate change, which the Bill proposed to make the subject of a determination by the Minister for Immigration. Questions were also raised about the implications for both Australia's security and humanitarian priorities, particularly whether the new visa category would attract migrants from around the world (which could include irregular migrants), and whether it would impact on Australia's humanitarian resettlement quota (Koser, 2012). The Bill did not proceed to a vote and lapsed.

Utilising existing policies

Some commentators on environmentally related migration have argued that 'there are actually a number of existing policy fields that can be relied upon to address the challenges it raises, including development strategy, humanitarian affairs, post-disaster interventions, or immigration and admission policies' (Piguet et al., 2011, p. 24). Each of these policy fields covers particular issues relevant to different stages of environmentally-related migration, but in light of the complexities that characterise the phenomenon, Warner (2010) has argued that institutional and policy 'silos' limit the effectiveness of existing responses. Warner has cited existing governance gaps in the protection of environmental migrants who are unable to return after rapid-onset disasters, and those whose movement is related to slow-onset processes.

To address these gaps, many commentators have highlighted the need for a stronger evidence-base, policy dialogue and collaboration between institutions and practitioners in different policy fields in order to understand environmental and climate change impacts on livelihoods and migration (Boano et al., 2008; Findlay & Geddes, 2011; Warner, 2010).

---

5   Australia, Migration (Climate Refugees) Amendment Bill 2007 (Cth), Schedule 1, Clause 2(2).

Due to their key relevance in this context, approaches to adaptation and migration have regularly been discussed in these arguments. Notwithstanding White's arguments about the potentially contentious nature of adaptation (White, 2011), commentators have suggested that not only can adaptation function as a way to reduce migration, but that migration can also function as an adaptation strategy that may significantly increase the resilience of communities to anticipated climate change impacts.

Discussion of migration and adaptation has often turned to the impact of sea-level rise on Pacific Island nations, as a part of the world in which 'long-term migration might be the only response for some communities vulnerable to climate change' (Elliott, 2010, p. 184).

Australia's humanitarian aid and development programs include a significant focus on the Pacific, including a number of projects aimed at building the resilience of communities and reducing disaster risk. However, its humanitarian action does not specifically address cross-border displacement due to natural disasters. From the migration policy side, migration from some Pacific Islands to Australia is long term and well established. In this context, Australia introduced a Seasonal Worker Program in 2012, which allows Australian businesses to recruit workers from Pacific states to both meet Australian workforce needs in particular sectors and to contribute to poverty reduction and economic development in Pacific countries. This program is not designed to address climate change adaptation, and has not been implemented in such terms. Similarly, New Zealand has introduced a Pacific Access Category which allows a number of Pacific Islanders to immigrate to New Zealand each year based on employment, not on climate change adaptation (Martin, 2010). These examples illustrate the potential utility of existing policies that could be adjusted to accommodate emerging priorities, and could be expanded, for example, in response to different issues, and possibly involve utilising migration as an adaptation strategy.

Finally, it is important to note that arguments for the utilisation of existing policies to address environmental and climate change migration should not be taken as rejecting the development of new normative legal and policy instruments outright. Rather, drawing on the conceptual challenges that the environment–migration nexus presents for the development of these instruments, it is argued that an absence of consensus on the desirability of such new standards does not imply that nothing can be done (Piguet et al., 2011; McAdam, 2010). How sustainable such existing policy settings are, in relation to future migration, is a key question.

Conclusions

A fundamental challenge for policymakers and decision-makers attempting to respond to environmentally related migration is the difficulty involved in conceptualising and defining the links between environmental and climate change factors and international migration, including irregular migration. Further, the lack of reliable empirical research and analysis on the issues means there is a weak evidence-base to underscore effective policy development or implementation.

Building the research base to determine the role of environmental factors among the range of other drivers that contribute to decision-making processes involved in regular and irregular migration across borders is complicated. Effective policy responses need to take into account the nature of particular environmental events or climate impacts, as well as the local social, political and economic contexts in which they occur.

Some authors have proposed that a range of existing national policies can be utilised to address the challenges raised by environmental migration. Given the multilayered nature of environmentally related migration, cooperation and coordination between different policy areas has been widely recommended to ensure that overlapping issues are captured.

A number of approaches to managing environmentally related migration have been put forward at both the international and national levels. However, all of these approaches have struggled to comprehensively address the multifaceted nature of the issues involved. One of the greatest challenges ahead will be to understand the nature of environmentally-related migration in order to develop policy responses that will effectively address potential future movement across borders.

Reference list

A question of climate refugees. Editorial. (2011). *New Scientist, 2180.* Retrieved from www.newscientist.com/article/mg21028103-600-a-question-of-climate-refugees/.

Appave, G. (2012). Emerging legal issues in international migration. In Opeskin, B., Perruchoud, R., & Redpath-Cross, J. (Eds), *Foundations of international migration law* (pp. 390–418). Cambridge: Cambridge University Press. doi.org/10.1017/CBO9781139084598.016

Bates, D. (2002). Envrionmental refugees? Classifying human migration caused by environmental change. *Population and Environment, 23*(5), 465–77. doi.org/10.1023/A:1015186001919

Bierman, F., & Boas, I. (2010). Preparing for a warmer world: Towards a global governance system to protect climate change refugees. *Global Environmental Politics, 10*(1), 60–88. doi.org/10.1162/glep. 2010.10.1.60

Black, R. (2001). *Environmental refugees: Myth or reality?* New Issues in Refugee Research, working paper no. 34. Sussex: United Kingdom.

Boano, C., Zetter, R., & Morris, T. (2008). *Environmentally displaced people: Understanding the linkages between environmental change, livelihoods and forced migration.* Oxford: Refugee Studies Centre, University of Oxford.

Brown, O. (2008). *Migration and climate change.* Geneva: International Organisation for Migration.

Castles, S. (2002). *Environmental change and forced migration: Making sense of the debate.* Geneva: UNHCR Evaluation and Policy Analysis Unit.

Castles, S. (2011). Concluding remarks on the climate change–migration nexus. In Piguet, E., Pécoud, A., & de Guchteneire, P. (Eds), *Migration and climate change* (pp. 415–27). Cambridge: Cambridge University Press.

Christian Aid. (2007). *Human tide: The real migration crisis.* London: Author.

Collinson, S. (2010). *Developing adequate humanitarian responses.* Washington DC: German Marshall Fund.

Crisp, J. (1999). *Who has counted the refugees?: UNHCR and the politics of numbers.* New Issues in Refugee Research, working paper, no. 12. Geneva: United Nations High Commissioner for Refugees.

Docherty, B., & Giannini, T. (2009). Confronting a rising tide: A proposal for a convention on climate change refugees. *Harvard Environmental Law Review, 33*(2), 349–403.

Dun, O., & Gemenne, F. (2008). Defining environmental migration: Why it matters so much, why it is controversial and some practical processes which may help to move forward. *Revue Asylon, 6.* Retrieved from www.reseau-terra.eu/article847.html.

El-Hinnawi, E. (1985). *Environmental refugees.* Nairobi: United Nations Environment Program.

Elliott, L. (2010). Climate migration and climate migrants: What threat, whose security? In McAdam, J. (Ed.), *Climate change and displacement: Multidisciplinary perspectives* (pp. 175–90). Oxford: Hart Publishing.

European Commission. (2013). *Commission staff working document: Climate change, environmental degradation, and migration.* Working paper. Brussels: Author.

Findlay, A., & Geddes, A. (2011). Critical views on the relationship between climate change and migration: Some insights from the experience of Bangladesh. In Piguet, E., Pécoud, A., & de Guchteneire, P. (Eds), *Migration and climate change* (pp. 138–59). Cambridge: UNESCO Publishing, Cambridge University Press.

Geddes, A., & Somerville, W. (2013). *Migration and environmental change: Assessing the developing European approach.* Migration Policy Institute, Europe policy brief series, no. 2. Brussels: Migration Policy Institute.

Gemenne, F. (2011). How they became the human face of climate change: Research and policy interactions in the birth of the 'environmental migration' concept. In Piguet, E., Pécoud, A., & de Guchteneire, P. (Eds), *Migration and climate change* (pp. 225–59). Cambridge: UNESCO Publishing, Cambridge University Press.

Hodgkinson, D., Burton, T., Anderson, H., & Young, L. (2010). The hour when the ship comes in: A convention for persons displaced by climate change. *Monash University Law Review, 36*(1), 69–119.

Hugo, G. (1996). Environmental concerns and international migration. *International Migration Review, 30*(1), 105–31. doi.org/10.2307/2547462

Hugo, G. (2010). Climate change-induced mobility and the existing migration regime in Asia and the Pacific. In McAdam, J. (Ed.), *Climate change and displacement: Multidisciplinary perspectives* (pp. 9–36). Oxford: Hart Publishing.

International Organisation for Migration. (2013). *Towards the 2013 high-level dialogue on international migration and development: Final report of the high-level dialogue series.* Geneva: Author.

Jacobson, J. (1988). *Environmental refugees: A yardstick of habitability.* Worldwatch institute paper, no. 86. Washington, DC: Worldwatch Institute.

Kälin, W., & Schrepfer, N. (2012). *Protecting people crossing borders in the context of climate change: Normative gaps and possible approaches.* Geneva: Office of the United Nations High Commissioner for Refugees.

Kibreab, G. (1997). Environmental causes and impact of refugee movements: A critique of the current debate. *Disasters, 21*(1), 20–38. doi.org/10.1111/1467-7717.00042

Kirsch-Wood, J., Korrebord, J., & Linde, A.-M. (2008). What humanitarians need to do. *Forced Migration Review, 31*, 40–41.

Kniveton, D., Schmidt-Verkerk, K., Smith, C., & Black, R. (2008). *Climate change and migration: Improving methodologies to estimate flows.* Geneva: International Organization for Migration.

Koser, K. (1996). Changing agendas in the study of forced migration: A report on the fifth international research and advisory panel. *Journal of Refugee Studies, 9*(4), 353–66. doi.org/10.1093/jrs/9.4.353

Koser, K. (2011). Climate change and internal displacement: Challenges to the normative framework. In Piguet, E., Pécoud, A., & de Guchteneire, P. (Eds), *Migration and climate change* (pp. 289–305). Cambridge: UNESCO Publishing, Cambridge University Press.

Koser, K. (2012). *Environmental change and migration: Implications for Australia*. Sydney: Lowy Institute for International Policy.

Koser, K. (2013). Who cares when migrants become internally displaced persons? Retrieved from Brookings Institute: www.brookings.edu/blog/up-front/2013/10/08/who-cares-when-migrants-become-internally-displaced-persons/.

Leighton, M. (2010). *Climate change and migration: Key issues for legal protection of migrants and displaced persons*. Washington DC: German Marshall Fund.

Leighton, M. (2011). Drought, desertification and migration: Past experiences, predicted impacts and human rights issues. In Piguet, E., Pécoud, A., & de Guchteneire, P. (Eds), *Migration and climate change* (pp. 331–58). Cambridge: UNESCO Publishing, Cambridge University Press.

Lonergan, S. (1998). *The role of environmental degradation in population displacement*. Environmental change and human security project report no. 4. Victoria, Canada: University of Victoria.

Martin, S. (2010). *Climate change and international migration*. Washington DC: German Marshall Fund.

McAdam, J. (2011, 29–30 March). *Climate change, displacement and the role of international law and policy*. Paper presented at the international dialogue on migration 2011: The future of migration: Building capacities for change, Geneva.

McAdam, J. (2012). *Climate change, forced migration and international law*. Oxford: Oxford University Press. doi.org/10.1093/acprof:oso/9780199587087.001.0001

McAdam, J., & Saul, B. (2010). *Displacement with dignity: International law and policy responses to climate change migration and security in Bangladesh*. University of New South Wales Faculty of Law research series, no. 63. Berkeley: Bepress.

McGregor, J. (1993). Refugees and the environment. In Black, R., & Robinson, V. (Eds), *Geography and refugees: Patterns and processes of change* (pp. 157–70). London: Belhaven.

Morrissey, J. (2009). *Environmental change and forced migration: A state of the art review.* Oxford: Refugee Studies Centre, University of Oxford.

Morrissey, J. (2012). Rethinking the 'debate on environmental refugees': From maximilists and minimalists to proponents and critics. *Journal of Political Ecology, 19*, 36–49. Retrieved from jpe.library.arizona.edu/volume_19/Morrissey.pdf.

Myers, N. (1993). Environmental refugees in a globally warming world: Estimating scope of what could well be a prominent international phenomenon. *Bio Science, 43*(11), 752–61. doi.org/10.2307/1312319

Myers, N. (1997). Environmental refugees. *Population and Environment, 18*(5), 509–24.

Myers, N. (2001). Environmental refugees: Our latest understanding. *Philosophical Transactions of the Royal Society B, 356*, 16.1–16.5.

Myers, N. (2005). *Environmental refugees: An emergent security issue.* Paper presented at the thirteenth economic forum, Prague.

Myers, N., & Kent, J. (1995). *Environmental exodus: An emergent crisis in the global arena.* Washington DC: The Climate Institute.

Newland, K. (2011). *Climate change & migration dynamics.* Washington DC: Migration Policy Institute & European University Institute.

Pacific Islands Forum Secretariat. (2008). Pacific Island forum leaders endorse the Niue declaration on climate change. Press statement retrieved from www.spc.int/ppapd/index.php?option=com_content&task=view&id=131.

Piguet, E. (2011). *The migration/climate change nexus: An assessment.* Paper presented at the international conference on rethinking migration: climate, resource conflicts and politics of migration/refugees in Europe, Berlin.

Piguet, E., Pécoud, A., & de Guchteneire, P. (2011). Introduction: Migration and climate change. In Piguet, E., Pécoud, A., & de Guchteneire, P. (Eds), *Migration and climate change* (pp. 1–33). Cambridge: UNESCO Publishing, Cambridge University Press.

Suhrke, A. (1992). *Environmental degradation, migration and conflict.* Paper presented at the Brookings Institute, Washington DC.

Suhrke, A. (1993). *Pressure points: Environmental degredation, migration and conflict,* Cambridge: American Academy of Art and Science.

Transatlantic study team on climate-induced migration. (2010). *Climate change and migration: Report of the transatlanticstudy team.* Washington DC: German Marshall Fund.

United Nations High Commissioner for Refugees. (1993). *The state of the world's refugees 1993: The challenge of protection.* Geneva: Author.

United Nations High Commissioner for Refugees. (2009). *Climate change, natural disasters and human displacement: A UNHCR perspective.* Geneva: Author.

Warner, K. (2010). *Assessing institutional and governance needs related to environmental change and human migration.* Washington DC: German Marshall Fund.

White, G. (2011). *Climate change and migration: Security and borders in a warming world.* Oxford: Oxford University Press. doi.org/10.1093/acprof:oso/9780199794829.001.0001

Zetter, R. (2007). More labels, fewer refugees: Remaking the refugee label in an era of globalization. *Journal of Refugee Studies, 20*(2), 172–92.

Zetter, R. (2010). Protecting people displaced by climate change: Some conceptual challenges. In McAdam, J. (Ed.), *Climate change and displacement: Multidisciplinary perspectives* (pp. 131–50). Oxford: Hart Publishing.

Legislative documents

Australia, Migration (Climate Refugees) Amendment Bill 2007 sch 1, cl 2(2).

Finland, Aliens Act (301/2004, amendments up to 458/2009 included), 30 April 2004. Retrieved from www.refworld.org/docid/4b4d93ad2.html.

Sweden, Aliens Act (2005:716), 31 March 2006. Retrieved from www.refworld.org/docid/3ae6b50a1c.html.

United Nations Commission on Human Rights. (1998). *Report of the representative of the Secretary-General, Mr. Francis M. Deng, submitted pursuant to commission resolution 1997/39. Addendum: Guiding principles on internal displacement.* Retrieved from www.refworld.org/docid/3d4f95e11.html.

United Nations General Assembly, International Covenant on Civil and Political Rights, 16 December 1966, United Nations, Treaty Series, vol. 999, p. 171. Retrieved from www.refworld.org/docid/3ae6b3aa0.html.

13

Conclusions

Khalid Koser and Marie McAuliffe

The purpose of this volume—like the research program from which it emerges—has been to address a gap in evidence of, and knowledge about, irregular migration, in order to inform policymaking, specifically in Australia. This concluding chapter assesses the extent to which this purpose has been achieved, and highlights remaining evidence, research, and policy gaps.

Addressing a gap in evidence and knowledge

On the whole, research on irregular migration has tended to focus on specific case studies or themes, and usually from a particular disciplinary approach. In contrast, this volume has tried to present a global and multidimensional perspective on irregular migration. Specific case studies of Afghanistan and Sri Lanka, both significant countries of origin for maritime asylum seekers to Australia in recent years, combine with wider studies on the causes of irregular migration globally. A chapter on Indonesia provides a more systematic understanding of migrant decision-making in transit. Several chapters adopt a global and comparative perspective on issues such as trends in asylum seeking. The entire migration 'cycle' is covered, from the decision to leave, through experiences in transit and applying for asylum in destination countries, to return. The chapters combine qualitative, quantitative, and mixed methods, and are written by scholars from diverse disciplinary backgrounds including public health, psychology, politics, geography, sociology and demography. The topics covered range from environmental drivers for migration, through media coverage of irregular migration, to unaccompanied minors.

Through this diversity, at the same time, a number of key unifying themes emerge. First, the chapters demonstrate how defining irregular migration is far from straightforward. The category covers a wider range of experiences than is often assumed. It includes both people who enter transit and destination countries with authorisation, and those who enter without authorisation. Asylum seekers, economic migrants, and transit migrants may all also be irregular migrants. Irregularity is not a fixed experience—regular migrants may become irregular, irregular migrants may be regularised. The contributions remind us that the concept includes people moving for different and sometimes mixed motivations, and with a wide diversity of profiles. There are often convergences in the manner that regular and irregular migrants move, whether arising from similar decision-making processes, to moving through similar networks and channels. A lack of data and research simply compounds such definitional challenges.

A second related theme is the multifaceted nature of irregular migration. As illustrated here, it involves different routes, modes of transportation, and geographies, even between the same origin and destination country. Motivations may vary between migrants, and even for the same migrant over time. Governments, international organisations, the private sector and non-state actors, some legal and others not, all have a stake in the causes and consequences of, as well as potential responses to, irregular migration. Irregular migration intersects with both state security and human security, and challenges existing legal, normative and institutional frameworks. It should not be a surprise that there is no easy policy solution to this multifaceted challenge.

Third, the chapters demonstrate the importance of context. The decision to migrate is rarely made in isolation from wider family contexts, in particular for unaccompanied minors. Irregular migration often takes place alongside other forms of regular migration. Understanding what drives irregular migration requires understanding the influence of global trends such as disparities in development, democracy and demography, the global jobs crisis, and revolutions in communications and transportation. Similarly, effective policymaking in response to irregular migration necessitates trade-offs with other public policy concerns such as security and economic growth. Even analysis of media coverage of irregular migration, usually assumed to be one-dimensional and negative, demonstrates how in fact coverage varies in response to wider contextual features such as recession and compassion in response to particular humanitarian disasters.

The contributions also point to remaining evidence and research gaps. More research is required on decision-making by (irregular) migrants, both before they leave home and when they are in transit. Experiences in transit as a whole remain understudied, despite clear indications that the number of migrants in transit worldwide is increasing. There is clearly more research required on media reporting on irregular migration, too. None of this research is easy, and the research represented here has on the one hand often adopted innovative methods in order to overcome some of the challenges; but on the other hand, it leaves the reader in no doubt of their shortcomings and the methodological challenges confronted. Equally, the contributions here reinforce why further research must be undertaken, in order to inform policy.

Informing policymaking

Policymaking obviously is shaped by influences other than just evidence and knowledge, and in certain circumstances may take place in spite of, rather than as a result of, the current body of research. Equally, well-informed policy may be ineffective; it may even result in negative unintended consequences because of changes in, for example, geopolitics or technology. Bridging the research–policy divide to develop effective and sustainable policy remains a perennial challenge in migration as in many other fields of public policy.

Such observations notwithstanding, at the very least it can be proposed that together the contributions to this volume have implications for policy, and more widely than in Australia alone.

One is apparent simply in restating the main messages that have emerged: irregular migration is complex, multifaceted, and deeply contextualised. It would be naïve to suggest that policy can ever be granular or dynamic enough to respond fully to this reality, but there are still implications here for how policy can be better planned, implemented and evaluated.

It should have become clear that irregular migration is a dynamic subset of migration, which is itself a dynamic subset of mobility. Understanding the interlinkages between irregular migration and wider global processes demonstrated by the contributions to this volume leads to the realisation that it cannot be managed in isolation from these processes. The chapters on Afghanistan and Sri Lanka in this volume imply, for example, that migration agencies may not always even be the best equipped to implement policies that seek to influence immigration; for example, in situations where the focus is on the root causes of migration such as climate change, conflict, relative deprivation or violent extremism. The chapters on transit migration suggest that, when it comes to evaluating the impacts of policy, the extent to which the rights of irregular migrants are being respected is just as relevant as reducing numbers. Similarly, the chapter on assisted voluntary return makes clear that the scale of return migration should not necessarily be a proxy for the sustainability of return.

There are good reasons why many states still attempt to manage migration (and in particular irregular migration) on a largely unilateral basis, given its intersection with sovereign issues of economic growth, citizenship, identity and security. But a second implication for policy that emerges from this volume is a recognition of the limits of bilateral or unilateral responses to multilateral challenges. It has been suggested here that policy interventions in origin and transit countries may be just as important as those in destination countries in reducing irregular migration (as well as respecting the right of migrants). As has been explained, irregular migration is in any case driven by global forces that necessitate at least regional and often global approaches. The implication of the chapter on environmental migration is that while adapting national laws and policies may be the most expedient response, ultimately it may be time to revisit the international protection regime.

This observation on the importance of a multilateral approach may also be extended to emphasising the importance of a multistakeholder approach, as illustrated here. Individual migrants rarely make the decision to move alone; thus, reaching families and communities is important for information campaigns. There is a range of intermediaries involved in migrant smuggling and human trafficking; thus, targeting just one operative will rarely disrupt the business. The media can influence public perceptions of migration and of the extent to which governments are able to manage borders and migration. Sustainable return depends on reintegration within local communities. Although not adequately reflected in the contributions to this volume, there is growing recognition of the pivotal role the private sector could play in contributing to more effective migration management.

A third implication arising from the various contributions is to guard against policy responses that view irregular migration exclusively as a security challenge. As has been acknowledged here and by several contributors, irregular migration can certainly pose challenges to state security by, for example, undermining the exercise of state sovereignty and disrupting managed migration programs and asylum systems. But as has also been made clear, development interventions, good governance in origin and transit countries, and promoting respect for rights may be just as effective as border management and restriction in undermining irregular migration. The risk of 'securitising' irregular migration is that it legitimises extraordinary responses, which themselves may often be counterproductive. Fitting environmental migration into existing frameworks for regular migration will be an important priority for the future.

That the contributions here have policy relevance should not be surprising as they emerge from papers commissioned by a research program with close links to policy and operational areas across government. Importantly, the findings in these papers were able to be combined with other knowledge and evidence, such as analysis of administrative data and classified material, to directly inform policy and operational deliberations. At the same time, some more conceptual implications also emerge, albeit not usually explicitly. For example, the sharp distinctions between traditional migration categories of 'regular' and 'irregular' or 'economic' and 'political' have been shown to be empirically blurred. Legal, normative and institutional arrangements are largely still based on these traditional categories, and need to adapt to new realities.

Beyond Australia

As stated, this volume arises from a research program explicitly established to inform Australian policy. To an extent, this has determined the papers commissioned by the program and by extension the chapters in this volume. Thus, they have focused on cases and themes of direct relevance to Australian policymaking on irregular migration. But that is not to say that these cases and themes are not also relevant elsewhere. There has, for example, been a significant increase in the number of Afghan asylum seekers in Europe during the last year; it is well known that Europe has faced a surge in maritime arrivals; and significant policy focus in Europe is on transit migration and decision-making in Greece and Turkey. Likewise, the events of May 2015, involving thousands of irregular migrants stranded in the Bay of Bengal and Andaman Sea, pointed to significant policy challenges facing South East Asia. The key messages and policy implications elucidated above also clearly apply to irregular migration, and policy responses, beyond Australia alone.

In at least three ways the genesis of this volume also has lessons beyond Australia. First, it is laudable both that the report of the Expert Panel identified a need for research as a priority (among only 22) for Australian policy, and the government responded by investing in the Irregular Migration Research Program. As this volume has amply demonstrated, there is a real dearth of evidence on and understanding of irregular migration patterns and processes, particularly in the Australian context, and further research is required. Some of the priorities have been identified here, and the Australian and other governments should continue to support research efforts.

Second, it is striking that the research program included international experts both as advisers and contributors. This approach risked international opprobrium at a time when Australia's asylum policies were quite controversial. But it also demonstrated a willingness to learn from the experiences of other countries and regions that have been confronted by far larger numbers of irregular migrants than Australia. The fact that international experts were willing to engage is a timely reminder in the face of Europe's migration crisis that proximity does not define responsibility. It also highlights the global nature of irregular migration, which is underscored by the increasing global mobility of irregular migrants—the rescue of migrants from Myanmar off the coast of Turkey in early 2016 is a case in point, and such examples are becoming less rare.

Third, the research program explicitly provided an opportunity for 'horizon-scanning' and 'blue-sky thinking'. The inclusion of chapters towards the end of this volume on media representations of irregular migration and the future challenges of environmental migration are illustrative. All too often migration policymaking is short-term and reactive. This is particularly problematic when recognising that, on the whole, migration presents challenges in the short term, and only realises dividends in the longer term.

It would be remiss not to conclude a section entitled 'Beyond Australia', and a volume focusing on 'irregular migration', without finally reflecting on the migration crisis in Europe, against which backdrop this volume will be published. The potential relevance of this volume certainly should not be overestimated—it has largely focused on a different set of challenges than those currently confronted in Europe and of course in a different context. But some of the research will be relevant to European policymakers, such as the work concerning decision-making by migrants in transit. The three key messages distilled here—complexity, multidimensionality and context—also resonate in Europe today. And the lessons posted here for policy, in particular the importance of guarding against viewing migration as a security issue unless justified, should also guide decisions currently being made by European politicians and policymakers.

www.ingramcontent.com/pod-product-compliance
Lightning Source LLC
Chambersburg PA
CBHW051436270326
41935CB00027B/1824